# MUSIC

## AN APPRECIATION

### SECOND BRIEF EDITION

BY THE AUTHOR

*The Norton Scores: An Anthology for Listening*
*Music: An Appreciation—Fifth Edition*

# MUSIC
## AN APPRECIATION

### SECOND BRIEF EDITION

Roger Kamien
*Queens College
of the City University of New York*
*Zubin Mehta Chair in Musicology,
The Hebrew University of Jerusalem*

McGraw-Hill, Inc.

New York   St. Louis   San Francisco   Auckland   Bogotá
Caracas   Lisbon   London   Madrid   Mexico City   Milan
Montreal   New Delhi   San Juan   Singapore   Sydney   Tokyo   Toronto

*For Anita, David, Joshua, and Adina*

# MUSIC: AN APPRECIATION
## SECOND BRIEF EDITION

This book is printed on acid-free paper.
Acknowledgments appear on page 393, and on this page by reference.

1 2 3 4 5 6 7 8 9 0  DOC DOC  9 0 9 8 7 6 5 4 3

ISBN 0–07–034819–7

This book was set in Palatino by York Graphic Services, Inc.
The editors were Cynthia Ward and Susan Gamer;
the designer was Joan E. O'Connor;
the production supervisor was Kathryn Porzio.
The photo editor was Elsa Peterson.
R. R. Donnelley & Sons Company was printer and binder.

*Cover Credit:* "Violin Concerto, 1951" by Raoul Dufy. Courtesy of Mrs. Charlotte Bergman in agreement with the Israel Museum, Jerusalem.

**Library of Congress Cataloging-in-Publication Data**

Kamien, Roger.
    Music: an appreciation / Roger Kamien.—2nd brief ed.
        p.        cm.
    Discography: p.
    Includes index.
    ISBN 0-07-034819-7 (acid-free paper)
    1. Music appreciation.        I. Title.
MT6.K22M9        1994
780—dc20                                        93-15089

INTERNATIONAL EDITION

When ordering this title, use ISBN 0-07-113421-2.

# CONTENTS

# APPENDIXES 355

# LISTENING OUTLINES
## LISTED BY COMPOSER

# PREFACE

M usic: *An Appreciation, Second Brief Edition*, is intended for introductory college courses lasting from eight to fifteen weeks. My
goal has been to write a book that is concise yet clear, accurate,
and engaging—useful both for study and in the classroom.

This text provides an approach to perceptive listening and an introduction to musical elements, forms, and stylistic periods. Its discussions of
composers' lives, individual styles, and representative works aim not
merely to impart facts but to stimulate readers' curiosity and enthusiasm
and heighten their love of music. Many listening outlines are included, to
help students concentrate more easily on the musical compositions discussed; and all the compositions with listening outlines are included on the
Brief Set of three cassettes and three compact disks accompanying the text.

The Second Brief Edition is a condensation of *Music: An Appreciation,*
Fifth Edition (it is about 330 pages shorter), and retains the general organization and the special features that have been so popular with readers.

## HOW THE SECOND BRIEF EDITION IS ORGANIZED

Part I of the Brief Edition examines the elements of music both in general
terms and with reference to attractive, brief illustrative pieces. Notation is
used sparingly here—usually in connection with familiar tunes that allow
students first to begin by analyzing music they have probably known since
childhood.

Parts II through VI deal with periods of music history from the Middle Ages and Renaissance through the present. Jazz, the American musical, and rock are considered within Part VI, The Twentieth Century; Part VII deals with nonwestern music. Each of Parts II through VI opens with a section providing background material and a stylistic overview of the period. Then, in the sections that follow, forms, trends, and representative composers and works are discussed.

Through exposure to a variety of compositions, students are encouraged to develop their listening skills. The color plates and black-and-white photographs help readers relate music to its cultural context.

A Glossary and Example Locator, a Chronology, and a guide to the accompanying recordings are provided as appendixes at the end of the book.

## KEY FEATURES

### Listening Outlines

A distinctive feature of *Music: An Appreciation* is the use of "listening outlines" to be followed while the compositions are heard. A listening outline focuses attention on musical events as they unfold and is easy to follow because it describes what students can readily hear. These outlines are useful for outside listening assignments as well as for classroom work. (A list of listening outlines is given on pages xvii–xix.)

### Opera Texts

The study of opera is aided in this book by excerpts from librettos; these appear with brief marginal notes that indicate the relationship between words and music and help readers follow the drama.

### Flexibility

The Second Brief Edition takes a chronological approach but can be adapted easily to individual teaching methods. Each stylistic period is subdivided into short, relatively independent sections that can be studied in any order; some could even be omitted.

Music examples—and music notation—can also be treated flexibly. Basic notation is described in Part I, and music examples are given throughout, providing visual aids for those who want them. But the discussions of compositions require no knowledge of music notation; students may prefer simply to read the text and skip the details of notation.

### Readability

Clarity of expression has been a chief goal. This is a book that students can feel comfortable with. They will recognize that it was written for them by a musician who loves music and who wants to convey its essentials without creating confusion or boredom.

The biographical sketches and descriptions of composers' individual styles attempt to give the flavor of each composer's personality and music, using anecdotes and quotations to enliven the discussion. Musical terms are defined simply and appear in **bold italic** type, and these terms and their definitions appear in the Glossary and Example Locator.

## NEW FEATURES IN THE SECOND BRIEF EDITION

The Second Brief Edition expands the range of music discussed by broadening the coverage of the American musical theater, music by women composers, and nonwestern music. The number of listening outlines has been increased to thirty, and new representative pieces are provided that will be attractive to students and effective for teaching. Now, every composition on the brief sets of recordings—three cassettes and three compact disks—is represented by a listening outline or vocal text. Timings and CD track numbers keyed to our recording sets have been added to listening outlines, vocal texts, and discussions of pieces. An innovative Glossary and Example Locator has been added as Appendix 1. This allows readers to combine a review of musical terms with easy reference to clear musical examples of these terms (elements, forms, genres, and compositional techniques) in the works included on our recording sets.

In Part II, on the Middle Ages and Renaissance, there is a new example of secular music: Estampie. Part III, on the baroque period, now has a listening outline for Bach's Organ Fugue in G Minor. Part V, on the classical period, now discusses the first movement of Mozart's Piano Concerto No. 23 in A Major, K. 488 (with a listening outline). Part V, on the romantic period, includes new sections on Clara Schumann, with her Romance in G Minor for Violin and Piano, Op. 22, as a representative work (with a listening outline); and on Franz Liszt, with his *Transcendental Étude* No. 10 in F minor as a representative work (with a listening outline). Part V also has new discussions of Robert Schumann's song *Im wunderschönen Monat Mai (In the Lovely Month of May)* from *Dichterliebe (Poet's Love)*, and the love scene from Act I of Wagner's *Die Walküre*.

Part VI, on the twentieth century, has a new section on the American musical, with the *Tonight* ensemble from Leonard Bernstein's *West Side Story* as an example (with a listening outline). There is a new listening outline for the Theme and Variations on *Simple Gifts* from Copland's *Appalachian Spring*. The section on music since 1950 now includes discussions of John Adams's minimalist opera *Nixon in China*; and Ellen Taaffe Zwilich's *Concerto Grosso 1985*, an example of ''quotation music'' (with a listening outline). New to this Second Brief Edition is Part VII, on nonwestern music, which includes sections on music in nonwestern cultures, music in sub-saharan Africa, and koto music of Japan.

The entire book has been carefully revised to reflect recent musical scholarship, and the discussion of electronic instruments has been updated. The Second Brief Edition also includes many new color and black-and-white photos.

## SUPPLEMENTARY MATERIALS

### Recordings

The Second Brief Edition is accompanied by a new expanded listening program produced by PolyGram: a Brief Set of three cassettes and three compact disks (3¾ hours in all) that include complete compositions or movements representing many of the works discussed in the text. The CD set is "internally tracked" so that the student or instructor can locate specific themes or sections within a composition at the push of a button. The cassettes have an announcement of composer and title before each composition. The recordings have all been chosen from the finest performances by leading artists and ensembles. So that the recordings can be easily used with the text, marginal notes in the text refer the reader to the appropriate CD track or side and band number.

Accompanying *Music: An Appreciation*, Fifth Edition, are a Basic Set of eight records, cassettes, and compact disks and a Supplementary Set of four records, cassettes, and compact disks, which may also be used to accompany the Second Brief Edition. These include all but one of the compositions discussed in the Second Brief Edition and are also keyed to the Second Brief Edition through marginal notes, as well as track, side and band numbers.

The format of the marginal references to the recordings is as follows:

**Brief sets:**
**Side 1, band 1**
**CD 1** 1

Basic sets:
Side 1, band 1
CD 1 1

The boxed numbers are CD track numbers. Note that **boldface** is used for the **brief sets** and lightface for the basic sets (lightface is also used for the supplementary sets). Subsequent marginal notations provide additional track numbers and include, when appropriate, time elapsed and brief descriptions:

Section B
**16** 25 3:20

This system of boldface track numbers referring to the brief CDs and lightface track numbers to the basic CDs is also used within the listening outlines.

## Study Guide and Student Workbook

The Study Guide/Workbook, developed by Professor Raoul Camus to interact with the text, provides students with listening exercises, self-tests, research projects, and unit quizzes.

## Instructor's Manual and Test Bank

The Instructor's Manual/Test Bank, also by Professor Camus, follows the organization of the text and provides objectives, suggested classroom activities, listening experiences, questions, discussion topics, student essays, and exams. The test file contains multiple-choice questions.

## Computerized Test Generator

The Test Generator, for IBM, MacIntosh, and Apple computers, contains all the questions found in the test bank within the Instructor's Manual.

## ACKNOWLEDGMENTS

I am grateful to the academic reviewers of the Second Brief Edition: Murry Alewine, Douglas Anderson, Charles Asche, Bruce Boone, Richard Burke, H. Joseph Butler, Marlan Carlson, C. Ann Carruthers, Caryl Conger, Lina Jeong Doo, Terry Fern, Truman Fisher, Douglas Graves, Roberto Gonzalez, Dirk Hillyer, Daniel Jacobson, Burton Karson, Richard Kassel, Laura McDowell, Bruce Mayhall, John Moore, Raymond Moore, Christine Moroni, Rebecca Nagel, Eric Nelson, Stephanie Berg Oram, Douglas Peterson, Dewayne Pigg, Christopher Pignoli, Nancy M. Reale, Cathy Risso, Tom Simon, John Slawson, Thomas Smialak, Larry Tynes, Eric Williams, Robert Zajkowski, and J. Douglas Zeller.

In addition, the contributions of the reviewers of *Music: An Appreciation,* Fifth Edition, and the generous help I received from colleagues in the music department of Queens College continue to be felt in this new Brief Edition.

I am also grateful to a number of people at McGraw-Hill: Cynthia Ward and Susan Gamer, editors; Joan O'Connor, designer; Kathy Porzio, production supervisor; and Patricia Rodney, editorial assistant, who compiled the lists of accompanying recordings.

Once again, Raoul Camus has prepared the excellent *Study Guide and Student Workbook* and *Instructor's Manual.*

As with each edition of *Music: An Appreciation,* the advice and encouragement of my wife, Anita Kamien, have helped to shape the Second Brief Edition.

*Roger Kamien*

# ELEMENTS I

All the musical elements come together when people play or sing.

# ELEMENTS 1

# SOUND: PITCH, DYNAMICS, AND TONE COLOR

Sounds bombard our ears every day—the squeaks and honks of traffic, a child's laugh, a dog's bark, the patter of rain. Through them we learn what's going on; we need them to communicate. By listening to speech, cries, and laughter, we learn what others think and feel. Silence—an absence of sound—also communicates. When we hear no sounds of traffic in the street, we assume that no cars are passing. When someone doesn't answer a question or breaks off in the middle of a sentence, we quickly notice and draw conclusions.

What is sound? What causes it, and how do we hear it? *Sound* begins with the vibration of an object, such as a table that is pounded or a string that is plucked. The vibrations are transmitted to our ears by a *medium*—usually air—and our eardrums start vibrating too. As a result, *impulses*, or signals, are sent to the brain, where they are selected, organized, and interpreted.

Music is part of the world of sound, an art based on the organization of sounds in time. We distinguish music from other sounds by recognizing the four main properties of musical sounds: *pitch* (highness or lowness); *dynamics* (loudness or softness), *tone color* (quality); and *duration*, or *rhythm* (time). We'll look now at pitch, dynamics, and tone color; duration is discussed in Section 3, "Rhythm."

## PITCH: HIGHNESS OR LOWNESS OF SOUND

*Pitch* is the relative highness or lowness that we hear in a sound. When you sing the beginning of *The Star-Spangled Banner*, for example, the pitch on *see* is higher than the pitch on *say:*

The pitch of a sound is decided by the *frequency* of its vibrations—that is, their speed, which is measured in cycles per second. The faster the vibrations, the higher the pitch; the slower the vibrations, the lower the pitch.

All other things being equal, smaller objects vibrate faster and have higher pitches: thus plucking a short string produces a higher pitch than plucking a long string.

In music, a sound that has a definite pitch is called a *tone*. It has a specific frequency, such as 440 cycles per second. The vibrations of a tone are regular and reach the ear at equal time intervals. By contrast, noiselike sounds (such as a squeal of brakes and a clash of cymbals) have an indefinite pitch and are produced by irregular vibrations.

Two tones will sound different when they have different pitches. The "distance" in pitch between any two tones is called an *interval.* When tones are separated by the interval called an *octave,* they sound very much alike. Sing the opening of *The Star-Spangled Banner* again. Notice that the tone you produce on *see* sounds like your tone on *say,* even though it's higher. An octave lies between them. The vibration frequency of the *say* tone is exactly half that of the *see* tone. If the *say* tone were 440 cycles per second, the *see* tone—an octave higher—would be 880 cycles per second. A tone an octave lower than the *say* tone would be half of 440, or 220 cycles per second. When sounded at the same time, two tones an octave apart blend so well that they seem almost to merge into one tone.

The octave is important in music. It is the interval between the first and last tones of the familiar scale:

$$do \quad re \quad mi \quad fa \quad sol \quad la \quad ti \quad do$$

If you sing this, starting with the low *do* and ending on the high *do* which "duplicates" it, you will fill the octave with seven different pitches, rather than sliding up like a siren. This group of seven tones (they are produced by the white keys of a piano) was the basis of western music for centuries. Eventually, five more pitches were added (the black keys on the piano), making twelve tones in all, each of which is "duplicated" in higher and lower octaves. (In nonwestern music, the octave may be divided into a different number of tones.)

The distance between the lowest and highest tones that a voice or an instrument can produce is called its *pitch range* or simply its *range.* The range of an average untrained voice is about 1½ octaves; a piano's range is over 7 octaves.

The organization of pitch is a composer's first resource. In Sections 5 and 6, where melody and harmony are explored, we will look at how pitch is organized. For now, we'll simply observe that composers can create a special mood in their music by using very low or very high pitches. For example, low pitches can intensify the sadness of a funeral march; high pitches can make a dance sound lighter; and a steady rise in pitch often increases musical tension.

Seven different tones are produced by the white keys of the piano.

Though most music we know is based on definite rather than indefinite pitches, noiselike sounds—such as those made by a bass drum or by cymbals—figure strongly in the rhythmic aspects of music. In parts of Africa, the indefinite pitches of drums are very important. And with recent developments in electronic music, indefinite pitches have come to play a vital role in western music as well.

## DYNAMICS

Degrees of loudness or softness in music are called *dynamics*—our second property of sound. Loudness is related to the *amplitude,* or width, of the vibration that produces a sound. When instruments are played more loudly or more softly, or when there is a change in how many instruments are heard, a dynamic change—which can be sudden or gradual—results. A performer can emphasize a tone by playing it more loudly than the tones around it; this is called a *dynamic accent.*

Skillful, subtle changes of dynamics add spirit and mood to performances; they may be written into the music, but often they are unwritten and are inspired by the performer's feelings. Today, the technology of musical instruments has greatly increased the range of dynamics.

When notating music, composers have traditionally used Italian words, and their abbreviations, to indicate dynamics. The most common terms are:

| Term | Abbreviation | Meaning |
|------|------|------|
| *pianissimo* | *pp* | very soft |
| *piano* | *p* | soft |
| *mezzo piano* | *mp* | moderately soft |
| *mezzo forte* | *mf* | moderately loud |
| *forte* | *f* | loud |
| *fortissimo* | *ff* | very loud |

For extremes of softness and loudness, composers use *ppp* or *pppp* and *fff* or *ffff*. The following notations indicate gradual changes in dynamics:

| Symbol | Term | Meaning |
|------|------|------|
| > | decrescendo (decresc.) *or* diminuendo (dim.) | gradually softer |
| < | crescendo (*cresc.*) | gradually louder |

Like many other elements in music, dynamic indications are not absolute: a tone has a dynamic level—is soft or loud—in relation to other tones around it.

## TONE COLOR

We can tell a trumpet from a flute even when they are playing the same tone at the same dynamic level. The quality that distinguishes them—our third property of sound—is called *tone color* or *timbre* (pronounced *tam'-ber*). Tone color is described by words like *bright, dark, brilliant, mellow,* and *rich.*

Changes in tone color create variety and contrast: for example, the same melody will have different expressive effects when it is played by one instrument and then another, or a new tone color may be used to highlight a new melody. Tone color also contributes to continuity; it is easier to recognize the return of a melody if the same instruments play it each time. And specific instruments can reinforce a melody's emotional impact—in fact, composers often invent melodies for particular instruments.

A practically unlimited variety of tone colors is available to composers: instruments (see Section 2) can be combined in various ways, and modern electronic techniques now allow composers to invent entirely new tone colors.

## LISTENING OUTLINES AND
## THE PROPERTIES OF SOUND

To understand the properties of musical sound, we must *listen for them.* In this book, listening outlines—which should be read *as you are listening to the music*—will help focus your attention on musical events as they unfold.

Each item in a listening outline describes some musical sound, such as dynamics, prominent instruments, pitch, or mood (but remember that indications of mood are subjective). Before you listen to a piece of music, glance over the entire outline; then, as you listen to each item, look ahead to see what's next.

Every listening outline is preceded by a description of the music's main features. Instrumentation, approximate duration, and recording notes (where important) are also given. Within the listening outline, at the left, are references to the recordings: time elapsed, in minutes and seconds (0:00); preceded by compact disk track numbers in small boxes. Boldface track numbers [1] refer to the brief set of CDs and lightface track numbers [1] to the basic set.

Following are our first two listening outlines.

## *LOHENGRIN*, PRELUDE TO ACT III, BY RICHARD WAGNER

**Brief sets:**
Side 1, band 1
CD 1 1

Basic sets:
Side 1, band 1
CD 1 1

Wagner makes wide and brilliant use of dynamic contrasts in the Prelude to Act III of his opera *Lohengrin* to set the scene for the wedding of the hero and heroine. The prelude opens with a feeling of exultation—great energy is conveyed by the massive sound of the full orchestra. Later, the music suddenly becomes calm and gentle as we hear fewer instruments, playing softly. This is followed by another sudden contrast when Wagner again employs the full orchestra.

# Listening Outline   To be read while music is heard

*LOHENGRIN*, PRELUDE TO ACT III (1848),
BY RICHARD WAGNER (1813–1883)

3 flutes, 3 oboes, 3 clarinets, 3 bassoons, 4 French horns, 3 trumpets, 3 trombones, bass tuba, timpani, triangle, cymbals, tambourine, 1st violins, 2d violins, violas, cellos, double basses

(Duration, 2:56)

| | | |
|---|---|---|
| 1 1 0:00 | 1. *a.* | Full orchestra, very loud *(ff)*, main melody in violins, cymbal crashes. |
| 2 2 0:22 | *b.* | Brass melody, pulsating accompaniment in strings. |
| 1:06 | *c.* | Full orchestra, main melody in violins, cymbal crashes. |
| 3 3 1:16 | 2. | Soft *(p)*, contrasting oboe melody. Melody repeated by flute. Clarinet and violins continue. |
| 4 4 2:13 | 3. *a.* | Full orchestra, very loud *(ff)*, main melody in violins, cymbal crashes. |
| 2:24 | *b.* | Brass melody, pulsating accompaniment in strings. |
| 2:47 | *c.* | Cymbals. Becomes softer (decrescendo). |

## *HOTTER THAN THAT*, BY LOUIS ARMSTRONG AND HIS HOT FIVE

**Brief sets:**
Side 1, band 2
CD 1 5

Basic sets:
Side 1, band 4
CD 1 10

A succession of different tone colors contributes to the variety within *Hotter Than That*, for jazz band. After an introduction played by the full band, we hear solos by the trumpet, clarinet, voice, guitar, and trombone. Louis Armstrong performs as both trumpeter and vocalist. His singing is like his trumpet playing in sound and style. Instead of lyrics, he sings nonsense syllables like *dat-a bat-a dip-da*. In one section, the guitarist, Lonnie Johnson, imitates the melodic phrases sung by Armstrong, whose voice takes on a guitarlike twang.

Unlike the preceding composition by Wagner, this music was improvised by the performers. Their point of departure was the tune *Hotter Than That*, by Lillian Hardin Armstrong, the band's pianist.

In item 2 of the outline, the trumpet is momentarily heard alone, without piano and guitar. This solo should not be mistaken for the entrance of the clarinet (item 3), which sounds like a high-pitched whine.

## Listening Outline    To be read while music is heard

*HOTTER THAN THAT* (1927),
BY LOUIS ARMSTRONG (1900–1971) AND HIS HOT FIVE

Voice, clarinet, trumpet, trombone, piano, banjo, guitar

(Duration, 3:00)

| | | |
|---|---|---|
| 5 10 0:00 | 1. | All instruments, trumpet predominates. |
| 0:09 | 2. | Trumpet accompanied by piano and guitar. Trumpet briefly alone, piano and guitar rejoin. |
| 6 11 0:43 | 3. | Clarinet, high-pitched whine, piano and guitar accompany. |
| 7 12 1:19 | 4. | Voice, guitar accompaniment. |
| 8 13 1:54 | 5. | Twangy voice imitated by guitar. Piano leads into |
| 9 14 2:17 | 6. *a.* | Muted trombone accompanied by piano and guitar. |
| 10 15 2:33 | *b.* | Trumpet, all instruments join. Guitar, trumpet, guitar at end. |

# PERFORMING MEDIA: VOICES AND INSTRUMENTS

ELEMENTS
**2**

## VOICES

Throughout history, singing has been the most widespread and familiar way of making music. Singers seem always to have had a magnetic appeal, and the exchange between singer and audience contains a bit of magic—something direct and spellbinding. The singer becomes an instrument with a unique ability to fuse words and musical tones.

For many reasons, it is difficult to sing well. In singing we use wider ranges of pitch and volume than in speaking, hold vowel sounds longer, and need a greater supply and control of breath. Air from the lungs is controlled by the lower abdominal muscles and the diaphragm. The air makes the vocal cords vibrate, and the lungs, throat, mouth, and nose produce the desired sound. The pitch of the tone varies with the tension of the vocal cords; the tighter they are, the higher the pitch.

The range of a singer's *voice* depends on both physical makeup and training. Professional singers can command 2 octaves or even more, whereas an untrained voice is usually limited to about 1½ octaves. Men's vocal cords are longer and thicker than women's, and this difference produces a lower range. The classification of voice ranges for women and men follows, arranged from highest to lowest; the four basic voice ranges are soprano, alto, tenor, and bass:

| Women | Men |
|---|---|
| *soprano* | *tenor* |
| *mezzo-soprano* | *baritone* |
| *alto (or contralto)* | *bass* |

Methods and styles of singing vary from culture to culture, and even within a culture: for instance, in the west, classical, popular, jazz, folk, and rock music are all sung differently.

Until the late 1600s, most of the music of western culture was vocal. Since then, instrumental music has rivaled vocal music in importance; but composers have continued to write vocal works—both solo and choral—with and without instrumental accompaniment (which can range from a single guitar or piano to an entire orchestra).

## MUSICAL INSTRUMENTS

An *instrument* may be defined as any mechanism—other than the voice—that produces musical sounds. Western instruments are usually classified in six broad categories: *string* (such as guitar and violin); *woodwind* (flute, clarinet); *brass* (trumpet, trombone); *percussion* (bass drum, cymbals); *keyboard* (organ, piano); and *electronic* (synthesizer).

Compositions are written for solo instruments and combinations of two or more instruments up to orchestras with over 100 musicians. A group may include instruments of only one category (say, strings) or several. Modern symphony orchestras have string, woodwind, brass, percussion, and sometimes keyboard instruments (see the illustration); bands consist mainly of brass, woodwind, and percussion instruments.

An instrument is often made in different sizes that produce different ranges. For instance, there are soprano, alto, tenor, baritone, and bass saxophones. A single instrument's tone color may vary according to the *register*—the part of its total range—in which it is played. A clarinet, for example, sounds dark and rich in its low register but brilliant and piercing in its high register. Most instruments have a wider range than the voice: many command 3 or 4 octaves, and some have 6 or 7. Instruments also produce tones more rapidly than the voice. When writing for a specific instrument, a composer must consider its range, its dynamics, and how quickly it produces tones.

Arrangements for a large orchestra. The diagram below shows a typical seating plan for an orchestra of about 100 instrumentalists, and the podium where the conductor stands. A variation of this seating plan is shown in the photograph above, of the New York Philharmonic orchestra: the violas, rather than the cellos, are in front at the conductor's (and the audience's) right.

| Woodwinds | Brass | Strings | Percussion |
|---|---|---|---|
| 3 flutes, 1 piccolo | 4 trumpets | 18 first violins | 4 timpani (1 player), |
| 3 oboes, 1 English horn | 6 French horns | 16 second violins | bass drum, snare |
| 3 clarinets, 1 bass clarinet | 4 trombones | 12 violas | drum, cymbals, |
| 3 bassoons, 1 contrabassoon | 1 tuba | 10 cellos | triangle, xylophone, |
|  |  | 8 double basses | celesta, glockenspiel, |
| 1 piano |  |  | etc. (2 to 4 players) |
| 2 harps |  |  |  |

People around the world use musical instruments that vary greatly in construction and tone color, and instruments have had many functions at different times and in different cultures. They may provide entertainment; they may accompany song, dance, ritual, and drama; they have sometimes been considered sacred or thought to have magic powers; they have been used for communication; and they have even been status symbols.

Instruments' popularity rises and falls with changing musical tastes and requirements. Today, only a fraction of all known instruments are used; but interest in music of earlier times has led to the resurrection of instruments like the harpsichord (an ancestor of the piano) and the recorder (a relative of the flute). In fact, modern musicians are flexible and far-ranging in their choice of instruments: some classical and rock composers are using nonwestern instruments, and some jazz musicians are turning to classical instruments while classical composers are using instruments associated with jazz.

## String Instruments

The *violin, viola, cello* (violoncello), and *double bass* (*bass fiddle,* or simply *bass*) form the symphony orchestra's string section. They differ in size, range, and tone color: the violin is smallest and has the highest range; the double bass is largest and has the lowest range. For symphonic music they are usually played with a *bow*—a slightly curved stick strung with horsehair (see the illustration)—but they may also be plucked. Here it will be helpful to consider the strings' construction and tone production; the violin can represent the entire family.

The violin consists of a hollow wooden *body* supporting four gut or wire strings which stretch, under tension, from a *tailpiece* at one end and over a

Violin and bow.

*bridge* (which holds them away from the *fingerboard*) to the other end, where they are wound around wooden *pegs*. Each string is tuned to a different pitch by turning its peg to make it tighter or looser (the greater the tension, the higher the pitch.) The musician makes a string vibrate by bowing it with the right hand (the speed and pressure of the bow stroke control dynamics and tone color), or by plucking it. The body amplifies and colors the tone. Pitch is controlled by pressing the strings against the fingerboard with the fingers of the left hand to vary the length of the vibrating portion (this is called **stopping** a string); thus each string can produce a range of pitches.

# STRINGS

The violin (above) is often used as a solo instrument. In the orchestra, the violins are divided into first and second violins, with the first violins frequently playing the main melody. One of the world's best-known violinists is Itzhak Perlman.

Although eighteenth-century composers generally used the cello in its bass and baritone registers, composers later exploited its upper registers as well. The cellist shown above is Yo-Yo Ma.

The body of the viola (left) is about 2 inches longer than that of the violin, and thus the viola's range is somewhat lower. Its tone color is darker, thicker, and a little less brilliant than the violin's.

The double bass (or bass; top left) has a very heavy tone and is less agile than other string instruments. It is often heard with the cello, but an octave lower.

The harp—with forty-seven strings stretched on a triangular frame—has a wide range of 6 octaves. The harpist plucks the strings with the fingers of both hands. Shown at top right is the harpist Maria Casale.

The guitar has six strings, which are plucked with the fingers of the right hand. Frets on the fingerboard mark the places where the strings are stopped (pressed) with the fingers of the left hand. The guitarist shown at right is the late Carlos Montoya.

How the string instruments are played—what performance techniques are used—determines which of many possible musical effects they produce. Plucking the string, for example, has already been mentioned; this is called *pizzicato. Double-stopping* is bowing two strings at once to sound two notes simultaneously; three notes (a *triple stop*) or four notes (a *quadruple stop*) can be sounded almost—but not quite—together by rotating the bow rapidly across three or all four strings. *Vibrato* is a throbbing tone produced by rocking the finger which is stopping a string so that the pitch fluctuates slightly; *tremolo* is rapidly repeated tones created by quick up-and-down strokes of the bow. *Harmonics* are very high-pitched tones produced by lightly touching certain points on the string. The musician can also muffle the tone by fitting a *mute* (a clamp) onto the bridge.

Some string instruments are always plucked rather than bowed. The most important are the *harp* (the only plucked string instrument usually in the symphony orchestra) and the *guitar.*

## Woodwind Instruments

The woodwind instruments are so named because they produce vibrations of air within a tube that was traditionally made of wood (although piccolos and flutes are now made of metal). They have little holes along their length that are opened or closed by the fingers or by pads controlled by a key mechanism; this varies the pitch by changing the length of the vibrating air column. Following are the woodwinds of the symphony orchestra, listed from highest (piccolo) to lowest (contrabassoon) in range; the brackets indicate closely related instruments, with the asterisk marking the more important one of each pair.

$\left\{\begin{array}{l} \textit{piccolo} \\ \textit{flute*} \end{array}\right.$
$\left\{\begin{array}{l} \textit{oboe*} \\ \textit{English horn} \end{array}\right.$
$\left\{\begin{array}{l} \textit{clarinet*} \\ \textit{bass clarinet} \end{array}\right.$
$\left\{\begin{array}{l} \textit{bassoon*} \\ \textit{contrabassoon} \end{array}\right.$

The woodwinds (unlike the strings) can produce only one note at a time. In symphonic music, they are frequently given melodic solos.

Woodwind instruments are great individualists and differ more in tone color than the strings do. Their unique sounds result largely from the way vibrations are produced. The flute and piccolo are played by blowing across the edge of the mouth hole (the *recorder,* a relative of the flute, has a "whistle" mouthpiece); but the rest of the woodwinds have a *reed*—a thin piece of cane that is set vibrating by a stream of air.

# WOODWINDS

The piccolo (top, left)—short for *flauto piccolo,* or *small flute*— is half the size of the flute and plays an octave higher. The piccolo's high register is shrill and whistlelike.

The flute has a high range and is very agile; it can produce rapid successions of tones. Its tone is full and velvety in the low register and bright and sparkling in the upper. Shown at top right is the flutist James Galway.

The recorder (left), like the flute and piccolo, has no reed. The recorder's tone resembles a flute's but is softer and gentler. Its five main sizes are sopranino, soprano, alto, tenor, and bass.

The oboe has a nasal, intense, expressive tone. Because the oboe's pitch is difficult to adjust, the entire orchestra is tuned to its A. The oboist above is Heinz Holliger.

The English horn (top left) is neither English nor a horn, but simply a low, or alto, oboe.

The clarinet can produce tones very rapidly and has a wide range of dynamics and tone color. The clarinetist shown at top right is Richard Stolzman.

The tone of the bassoon (bottom left) is deeply nasal.

The bass clarinet (bottom right) is larger than the clarinet and has a much lower range.

The contrabassoon can produce the lowest pitch in the orchestra.

The saxophone has a single-reed mouthpiece like a clarinet's, but its tube is made of brass. Its tone is rich, husky, and speechlike. Shown here is the jazz saxophonist Sonny Rollins.

In *single-reed woodwinds* (such as the clarinet and the bass clarinet), the reed is fastened over a hole in the mouthpiece and vibrates when the player blows into the instrument. (*Saxophones*—instruments that are used mainly in bands—are also single-reed woodwinds.) In *double-reed woodwinds* (oboe, English horn, bassoon, and contrabassoon), two pieces of cane are held between the player's lips. Tone colors differ greatly not only between single-reed and double-reed woodwinds but also among the various registers of each woodwind instrument. In general, low registers of the woodwinds tend to be breathy and thick, and their top registers more penetrating.

## Brass Instruments

From high register to low, the main instruments of the orchestra's brass section are the **trumpet, French horn** (sometimes called simply a *horn*), **trombone,** and **tuba.** Other brasses, such as the *cornet, baritone horn, euphonium,* and *bass,* are used mainly in concert and marching bands.

The brasses are played by blowing into a cup- or funnel-shaped mouthpiece. The vibrations come from the musician's lips and are amplified and colored in a coiled tube that is flared at the end to form a *bell.* Pitch is regulated both by varying lip tension and by using *slides* and *valves* to change the length of the tube (the longer the tube, the lower the pitch); the trombone uses a slide which is pulled in or pushed out, and the trumpet, French horn, and tuba have three or four valves to divert air through various lengths of tubing. (Valves came into use in the mid-nineteenth century, making these instruments much more flexible and allowing them to produce many more tones.) Brass players can also alter tone by inserting a *mute*—a hollow, funnel-shaped piece of wood or plastic—into the bell.

Brasses are powerful instruments, often used at climaxes and for bold and heroic statements; but they cannot play as rapidly as most of the strings or woodwinds and serve less often as soloists.

## Percussion Instruments

Most percussion instruments are struck by hand, with sticks, or with hammers, though some are shaken or rubbed. Percussion instruments of *definite pitch* produce tones; those of *indefinite pitch* produce noiselike sounds.

| Definite Pitch | Indefinite Pitch |
|---|---|
| **timpani (kettledrums)** | **snare drum (side drum)** |
| *glockenspiel* | *bass drum* |
| *xylophone* | *tambourine* |
| *celesta* | *triangle* |
| *chimes* | *cymbals* |
| | *gong (tam-tam)* |

In percussion instruments, vibrations are set up in stretched membranes (like the calfskin or plastic of the kettledrum) or in plates or bars (metal, wooden, etc.). Extremely loud sounds can be made by some percussion instruments, but percussion sounds die away relatively quickly. In a symphony orchestra, one percussionist may play several different instruments.

Percussion instruments have long been used to emphasize rhythm and heighten climaxes. But until about 1900, they played a far less important role in western music than strings, woodwinds, and brasses. In this century, composers have been more willing to use the special colors of the percussion group. Yet western musicians barely approach the incredibly varied use of such percussion found in Africa and Asia.

# BRASS

The trumpet sounds brilliant, brassy, and penetrating. The trumpeter shown at left, top, is Wynton Marsalis.

The trombone (left, middle) has a tone that combines the trumpet's brilliance with the French horn's mellowness.

The thick, heavy tone of the tuba (left, bottom) is used to add weight to the lowest orchestral register.

The French horn (above) has a tone that is less brassy, more mellow, and more rounded than the trumpet's.

# PERCUSSION

The timpani (kettledrums; top) are the only orchestral drums of definite pitch. A calfskin or plastic head is stretched over a copper, hemispherical shell. The pitch of the timpani is changed by varying the tension of the head. Screws around the shell's rim are tightened or loosened by hand or by a foot pedal. One percussionist generally plays two to four timpani, each tuned to a different pitch.

The metal bars of the glockenspiel (orchestral bells; middle) are struck with two hammers to produce a tone that is bright and silvery.

The xylophone (bottom) consists of a set of wooden bars which are struck with two hard hammers to produce a dry, wooden tone.

(Innervisions)

(Randy Matusow)

(Clemens Kalischer)

(Randy Matusow)

*Opposite page:*

The celesta (top left) looks like a small upright piano, but its sounding mechanism is like a glockenspiel's. Metal bars are struck by hammers that are controlled by a keyboard. The celesta's tone is tinkling and graceful.

Chimes (top right) are a set of metal tubes hung from a frame. They are struck with a hammer and sound like church bells.

The dry rattling sound of the snare drum (or side drum; bottom left) is produced by the vibration of snares—strings, which are tightly stretched against the bottom head. The snare drum is often used in marches.

The bass drum (bottom right)—the largest of the orchestral drums—is almost 3 feet in diameter.

*Above:*

The tambourine (top left) is often used to create Spanish or Gypsy effects. The player shakes it or strikes its head with the knuckles.

The triangle (top right) is struck with a metal beater and makes a tinkling, bell-like sound.

Cymbals (bottom left) are round brass plates. They are usually struck together with a sliding motion, and their sound penetrates like a sharp crash.

When struck by a bass drum's stick with a soft head, the gong (or tam-tam; bottom right) produces long-lasting sounds that can seem solemn, mysterious, or frightening.

# KEYBOARD INSTRUMENTS

The piano is exceptionally versatile. Shown above is the pianist Mitsuko Uchida.

The harpsichord (below) has plucked strings controlled by one or two keyboards.

A pipe organ has many sets of pipes, controlled by several keyboards.

## Keyboard Instruments

The piano, harpsichord, organ, and accordion are the best-known keyboard instruments. Though quite different from each other, each has a keyboard which allows several tones to be played at once quickly and easily.

The *piano* was invented around 1700 and mechanically perfected by the 1850s. It produces sound through vibrating strings held under tension by an iron frame: striking a key causes a felt-covered hammer to hit a string (the harder the pianist strikes the key, the louder the sound); releasing the key causes a felt damper to come down on the string and end the tone. Pianos have two or three pedals; the *damper pedal* lets the pianist sustain a tone even after releasing the key, the *una corda pedal* (or *soft pedal*) veils the sound, and the *sostenuto* pedal (which not all pianos have) sustains some tones but not others.

Pianos are exceptionally versatile; the eighty-eight keys span more than 7 octaves, the dynamic range is very broad, and the pianist can play many notes at once, including a melody and its accompaniment. Today, the piano is very popular as a solo instrument, for accompaniments, and in ensembles, including the symphony orchestra.

The *harpsichord* was important from about 1500 to 1775 (when it was gradually replaced by the piano) and has been revived in the twentieth century for performance of early music and in some new works. It has strings that are plucked by small wedges called *plectra*, controlled by one or two keyboards.

23

The *pipe organ* was most prominent from 1600 to 1750 (when it was known as the "king of instruments") but is still in wide use today, particularly in religious services. It has a very wide range of pitch, dynamics, and tone color. There are several keyboards (including a pedal keyboard) that control valves from which air is blown across or through openings in the pipes; different sets of pipes—each with a particular tone color—are brought into play by pulling knobs called *stops;* dynamics are changed by adding or reducing the number of pipes, moving from one keyboard to another, or opening and closing shutters around some of the pipes.

The *accordion* has free steel reeds controlled by a treble keyboard with piano keys (played by the right hand) and a bass keyboard with buttons (played by the left hand). Air from a bellows makes the reeds vibrate.

### Electronic Instruments

*Electronic instruments* produce or amplify sound electronically; they were invented as early as 1904 but have had a significant impact on music only since 1950. Today, electronic and computer technologies are continually developing and increasingly blending together. Electronic instruments for performing and composing music include amplified instruments, such as the electric piano, organ, and guitar; tape studios; synthesizers; computers; and various "hybrid" technologies.

The *tape studio* was important in the 1950s. (In Part VI, we'll study Edgard Varèse's *Poème électronique,* created in a tape studio in 1958.) The raw material in tape studios consisted of recorded sounds—electronic or "real" (flutes, bird calls, etc.)—of definite and indefinite pitch. The composer could speed them up, slow them down, alter their pitch and duration, give them echos, filter them to change tone color, mix them, and cut and splice the tape. But splicing and rerecording were difficult, inaccurate, and time-consuming, and many composers of the 1960s turned to synthesizers, which appeared around 1955.

*Synthesizers* are electronic systems that can generate, modify, and control a huge variety of musical sounds and noises; they give the composer complete control over pitch, tone color, loudness, and duration. Most of them can be played with a keyboard. Synthesizers vary in size and capacity. During the 1960s and 1970s, relatively small, inexpensive transistorized synthesizers such as the Moog and Buchla were installed in electronic music studios at universities and advertising agencies, played in live rock concerts and concerts of electronic music, and used to create film and television scores. Highly sophisticated computerized synthesizers now exist, and various technologies are in use.

*Analog synthesis*—the earliest of the synthesizer technologies, which predominated until about 1980—uses a mixture of complex sounds that are shaped by filtering. Like all analog technology, it is based on representing data in terms of measurable physical quantities, in this case sound waves.

(Patricia Sener)

Today's electronic music studios integrate a wide variety of equipment, including tape recorders, synthesizers, computers, and devices for mixing and filtering sound.

*Digital frequency modulation (FM) synthesis*, invented by John Chowning, was patented by Yamaha and has been associated with Yamaha instruments. Like all digital technology, it is based on representing physical quantities—here, points on sound waves—as numbers.

*Effects devices*, which include reverberators, echo devices, and stereo splitters, are often integrated into synthesizers and the synthesis process. They are used in almost all recorded music (especially popular music) and in some live music.

*Sampling* is considered a synthesizer technology, since it involves placing brief digital recordings of live sounds under the control of a synthesizer keyboard; but although the sounds can be modified during playback, no actual synthesis is present. Sampling can be seen as an advanced form of composing by tape splicing: it allows the composer to record short segments of sounds (these are the "samples") digitally and then manipulate them. Sampling has been integrated into relatively inexpensive computer-linked keyboards and is one of the most important aspects of today's electronic music making.

A significant development in synthesizing technology is known as *musical instrument digital interface (MIDI)*: this is a standard adopted by manufacturers for interfacing synthesizer equipment. MIDI has allowed the device actually played on to be separated from tone generation; thus there are now keyboards that look, feel, and play like a piano; wind controllers played like a woodwind instrument; and string controllers played like a violin or cello. Also, control signals can be fed to and from a MIDI instrument into and out of a personal computer, and users can store and edit music and convert to and from musical notation.

Historically, *computers* were the third means of producing sounds on audiotape; they were developed for this purpose after the tape studio and synthesizers. Since the vibrating waves which produce any sound can be represented by a series of numbers, a computer can be programmed to accept musical specifications fed into it by a composer; it then changes these specifications into numbers that represent the final sounds. Later, the numbers are passed through a converter so that the music may be heard or recorded.

The 1970s and 1980s saw the development of small computers with which composers could instantly hear the music they programmed; since then, computers have become even more sophisticated. Computers are used for music synthesis (mainly to produce sounds not otherwise obtainable), to help composers write scores (following rules selected by the composer), to store samples of audio signals, to control synthesizing mechanisms, and so on.

Obviously, it is not entirely possible (or particularly useful) to consider modern electronic music devices and processes separately: the distinction between synthesizer technology and computer technology is not clear-cut. To increase the variety of sound and the composer's control over it, today's electronic music studios contain and integrate a wide variety of equipment, including tape recorders, synthesizers, computers, and devices for mixing and filtering sound.

All this equipment enables the composer to exploit the entire spectrum of sound as never before. But the quality of the music produced still depends on the imagination and organizing power of the human mind.

# [ ELEMENTS 3 ] RHYTHM

Rhythm is basic to life. We see it in the cycle of day and night, the four seasons, the rise and fall of tides. More personally, we find it in our heartbeats, and we feel it when we breathe and walk. The essence of rhythm is a recurring pattern of tension and release, of expectation and fulfillment. This rhythmic alternation seems to pervade the flow of time. Time, as we live it, has fantastic diversity; each hour has 60 minutes, but how different one hour may seem from another!

Rhythm forms the lifeblood of music, too. In its widest sense, *rhythm* is the ordered flow of music through time. How musical elements change in time, and their rate of change, has to do with rhythm, which is our fourth property of sound. Rhythm has several interrelated aspects which we'll consider one at a time: beat, meter, accent and syncopation, and tempo.

Beats can be shown as a succession of marks on a time line.

## BEAT

When you clap your hands or tap your foot to music, you are responding to its beat. **Beat** is a regular, recurrent pulsation that divides music into equal units of time. Beats can be represented by marks on a time line (see the illustration). In music, such beats occur as often as every ¼ second or as seldom as every 1½ seconds. Sometimes the beat is powerful and easy to feel, as in marches or rock music. Or it may be barely noticeable, suggesting floating or aimlessness.

The pulse of music is communicated in different ways. Sometimes the beat is explicitly pounded out—by a bass drum in a marching band, for instance. At other times, however, the beat is sensed rather than actually heard.

Sing the beginning of the song *America* up to the words *Land where my fathers died:*

| My | coun- | try, | 'tis | | of | thee, | Sweet | land | of | | lib- | | er- | ty, |
|----|-------|------|------|---|-----|-------|-------|------|-----|---|------|---|-----|-----|
| \| | \| | \| | \| | \| | \| | \| | \| | \| | \| | | \| | | \| | \| |
| Of | thee | I | sing. | | | Land (etc.) | | | | | | | | |
| \| | \| | \| | \| | \| | \| | \| | | | | | | | | |

Each of the marks represents a beat. Did you notice that you automatically held *sing* for 3 beats? You *sensed* the beat because you were aware of it and expected it to continue.

Beats form the background against which the composer places notes of varying length, and they are the basic unit of time by which all notes are measured. Notes last a fraction of a beat, or an entire beat, or more than a beat. In the example from *America*, the syllables, or notes, range from ½ beat for *of* to 3 beats for *sing*.

Combinations of different note lengths create rhythm. Earlier, **rhythm** was defined as the ordered flow of music through time; more specifically, it can be defined as the particular arrangement of note lengths in a piece of music. Rhythm is an essential feature of a melody's "personality." Indeed, we might be able to recognize *America* merely by clapping out its rhythm without actually singing the tones. The *beat* of *America* is an even, regular pulsation. But its *rhythm* flows freely, sometimes matching the beat, sometimes not.

## METER

In music, some beats feel stronger or more stressed—that is, more empha-sized—than others, and we find repeated patterns of a strong beat plus one or more weaker beats. The organization of beats into regular groups is called *meter.* A group containing a fixed number of beats is called a *measure.* The first, or stressed, beat of the measure is called the *down-beat.* There are several types of meter, based on the number of beats in a measure.

When a measure has 2 beats, it is said to be in *duple meter;* we count **1**–2, **1**–2, etc., as in the following example (the vertical lines indicate the measures):

| Ma- ry | had | a | lit- tle | lamb, | lit- tle | lamb, | lit- tle | lamb, |
|---|---|---|---|---|---|---|---|---|
| **1** | 2 | | \| **1** | 2 | \| **1** | 2 | \| **1** | 2       \| |

A pattern of 3 beats to the measure is known as *triple meter;* we count **1**–2–3, **1**–2–3, etc. *America* is in triple meter:

| My | coun- try, | 'tis | | of | thee, |
|---|---|---|---|---|---|
| **1** | 2      3 | \| **1** | 2 | 3 | \| |

| Sweet | land | of | lib- | | er- ty, |
|---|---|---|---|---|---|
| **1** | 2 | 3 | \| **1** | 2 | 3        \| |

| Of | thee | I | sing. | |
|---|---|---|---|---|
| **1** | 2 | 3 | \| **1** | 2      3     \| |

*Quadruple meter* has 4 beats to the measure. As usual, the downbeat is strongest, but there is another, slighter stress on the third beat; we count **1**–2–3–4, **1**–2–3–4, etc. In the following example, the first word is on the *upbeat,* an unaccented pulse preceding the downbeat:

| Mine | eyes | have | seen | the | glo- ry | of | the | com- ing | of | the | Lord; | He | is |
|---|---|---|---|---|---|---|---|---|---|---|---|---|---|
| | \| **1** | 2 | 3 | | 4 | | \| **1** | 2 | | 3 | | 4 | \| |

*Sextuple meter* has 6 rather quick beats to the measure. The downbeat is strongest, but the fourth beat also has a stress; we count **1**–2–3–4–5–6. Actually, the measure is subdivided into two 3-beat groups, **1**–2–3/4–5–6, so that sextuple meter is a combination of duple and triple meter. For example:

| Oh, | give | me | a | home | | where the buf- | fa- lo | | roam, | | where the |
|---|---|---|---|---|---|---|---|---|---|---|---|
| \| **1** | 2 | 3 | 4 | 5 | 6 | \| **1** | 2      3 | 4 | 5 | 6 | \| |

*Quintuple meter* (5 beats to the measure) and *septuple meter* (7 beats to the measure) also combine duple and triple meter. In quintuple meter, for example, the measure is subdivided into 2- and 3-beat groups: **1**–2–**3**/**4**–5 or **1**–2/**3**–4–5. These meters occur frequently in twentieth-century music but only occasionally in earlier music.

## ACCENT AND SYNCOPATION

An important aspect of rhythm is how individual notes are stressed. One way to emphasize a note is by giving it a dynamic *accent,* that is, by playing it more loudly than the notes around it. A note can also be emphasized by being held longer or being higher in pitch than nearby notes.

When an accented note comes where we would normally *not* expect it, the effect is known as *syncopation.* A syncopation occurs when an "off-beat" note is accented (that is, when the stress comes *between* beats). In the following example, syncopation occurs on the accented *my*, which comes between beats 1 and 2:

| Give | **my** | re- | gards | to | | Broad- | | way | | |
|------|--------|-----|-------|-----|-----|--------|-----|-----|-----|-----|
| 1 | 2 | 3 | 4 | | \| 1 | 2 | 3 | 4 | \| |

A syncopation also occurs when a weak beat is accented (as in 1–**2**–3–4 and 1–2–3–**4**). It creates rhythmic excitement and is one of the most characteristic features of jazz.

## TEMPO

*Tempo*—the speed of the beat—is the basic pace of the music. We associate fast tempos with energy, drive, and excitement, and slow tempos with solemnity, lyricism, or calmness.

A *tempo indication* is usually given at the beginning of a piece. As with dynamics, the terms that show tempo are in Italian:

| Term | Meaning |
|------|---------|
| *largo* | very slow, broad |
| *grave* | very slow, solemn |
| *adagio* | slow |
| *andante* | moderately slow, a walking pace |
| *moderato* | moderate |
| *allegretto* | moderately fast |
| *allegro* | fast |
| *vivace* | lively |
| *presto* | very fast |
| *prestissimo* | as fast as possible |

Tempo indications are often made more specific by the use of qualifiers, such as *molto (much)* and *non troppo (not too much)*: thus *allegro molto* means *very fast* and *allegro non troppo* means *not too fast*. The same tempo is not always used throughout a piece. A gradual speeding up may be indicated by **accelerando** *(becoming faster),* and a gradual slowing down by **ritardando** *(becoming slower).*

All these terms (again, like dynamics) are relative and approximate; different performers interpret them differently, and there is no one "right" tempo for a piece. This is true even though, since about 1816, composers have been able to indicate tempo by means of a metronome setting. A **metronome** is a device which ticks or flashes a light at any desired musical speed, and a metronome setting indicates the exact number of beats per minute.

# ELEMENTS 4

# MUSIC NOTATION

We use written words to express our thoughts and communicate with others when we cannot be with them. In music, ideas are also written down, or *notated*, so that performers can play pieces unknown to them. **Notation** is a system of writing music so that specific pitches and rhythms can be communicated. It is explained here—very briefly—primarily to help you recognize rising and falling melodic lines and long and short notes so that you can follow the music examples in this book. (You will find it helpful to review the material on pitch in Section 1, pages 2–4; and on rhythm in Section 3 above.)

The twelve pitches of the octave and their positions on the piano keyboard.

## NOTATING PITCH

With music notation, we can indicate exact pitches by the upward or downward placement of symbols—called *notes*—on a *staff*. A **note** is an oval. (Its duration is indicated by whether it is black or white or has a *stem* and *flags*, as will be explained later, under "Notating Rhythm.") A **staff** (plural, *staves*) is a set of five horizontal lines. Notes are positioned either on the lines of the staff or between them, in the spaces; the higher a note is placed on the staff, the higher its pitch:

If a pitch falls above or below the range indicated by the staff, short, horizontal **ledger lines** are used:

Seven of the twelve pitches (tones) that fill the octave in western music are named after the first seven letters of the alphabet: A, B, C, D, E, F, G. This sequence is repeated over and over to represent the "same" tones in higher and lower octaves, and it corresponds to the white keys of the piano. The other five tones of the octave correspond to the black keys of the piano and are indicated by one of the same seven letters plus a **sharp sign** (♯) or a **flat sign** (♭) (see the illustration on the opposite page). Thus the pitch between C and D may be called C sharp (C♯; higher than C) or D flat (D♭; lower than D). A **natural sign** (♮) is used to cancel a previous sharp or flat sign.

A *clef* is placed at the beginning of the staff to show the pitch of each line and space. The two most common clefs are the **treble clef,** used for relatively high ranges (such as those played by a pianist's right hand), and the **bass clef,** used for relatively low ranges (played by the pianist's left hand):

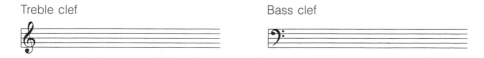

Treble clef                                    Bass clef

Keyboard music calls for a wide range of pitches to be played by both hands; for such music, the **grand staff**—a combination of the treble and bass staves—is used. The illustration on the following page shows how the notes on the grand staff are related to the piano keyboard. Note that the C nearest to the middle of the keyboard is called **middle C.**

Notes on the grand staff and their positions on the piano keyboard.

## NOTATING RHYTHM

Music notation does not indicate the exact duration of tones; instead, it shows how long one tone lasts in relation to others in the same piece. A single note on the staff lasts longer or shorter depending on how it looks— on whether it is white or black and has a *stem* or *flags.*

The chart below shows the relationships of the duration symbols:

One whole note lasts as long as 2 half notes or 4 quarter notes, and so on. As shown, the flags of several eighth notes or sixteenth notes in succession are usually joined by a horizontal *beam.*

32

To lengthen the duration of a tone (and add rhythmic variety), we can make it a ***dotted note;*** adding a dot (·) to the right of a note increases its duration by half. Thus, 1 quarter note ordinarily equals 2 eighth notes, but 1 dotted quarter note equals 3 eighth notes:

Frequently, a dotted note is followed by a note that is much shorter; this long-short pattern, called ***dotted rhythm,*** strongly emphasizes the beat (and is therefore often used in marches).

A *tie* (⌣) is another way to lengthen the duration of a note. When two notes in a row are the same pitch and are connected by a tie, the first note is lengthened by the duration of the second. In the following example, the tone on *dell* lasts as long as 1 dotted quarter note plus 1 quarter note; the two tied notes become one continuous sound:

We can also add rhythmic variety by shortening the duration of a note. One method is the ***triplet,*** three notes of equal duration notated as a group within a curved line and the number 3. Such a group lasts only as long as if it were two notes of equal value:

## NOTATING SILENCE (RESTS)

Duration of silence is notated by using a symbol called a ***rest.*** Rests are pauses; their durations correspond to those of notes:

whole rest    half rest

quarter rest    eighth rest    sixteenth rest

A page from the orchestral score of Tchaikovsky's *Romeo and Juliet.*

## NOTATING METER

A *time signature* (or *meter signature*) shows the meter of a piece. It appears at the beginning of the staff at the start of a piece (and again later if the meter changes) and consists of two numbers, one on top of the other. The upper number tells how many beats fall in a measure; the lower number tells what kind of note gets the beat (2 = a half note, for instance, and 4 = a quarter note). Thus a $\frac{2}{4}$ time signature shows that there are 2 beats to the measure (duple meter) and a quarter note gets 1 beat. Duple meter may also be shown as $\frac{2}{2}$ (or by its symbol, ¢); quadruple meter is usually $\frac{4}{4}$ (or **c**). The most common triple meter is $\frac{3}{4}$.

## THE SCORE

An orchestral *score* shows the music for each instrumental or vocal category in a performing group; often, a score will show more than twenty different staves of notation (see the illustration on the opposite page).

# MELODY

ELEMENTS

# 5

For many of us, music means melody. Though it is easier to recognize than define, we do know that a *melody* is a series of single notes which add up to a recognizable whole. A melody begins, moves, and ends; it has direction, shape, and continuity. The up-and-down movement of its pitches conveys tension and release, expectation and arrival. This is the melodic curve, or line.

As you get further into the music explored in this book, you'll find a wealth of melodies: vocal and instrumental, long and short, simple and complex. This section will help you sort them out by introducing some terms and basic melodic principles.

A melody moves by small intervals called *steps* or larger ones called *leaps*. A *step* is the interval between two adjacent tones in the *do-re-mi* scale (from *do* to *re*, *re* to *mi*, etc.). Any interval larger than a step is a *leap* (*do* to *mi*, for example). Besides moving up or down by step or leap, a melody may simply repeat the same note. A melody's range—the distance between its lowest and highest tones—may be wide or narrow; melodies written for instruments tend to have a wider range than those for voices, and they frequently have wide leaps and rapid notes that would be difficult to sing. Often the highest tone of a melody will be the *climax,* or emotional focal point.

Note durations as well as pitches contribute to the distinctive character of a melody, and the specific order of long and short notes is important. A well-known melody can be almost unrecognizable if it is not sung or played in proper rhythm.

How the tones are performed can also vary the effect of a melody: they may be sung or played in a smooth, connected style called *legato* or in a short, detached style called *staccato.*

Many melodies are made up of shorter parts called *phrases.* Phrases may have similar pitch and rhythm patterns that help unify the melody, or they may contrast, furnishing variety. They often appear in balanced pairs (a phrase of rising pitches, say, followed by one of falling pitches). In analyzing music, letters are customarily used to represent sections of a piece: lowercase letters (a, b, etc.) for phrases and other relatively short sections, and capital letters (A, B, etc.) for longer sections. If two sections, such as phrases, differ significantly, we use different letters: a b. If one exactly repeats another, the letter is repeated: a a. If a section is a varied repetition of a previous one, the repeated letter has a prime mark: a a'. A repetition of a melodic pattern at a higher or lower pitch is called a *sequence.*

A resting place at the end of a phrase—a point of arrival—is called a *cadence;* it may be partial, setting up expectations (an *incomplete cadence*), or it may give a sense of finality (a *complete cadence*).

Now let's consider some examples of familiar melodies, starting with *Row, Row, Row Your Boat* (a b):

Sing it only up to the word *stream*. Notice that on *stream* the melody comes to a resting place which ends the first phrase (a); but it seems incomplete, as though it had posed a question. Now sing the rest—the second phrase (b), beginning on *merrily*—and notice how it ends conclusively and seems to answer the question. Thus the first phrase ends with an incomplete cadence and the second with a complete cadence. Each phrase is the same length, a formula typical of many melodies called *tunes;* the two phrases create a feeling of symmetry and balance, one beginning with repeated notes and then moving upward by step, the second moving downward by leap and then by step. The climax comes on the first *merrily*.

Next, sing the nursery tune *Mary Had a Little Lamb* (a a'):

It also has two balancing phrases, the first phrase (a) ending with an incomplete cadence and the second with a complete cadence. But here the second phrase (a') begins exactly like the first before proceeding to a different, more conclusive ending. Melodic repetition, both exact and (as here) varied, plays an important unifying role in music.

Our final example, *America* (a b), has phrases that are *not* of equal length:

The second phrase (starting from *Land*) is longer than the first and creates a feeling of continuation rather than balance or symmetry. An interesting aspect of *America* is the way a repeated rhythmic pattern (for *My country, 'tis of thee, Sweet land of liberty, Land where my fathers died,* and *Land of the Pilgrims' pride*) unifies the melody. *America* also contains a sequence: the melody for *Land of the Pilgrims' pride* is simply a repetition a little lower of the preceding *Land where my fathers died.*

These three melodies are complete in themselves. Frequently, however, a melody will serve as a starting point for a more extended piece of music and, in stretching out, will go through all kinds of changes. This kind of melody is called a *theme.*

(Larry Busacca/Retna Ltd.)

The singer Tracy Chapman blends melody and harmony by accompanying herself on the guitar.

# HARMONY

When folksingers accompany themselves on a guitar, they add support, depth, and richness to the melody; we call this *harmonizing*. Most music in western culture is a blend of melody and harmony (much nonwestern music, on the other hand, emphasizes melody and rhythm rather than harmony).

*Harmony* refers to the way chords are constructed and how they follow each other. A *chord* is a combination of three or more tones sounded at once. Essentially, a chord is a group of simultaneous tones, and a melody is a series of individual tones heard one after another. As a melody unfolds, it gives clues for harmonizing, but it does not always dictate a specific series—or *progression*—of chords; a melody may be harmonized in several musically convincing ways. Chord progressions enrich a melody by adding emphasis, surprise, suspense, or finality. New chords and progressions continually enter the language of music, but the basic chordal vocabulary has remained fairly constant. We'll look now at a few principles of harmony.

# ELEMENTS

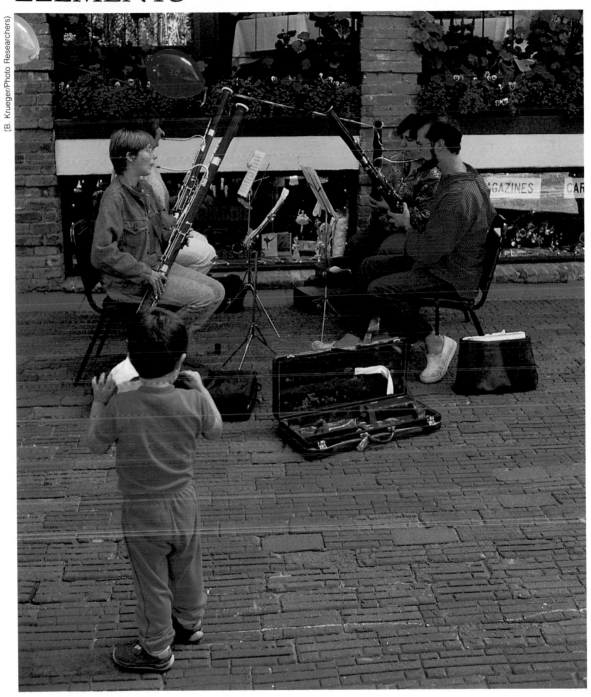

Street musicians. Informal music making is a source of pleasure for both players and listeners.

The audience at a concert of the United States Marines Band. Whether in a public park or a concert hall, live performances have a special electricity.

(Paul Conklin/Uniphoto)

## BROKEN CHORDS (ARPEGGIOS)

When the individual tones of a chord are sounded one after another, it is called a **broken chord,** or **arpeggio.** *The Star-Spangled Banner* begins with a broken chord:

In this example, the notes of the tonic chord are heard in succession rather than together.

Throughout this book, the importance of harmony will be more and more apparent. It helps give music variety and movement; and its effects are endless, varying with the style of a particular era and the desires of individual composers.

ELEMENTS

# 7 KEY

Almost all familiar melodies are built around a central tone toward which the other tones gravitate and on which the melody usually ends. To feel this gravitational pull (which is rooted in cultural conditioning), sing *America* (page 37), pausing for a few seconds between *freedom* and *ring;* you will probably feel uneasy until you supply the last tone. This central tone is the **keynote,** or **tonic.** A keynote can be any of the twelve tones of the octave; when, for example, a piece is in the key of C, the tonic or keynote is C.

   *Key* involves not only the central tone but also a central chord and scale. *Chord* was defined in Section 6 above; the basic chord of a piece in C is a tonic triad with C as its root, or bottom tone. A **scale** is made up of the basic pitches of a piece of music arranged in order from low to high or high to low. A piece in the key of C has a basic scale, *do-re-mi-fa-sol-la-ti-do,* with C as its *do,* or tonic. *Key,* then, refers to the presence of a central note, scale, and chord within a piece, and all the other tones are heard in relationship to them. Another term for key is **tonality.** After 1900, some composers abandoned tonality; but even today much of the music we hear is tonal.

| whole step | whole step | half step | whole step | whole step | whole step | half step |
|---|---|---|---|---|---|---|

do    re    mi   fa    sol    la    ti   do

Pattern of whole and half steps making up the major scale.

## THE MAJOR SCALE

The basic scales of western music from the late 1600s to 1900 were the *major* and *minor*, and they continue to be widely used today.

The *major scale*—the familiar *do-re-mi*, etc.—has two kinds of intervals in a specific pattern: the *half step,* the smallest interval traditionally used in western music; and the *whole step,* twice as large as the half step. The illustrations on this page show the pattern of whole and half steps in the major scale (above) and a major scale with C as the beginning tone (below).

Major scale beginning on C.

The C major scale uses only the white keys of the piano (the half steps come between E and F and between B and C, which are not separated by black keys). We can construct similar major scales by starting the same pattern of intervals on any of the twelve tones of the octave (thus there are twelve possible major scales); the other major scales use one or more black keys of the piano, but the pattern sounds the same.

## THE MINOR SCALE

Along with the major scale, the minor scale is fundamental to western music. The *minor scale*—like the major—consists of seven different tones and an eighth tone that duplicates the first an octave higher, but it differs from the major scale in its pattern of intervals, or whole and half steps. Since (again, like the major) it can begin on any of the twelve tones of the octave, there are twelve possible minor scales. Here is a comparison between a major and a minor scale both starting on C.

C major scale:

| | whole step | whole step | half step | whole step | whole step | whole step | half step |
|---|---|---|---|---|---|---|---|
| C | D | E F | | G | A | B | C |

C minor scale:

| | whole step | half step | whole step | whole step | half step | whole step | whole step |
|---|---|---|---|---|---|---|---|
| C | D E♭ | | F | G A♭ | | B♭ | C |

The crucial difference is that in the minor scale there is only a half step between the second and third tones; this greatly changes the sound of the scale and the mood of music using it. Music based on minor scales tends to sound serious or melancholy; also, the tonic triad built from a minor scale is a minor chord, which sounds darker than a major chord.

*Joshua Fought the Battle of Jericho* is a tune based on a minor scale:

Josh-ua fought the bat-tle of Jer-i-cho, Jer-i-cho, Jer-i-cho;

Josh-ua fought the bat-tle of Jer-i-cho, and the walls came tum-bl-ing down.

## THE KEY SIGNATURE

When a piece of music is based on a major scale, we say that it is in a *major key;* when it is based on a minor scale, it is said to be in a *minor key.* Thus a piece based on (for example) a major scale with D as its keynote is in the key of D major; a piece based on a minor scale with the keynote F is in the key of F minor. Each major and minor scale has a specific number of sharps or flats, from none to seven; and to indicate the key of a piece, a *key signature*—consisting of sharp and flat signs following the clef at the beginning of the staff—is used. To illustrate, here is the key signature for D major, which contains two sharps:

Key signatures make it unnecessary to put a sharp or flat sign before every sharped or flatted note in the piece.

## THE CHROMATIC SCALE

The twelve tones of the octave—*all* the black and white keys in one octave on the piano—form the *chromatic scale.* The tones of the chromatic scale (unlike those of the major or minor scale) are all the same distance apart, one half step:

The word *chromatic* comes from the Greek *chroma, color;* and the traditional function of the chromatic scale is to color or embellish the tones of the major and minor scales. The chromatic scale does not define a key, but it gives a sense of motion and tension. It has long been used to evoke grief, loss, or sorrow. In the twentieth century the chromatic scale has also become independent of major and minor scales and is used as the basis for entire compositions.

## MODULATION: CHANGE OF KEY

Most short melodies remain in one key from start to end; but in longer pieces, variety and contrast are created by using more than one key. A shift from one key to another within the same piece is called a *modulation.*

A modulation is like a temporary shift in the center of gravity—it brings a new central tone, chord, and scale. Though modulations are sometimes subtle and difficult to hear, they produce subconscious effects that increase our enjoyment.

## TONIC KEY

No matter how often a piece changes key, there is usually one main key, called the *tonic* or *home key.* The tonic key is the central key around which the whole piece is organized. Traditionally, a piece would usually begin in the home key and practically always end in it. A composition in the key of C major, for example, would begin in the home key, modulate to several other keys—say, G major and A minor—and finally conclude in the home key of C major. The other keys are subordinate to the tonic.

Modulating away from the tonic key is like visiting: we may enjoy ourselves during the visit, but after a while we're glad to go home. In music, modulations set up tensions that are resolved by returning to the home key. For centuries, the idea of a central key was a basic principle of music. But after 1900, some composers wrote music that ignored the traditional system. The results of this revolutionary step are explored in Part VI, The Twentieth Century.

## ELEMENTS
## 8
# MUSICAL TEXTURE

At any moment within a piece, we may hear one unaccompanied melody, several melodies, or one melody with harmony. The term *musical texture* describes these possibilities; it refers to how many different layers of sound are heard at once, whether they are melody or harmony, and how they are related to each other. Texture is described as transparent, dense, thin, thick, heavy, or light; and variations in texture create contrast and drama. We'll now look at three basic textures: *monophonic, polyphonic,* and *homophonic.*

## MONOPHONIC TEXTURE

The texture of a single unaccompanied melodic line is *monophonic,* meaning literally *one sound.* If you sing alone, you make monophonic music. Performance of a single melodic line by more than one instrument or voice is playing or singing in *unison* and results in a fuller, richer-sounding monophonic texture.

## POLYPHONIC TEXTURE

Simultaneous performance of two or more melodic lines of relatively equal interest produces **polyphonic** (*many-sounding*) texture. In polyphony several melodic lines compete for attention, adding a dimension that has been compared to perspective in painting: each line enriches the others. The technique of combining several melodic lines into a meaningful whole is called **counterpoint** (and the term *contrapuntal texture* is sometimes used in place of *polyphonic texture*). To fully enjoy polyphony, you may have to hear a piece several times; it's often helpful to listen first for the top line, then for the bottom line, and then for the middle lines.

Polyphonic music often contains **imitation,** which occurs when a melodic idea is presented by one voice or instrument and then restated immediately by another. A *round*—a song in which several people sing the same melody but each starts at a different time—uses imitation; *Row, Row, Row Your Boat* is a familiar example:

Here, the imitation is "strict": each voice sings exactly the same melody. But in polyphonic texture imitation is often freer, with the imitating line starting like the first one but then going off on its own.

## HOMOPHONIC TEXTURE

When we hear one main melody accompanied by chords, the texture is *homophonic.* Attention is focused on the melody, which is supported and colored by sounds of subordinate interest. When harmonized by chords, *Row, Row, Row Your Boat* is an example of homophonic texture:

Accompaniments in homophonic music vary widely in character and importance, from subdued background chords to surging sounds that almost hide the main melody. When a subordinate line asserts its individuality and competes for the listener's attention, the texture is probably best described as being between homophonic and polyphonic.

## CHANGES OF TEXTURE

Changing textures within a composition creates variety and contrast, as was noted above. A composer may, for instance, begin with a melody and a simple accompaniment and later weave the melody into a polyphonic web—or contrast a single voice with massive chords sung by a chorus. Georges Bizet's *Farandole* from *L'Arlésienne* Suite No. 2, is a good example of textural variety.

### *FARANDOLE* FROM *L'ARLÉSIENNE* (*THE WOMAN FROM ARLES*) SUITE NO. 2, BY GEORGES BIZET

Brief sets:
Side 1, band 3
CD 1 ⑪

Basic sets:
Side 1, band 10
CD 1 ㉖

The *Farandole* comes from Bizet's music for the play *L'Arlésienne (The Woman from Arles)*, which is set in southern France. Two contrasting themes are heard in this exciting orchestral piece. The first, in minor, is a march theme adapted from a southern French folk song. The lively second theme, in major, has the character of the *farandole*, a southern French dance.

Many changes of texture contribute to the *Farandole*'s exciting mood. The piece contains two kinds of homophonic texture: in one, the accompaniment and melody have the same rhythm; in the other, the rhythm of the accompaniment differs from that of the melody. The *Farandole* opens with the march theme and its accompaniment in the same rhythm. But when the lively dance theme is first presented, its accompanying chords do not duplicate the rhythm of the melody; instead, they simply mark the beat.

The *Farandole* also includes two kinds of polyphony: with and without imitation. Soon after the opening, the march theme is presented by the violins and then is imitated by the violas. At the end of the piece, polyphony results when the march and dance themes—previously heard in alternation—are presented simultaneously. In this concluding section, both themes are in major.

The *Farandole* also contains monophonic texture, which sets off the homophony and polyphony. Monophony is heard when the march theme is played by the strings in unison.

## Listening Outline   To be read while music is heard

FARANDOLE FROM *L'ARLÉSIENNE (THE WOMAN FROM ARLES)*
SUITE NO. 2 (1879), BY GEORGES BIZET (1839–1875)*

Allegro deciso (forceful allegro), march tempo, quadruple meter ($\frac{1}{4}$), D minor

Piccolo, 2 flutes, 2 oboes, 2 clarinets, 2 bassoons, 4 French horns, 2 trumpets, 2 cornets, 3 trombones, timpani, tambourine, bass drum, cymbals, 1st violins, 2d violins, violas, cellos, double basses

(Duration, 3:01)

| 11 | 26 | 0:00 | 1. *a.* Full orchestra, *ff,* march theme; homophonic (accompaniment in same rhythm as melody), minor.

| 12 | 27 | 0:16 | *b.* Violins imitated by violas, march theme; polyphonic, minor.

*L'Arlésienne* Suites No. 1 and No. 2 are sets of pieces from the theater music composed by Bizet. Suite No. 2 was arranged by Bizet's friend Ernest Guiraud after the composer's death.

13 28 0:33      2. *a.* High woodwinds, *ppp,* dance theme; faster tempo, homophonic
(accompanying chords on beat), major; decorative rushes in violins, long
crescendo to *ff* as dance theme is repeated.

*ppp*    *poco a poco crescendo* ------------------------------------------------------------------------

        1:13         *b.* Full orchestra, *fff,* dance theme.
14 29 1:23      3. *a.* Strings only, *ff,* march theme in faster tempo; monophonic, minor.
        1:34         *b.* High woodwinds, *ppp,* dance theme; homophonic.
        1:39         *c.* Strings only, *ff,* continue march theme; monophonic, then homophonic as
lower strings accompany melody.
        1:50         *d.* High woodwinds, *ppp,* dance theme; homophonic. Crescendo to
15 30 2:12      4. Full orchestra, *fff,* dance and march themes combined; polyphonic, major.
Homophonic ending.

ELEMENTS

# MUSICAL FORM

The word *form* is associated with shape, structure, organization, and co-
herence. Form calls to mind, for instance, the human body or the balanced
arrangement of figures in a painting. *Form* in music is the organization of
musical ideas in time. In the flow of time, a composer creates something
cohesive out of the musical elements—pitch, tone color, dynamics, melody, harmony, and texture. In a logically organized piece of music, one
thought grows from another and all the parts are interrelated; we perceive
the form of the piece by recalling the various parts and how they relate,
and with repeated listening the form becomes clearer and takes on an emotional meaning.

## TECHNIQUES THAT CREATE MUSICAL FORM

Both in short tunes (such as those we explored in Section 5) and in much
longer compositions, repetition, contrast, and variation are essential techniques. *Repetition* creates a sense of unity; *contrast* provides variety; and
*variation,* in keeping some elements of a musical thought while changing
others, provides both unity and variety.

## Repetition

Musical repetition appeals to the pleasure we get in recognizing and remembering something, and the repetition of melodies or extended sections is a technique widely used for binding a composition together. The passage of time influences our reaction to repetition: when a musical idea returns, the effect is not duplication but balance and symmetry.

## Contrast

Forward motion, conflict, and change of mood all come from contrast. Opposition—of loud and soft, strings and woodwinds, fast and slow, major and minor—propels and develops musical ideas. Sometimes such contrast is complete, but at other times the opposites have common elements that give a sense of continuity.

## Variation

In the variation of a musical idea, some of its features will be retained while others are changed. For example, a melody might be restated with a different accompaniment, or its pitches might stay the same while its rhythm is changed. A whole composition can be created from variations on one idea.

## TYPES OF MUSICAL FORM

Composers have traditionally organized musical ideas by using certain forms or patterns, and listeners can respond more fully when they recognize these patterns. It's important to note, though, that two compositions having the same form may be different in every other respect. We'll look now at two basic types of musical form. (Remember, from Section 5, that lowercase letters represent phrases or short sections and capital letters represent longer sections.)

### Three-Part (Ternary) Form: A B A

During the last few centuries *three-part form (A B A)* has probably been used most frequently. It can be represented as *statement* (A), *contrast* or *departure* (B), *return* (A). When the return of A is varied, the form is outlined A B A' (Wagner's Prelude to Act III of *Lohengrin*, analyzed in Section 1, is in A B A' form). The contrast between A and B can be of any kind; A and B can be of equal or unequal length; and the way A returns after B differs from piece to piece—A may come unexpectedly, or it may be clearly signaled (if B comes to a definite end with a cadence and a pause), or there may be a transition smoothly linking the two.

The sections of an A B A composition can be subdivided; for example, as follows:

A       B       A
a b a   c d c   a b a

In some pieces, a listener might mistake subsection b within the first A for the arrival of B; but as the music progresses, the greater contrast one hears with B will make it clear that b is a subsection.

## DANCE OF THE REED PIPES FROM NUTCRACKER SUITE, BY PETER ILYICH TCHAIKOVSKY

**Brief sets:**
**Side 1, band 4**
**CD 1** 16

Basic sets:
Side 1, band 11
CD 1 31

The *Nutcracker* Suite is a set of dances from Tchaikovsky's fairy-tale ballet *The Nutcracker. Dance of the Reed Pipes* is a particularly clear example of A B A' form. Section A features three flutes playing a staccato melody which conveys a light, airy feeling and is repeated several times. The B section contrasts in tone color, melody, and key—it features a trumpet melody accompanied by brasses and cymbals. This melody moves by step within a narrow range, in contrast to the opening flute melody, which has a wide range and many leaps as well as steps. The F sharp minor key of the middle section contrasts with the D major key of the opening section. The concluding A' section, in D major, is a shortened version of the opening A section.

# Listening Outline   To be read while music is heard

DANCE OF THE REED PIPES FROM NUTCRACKER SUITE (1892),
BY PETER ILYICH TCHAIKOVSKY (1840–1893)

Three-part (ternary) form: A B A'

Moderato assai (very moderate), duple meter ($\frac{2}{4}$), D major

3 flutes, 2 oboes, English horn, 2 clarinets, bass clarinet, 2 bassoons, 4 French horns, 2 trumpets, 3 trombones, tuba, timpani, cymbals, 1st violins, 2d violins, violas, cellos, double basses

(Duration, 2:34)

A

16 31 0:00    1. *a.* Low pizzicato strings, *p,* introduce
       0:04          *b.* 3 flutes, staccato melody in major, pizzicato strings accompany. Melody repeated.

0:31 c. English horn melody, legato, flutes accompany, staccato.

0:45 d. 3 flutes, staccato melody, pizzicato strings accompany. Melody repeated. Cadence.

**B**

[17] [32] 1:13 2. a. Trumpet melody in minor, brasses and cymbals accompany.

1:26 b. Strings repeat trumpet melody. Flutes lead back to

**A′**

[18] [33] 1:46 3. 3 flutes, staccato melody in major, strings accompany. Melody repeated. Cadence.

## Two-Part (Binary) Form: A B

A composition divided into two large sections is in *two-part form (A B)*. Two-part form gives a sense of *statement* (A) and *counterstatement* (B). If either of its large sections is immediately repeated, or if both are, the form might be represented by A A B, A B B, or A A B B. As in three-part form, differences between A and B may be of any kind, and the two sections may be equal or unequal in length and may have subsections. The B section almost always returns to the home key and gives a sense of finality.

## *BADINERIE* FROM SUITE NO. 2 IN B MINOR, BY JOHANN SEBASTIAN BACH

The *Badinerie* (French for *jest* or *banter*) is the lighthearted finale of Bach's Suite No. 2 in B Minor for solo flute, string orchestra, and harpsichord. It is in two-part (binary) form and is outlined A A B B, because each part is repeated. Parts A and B differ in key and length but are similar in melody and rhythm. The first part begins in B minor and then modulates to F sharp minor, and the longer second part begins in F sharp minor and then modulates back to the tonic key of B minor. Section A opens with a descending phrase that reappears at the beginning of section B but at a lower pitch. Each section of this playful miniature is rounded off by a cadence.

Brief sets:
**Side 1, band 5**
**CD 1** [19]

Basic sets:
Side 1, band 12
CD 1 [34]

51

# Listening Outline To be read while music is heard

*BADINERIE* FROM SUITE NO. 2 IN B MINOR (LATE 1730s),
BY JOHANN SEBASTIAN BACH (1685–1750)

Two-part (binary) form: A A B B

Duple meter ($\frac{2}{4}$), B minor

Solo flute, string orchestra, harpsichord

(Duration, 1:23)

A
19 34 0:00

1. Flute, descending phrase in minor,

phrase repeated, running notes lead to cadence in minor. Section A repeated.

B
20 35 0:31

2. Descending phrase, lower in pitch than section A,

running notes, flute melody descends and leads to cadence in minor. Section B repeated.

## LISTENING FOR FORM

Music is continuous in its flow and does not always fall into clearly defined units. Short pieces, especially, may seem elusive, and some music seems to fit none of the usual patterns. But such music is not formless—it has unique forms that can be discovered through repeated hearings. It's important for listeners to rely on memory, to put related ideas together by recognizing and recalling them and finding their relationships. Through alert listening the overall shape of the ideas will be made clear.

# MUSICAL STYLE

In music, *style* refers to a characteristic way of using melody, rhythm, tone color, dynamics, harmony, texture, and form. How these elements are put together can result in a distinctive or unique sound, and we can speak of the musical style of one composer, a group of composers, a country, or a period in history. Compositions created in the same part of the world or at about the same time are often similar in style, but individuals using the same musical vocabulary can create a personal manner of expression.

Musical styles change from one historical era to the next, but these changes are continuous, so that any boundary between one stylistic period and another is only approximate. Although there are some sudden turning points, even the most revolutionary new styles are usually foreshadowed in earlier compositions; and few changes of style sweep away the past entirely.

Western art music can be divided into the following stylistic periods:

Middle Ages (450–1450)
Renaissance (1450–1600)
Baroque (1600–1750)
Classical (1750–1820)
Romantic (1820–1900)
Twentieth century to 1950
1950 to the present

The following chapters describe the general features of each period and show how it differs from the preceding one. Awareness of the characteristics of a style will let you know what to listen for in a composition and help you recognize innovative or unique features.

Music is probably as old as the human race; and we know—from art and other evidence—that it existed in ancient Egypt, Israel, Greece, and Rome, but hardly any notated music has survived from these civilizations. The first stylistic period to be considered in this book is the European Middle Ages, from which notated music *has* come down to us—allowing compositions created over 1,000 years ago to come alive today.

# THE MIDDLE AGES AND RENAISSANCE

Sacred music predominated during the Middle Ages. This miniature from a twelfth-century psalter shows King David playing the harp, and ten other musicians.

# MUSIC IN THE MIDDLE AGES (450–1450)

A thousand years of European history are spanned by the phrase *Middle Ages*. The "dark ages"—a time of migration, upheavals, and wars—began about 450 with the disintegration of the Roman Empire. But the later Middle Ages (until about 1450) were a period of cultural growth: romanesque churches and monasteries (1000–1150) and gothic cathedrals (1150–1450) were constructed, towns grew, and universities were founded.

During the Middle Ages a very sharp division existed among three main social classes: nobility, peasantry, and clergy. The nobles were sheltered within fortified castles; but the peasants lived miserably, and many were bound to the soil and subject to feudal overlords. This was an age of faith: all segments of society felt the powerful influence of the Roman Catholic church. Monks in monasteries held a virtual monopoly on learning; most people, including the nobility, were illiterate. Just as the cathedral dominated the medieval landscape and the medieval mind, so was it the center of musical life. Most important musicians were priests and worked for the church. Boys received music education in church schools, and an important occupation in monasteries was liturgical singing. Women were not allowed to sing in church but did make music in convents, and some—like Hildegard of Bingen (1098–1179), abbess of Rupertsberg—wrote music for their choirs.

Although most medieval music was vocal—the church frowned on instruments because of their earlier role in pagan rites—instruments did serve as accompaniment and after about 1100 were used increasingly in church. (The organ was most prominent.) In the later Middle Ages, instruments were a source of controversy between composers, who wanted to create elaborate compositions, and the church, which wanted music only as a discreet accompaniment to the religious service.

## THE CHURCH MODES

The *church modes* were the basic scales of western music in the Middle Ages and (despite their name) were used in secular as well as sacred music. Like major and minor scales, they consist of seven different tones and an eighth tone that duplicates the first an octave higher; but their patterns of whole and half steps are different. (Much western folk music follows the patterns of the church modes: for example, *What Shall We Do with the Drunken Sailor?* is in a mode called *Dorian; When Johnny Comes Marching Home* is in the *Aeolian* mode.)

Architecture changed during the Middle Ages from the romanesque style, seen in the eleventh-century nave at the left, to the gothic of the thirteenth-century Cathedral of Reims, above.

## GREGORIAN CHANT

For over 1,000 years (though it is not common today), the official music of the Roman Catholic church has been *Gregorian chant,* which consists of melody set to sacred Latin texts and sung without accompaniment. (It is monophonic in texture.) Gregorian chant was meant to create the atmosphere for specific prayers and rituals in the church service and has a calm, otherworldly quality (resulting partly from the use of church modes) that represents the voice of the church rather than any individual. Its rhythm is

(Bildarchiv Foto Marburg)

During the Middle Ages, artists were concerned more with religious symbolism than with lifelike representation. Sculptures from the late-twelfth-century church of St. Trophime in Arles (in southern France) show Christ surrounded by symbols of the four evangelists.

flexible, without meter, and has little sense of beat; this gives it a floating, almost improvisational character. Melodies may be simple or elaborate but tend to move by step within a narrow range of pitches.

Gregorian chant is named after Pope Gregory I (the Great, reigned 590–604), who was credited by medieval legend with having created it; actually, however, it evolved over many centuries. At first, the chants were passed along by oral tradition, but later they were notated (the illustration on page 59 shows an example of medieval chant notation). Most of the several thousand chants known today date from A.D. 600 to 1300, and the earliest surviving manuscripts date from about the ninth century. The composers—like the artists who decorated the early medieval churches—remain almost completely unknown.

### ALLELUIA: VIDIMUS STELLAM
### (WE HAVE SEEN HIS STAR)

An elaborate and jubilant Gregorian chant is the Alleluia from the Mass for Epiphany. The word *alleluia* is a Latinized form of the Hebrew *hallelujah* (*praise ye the Lord*).

**Brief sets:**
**Side 1, band 6**
**CD 1** 21

Basic sets:
Side 1, band 13
CD 1 36

Medieval chant notation for *Alleluia: Vidimus stellam.*

In this chant (shown above in medieval notation), many notes are sung to single syllables of text. The long series of tones on *ia* is an expression of wordless joy and religious ecstasy. The monophonic texture of the chant is varied by an alternation between a soloist and a choir singing in unison. The chant is in A B A form; the opening Alleluia melody is repeated after a middle section that is set to a Biblical verse.

|  |  |  |
|---|---|---|
| Solo voice: *Alleluia* phrase. | | A |
| Chorus: Long series of tones on *ia*. | | 21 36 0:00 |

| | | B |
|---|---|---|
| Chorus: *Vidimus stellam* | We have seen His star | 22 37 0:23 |
| *ejus in Oriente,* | in the East | |
| *et venimus cum muneribus* | and are come with gifts | |
| *adorare Dominum.* | to worship the Lord. | |

|  |  |
|---|---|
| | A |
| Chorus: *Alleluia* phrase with long series of tones on *ia*. | 23 38 1:43 |

**A**
Alleluia
[Soloist]                                          [Choir]

Al - le - lu - ia.

## SECULAR MUSIC IN THE MIDDLE AGES

Despite the domination of Gregorian chant (and despite the fact that for centuries only sacred music was notated), there was much music outside the church. The first large body of secular songs that survives in decipherable notation was composed during the twelfth and thirteenth centuries by French nobles called *troubadours* and *trouvères*. Most of these songs are about love, but there are also songs about the Crusades, dance songs, and spinning songs. In southern France, there were women troubadours—such as Beatriz de Dia—who addressed their songs to men. The notation of troubadour and trouvère melodies does not indicate rhythm, but it's likely

(Heidelberg University Library)

Many secular songs in the Middle Ages dealt with love. The illustration shows the German poet-composer Frauenlob (c. 1255–1318) with a group of musicians.

that many had a regular meter with a clearly defined beat (thus they differ from the nonmetrical rhythm of Gregorian chant).

There was also music performed by wandering minstrels—*jongleurs*—who were acrobats as well and were on the lowest social level. The jongleurs usually sang songs written by others and played instrumental dances on harps, fiddles (bowed string instruments), and lutes (plucked string instruments).

## ESTAMPIE (THIRTEENTH CENTURY)

The *estampie*, a medieval dance, is one of the earliest surviving forms of instrumental music. In the manuscript for this estampie, a single melodic line is notated and, as usual, no instrument is specified. In our recording, the melody is played on a *rebec* (a bowed string instrument) and a *pipe* (a tubular wind instrument). Since medieval minstrels probably improvised modest accompaniments to dance tunes, the performers have added a drone—two simultaneous, repeated notes at the interval of a fifth, played on a *psaltery* (a plucked or struck string instrument). The estampie is in triple meter and has a strong, fast beat.

Basic sets:
Side1, band 14
CD 1 39

## THE DEVELOPMENT OF POLYPHONY: ORGANUM

For centuries, western music was basically monophonic. But sometime between 700 and 900, the first steps were taken in a revolution that eventually transformed western music: monastery choirs began to add a second melodic line to Gregorian chant. Medieval music that consists of Gregorian chant and one or more additional melodic lines is called *organum.*

At first, the second line was improvised and simply duplicated the chant melody at a different pitch—the two lines were parallel, note against note, at an interval of a fourth (such as *do* to *fa*) or a fifth (such as *do* to *sol*):

Sit  glo - ri - a  Do - mi - ni  in  se - cu - la

Between 900 and 1200, however, organum became truly polyphonic, as the additional melody became more independent. The second melody might develop its own curve instead of remaining strictly parallel to the main melody (sometimes its motion was contrary to that of the chant). Around 1100, the two lines were no longer restricted to note-against-note style but could differ rhythmically. The chant, on the bottom, was often sung in very long notes while the added melody, on top, moved in shorter notes.

After 1150, Paris became the center of polyphonic music. Two successive choirmasters of the Cathedral of Notre Dame—Leonin and Perotin, the first notable composers known by name—and their followers are referred to as the *school of Notre Dame*, and from about 1170 to 1200 these Notre Dame composers developed rhythmic innovations. Earlier polyphonic music probably had the free, unmeasured rhythms of Gregorian chant; but Leonin and Perotin, for the first time in music history, used *measured rhythm*, with definite time values and a clearly defined meter.

Medieval polyphony had relatively few triads, which were later to become the basic consonant chords. A triad contains two intervals of a third (such as *do* to *mi* and *mi* to *sol*); medieval music theorists considered this a dissonance—though in the later Middle Ages triads and thirds were used more often, making polyphonic music fuller and richer (by our standards).

## FOURTEENTH-CENTURY MUSIC: THE "NEW ART" IN FRANCE

The fourteenth century was a time of disintegration in Europe: it saw the Hundred Years' War (1337–1453), the black death (bubonic plague), and a weakening of both the feudal system and the authority of the church. Given this atmosphere, it's not surprising that secular music became more important than sacred music in the fourteenth century.

Composers wrote polyphonic music that was *not* based on Gregorian chant, including drinking songs and pieces that imitated bird calls, barks of dogs, and hunters' shouts. By the early fourteenth century they had evolved a new system of music notation that allowed them to specify almost any rhythmic pattern. Syncopation—rarely used earlier—now became important. Changes in musical style in the fourteenth century were so profound that French and Italian music was called the *new art* (*ars nova*, in Latin). We'll study a mass by Guillaume de Machaut, the foremost French composer of the time.

## *NOTRE DAME* MASS (MID-FOURTEENTH CENTURY), BY GUILLAUME DE MACHAUT

Guillaume de Machaut (about 1300–1377), who was famous as both musician and poet, was born in the French province of Champagne. Though a priest, he spent most of his life as a court official for various royal families. Machaut traveled to many courts and presented beautifully decorated copies of his music to noble patrons; these make him one of the first important composers whose works have survived. The decline of the church is reflected in his output, which consists mainly of love songs for one or two voices and instrumental accompaniment. But he also wrote sacred music, and his *Notre Dame* Mass, the best-known composition of the fourteenth century, is of great historical importance: it is the first polyphonic treatment of the mass ordinary by a known composer.

The **mass ordinary** consists of texts that remain the same from day to day throughout most of the church year. The five sung prayers of the ordinary are the Kyrie, Gloria, Credo, Sanctus, and Agnus Dei. Since the fourteenth century, these five texts have often been set to polyphonic music and have inspired some of the greatest choral works. In each age, composers have responded to the mass in their own particular style. This centuries-old tradition of the mass gives invaluable insight into the long span of music and its changing styles.

The *Notre Dame* Mass is written for four voices, some of which were probably performed or doubled by instruments. How Machaut wanted his mass performed and which instruments were used to support the voices are unknown. We also do not know when or why the mass was composed. We'll examine the Agnus Dei of the mass as an example of fourteenth-century polyphony.

### Agnus Dei

Machaut's music for the Agnus Dei—a prayer for mercy and peace—is solemn and elaborate. It is in triple meter; complex rhythmic patterns contribute to its intensity. The two upper parts are rhythmically active and

Brief sets:
Side 1, band 7
CD 1 24

Basic sets:
Side 2, band 2
CD 1 41

contain syncopation, a characteristic of fourteenth-century music. The two lower parts move in longer notes and play a supporting role. In our recording, one low part is played on an instrument, and the other three parts are sung by vocal soloists who are reinforced by instruments.

The Agnus Dei is based on a Gregorian chant, which Machaut furnished with new rhythmic patterns and placed in the tenor, one of the two lower parts. Since the chant, or cantus firmus, is rhythmically altered within a polyphonic web, it is more a musical framework than a tune to be recognized. The harmonies of the Agnus Dei include stark dissonances, hollow-sounding chords, and full triads. Thus the Agnus Dei sounds fuller than some earlier medieval works.

Like the chant melody on which it is based, the Agnus Dei is in three sections. It may be outlined as follows:

Agnus Dei (I)    Agnus Dei (II)    Agnus Dei (III)
    A             B              A

The same text appears in each section, except for a change from *miserere nobis (have mercy on us)* to *dona nobis pacem (grant us peace)* in the concluding Agnus Dei (III). A and B are similar in mood, rhythm, and texture and end with the same hollow-sounding chord. The division into three sections is thought to symbolize the Trinity. In Machaut's time, music was meant to appeal to the mind as much as to the ear.

A
24 41 0:00

*Agnus dei, qui tollis peccata mundi: miserere nobis.*

Lamb of God, who taketh away the sins of the world, have mercy on us.

B
25 42 0:59

*Agnus dei, qui tollis peccata mundi: miserere nobis.*

Lamb of God, who taketh away the sins of the world, have mercy on us.

A
26 43 2:21

*Agnus dei, qui tollis peccata mundi: dona nobis pacem.*

Lamb of God, who taketh away the sins of the world, grant us peace.

# MUSIC IN THE RENAISSANCE (1450–1600)

The fifteenth and sixteenth centuries in Europe have come to be known as the *Renaissance*. People then spoke of a "rebirth," or "renaissance," of creativity; it was a period of exploration and adventure which saw the voyages of Columbus and Magellan and produced Leonardo da Vinci—who was a painter, sculptor, architect, engineer, and scientist, and fine musician.

Renaissance sculptors and painters once again depicted the nude human body, which had been a subject of shame and concealment during the Middle Ages. Above: *The Birth of Venus* (1480), by Botticelli.

*David* (1504), by Michelangelo.

(Schloss Rohrau, Vienna)

During the Renaissance, music was an important leisure activity; every educated person was expected to play an instrument and read musical notation. *The Concert*, a sixteenth-century painting by the "Master of the Female Half-Lengths," shows a flutist, a lutenist, and a singer.

The dominant intellectual movement, called *humanism*, focused on human life and accomplishments, and the humanists—though devout Christians—were captivated by the pagan cultures of ancient Greece and Rome. Humanism strongly influenced Renaissance art: for example, sculptors and painters once again depicted the nude human body, and they treated the madonna not as childlike or unearthly but as a beautiful young woman.

The Catholic church was far less powerful during the Renaissance than it had been during the Middle Ages, for the unity of Christendom was exploded by the Protestant Reformation led by Martin Luther (1483–1546). No longer did the church monopolize learning. Aristocrats and the upper middle class now considered education a status symbol, and they hired scholars to teach their children. The invention of printing with movable type (around 1450) accelerated the spread of learning. Before 1450, books were rare and extremely expensive because they were copied by hand. By 1500, 15 to 20 million copies of 40,000 editions had been printed in Europe.

The Renaissance in music occurred between 1450 and 1600 (though some historians place its beginning as early as 1400). As with the other arts, musical horizons were expanded: printing widened the circulation of music, and the number of composers and performers increased. Indeed, every educated person was expected to be trained in music, in keeping with the Renaissance ideal of the "universal man." As in the past, musicians worked in churches, courts, and towns; but though the church remained an important patron (and church choirs increased in size), musical activity gradually shifted to the courts.

## CHARACTERISTICS OF RENAISSANCE MUSIC

### Words and Music

In the Renaissance, as in the Middle Ages, vocal music was more important than instrumental music. The humanistic interest in language influenced vocal music, creating a close relationship between words and music: Renaissance composers (much more than medieval composers) wrote music to enhance the meaning and emotion of the text.

Renaissance composers often used *word painting*, a musical representation of specific poetic images. For example, the words *descending from heaven* might be set to a descending melodic line, and *running* might be heard with a series of rapid notes. Yet, despite this emphasis on capturing the emotion and imagery of a text, Renaissance music may seem calm and restrained to us. While there *is* a wide range of emotion in Renaissance music, it usually is expressed in a moderate, balanced way, with *no* extreme contrasts of dynamics, tone color, or rhythm.

### Texture

The texture of Renaissance music is chiefly polyphonic. A typical choral piece has four, five, or six voice parts of nearly equal melodic interest. Imitation among the voices is common: each presents the same melodic idea in turn, as in a round. Homophonic texture, with successions of chords, is also used, especially in light music, like dances. The texture may vary within a piece to provide contrast and bring out aspects of the text.

Renaissance music sounds fuller than medieval music. The bass register was used for the first time, expanding the pitch range to more than 4 octaves. With this new emphasis on the bass line came richer harmony. Composers began to think in terms of chords as well as individual melodies. Now all the melodic lines were conceived at the same time. (During the Middle Ages, a melodic line was conceived and then another was added on top of it, with relatively little attention to total harmonic effect.)

Renaissance music sounds mild and relaxed, because stable, consonant chords are favored; triads occur often, while dissonances are played down.

Renaissance choral music did not need instrumental accompaniment, and this period is thus sometimes called the "golden age" of *a capella* (*unaccompanied*) choral music. Even so, instruments were often combined with voices. They might duplicate the vocal lines to reinforce the sound, or they might take the part of a missing singer. But parts written exclusively for instruments are rarely found in Renaissance choral music.

### Rhythm and Melody

In Renaissance music, rhythm is more a gentle flow than a sharply defined beat. This is because each melodic line has great rhythmic independence: when one singer is at the beginning of his or her melodic phrase, the others may already be in the middle of theirs. This technique makes singing Renaissance music both a pleasure and a challenge, for each singer must maintain an individual rhythm. But pitch patterns in Renaissance melodies are easy to sing. The melody usually moves along a scale with few large leaps.

## SACRED MUSIC IN THE RENAISSANCE

The two main forms of sacred Renaissance music are both polyphonic choral works. The *motet* is set to a sacred Latin text other than the ordinary of the mass; the *mass* is made up of five sections—Kyrie, Gloria, Credo, Sanctus, and Agnus Dei. The motet and the mass are alike in style, but the mass is longer.

### The Renaissance Motet

*AVE MARIA . . . VIRGO SERENA*
*(HAIL, MARY . . . SERENE VIRGIN; 1502),*
**BY JOSQUIN DESPREZ**

**Brief sets:**
**Side 1, band 8**
**CD 1** 27

Basic sets:
Side 2, band 3
CD 1 44

Josquin Desprez (about 1440–1521) was a master of Renaissance music. Like many leading composers of the time, he was Flemish and had an international career; he spent much of his life in Italy, serving in ducal chapels and in the Papal Choir, and in his later years he worked for Louis XII of France and held several church posts in Flanders. His compositions, which included masses, motets, and secular vocal pieces, strongly influenced other composers and were praised enthusiastically by music lovers (including Martin Luther).

Josquin's four-voice motet *Ave Maria . . . virgo serena* is an outstanding Renaissance choral work. This Latin prayer to the Virgin is set to delicate and serene music. The opening uses polyphonic imitation, a technique typical of the period. The short melodic phrase on *Ave Maria* is presented by the soprano voice and then imitated in turn by the alto, tenor, and bass. The next two words, *gratia plena (full of grace),* have a different melody, which also is passed from voice to voice. Notice that each voice enters while the preceding one is in the middle of its melody. This overlapping creates a feeling of continuous flow. Josquin adapted the melody for the opening phrases from a Gregorian chant, but the rest of the motet was not based on a chant melody.

Josquin skillfully varies the texture of this motet; two, three, or four voices are heard at one time. In addition to the imitation among individual voices, there is imitation between pairs of voices: duets between the high voices are imitated by the two lower parts. Sometimes the texture almost becomes homophonic, as at the words *Ave, vera virginitas.* Here, also, is a change from duple to triple meter, and the tempo momentarily becomes more animated. But soon the music returns to duple meter and a more peaceful mood. *Ave Maria* ends with slow chords that express Josquin's personal plea to the Virgin: *O Mother of God, remember me. Amen.*

| | | |
|---|---|---|
| **27** **44** 0:00 | *Ava Maria*<br>*gratia plena*<br>*dominus tecum,*<br>*virgo serena.* | Hail Mary,<br>full of grace,<br>the Lord is with thee,<br>serene Virgin. | Each soprano phrase<br>imitated in turn by<br>alto, tenor, and bass.<br>Duple meter. |
| 0:49 | *Ave, cuius conceptio,* | Hail, whose conception, | High duet imitated by<br>three lower voices. |
| | *solemni plena gaudio,*<br>*coelestia terrestria*<br>*nova replet laetitia.* | full of great jubilation,<br>fills Heaven and Earth<br>with new joy. | All four voices.<br>Increased rhythmic<br>animation reflects<br>"new joy." |
| 1:32 | *Ave, cuius nativitas*<br>*nostra fuit solemnitas,*<br>*ut lucifer lux oriens*<br>*verum solem praeveniens.* | Hail, whose birth<br>brought us joy,<br>as Lucifer, the morning star,<br>went before the true sun. | High duet imitated by<br>low duet.<br>Soprano phrase<br>imitated by alto,<br>tenor, and bass. |
| 2:17 | *Ave, pia humilitas,*<br>*sine viro fecunditas,*<br>*cuius annuntiatio*<br>*nostra fuit salvatio.* | Hail, pious humility,<br>fruitful without a man,<br>whose Annunciation<br>brought us salvation. | High duet imitated by<br>low duet.<br>High duet.<br>Low duet. |
| **28** **45** 2:50 | *Ave, vera virginitas,*<br>*immaculata castitas,*<br>*cuius purificatio*<br>*nostra fuit purgatio.* | Hail, true virginity,<br>immaculate chastity,<br>whose purification<br>brought our cleansing. | Triple meter. |
| **29** **46** 3:16 | *Ave, praeclara omnibus*<br>*angelicis virtutibus,*<br>*cuius assumptio*<br>*nostra glorificatio* | Hail, glorious one<br>in all angelic virtues,<br>whose Assumption<br>was our glorification. | Duple meter, high<br>duets imitated by<br>lower voices.<br>Brief pause. |
| | *O mater Dei,*<br>*memento mei. Amen.* | O Mother of God,<br>remember me. Amen. | Sustained chords. |

## The Renaissance Mass

### *POPE MARCELLUS* MASS (1562–1563), BY GIOVANNI PIERLUIGI PALESTRINA

During the sixteenth century, Italian composers attained the excellence of earlier Flemish masters such as Josquin. Among the most important Italian Renaissance composers was Giovanni Pierluigi Palestrina (about 1525–1594), who devoted himself to church music and accordingly had a career centered in Rome (one of his positions was music director of St. Peter's). Palestrina's music includes 104 masses and some 450 other sacred works; its restraint and serenity reflect an emphasis on spirituality (for centuries, church authorities have regarded his masses as models of church music), and its technical perfection is a model for students of counterpoint.

# THE MIDDLE AGES

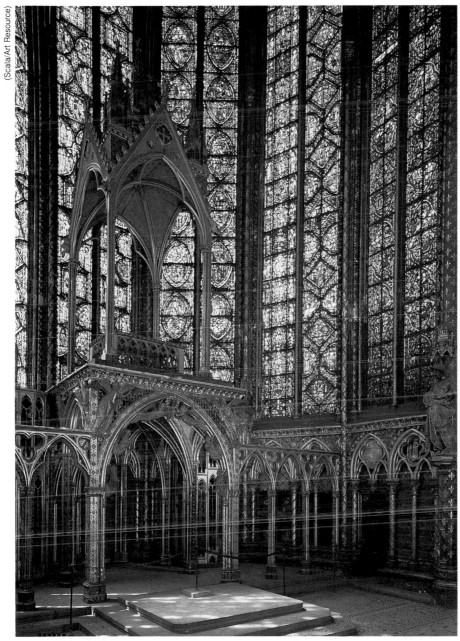

Interior of the Sainte-Chapelle in Paris (1243–1248). During the Middle Ages, religious teachings were imparted, and beliefs were strengthened, by the biblical scenes depicted in stained-glass windows.

*Madonna and Child Enthroned,* by an anonymous Byzantine artist (late thirteenth century). Like Gregorian chant, medieval painting often expressed an otherworldly feeling. It represented the voice of the church, rather than of any individuals.

# THE RENAISSANCE

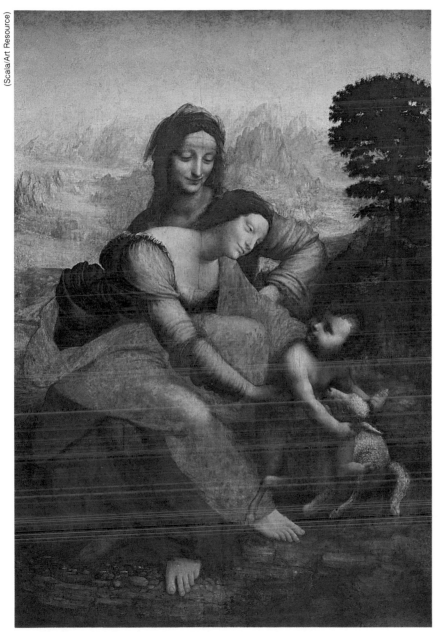

*Saint Anne, the Virgin, and Child* (1506–1510), by Leonardo da Vinci. The Renaissance was an age of curiosity and individualism, exemplified in the remarkable life of Leonardo da Vinci (1452–1519), who was an important painter, a sculptor, an architect, an engineer, and a scientist—and a fine musician as well. Renaissance painters emphasized balance and human beauty and used perspective to create an illusion of depth.

An important form of vocal music was the **madrigal,** a piece for several solo voices set to a short poem, usually about love. Like a motet, it has homophonic and polyphonic textures, but it more often uses word painting and unusual harmonies. Madrigals began in Italy around 1520 and were published there by the thousands in the sixteenth century. In 1588 a volume of translated Italian madrigals was published in London, setting off a spurt of madrigal writing by English composers. The English madrigal became lighter and more humorous than its Italian model, with simpler melody and harmony.

### *AS VESTA WAS DESCENDING* (1601), BY THOMAS WEELKES

**Brief sets:**
**Side 1, band 9**
**CD 1** 30

Basic sets:
Side 2, band 4
CD 1 47

Among the finest English madrigalists was Thomas Weelkes (about 1575–1623), an organist and church composer. Weelkes's *As Vesta Was Descending* comes from *The Triumphes of Oriana* (1601), an anthology of English madrigals written to honor Queen Elizabeth, who was often called Oriana. The text of this six-voice madrigal pictures Vesta (the Roman goddess of the hearth) coming down a hill with her attendants, "Diana's darlings." (Diana was the Roman goddess of chastity, hunting, and the moon.) At the same time, the "maiden queen," Oriana (Elizabeth), is climbing the hill with her shepherd gallants. Vesta's attendants desert her and race down the hill to join Oriana.

*As Vesta Was Descending* has the light mood typical of English madrigals. Word painting is plentiful. For example, the word *descending* is sung to downward scales, and *ascending* to upward ones.

When Vesta's attendants run down the hill, "first *two* by *two*, then *three* by *three together*, leaving their goddess all *alone*," we hear first *two* voices, then *three* voices, then *six* voices, and finally a *solo* voice. In the extended concluding section, "*Long* live fair Oriana," a joyous phrase is imitated among the voices. And in the bass this phrase is sung in long notes, with the longest note on the word *long*.

As Vesta was from Latmos hill descending,
she spied a maiden queen the same ascending,
attended on by all the shepherds swain,
to whom Diana's darlings
came running down amain.

First two by two,
then three by three together,

leaving their goddess all alone, hasted thither,
and mingling with the shepherds of her train
with mirthful tunes her presence entertain.
Then sang the shepherds and nymphs of Diana,
Long live fair Oriana!

30 47
Descending scales
Ascending scales.

Rapid descending
figures.
Two voices.
Three voices; all
voices.
Solo voice.

Brief joyful phrase
imitated among
voices; long notes
in bass.

## Instrumental Music

Though still subordinate to vocal music, instrumental music did become
more important during the Renaissance. Traditionally, instruments accompanied voices or played music intended for singing, and even in the early
1500s instrumental music was largely adapted from vocal music. But during the sixteenth century instrumental music became increasingly emancipated from vocal models: more music was written specifically for instruments, composers began to exploit instruments' particular capacities when
writing instrumental solos, and purely instrumental forms (such as theme
and variations) were developed. Much of this instrumental music was intended for dancing—a popular Renaissance entertainment—and a wealth
of dance music has come down to us.

Renaissance instruments produced softer, less brilliant sounds than the
instruments we hear today. Most came in families of three to eight, ranging
from soprano to bass (recorders and viols—bowed string instruments—
were among the most important), and often several members of a family
were played together. But composers did not specify instruments: a piece
might be performed by different instruments, depending on what was
available, and today's standardized orchestras and other ensembles did
not exist.

## RICERCAR IN THE TWELFTH MODE
## (SIXTEENTH CENTURY), BY ANDREA GABRIELI

Andrea Gabrieli (about 1520–1586) was organist at St. Mark's Cathedral in
Venice from 1564 until his death. He was an important composer of both
sacred and secular vocal music, as well as instrumental music.

Basic sets:
Side 2, band 5
CD 1 48

Gabrieli's Ricercar in the Twelfth Mode was written for four unspecified instruments (soprano, alto, tenor, and bass). In our recording, the ricercar is performed by a group of recorders ranging from soprano to bass. (A *ricercar* is a polyphonic instrumental composition employing imitation. That this one is "in the twelfth mode" means that it is based on a scale corresponding to C major.)

This short, lively piece is composed of several contrasting sections; its form is A B CC A. Gabrieli unifies the ricercar by bringing back the opening material (A) after the two middle sections. Most of section C is in triple meter and contrasts with the duple meter of sections A and B. The work features imitation among the individual instruments and rapid echoes between the two lower and two upper parts. Though relatively simple, the piece is an early step toward the more elaborate instrumental music that developed in the baroque period.

# III

# THE BAROQUE PERIOD

III

During the late baroque period, instrumental music became, for the first time, as important as vocal music. Jan Vermeer's painting *A Lady and Gentleman at the Virginals* (1664) shows a virginal, which is a type of small harpsichord, and a viola da gamba.

# [ 1 ] BAROQUE MUSIC (1600–1750)

Though the word *baroque* has at various times meant bizarre, flamboyant, and elaborately ornamented, modern historians use it simply to indicate a particular style in the arts. An oversimplified but useful characterization of baroque style is that it fills space—canvas, stone, or sound—with action and movement. Painters, sculptors, and architects became interested in forming a total illusion, like a stage setting. Artists such as Bernini, Rubens, and Rembrandt exploited their materials to expand the potential of color, detail, ornament, and depth; they wanted to create totally structured worlds.

Such a style was very well suited to the wishes of the aristocracy, who also thought in terms of completely integrated structures. In France, for example, Louis XIV held court in the Palace of Versailles, a magnificent setting that fused baroque painting, sculpture, and architecture into a symbol of royal wealth and power. The baroque style was also shaped by the needs of churches, which used the emotional and theatrical qualities of art to make worship more attractive. The middle class, too, influenced the development of the baroque style. In the Netherlands, for instance, prosperous merchants and doctors commissioned realistic depictions of landscapes and scenes from everyday life.

It's also helpful to think of baroque style against the backdrop of seventeenth-century scientific discovery. The work of Galileo (1564–1642) and Newton (1642–1727) represented a new approach to science based on the union of mathematics and experiment; they discovered mathematical laws governing bodies in motion. Such scientific advances led to new inventions and the gradual improvement of medicine, mining, navigation, and industry during the baroque era. Baroque art is a complex mixture of rationalism, sensuality, materialism, and spirituality.

In music, the baroque style flourished from about 1600 to 1750. Its two giants were George Frideric Handel and Johann Sebastian Bach (Bach's death in 1750 marks the end of the period), but many other masters—Monteverdi, Purcell, Corelli, Vivaldi—were largely forgotten until the "baroque revival" of the 1940s and 1950s.

During the baroque period (and until about 1800), most music was written to order; it was commissioned by aristocratic courts, churches, opera houses, and municipalities, all of which also employed musicians—and invariably demanded *new* music. Thus composers were an integral part of baroque society; and even though they wrote their music for specific needs of their patrons, its quality is so high that much of it has become standard in today's concert repertory.

(Michael J. Howell)

The Palace of Versailles, in France, fused baroque architecture, sculpture, and painting into a symbol of royal wealth and power.

(Alinari-Anderson/Art Resource)

Bernini's *David Slaying Goliath* (1623) fills space with action and movement. It is far more dynamic than Michelangelo's *David*, shown on page 65.

79

The baroque period can be divided into three phases: early (1600–1640), middle (1640–1680), and late (1680–1750). The early phase was one of the most revolutionary periods in music history. Italian composers of the early baroque invented opera—a drama sung to orchestral accompaniment—and the operas of Claudio Monteverdi (1567–1643) convey unprecedented passion and dramatic contrast. Early baroque composers favored homophonic textures, which they felt could project words more clearly than the polyphony typical of Renaissance music; and, to depict extreme emotions, they used dissonances with a new freedom. They also stressed contrasts of sound—solo singers against a chorus, voices against instruments.

During the middle phase (1640–1680), the new musical style spread from Italy throughout Europe. The church modes of the Middle Ages gradually gave way to major and minor scales, which were the tonal basis for most compositions by about 1680; and instrumental music took on a new importance.

We will focus mainly on the late baroque period (1680–1750), which produced most of the baroque music heard today. Many aspects of harmony (including the emphasis on the dominant-tonic attraction) arose during this period, and for the first time instrumental music became as important as vocal music. Polyphony returned to favor; in fact, late baroque composers gloried in it.

Let's look more closely at some features of late baroque style. (From now on, the word *baroque* will pertain to the late baroque phase.)

## CHARACTERISTICS OF BAROQUE MUSIC

### Unity of Mood

A baroque piece usually expresses one basic mood—what begins joyfully will remain joyful throughout. Emotional states like joy, grief, and agitation were represented. (At the time, these moods were called *affections*.) Composers molded a musical language to depict the affections; specific rhythms or melodic patterns were associated with specific moods. This common language gives a family resemblance to much late baroque music.

The prime exception to this baroque principle of unity of mood occurs in vocal music. Drastic changes of emotion in a text may inspire corresponding changes in the music. But even in such cases, one mood is maintained at some length before it yields to another.

### Rhythm

Unity of mood in baroque music is conveyed, first of all, by continuity of rhythm. Rhythmic patterns heard at the beginning of a piece are repeated throughout it. This rhythmic continuity provides a compelling drive and energy—the forward motion is rarely interrupted. The beat is emphasized far more in baroque music than in most Renaissance music, for example.

## Melody

Baroque melody also creates a feeling of continuity. An opening melody will be heard again and again in the course of a piece. Even when a melody is varied, its character tends to remain constant. There is a continuous expanding, unfolding, and unwinding of melody. This sense of directed motion is frequently the result of a melodic sequence—successive repetition of a musical idea at higher or lower pitch levels. Many baroque melodies sound elaborate and ornamental, and they are not easy to sing or remember. The baroque melody gives an impression of dynamic expansion rather than of balance and symmetry. A short opening phrase is often followed by a longer phrase with an unbroken flow of rapid notes.

## Terraced Dynamics

Paralleling continuity of rhythm and melody in baroque music is a continuity of dynamic level: the volume tends to stay constant for a stretch of time. When the dynamics do shift, it's sudden, like stepping physically from one level to another. This alternation between loud and soft is called *terraced dynamics*. *Gradual* changes through crescendo and decrescendo are *not* typical of baroque music. However, singers and instrumentalists no doubt made some subtle, expressive dynamic inflections.

The main keyboard instruments of the baroque period were the organ and harpsichord, both well suited for continuity of dynamic level. An organist or harpsichordist could not obtain a crescendo or decrescendo by varying finger pressure, as pianists today can. A third keyboard instrument, the clavichord, could make gradual dynamic changes, but only within a narrow range—from about *ppp* to *mp*. The clavichord produced sounds by means of brass blades striking the strings. It was usually not played in large halls, since its tone was too weak. But for use by amateurs at home it was ideal; its cost was low and its expressive sound satisfying. It had especially wide popularity in Germany.

## Texture

Late baroque music is predominantly polyphonic in texture: two or more melodic lines compete for the listener's attention. Usually, the soprano and bass lines are the most important. Imitation between the various lines, or "voices," of the texture is very common. A melodic idea heard in one voice is likely to make an appearance in the other voices as well.

However, not all late baroque music was polyphonic. A piece might shift in texture, especially in vocal music, where changes of mood in the words demand musical contrast. Also, baroque composers differed in their treatment of musical texture. Bach inclined toward a consistently polyphonic texture, whereas Handel used much more contrast between polyphonic and homophonic sections.

## Chords and the Basso Continuo (Figured Bass)

Chords became increasingly important during the baroque period. In earlier times, there had been more concern with the beauty of individual melodic lines than with chords formed when the lines were heard together. In a sense, chords were mere by-products of the motion of melodic lines. But in the baroque period chords became significant in themselves. As composers wrote a melodic line, they thought of chords to mesh with it. Indeed, sometimes they composed a melody to fit a specific chord progression. This interest in chords gave new prominence to the bass part, which served as the foundation of the harmony. The whole musical structure rested on the bass part.

The new emphasis on chords and the bass part resulted in the most characteristic feature of baroque music, an accompaniment called the **basso continuo,** or **figured bass.** This is made up of a bass part together with numbers (figures) which specify the chords to be played above it. The continuo—to use the common abbreviation for *basso continuo*—is usually played by at least two instruments: an organ or a harpsichord and a low melodic instrument like the cello or bassoon. With the left hand, the organist or harpsichordist plays the bass part, which is also performed by the cello or bassoon. With the right hand, the keyboard player improvises chords or even a melodic line, following the indications of the numbers. These numbers specify only a basic chord, not the exact way in which the chord should be played. Thus, the performer is given a great deal of freedom. (This shorthand system is similar in principle to the chord indications found on the modern song sheets from which jazz pianists improvise.) Shown below is the beginning of the continuo part of Bach's *Brandenburg* Concerto No. 5, first movement (studied in Section 2), and one possible performance or "realization" of this part by a harpsichordist.

Basso Continuo Part

Harpsichord Realization

The basso continuo offered the advantage of emphasizing the all-important bass part, besides providing a steady flow of chords. Practically, the use of numbers, rather than chords with all their notes written out, saved time for busy baroque composers. It also saved paper at a time when paper was expensive.

## Words and Music

Like their Renaissance predecessors, baroque composers used music to depict the meaning of specific words. The word *heaven* might be set to a high tone, and the word *hell* to a low tone. Rising scales represented upward motion; descending scales depicted the reverse. Descending chromatic scales were associated with pain and grief. This descriptive musical language was quite standardized: a lament for a lost love might call forth the same descending chromatic scale used to depict suffering in the *Crucifixus* of the mass.

Baroque composers emphasized words by writing many rapid notes for a single syllable of text; this technique also displayed a singer's virtuosity. The individual words and phrases of a text are repeated over and over as the music continuously unfolds.

## THE BAROQUE ORCHESTRA

During the baroque period, the orchestra evolved into a performing group based on instruments of the violin family. By modern standards, the baroque orchestra was small, consisting of from ten to thirty or forty players. Its instrumental makeup was flexible and could vary from piece to piece. At its nucleus were the basso continuo (harpsichord plus cello, double bass, or bassoon) and upper strings (first and second violins and violas). Use of woodwind, brass, and percussion instruments was variable. To the strings and continuo could be added recorders, flutes, oboes, trumpets, horns, trombones, or timpani. One piece might use only a single flute, while another would call for two oboes, three trumpets, and timpani. Trumpets and timpani joined the orchestra mainly when the music was festive. This flexibility contrasts with the standardized orchestra of later periods, composed of four sections: strings, woodwinds, brasses, and percussion.

The baroque trumpet had no valves but was given rapid, complex melodic lines to play in a high register. Because the instrument was difficult to play and had a traditional association with royalty, the trumpeter was the aristocrat of the baroque orchestra. When prisoners of war were exchanged, trumpeters, if they had been captured, were treated like military officers.

Bach, Handel, Vivaldi, and others chose their orchestral instruments with care and obtained beautiful effects from specific tone colors. They loved to experiment with different combinations of instruments. However, in the baroque period tone color was distinctly subordinate to other musical elements—melody, rhythm, and harmony. Composers frequently rearranged their own or other composers' works for different instruments. A piece for string orchestra might become an organ solo, losing little in the process. Often, one instrument was treated like another. An oboe would play the same melody as the violins, or the flute and trumpet would imitate each other for extended sections of a piece.

## BAROQUE FORMS

It has been noted that a piece of baroque music—particularly instrumental music—usually has unity of mood. Yet many baroque compositions include a set of pieces, or movements, that contrast. A *movement* is a piece that sounds fairly complete and independent but is part of a larger composition. Usually, each movement has its own themes, comes to a definite end, and is separated from the next movement by a brief pause. Thus, a baroque composition in three movements may contain contrasts between a fast and energetic opening, a slow and solemn middle, and a conclusion that is quick, light, and humorous.

All the form types described in ''Musical Form'' in Part I appear in baroque music. Three-part form (A B A), two-part form (A B), and continuous or undivided form are all common. A variation form found in many baroque works is the **ground bass,** or **basso ostinato** (*obstinate*, or *persistent, bass*), a musical idea repeated over and over in the bass while the melodies above it constantly change. (One famous example of the ground bass is the aria *Dido's Lament* from *Dido and Aeneas*, an opera by the English composer Henry Purcell, who lived from about 1659 to 1695.)

Regardless of form, baroque music features contrasts between bodies of sound. Often there is a quite regular alternation between a small and a large group of instruments, or between instruments and voices with instrumental accompaniment. This exploration of contrasting sounds was pursued with great imagination and provides a key to the understanding and enjoyment of baroque music.

Basic sets:
Side 2, band 8
CD 1 57

# THE CONCERTO GROSSO AND RITORNELLO FORM

We've seen that the contrast between loud and soft sounds—between large and small groups of performers—is a basic principle of baroque music. This principle governs the concerto grosso, an important form of orchestral music in the late baroque period. In the *concerto grosso*, a small group of soloists is pitted against a larger group of players called the *tutti (all)*. Usually, between two and four soloists play with anywhere from eight to twenty or more musicians for the tutti. The tutti consists mainly of string instruments, with a harpsichord as part of the basso continuo. A concerto grosso presents a contrast of texture between the tutti and the soloists, who assert their individuality and appeal for attention through brilliant and fanciful melodic lines. The soloists were the best and highest-paid members of the baroque orchestra, because their parts were more difficult than those of the other players. Concerti grossi were frequently performed by private orchestras in aristocratic palaces.

The concerto grosso consists of *several movements that contrast in tempo and character*. Most often there are three movements: (1) fast, (2) slow, (3) fast. The opening movement is usually vigorous and determined, clearly showing the contrast between tutti and soloists. The slow movement is quieter than the first, often lyrical and intimate. The last movement is lively and carefree, sometimes dancelike.

The first and last movements of concerti grossi are often in *ritornello form*, which is based on alternation between tutti and solo sections. In ritornello form the tutti opens with a theme called the *ritornello (refrain)*. This theme, always played by the tutti, returns in different keys throughout the movement. But it usually returns in fragments, not complete. Only at the end of the movement does the entire ritornello return in the home key. Although the number of times a ritornello (tutti) returns varies from piece to piece, a typical concerto grosso movement might be outlined as follows:

1. *a*. Tutti (*f*), ritornello in home key
   *b*. Solo
2. *a*. Tutti (*f*), ritornello fragment
   *b*. Solo
3. *a*. Tutti (*f*), ritornello fragment
   *b*. Solo
4. Tutti (*f*), ritornello in home key

In contrast to the tutti's ritornello, the solo sections offer fresh melodic ideas, softer dynamics, rapid scales, and broken chords. Soloists may also expand short melodic ideas from the tutti. The opening movement of Bach's *Brandenburg* Concerto No. 5 is a fine example of ritornello form in the concerto grosso.

## *BRANDENBURG* CONCERTO NO. 5 IN D MAJOR (1721), BY JOHANN SEBASTIAN BACH

Bach's six *Brandenburg* Concertos are so called because he dedicated them to the margrave of Brandenburg—although he had actually composed them for the orchestra of his own employer, the prince of Cöthen. Each of the six is written for a different and unusual combination of instruments.

The *Brandenburg* Concerto No. 5 uses a string orchestra and a group of soloists consisting of a flute, a violin, and a harpsichord. This was the first time that a harpsichord had been given the solo role in a concerto grosso. In 1719, the prince of Cöthen bought a new harpsichord; Bach probably wanted to show off this instrument (as well as his skill as a keyboard player), and so he gave it a solo spot. The tutti is written for violins, violas, cellos, and double bass. During the tutti sections the solo violinist plays along, as does the harpsichordist, who realizes the figured bass.

The *Brandenburg* Concerto No. 5 has three movements: (1) fast, (2) slow, (3) fast. We'll focus on the first movement.

### First Movement:

### Allegro

**Brief sets:**
**Side 1, band 10**
**CD 1** 31

Basic sets:
Side 3, band 1
CD 2 1

The allegro movement opens with the ritornello, which is an almost continuous flow of rapid notes. After the ritornello ends very definitely, the soloists present short melodic ideas, the flute and violin imitating each other playfully. The appearance of the soloists brings a lower dynamic level and the new tone color of the flute. After a while, the tutti returns loudly with a brief fragment of the ritornello, only to give way again to the soloists. This alternation between brief, loud ritornello fragments in the tutti and longer, softer solo sections continues throughout the movement.

The soloists' music tends to be brilliant, fanciful, and personal, compared with the more vigorous and straightforward tutti sections. Solo sections are also more polyphonic than the tutti and stress imitation between flute and violin. The soloists play new material of their own or varied fragments from the ritornello. These solo sections build tension and make the listener anticipate the tutti's return. Listen especially for the suspenseful solo section that begins with a new theme in minor and ends with fluttery trills in the flute and violin. (A **trill** is an ornament consisting of the rapid alternation of two tones a whole or half step apart.)

Only the harpsichord plays during the long final solo section. And it is spectacular! Bach builds a tense high point for the movement through irresistible rhythm and dazzling scale passages that require a virtuoso's skill. His audience must have marveled at this brilliant harpsichord solo within a concerto grosso. Audiences still do.

# Listening Outline  To be read while music is heard

*BRANDENBURG* CONCERTO NO. 5 IN D MAJOR (1721),
BY JOHANN SEBASTIAN BACH

First Movement: Allegro

Ritornello form, duple meter (²⁄₂), D major

Flute, violin, harpsichord (solo group); string orchestra, continuo (tutti)

(Duration, 9:43)

Tutti
`31` `1` 0:00        1. *a.* Strings, *f,* ritornello.

Solo
`32` `2` 0:20        *b.* Flute, violin, harpsichord, major key.
Tutti
        0:45        2. *a.* Strings, *f,* ritornello fragment.
Solo
`33` `3` 0:49        *b.* Flute, violin, harpsichord, varied ritornello fragment.
Tutti
        1:10        3. *a.* Strings, *f,* ritornello fragment.

Trills in flute and violin lead to

BAROQUE

3

# THE FUGUE

One cornerstone of baroque music is the fugue, which can be written for a group of instruments or voices, or for a single instrument like an organ or harpsichord. A *fugue* is a polyphonic composition based on one main theme, called a *subject.* Throughout a fugue, different melodic lines, or "voices," imitate the subject. The top melodic line—whether sung or played—is the soprano voice, and the bottom is the bass. A fugue's texture usually includes three, four, or five voices. Though the subject remains fairly constant throughout, it takes on new meanings when shifted to different keys or combined with different melodic and rhythmic ideas.

The form of a fugue is extremely flexible; in fact, the only constant feature of fugues is how they begin—the subject is almost always presented in a single, unaccompanied voice. By thus highlighting the subject, the composer tells us what to remember and listen for. In getting to know a fugue, try to follow its subject through the different levels of texture. After its first presentation, the subject is imitated in turn by all the remaining voices.

The opening of a fugue in four voices may be represented as follows:

Soprano      Subject _____ . . . . . . . . . . . . . . . . . . . . . . . . . . .   etc.

Alto                        Subject _____ . . . . . . . . . . . . . . . . . . . .   etc.

Tenor                              Subject _____ . . . . . . . . . . . .   etc.

Bass                                     Subject _____ . . . . . . . .   etc.

In this case, the top voice announces the subject and then the lower voices imitate it. However, the subject may be announced by *any* voice—top, bottom, or middle—and the order in which the remaining voices imitate it is also completely flexible.

This may seem reminiscent of a round like *Row, Row, Row Your Boat*, but in a fugue the game of follow the leader (exact imitation of the subject) does not continue indefinitely. The dotted lines in the diagram show that *after a voice has presented the subject, it is free to go its own way with different melodic material.* A fugue's opening differs from a round's in another way: in a round, each voice presents the melody on the same tones. If the melody begins with the tones C–D–E, each voice will begin with these tones, whether at a higher or lower register. But in the opening of a fugue, *the subject is presented in two different scales.* The first time, it is based on the notes of the *tonic scale.* But when the second voice presents the subject, it is in the *dominant scale*—five scale steps higher than the tonic —and it is then called the **answer.** A subject beginning with the notes C–D–E, for example, would be imitated by an answer five steps higher, on G–A–B. This alternation of subject and answer between the two scales creates variety.

In many fugues, the subject in one voice is constantly accompanied in another voice by a different melodic idea called a **countersubject.** A constant companion, the countersubject always appears with the subject— sometimes below it, sometimes above it.

After the opening of a fugue, when each voice has taken its turn at presenting the subject, a composer is free to decide how often the subject will be presented, in which voices, and in which keys. Between presentations of the subject, there are often transitional sections called **episodes,** which offer either new material or fragments of the subject or countersubject. Episodes do *not* present the subject in its entirety. They lend variety to the fugue and make reappearances of the subject sound fresh. Bach called one composer of fugues "pedantic" because he "had not shown enough fire to reanimate the theme by episodes."

Several musical procedures commonly appear in fugues. One is *stretto,* in which a subject is imitated before it is completed; one voice tries to catch the other. Another common procedure is *pedal point* (or *organ point*), in which a single tone, usually in the bass, is held while the other voices produce a series of changing harmonies against it. (The term is taken from organ music, where a sustained low tone is produced by the organist's foot on a key of the pedal keyboard.)

A fugue subject can be varied in four principal ways:

1.  It can be turned upside down, a procedure known as *inversion.* If the subject moves *upward* by leap, the inversion will move *downward* the same distance; if the subject moves *downward* by step, the inversion will move *upward* by step. In inversion, each interval in the subject is reversed in direction.
2.  The subject may be presented *retrograde,* that is, by beginning with the last note of the subject and proceeding backward to the first note.
3.  The subject may be presented in *augmentation,* in which the original time values are lengthened.
4.  The subject may appear in *diminution,* that is, with shortened time values.

Fugues usually convey a single mood and a sense of continuous flow. They may be written as independent works or as single movements within larger compositions. Very often an independent fugue is introduced by a short piece called a *prelude.*

Bach and Handel each wrote hundreds of fugues; their fugues represent the peak among works in the form. In the baroque period, as a friend of Bach's observed, "Skill in fugue was so indispensable in a composer that no one could have attained a musical post who had not worked out a given subject in all kinds of counterpoint and in a regular fugue." Fugal writing has continued into the nineteenth and twentieth centuries; it is not used as frequently as in the baroque period, yet to this day musicians study how to write fugues as part of their training.

## ORGAN FUGUE IN G MINOR (*LITTLE* FUGUE; ABOUT 1709), BY JOHANN SEBASTIAN BACH

**Brief sets:**
**Side 1, band 11**
**CD 1** [36]

Basic sets:
Side 2, band 10
CD 1 [64]

One of Bach's best-known organ pieces is the *Little* Fugue in G Minor, so called to differentiate it from another, longer fugue in the same key. The opening section of this fugue corresponds to the diagram on page 89.

Each of the fugue's four voices takes its turn presenting the tuneful subject, which is announced in the top voice and then appears in progressively lower voices until it reaches the bass, where it is played by the organist's feet on the pedal keyboard. Like many baroque melodies, the subject gathers momentum as it goes along, beginning with relatively long time values (quarter notes) and then proceeding to shorter ones (eighth and sixteenth notes). Starting with its second appearance, the subject is accompanied by a countersubject that moves in short time values.

After the opening section, the subject appears five more times, each time preceded by an episode. The first episode uses both new material and a melodic idea from the countersubject. This episode contains downward sequences, which are melodic patterns repeated in the same voice but at lower pitches.

For harmonic contrast, Bach twice presents the subject in major keys rather than minor. The final statement of the subject—in minor—exploits the powerful bass tones of the pedal keyboard. Though the fugue is in minor, it ends with a major chord. This was a frequent practice in the baroque period; major chords were thought more conclusive than minor.

## Listening Outline   To be read while music is heard

ORGAN FUGUE IN G MINOR (*LITTLE* FUGUE; 1709?),
BY JOHANN SEBASTIAN BACH

Fugue, quadruple meter ($\frac{4}{4}$), G minor
Organ

(Duration, 4:04)

36  64  0:00          1. *a.* Subject, soprano voice alone, minor key.

0:18  *b.* Subject in alto, countersubject in running notes in soprano.

0:41  *c.* Subject in tenor, countersubject above it.
0:58  *d.* Subject in bass (pedals), countersubject in tenor.
37 65 1:14  *e.* Brief episode, downward sequence.

1:24  2. *a.* Subject begins in tenor, continues in soprano, accompanied by sustained tone in bass; subject leads to
1:43  *b.* Brief episode, running notes in a downward sequence.
38 66 1:52  3. *a.* Subject in alto, major key; countersubject in soprano; subject leads to
2:17  *b.* Episode in major, upward leaps and running notes.
2:29  *c.* Subject in bass (pedals), major key, countersubject and long trill above it.
2:45  *d.* Longer episode, downward sequence; begins in major, ends in minor.
3:03  4. *a.* Subject in soprano, minor key, countersubject below it.
3:19  *b.* Most extended episode, running notes in a downward sequence; upward sequences lead to sustained high tones which usher in
3:49  *c.* Subject in bass (pedals), countersubject in soprano. Fugue ends with major chord.

# THE ELEMENTS OF OPERA

The baroque era witnessed the development of a major innovation in music—*opera,* or drama that is sung to orchestral accompaniment. In Section 5, we'll look at baroque opera; but first, a general discussion of opera is in order.

In opera, characters and plot are revealed through song rather than speech. Once we accept this convention, opera offers us great pleasure, since the music not only delights the ear but also depicts mood, character, and action and heightens the emotional effect of the story. Opera demands performers who can sing and act simultaneously, and in addition to solo singers—the stars—it uses secondary soloists, choruses, nonsinging "extras," and sometimes dancers, all in costume. In the orchestra pit are the instrumentalists and the conductor. Scenery, lighting, and stage machinery are intricate, since operas often include fires, floods, storms, and supernatural effects. A large opera's personnel—from conductor to stage director and assorted vocal coaches, rehearsal accompanists, technicians, and stagehands—may reach a startling total of several hundred people.

The creation of an opera results from the joint efforts of a composer and a dramatist. The text, called a *libretto,* is usually written by the dramatist, or *librettist,* and then set to music by the composer, but the two usually collaborate to ensure that the text meets the composer's musical needs. W. H. Auden has observed—correctly—that "no good opera plot can be sensible." Opera characters are people overwhelmed by love, lust, hatred, and revenge; they wear fantastic disguises and commit extraordinary acts of violence. Yet the music makes them human and real. A great opera composer is a master of musical timing and characterization and has a keen sense of the theater; through the music, the composer paces and controls the drama.

Some operas are serious, some comic, some both. Most are entirely sung, though some contain spoken dialogue. The range of characters is broad—gods, empresses, dukes, servants, priests, prostitutes, peasants, clowns, cowboys. For the opera soloists who create all these roles, the basic voice categories (soprano, alto, tenor, and bass) are divided more finely: the *voice categories of opera* include coloratura soprano (with a very high range), lyric soprano and lyric tenor, dramatic soprano and dramatic tenor, basso buffo (who takes comic roles), and basso profundo (with a very low range).

Like plays, operas have from one to five acts subdivided into scenes. An act presents a variety of vocal and orchestral contrasts. For many opera fans, the main attraction is the *aria,* a song for solo voice with orchestral accompaniment, usually lasting several minutes. An aria is an outpouring of melody that expresses an emotional state; it is a complete piece with a definite beginning, high point, and end (at which the audience often gives an ovation). Composers often lead into an aria with a *recitative,* a vocal line that imitates speech and is used to move the action forward. In a recitative, words are sung quickly, often on repeated tones, and with one note to each syllable—as opposed to an aria, where one syllable may be stretched over many notes. Besides arias, there are compositions for two or more singers: duets (two singers), trios (three), quartets (four), quintets (five), and sextets (six). Pieces for three or more singers are called *ensembles.* The opera chorus—courtiers, sailors, peasants, prisoners, or whatever—creates atmosphere and comments on the action.

The nerve center of an opera performance is the orchestra pit—a sunken area directly in front of the stage. An opera orchestra has the same instruments as a symphony orchestra but usually a smaller string section. It supports the singers, depicts mood and atmosphere, and highlights the drama. The conductor's awesome responsibility is to hold everything together. (A *conductor* beats time, indicates expression, cues in musicians, and controls the balance among instruments or voices.)

Most operas open with a purely orchestral composition that is called an *overture* or *prelude* (orchestral introductions to acts other than the first are always called *preludes*). Since the eighteenth century, the music for the overture has been drawn from material in the opera itself. Many overtures are complete compositions that frequently appear on symphony orchestra programs.

## BAROQUE
# 5 OPERA IN THE BAROQUE ERA

Opera was born in Italy. Its "parents" were a small group of nobles, poets, and composers called the **Camerata** (Italian for *fellowship* or *society*) who began meeting in Florence around 1575 to create a new vocal style based on the music of ancient Greek tragedy. (Since no ancient Greek music had survived, they relied on literary accounts of it.) This new style followed the rhythms and pitch fluctuations of speech. It was sung by a soloist with only a simple chordal accompaniment and was thus homophonic; the Camerata rejected polyphony because it would obscure the all-important text.

*Euridice*, by Jacopo Peri, which was performed in Florence in 1600, is the earliest opera that has been preserved; seven years later, Monteverdi composed *Orfeo*, the first *great* opera. Both are based on the Greek myth of Orpheus and Eurydice.

Much baroque opera was composed for ceremonial occasions at court; its subject matter, classical mythology and ancient history, fascinated aristocratic patrons and also flattered them, since they identified with the Greek and Roman heroes and gods. But in 1637, the first public opera house opened in Venice, and between then and 1700 there were seventeen opera houses in Venice alone and many in other Italian cities—ample evidence that opera was born in the right place at the right time. Court opera was designed to display magnificence and splendor; similarly, the public opera houses had stage machinery and sets that bordered on the colossal: gods would ride across the sky in chariots, ships would toss, boulders would split.

Baroque opera marked the rise of virtuoso singers, particularly the **castrato**, a male singer castrated before puberty. (A **virtuoso** is a performing artist of extraordinary technical mastery.) Castration of boy singers was common in Italy from 1600 to 1800, usually with the consent of impoverished parents who hoped their sons would go on to wealth and stardom. A castrato (plural, *castrati*) combined the lung power of a man with the vocal range of a woman and had a unique sound—not like a woman's—that intrigued listeners. Some baroque operas cannot be done today, because contemporary singers are unable to manage the fiendishly difficult castrato parts.

Late baroque operas consisted largely of arias linked by recitatives. Usually, the recitative is speechlike and accompanied only by a basso continuo, this is a *secco recitative.* When the recitative is supported by strings as well as continuo, it is called an *accompanied recitative.* The form of a typical aria is A B A, and an aria in A B A form is called a *da capo aria:* after the B section, the term *da capo* is written, meaning *from the beginning* and indicating a repetition of the A section. However, the repetition was not literal, because the singer was expected to *embellish* the returning melody with ornamental tones.

By combining virtuosity, nobility, and extravagance, baroque opera expressed the spirit of a grand age.

## ORFEO (ORPHEUS, 1607), BY CLAUDIO MONTEVERDI

The earliest operatic masterpiece, *Orfeo,* was created by Claudio Monteverdi (1567–1643), a monumental figure in the history of music whose works not only were highly influential in their time but also form a bridge between the sixteenth and seventeenth centuries. He composed *Orfeo* for the court of Mantua, where he was music director—a position which evidently earned him little money and even less respect. Later, life improved for him; in 1613, he was appointed music director of St. Mark's in Venice, the most important church position in Italy, and he remained there until his death.

Only three of Monteverdi's twelve operas are preserved, but they truly blend music and drama. To achieve emotional intensity, he used dissonance with unprecedented freedom and daring and introduced new orchestral effects, and his vocal lines respond marvelously to the inflections of Italian while maintaining melodic flow.

Fittingly enough, Monteverdi's first opera is about Orpheus, the supremely gifted musician of Greek myth. Orpheus, son of the god Apollo, is ecstatically happy after his marriage to Eurydice. But this joy is shattered when his bride is killed by a poisonous snake. Orpheus goes down to hades hoping to bring her back to life. Because of his beautiful music, he is granted this privilege—on the condition that he not look back at Eurydice while leading her out of hades. But in a moment of anxiety, Orpheus does look back, and Eurydice vanishes. Nonetheless, there is a happy ending, of sorts. Apollo pities Orpheus and brings him to heaven, where he can gaze eternally at Eurydice's radiance in the sun and stars.

When *Orfeo* was composed, in 1607, no expense was spared to make it a lavish production. There were star soloists, a chorus, dancers, and a large orchestra (for the time) of about forty players. The aristocratic audience was wildly enthusiastic and recognized the historic significance of the performance.

Monteverdi creates variety in *Orfeo* by using many kinds of music—recitatives, arias, duets, choruses, and instrumental interludes. He uses the opera orchestra to establish atmosphere, character, and dramatic situation. With the simplest of musical means, Monteverdi makes his characters come alive. Through vocal line alone he quickly characterizes the hero's joy and despair. Monteverdi sets his text in a very flexible way, freely alternating recitatives with more melodious passages, depending on the meaning of the words.

## Act II

### Recitative: *Tu se' morta (You are dead)*

**Brief sets:**
**Side 2, band 1**
**CD 1 39**

Basic sets:
Side 2, band 7
CD 1 56

Monteverdi's mastery of the then-novel technique of recitative is shown in *Tu se' morta,* which is sung by Orpheus after he is told of Eurydice's death. Orpheus resolves to bring Eurydice back from hades, and he bids an anguished farewell to the earth, sky, and sun. His vocal line is accompanied only by a basso continuo played by a small portable organ and a bass lute. (In modern performances, other instruments are sometimes substituted for these.)

The texture is homophonic: the accompaniment simply gives harmonic support to the voice. The vocal line is rhythmically free, with little sense of beat or meter, and its phrases are irregular in length. This flexible setting of text is meant to suggest the passionate speech of an actor declaiming his lines. Monteverdi frequently uses word painting, the musical representation of poetic images that was favored by baroque composers. For example, words like *stelle (stars)* and *sole (sun)* are sung to climactic high tones, while *abissi (abysses)* and *morte (death)* are sung to somber, low tones. Three times during the recitative the melodic line rises to a climax and then descends. In these ways, Orpheus's passion is conveyed very vividly.

| | |
|---|---|
| *Tu se' morta, se' morta, mia vita,* | You are dead, you are dead, my dearest, |
| *ed io respiro; tu se' da me partita,* | And I breathe; you have left me, |
| *se' da me partita per mai più,* | You have left me forevermore, |
| *mai più non tornare, ed io rimango—* | Never to return, and I remain— |
| *no, no, che se i versi alcuna cosa ponno,* | No, no, if my verses have any power, |
| *n'andrò sicuro a' più profondi abissi,* | I will go confidently to the deepest abysses, |
| *e, intenerito il cor del re de l'ombre,* | And, having melted the heart of the king of shadows, |
| *meco trarrotti a riveder le stelle,* | Will bring you back to me to see the stars again, |
| *o se ciò negherammi empio destino, rimarrò teco in compagnia di morte.* | Or, if pitiless fate denies me this, I will remain with you in the company of death. |
| *Addio terra, addio cielo, e sole, addio.* | Farewell earth, farewell sky, and sun, farewell. |

39 56

# THE BAROQUE SONATA

BAROQUE

6

One of the main developments in instrumental music was the baroque **sonata,** a composition in several movements for one to eight instruments. (In later periods, the term *sonata* took on a more restricted meaning.) Composers often wrote ***trio sonatas,*** so called because they had three melodic lines: two high ones and a basso continuo. A trio sonata is actually played by four instruments, however—two high instruments, such as violins, flutes, or oboes; and a keyboard instrument plus a cello or bassoon for the continuo.

## TRIO SONATA IN E MINOR, OP.* 3, NO. 7 (1689), BY ARCANGELO CORELLI

Arcangelo Corelli (1653–1713), the most prominent Italian violinist and composer of string music around 1700, was also an eminent teacher who laid the foundations of modern violin technique; he wrote only instrumental music—sixty sonatas and twelve concertos, all for strings.

Corelli's Trio Sonata in E Minor, Op. 3, No. 7, is a fine example of the baroque trio sonata. The basso continuo is for organ and cello; the upper lines are taken by two violins in the same high register. The violins are the center of attention; they seem to be rivals, taking turns at the melodic ideas, intertwining, and sometimes rising above each other in pitch. Though the bass line is subordinate to the two upper voices, it is no mere accompaniment. It imitates melodic ideas presented by the violins.

The sonata consists of four short movements: (1) slow, (2) fast, (3) slow, (4) fast. All are in the same key, but they differ in meter, mood, and tempo. Each movement alone, however, has only a single mood.

Supplementary sets:
Movements 1–4
Side 2, bands 1–4
CD 1 34 – 37

A solemn, dignified slow movement in quadruple meter opens the sonata. The main motive is presented by the first violin and immediately imitated in turn by the other instruments before it has been completed.

The second movement, a vigorous allegro, is fuguelike and in duple meter. Fugal second movements were characteristic of trio sonatas.

The third movement is a songlike adagio in triple meter. The two violins play in a high register until the concluding measures, when they sustain a single low tone while the cello plays a slow descending scale.

The lightest movement is the concluding allegro, a dancelike piece in triple meter, in A A B B form. Section B is almost twice as long as A. At the end of section B, Corelli uses his only dynamic change in the sonata: the concluding phrase is repeated softly, like an echo.

## BAROQUE 7

# ANTONIO VIVALDI

Antonio Vivaldi (1678–1741), a towering figure of the late Italian baroque, was the son of a violinist at St. Mark's Cathedral in Venice. He became a priest, but left the ministry after about a year because of poor health; for most of his life, he was a violin teacher, composer, and conductor at a Venetian music school for orphaned and illegitimate girls. It was for the school's all-female orchestra—considered one of the best in Italy—that he composed many of his finest works. Though he was famous and influential as a virtuoso violinist and composer, his popularity waned shortly before his death in 1741; he died in poverty and was almost forgotten until the baroque revival of the 1940s and 1950s.

Vivaldi is best known for his 450 or so concerti grossi and solo concertos (a *solo concerto* is a piece for a *single* soloist and an orchestra). He exploited the resources of the violin and many other instruments and is noted for vigorous, tuneful fast movements and impassioned, lyrical slow movements.

## LA PRIMAVERA (SPRING), CONCERTO FOR VIOLIN AND STRING ORCHESTRA, OP.* 8, NO. 1, FROM *THE FOUR SEASONS* (1725)

Vivaldi's most popular work is the concerto *La Primavera (Spring)* from *The Four Seasons*, a set of four solo concertos for violin, string orchestra, and basso continuo. Each of these concertos depicts sounds and events associated with one of the seasons, such as the bird songs of spring and the gentle breezes of summer. The descriptive effects in the music correspond to images and ideas in sonnets that preface each concerto. To make his intentions clear, Vivaldi placed lines from the poems at the appropriate passages in the musical score and even added such descriptive labels as *the sleeping goatherd* and *the barking dog*. These concertos are examples of baroque *program music*—instrumental music associated with a story, poem, idea, or scene. They are forerunners of the more elaborate program music that developed during the romantic period.

Like most of Vivaldi's concertos, *Spring* has three movements: (1) fast, (2) slow, (3) fast. Both the first movement (which we'll study) and the last are in ritornello form.

### First Movement:

### Allegro

The allegro, in E major, opens with an energetic orchestral ritornello depicting the arrival of spring. Each of the ritornello's two phrases is played loudly and then repeated softly, in the terraced dynamics typical of baroque music. After the ritornello, the movement alternates between extended solo sections containing musical tone painting and brief tutti sections presenting part of the ritornello theme. In the first solo section, bird songs are imitated by high trills and repeated notes played by the violin soloist and two violins from the orchestra. In the second descriptive episode, murmuring streams are suggested by soft running notes in the violins. The next solo section contains string tremolos and rapid scales representing thunder and lightning. Following the storm, the ritornello appears in minor instead of in major. All the pictorial passages provide contrasts of texture and dynamics between returns of the ritornello theme. Tunefulness, rhythmic vitality, and light, homophonic texture evoke springtime.

Brief sets:
Side 2, band 2
CD 1 40

Basic sets:
Side 2, band 9
CD 1 59

"The abbreviation *op.* stands for *opus*, Latin for *work*. An opus number is a way of identifying a piece or set of pieces. Usually, within a composer's output, the higher a composition's opus number, the later it was written.

# Listening Outline   To be read while music is heard

*LA PRIMAVERA (SPRING),*
CONCERTO FOR VIOLIN AND STRING ORCHESTRA, OP. 8, NO. 1,
FROM *THE FOUR SEASONS* (1725), BY ANTONIO VIVALDI

First Movement: Allegro

Ritornello form, quadruple meter ($\frac{4}{4}$), E major

Solo violin, string orchestra, harpsichord (basso continuo)

(Duration, 3:15)

Spring
has come
`40` `59` 0:00    1. *a.* Tutti, ritornello opening phrase, *f,* repeated p

closing phrase with syncopations, *f,* repeated *p,* major key.

Song of
the birds
`41` `60` 0:30    *b.* Solo violin joined by two violins from orchestra, high trills and repeated notes.
   1:03   2. *a.* Tutti, ritornello closing phrase, *f.*
Murmuring
streams
`42` `61` 1:10    *b.* Violins, *p,* running notes, cellos, *p,* running notes below sustained tones in violins.
   1:33   3. *a.* Tutti, ritornello closing phrase, *f.*
Thunder
and lightning
`43` `62` 1:40    *b.* String tremolos, *f,* upward rushing scales introduce high solo violin, brilliant virtuoso passages answered by low string tremolos.
   2:06   4. *a.* Tutti, ritornello closing phrase in minor key, *f.*
Song of
the birds
`44` `63` 2:13    *b.* Solo violin joined by two violins from orchestra, high repeated notes and trills, minor key.
   2:30   5. *a.* Tutti, ritornello opening phrase varied, *f,* ends in major key.
   2:40      *b.* Solo violin, running notes accompanied by basso continuo.
   2:54   6. Tutti, ritornello closing phrase, *f,* repeated *p,* major key.

# JOHANN SEBASTIAN BACH

The masterpieces of Johann Sebastian Bach (1685–1750) mark the high point of baroque music. Bach came from a long line of musicians and passed on this musical heritage; four of his sons were also composers. He was born in Eisenach, Germany, and began his musical career as a church organist and then as court organist and later concertmaster of the court orchestra in Weimar.

His most lucrative and prestigious post was as court conductor for the prince of Cöthen—more important, this was the first position in which he was not involved with church or organ music. For six years (1717–1723) he directed and composed for the prince's small orchestra; the *Brandenburg* Concertos grew out of this productive period.

Bach's next position was as cantor (director of music) of St. Thomas Church in Leipzig, with responsibility for the four main municipal churches. Bach remained here for the last twenty-seven years of his life. He rehearsed, conducted, and usually composed an extended work for chorus, soloists, and orchestra for each Sunday and church holiday and was responsible for the musical education of some fifty-five students in the St. Thomas school. He also became director of the Leipzig Collegium Musicum, a student organization that gave weekly concerts at a coffeehouse. An eminent teacher of organ and composition, he gave organ recitals and was often asked to judge the construction of organs. In his last years, his eyesight deteriorated, yet he continued to compose, conduct, and teach; when he died in 1750, he had become completely blind.

Bach was a deeply religious man—a Lutheran—who wrote the letters *J. J.*, standing for *Jesu Juva (Jesus help)*, at the beginning of each of his sacred compositions and *S. D. G.* for *Soli Deo Gloria (to God alone the glory)* at the end. His love of music was so great that as a young man he would walk up to 30 miles to hear a famous organist. He was married twice and had twenty children, of whom nine survived him and four became well-known musicians.

Bach was by no means considered the greatest composer of his day, though he was recognized as the most eminent organist, harpsichordist, and improviser (*improvisation* is the term used for music created at the same time as it is performed). He was little known outside Germany; and by the time of his maturity, the baroque style had started to go out of fashion and many people thought his works too heavy, complex, and polyphonic. His music was largely forgotten for years after his death, though a few later composers were aware of his genius; but in 1829 Felix Mendelssohn presented the *St. Matthew Passion*, and Bach's music has been the daily bread of every serious musician since then.

101

(Bärenreiter Bild-Archiv)

Johann Sebastian Bach.

## BACH'S MUSIC

Bach created masterpieces in every baroque form except opera. Throughout, he fused technical mastery with emotional depth. The excellence and number of his compositions for orchestra, small groups, and various solo instruments show how prominent instrumental music had become in the baroque period. His vocal music—the bulk of his output—was written mostly for the Lutheran church and was often based on familiar hymns. But his personal style was drawn from Italian concertos and French dance pieces as well as German church music.

Bach's works are unique in their combination of polyphonic texture and rich harmony and are used as models by music students today. Baroque music leans toward unity of mood, and this is particularly true of Bach, who liked to elaborate a single musical idea in a piece, creating unity by an insistent rhythmic drive. By his time, there was little difference in style between sacred and secular music; he often created sacred music simply by rearranging secular works, and his church music uses operatic forms like aria and recitative. Sometimes he composed music to demonstrate what could be done with a specific form (his *Art of the Fugue*, for example) or instrument (for instance, his six suites for solo cello). His *Well-Tempered Clavier*, a collection of forty-eight preludes and fugues, two in each major key and each minor key, was composed to explore and demonstrate a system of tuning (the title means, roughly, *The Well-Tuned Keyboard Instrument*).

# THE BAROQUE PERIOD

(Metropolitan Museum of Art, Harris Brisbane Dick Fund, 1946)

*Rape of the Sabine Women* (1636–1637), by Nicolas Poussin. The French painter Poussin combined dynamic motion with logic and balance.

*Adoration of the Magi* (1634), by Peter Paul Rubens. Baroque artists became interested in forming a total illusion, like a stage setting. Both baroque painting and baroque opera were often created for the nobility and designed to display magnificent extravagance.

### Second Movement: Air

Basic sets:
Side 4, band 1
CD 2 [17]
Section A
[17] 0:00
Section B
[18] 1:32

The second movement, the air, contains one of Bach's best-loved melodies. It is scored for only strings and continuo and is serene and lyrical, in contrast to the majestic and bustling French overture. The title suggests that the movement is written in the style of an Italian aria. Like the opening movement, the air is not related to dance. In its A A B B form, the B section is twice as long as the A section. The air combines a steadily moving bass (which proceeds in upward and downward octave leaps) with a rhapsodic and rhythmically irregular melody in the violins.

### Third Movement: Gavotte

All the movements that follow the overture and the air are inspired by dance, beginning with the gavotte, which is written in duple meter and in a moderate tempo and uses the full orchestra again. It may be outlined as follows: gavotte I (A A B B); gavotte II (C C D D); gavotte I (A B). Notice the contrast between the sections for full orchestra and those without trumpets and timpani.

### Fourth Movement: Bourrée

Basic sets:
Side 4, band 2
CD 2 [19]
Section A
[19] 0:00
Section B
[20] 0:17

The bourrée is an even livelier dance, also in duple meter. Its form is A A B B, and it is the shortest movement of the suite. Section A employs the full orchestra, including trumpets and timpani. Section B is three times as long as section A and alternates loud tutti passages with softer passages for strings and oboes.

### Fifth Movement: Gigue

Basic sets:
Side 4, band 3
CD 2 [21]
Section A
[21] 0:00
Section B
[22] 0:55

The suite concludes with a rollicking gigue in $\frac{6}{8}$ time, which is also in the form A A B B. Here, Bach's manner is simple and direct. Listen for the splendid effect when timpani and trumpets periodically join the rest of the orchestra.

## BAROQUE 10
# THE CHORALE AND CHURCH CANTATA

In Bach's time, the Lutheran church service (which lasted about 4 hours) was filled with music, and his church had not only a choir of twelve or so boys and men but also an orchestra of fourteen to twenty-one players.

Each service included several *chorales,* hymn tunes sung to a German religious text. These were often preceded by a *chorale prelude,* a short composition played by the organist and based on a hymn tune. Chorales were also employed in the principal means of musical expression in the service—the church *cantata.*

The cantata for Lutheran services of Bach's day was usually written for chorus, vocal soloists, organ, and small orchestra. Its text, in German, was original or drawn from the Bible or familiar hymns and was meant to reinforce the sermon. It might last about half an hour and include choruses, recitatives, arias, and duets—in fact, it resembled baroque opera.

The cantor, or music director, had to provide cantatas for every Sunday and holiday; Bach wrote about 295, of which about 195 are still in existence.

## CANTATA NO. 140: *WACHET AUF, RUFT UNS DIE STIMME (AWAKE, A VOICE IS CALLING US; 1731),* BY JOHANN SEBASTIAN BACH

*Wachet auf, ruft uns die Stimme* (Cantata No. 140), one of Bach's best-known cantatas, is based on a chorale tune which was then about 130 years old and widely familiar. It has the form A A B, and the last movement of the cantata presents it unadorned:

Last movement:
**Brief sets:**
**Side 2, band 4**
**CD 1** 48

Basic sets:
Side 3, band 6
CD 2 16

**A** (repeated)

**B**

There are nine melodic phrases; 1 to 3, the A section, are repeated immediately; phrase 3 reappears at the end of the B section (phrase 9) and beautifully rounds off the melody.

The cantata has seven movements: (1) chorus and orchestra, (2) recitative for tenor, (3) duet for bass (Jesus) and soprano (the soul), (4) tenor chorale, (5) recitative for bass (Jesus), (6) duet for bass (Jesus) and soprano (soul), (7) chorale (chorus doubled by orchestra). We'll consider movements 1, 4, and 7.

### First Movement: Chorus and Orchestra
### 2 oboes, English horn, French horn, 1st violins, 2d violins, violas, basso continuo (organ, bassoon, cello)

Basic sets:
Side 3, band 4
CD 2 [10]

In the chorale text of the first movement, watchmen on the towers of Jerusalem call on the wise virgins (Christians) to awake because the bridegroom (Christ) is coming. The movement opens with an orchestral ritornello that may have been intended to suggest a procession or march. There are dotted rhythms (long-short, long-short), a rising figure with syncopation, and a series of rising scales.

At the ritornello's closing cadence the sopranos enter and sing the first phrase of the chorale in long notes. Soon the three lower voices engage in an imitative dialogue based on a new motive in shorter note values. Throughout, the orchestra continues to play still shorter notes.

Thus there are three layers of sound: the chorale phrases in long notes in the soprano; the imitative dialogue in shorter note values in the three lower voices; and the ever-busy orchestra playing motives from the ritornello in even shorter notes. The chorale tune (in the soprano) is presented not as a continuous whole but rather phrase by phrase, with breaks between. After each phrase, the voices pause while the orchestra continues to play interludes made up of either the whole ritornello or sections from it. Sometimes the motives in the three lower voices illustrate the text, as when they have rising scale figures at the word *hoch (high)* and exclamations at the repeated *wo (where)*.

Once during the movement, the three lower voices become emancipated from the soprano and jubilantly sing a melody in rapid notes on *Alleluja*. This, perhaps, is the most exciting moment in the movement.

| | | | |
|---|---|---|---|
| [10] 0:00 | | | Orchestral ritornello. |
| [11] 0:28 | *Wachet auf, ruft uns die Stimme* | "Awake," the voice of watchmen | |
| | | | Brief orchestral interlude. |
| 0:50 | *der Wächter sehr hoch auf der Zinne* | calls us from high on the tower, | Rising scales in lower voices depict *hoch (high)*. |
| | | | Brief orchestral interlude. |

| | | | |
|---|---|---|---|
| *wach auf, du Stadt Jerusalem!* | "Awake, you city of Jerusalem!" | | |
| | | Orchestral ritornello. | 1:36 |
| *Mitternacht heisst diese Stunde;* | Midnight is this very hour; | | 2:01 |
| | | Brief orchestral interlude. | |
| *sie rufen uns mit hellem Munde:* | they call to us with bright voices: | | |
| | | Brief orchestral interlude. | |
| *wo seid ihr klugen Jungfrauen?* | "Where are you, wise virgins?" | | |
| | | Long orchestral interlude. | 3:07 |
| *Wohl auf, der Bräut'gam kömmt,* | Take cheer, the Bridegroom comes, | | |
| | | Brief orchestral interlude. | |
| *steht auf, die Lampen nehmt!* | arise, take up your lamps! | | |
| *Alleluja!* | Hallelujah! | Altos, jubilant melody in rapid notes. Imitation by tenors, then basses. | [12] 4.00 |
| *Alleluja!* | Hallelujah! | Sopranos, chorale in long notes. | 4:26 |
| | | Orchestral interlude. | |
| *Macht euch bereit* | Prepare yourselves | | |
| | | Orchestral interlude. | |
| *zu der Hochzeit* | for the wedding, | | |
| | | Brief orchestral interlude. | |
| *ihr müsset ihm entgegen gehn.* | you must go forth to meet him. | | |
| | | Orchestral ritornello. | 5:36 |

## Fourth Movement: Tenor Chorale
### Violins and violas in unison, basso continuo

The chorale tune returns in the fourth movement, the most popular of the cantata. Bach liked this section so much that toward the end of his life he rearranged it as a chorale prelude for organ. With miraculous ease, he sets two contrasting melodies against each other. First we hear the unison strings supported by the continuo playing the ritornello, a warm, flowing melody that Bach may have intended as a dancelike procession of the maidens as they "all follow to the joyful hall and share in the Lord's supper." This melody is repeated and varied throughout while the tenors sing the chorale tune against it.

Brief sets:
Side 2, band 3
CD 1 [45]

Basic sets:
Side 3, band 5
CD 2 [13]

Zi - on hört die Wäch - ter sin - gen

The chorale tune moves in faster rhythmic values than it did in the opening movement, but here, too, it is broken into component phrases linked by the instrumental melody. It's helpful to listen several times to this movement, first focusing on the rapid rhythms of the graceful string melody, then on the sturdy, slower rhythms of the chorale tune, and finally on all lines at once.

| | | | |
|---|---|---|---|
| **45** 13 0:00 | | | String ritornello. |
| **46** 14 0:39 | *Zion hört die Wächter singen,* | Zion hears the watchmen singing, | |
| | *das Herz tut ihr vor Freuden springen,* | for joy her very heart is springing, | |
| | *sie wachet und steht eilend auf.* | she wakes and rises hastily. | |
| | | | Ritornello. |
| 1:45 | *Ihr Freund kommt von Himmel prächtig,* | From heaven comes her friend resplendent, | |
| | *von Gnaden stark, von Wahrheit mächtig,* | sturdy in grace, mighty in truth, | |
| | *Ihr Licht wird hell, ihr Stern geht auf.* | her light shines bright, her star ascends. | |
| | | | Ritornello. |
| **47** 15 2:36 | *Nun komm, du werte Kron,* | Now come, you worthy crown, | |
| | *Herr Jesu, Gottes Sohn.* | Lord Jesus, God's own Son, | |
| 2:53 | *Hosianna!* | Hosanna! | |
| | | | Ritornello in minor. |
| 3:15 | *Wir folgen all' zum Freudensaal und halten mit das Abendmahl.* | We all follow to the joyful hall and share the Lord's Supper. | |
| | | | Ritornello. |

108

## Seventh Movement: Chorale
### Chorus doubled by orchestra

Bach rounds off Cantata No. 140 by bringing back the chorale once more. For the first time since the first movement, all voices and instruments take part. Here the chorale is set in a relatively simple, homophonic texture for four voices, with the instruments simply doubling them, not playing melodies of their own. Now the chorale is heard as a continuous melody, without interludes between its phrases. The rich sound, full harmonies, and regular rhythms express praise of God, faith in him, and joy in being in his kingdom. No doubt the congregation joined in the singing of the final chorale, which so firmly expressed their unity and belief.

Brief sets:
Side 2, band 4
CD 1 [48]

Basic sets:
Side 3, band 6
CD 2 [16]

| | |
|---|---|
| *Gloria sei dir gesungen* | Gloria be sung to you |
| *mit Menschen- und englischen Zungen,* | with men's and angel's tongues, |
| *mit Harfen und mit Zimbeln schon.* | with harps and beautiful cymbals. |
| *Von zwölf Perlen sind die Pforten* | Of twelve pearls are the gates |
| *an deiner Stadt; wir sind Konsorten* | at your city; we are consorts |
| *der Engel hoch um deinen Thron.* | of the angels high about your throne. |
| *Kein Aug' hat je gespürt,* | No eye has ever sensed, |
| *kein Ohr hat je gehört* | no ear has ever heard |
| *solche Freude.* | such a delight. |
| *Des sind wir froh,* | Of this we rejoice, |
| *io, io!* | io, io, |
| *ewig in dulci jubilo.* | forever in sweet joy. |

[48] [16]

# THE ORATORIO

BAROQUE 11

Together with the opera and cantata, the oratorio stands as a major development in baroque vocal music. Like opera, the *oratorio* is a large-scale composition for chorus, vocal soloists, and orchestra; it is usually set to a narrative text. Oratorio differs from opera in that it has no acting, scenery, or costumes. Most oratorios are based on biblical stories, but usually they are not intended for religious services. Today they are performed in either concert halls or churches.

An oratorio has a succession of choruses, arias, duets, recitatives, and orchestral interludes. The chorus is especially important and serves to comment on or participate in the drama. A narrator's recitatives usually relate the story and connect one piece with another. Oratorios are longer than cantatas (they sometimes last over 2 hours) and have more of a story line.

Oratorios first appeared in early seventeenth-century Italy as musical dramatizations of biblical stories and were performed in prayer halls called *oratorios*. During the baroque period, the oratorio spread to other countries and assumed many forms. *Messiah*, by George Frideric Handel, has for decades been the best-known and most-loved oratorio.

BAROQUE

# 12  GEORGE FRIDERIC HANDEL

George Frideric Handel (1685–1759), a master of Italian opera and English oratorio, was born one month before J. S. Bach, in Halle, Germany. He was not from a musical family—his father wanted him to study law—but by the time he was nine, his musical talent was so outstanding that he was allowed to study with a local organist and composer. By eleven, he himself was able to compose and give organ lessons. At eighteen, he set out for Hamburg, where he was drawn to the renowned opera house, and became a violinist and harpsichordist in the orchestra. When he was twenty, one of his operas was successfully produced.

At twenty-one, Handel went to Italy; there he wrote widely acclaimed operas and mingled with princes, cardinals, and famous musicians. Returning to Germany in 1710, he took a well-paid position as music director for Elector Georg Ludwig of Hanover; but after a month he asked for a leave to go to London, where his opera *Rinaldo* was being produced. It was a triumph, and a year later Handel asked for another English leave—which was granted for a "reasonable time" that turned out to be the next half-century (1712–1759).

Handel became England's most important composer and a favorite of Queen Anne. He was the director of the Royal Academy of Music (a commercial opera company) and composed a number of brilliant operas for outstanding sopranos and castrati. When the Royal Academy folded, he formed his own company to produce his works (for years, he had a triple career as impresario, composer, and performer.) It eventually went bankrupt and Handel suffered a breakdown; but he recovered and managed to continue producing operas on his own. To these he added his oratorios, opening a glowing new chapter in music history.

Late in life, Handel was still conducting and giving organ concerts, though he was almost blind. When he died in 1759, 3,000 mourners attended his funeral in Westminster Abbey. He was stubborn, wealthy, generous, and cultivated. But above all, he was a master composer whose dramatic sense has rarely been equaled.

(Metropolitan Museum of Art, bequest of Alexandrine Sinsheimer, 1959)

George Frideric Handel.

## HANDEL'S MUSIC

Handel shares Bach's stature among composers of the late baroque. Although he wrote a great deal of instrumental music—suites, organ concertos, concerti grossi—the core of his huge output consists of English oratorios and Italian operas.

His oratorios are usually based on stories from the Old Testament and have titles like *Israel in Egypt* and *Joshua*; but they are not church music—they were for paying audiences in public theaters. Most have plots and characters, though they were performed without acting, scenery, or costumes. (*Messiah*, which deals with a New Testament subject and has no plot, is an exception.) The chorus is the focus of a Handelian oratorio and is combined flexibly and imaginatively with the orchestra. Handel's music has more changes in texture than Bach's. He liked to combine two different melodic ideas polyphonically, and he achieved sharp changes of mood by shifting between minor and major keys.

Handel's thirty-nine Italian operas are less well known today than his oratorios; but after two centuries of neglect, they are being revived successfully by modern opera companies. Their arias—often written to display the virtuosity of singers—show his outstanding ability to evoke a mood or emotion.

## *MESSIAH* (1741)

*Messiah* lasts about 2½ hours and was composed in just twenty-four days. Handel wrote it before going to Ireland to attend performances of his own works that were being given to dedicate a concert hall. About five months after his arrival in Dublin (in 1742), Handel gave the first performance of *Messiah;* the occasion was a benefit for people in debtors' prisons. The rehearsals attracted wide attention: one newspaper commented that *Messiah* was thought "by the greatest Judges to be the finest Composition of Musick that ever was heard." Normally, the concert hall held 600 people; but to increase the capacity, women were asked not to wear hoopskirts, and men were asked to leave their swords at home.

Although the premiere was a success, the first London performance (1743) was poorly received, mainly because of religious opposition to the use of a Christian text in a theater. It took *Messiah* almost a decade to find popularity in London. Not until it was performed yearly at a benefit for a London orphanage did it achieve its unique status. A contemporary wrote that *Messiah* "fed the hungry, clothed the naked, fostered the orphan."

*Messiah* is in three parts. Part I starts with the prophecy of the Messiah's coming and makes celestial announcements of Christ's birth and the redemption of humanity through his appearance. Part II has been aptly described by one Handel scholar as "the accomplishment of redemption by the sacrifice of Jesus, mankind's rejection of God's offer and mankind's utter defeat when trying to oppose the power of the Almighty." Part III expresses faith in the certainty of eternal life through Christ as redeemer.

Unlike most of Handel's oratorios, *Messiah* is meditative rather than dramatic; it lacks plot action and specific characters. *Messiah* is Handel's only English oratorio that uses the New Testament as well as the Old. Charles Jennings, a millionaire and amateur literary man, compiled the text by taking widely separated passages from the Bible—Isaiah, Psalms, and Job from the Old Testament; Luke, I Corinthians, and the Book of Revelations from the New.

Over the years, Handel rewrote some movements in *Messiah* for different performers and performances. In Handel's own time, it was performed with a smaller orchestra and chorus than we are used to. Handel's own chorus included twenty singers, all male, and his small orchestra had only strings and continuo, with trumpets and timpani used in some sections. Today we sometimes hear arranged versions; Mozart made one, and still later versions are often played by orchestras of one hundred and choruses of several hundred.

*Messiah* has over fifty movements, and Handel ensures variety by skillfully contrasting and grouping them. We will focus on two movements from Part I and the famous *Hallelujah* chorus which ends Part II.

*Ev'ry Valley Shall Be Exalted*
**Aria for tenor**
**Andante**

Ev'ry valley shall be exalted, and ev'ry mountain and hill made low, the
crooked straight, and the rough places plain. (Isaiah 40:4)

Like many baroque arias, *Ev'ry valley shall be exalted* opens and closes with
an orchestral ritornello. This aria is striking in its vivid word painting, so
characteristic of baroque music. On a single syllable of *exalted (raised up)*,
forty-six rapid notes form a rising musical line.

**Brief sets:**
**Side 2, band 5**
**CD 1** 49

Basic sets:
Side 4, band 6
CD 2 27

Notice, too, the rising and falling direction of the phrase *and every mountain and hill made low:*

*The crooked straight* is represented as follows:

*Plain (smooth* or *level)*, in the line *and the rough places plain,* is expressed by
sustained tones and a long, legato melodic line.

### *For unto Us a Child Is Born*
### Chorus

> For unto us a Child is born, unto us a Son is given, and the government shall
> be upon His shoulder, and His Name shall be called: Wonderful, Counsellor,
> the Mighty God, the Everlasting Father, the Prince of Peace! (Isaiah 9:6)

Basic sets:
Side 4, band 7
CD 2 [28]

The twelfth movement, *For unto us a Child is born*, is among Handel's most
joyful music. The texture is light, often with only one or two voices singing
at a time. After the sopranos announce a motive, it is imitated by the
tenors; then both voices—with different rhythms—are combined.

[29] 0:58

The words *and the government shall be upon His shoulder* bring a new melodic idea in dotted rhythm:

[30] 1:15

Handel keeps the dynamics subdued until the choral exclamation on *Wonderful, Counsellor*, when all voices sing in the same rhythm. This change of
texture and dynamics is a master's stroke.

With such a close fusion of words and music, it may be disconcerting to
learn that most of the melodic ideas in this chorus came from Handel's
Italian duet for the words *No, I will not trust you, blind love, cruel Beauty!
You are too treacherous, too charming a deity!* (The musical idea for *Wonderful* is new.) But remember that in Handel's time there was little difference
in style between sacred and secular music.

### *Hallelujah* Chorus

Brief sets:
Side 2, band 6
CD 1 [50]

Basic sets:
Side 4, band 8
CD 2 [31]

In the *Hallelujah* chorus, Handel offers sweeping variety by sudden
changes among monophonic, polyphonic, and homophonic textures. The
monophonic texture is very full-sounding as all the voices and instruments
perform in unison at *for the Lord God Omnipotent reigneth*. The texture
becomes polyphonic when this proclamation is set against joyful repeated
exclamations of *Hallelujah* in quick rhythms. Polyphony gives way to ho-

mophony as the chorus sings *The kingdom of this world* to hymnlike music. Words and phrases are repeated over and over, as has been common practice in choral music for several centuries. (Below, braces connect lines sung at the same time.) Handel took his text from the Revelation of St. John, which celebrates God as the almighty and everlasting ruler.

| | Orchestral introduction | 50 31 |
|---|---|---|
| Hallelujah! | Chorus joins, homophonic, quick exclamations | |
| for the Lord God Omnipotent reigneth; | Monophonic, longer notes | 51 32 |
| Hallelujah! | Homophonic, quick exclamations | |
| for the Lord God Omnipotent reigneth; | Monophonic, longer notes | |
| Hallelujah! | Homophonic, quick exclamations | 52 33 |
| { for the Lord God Omnipotent reigneth; <br> { Hallelujah! | Longer-note melody against quick exclamations, polyphonic | |
| The kingdom of this world is become the Kingdom of our Lord and of His Christ: | Hymnlike in longer notes, homophonic | 53 34 |
| and He shall reign for ever and ever, | Bass melody, monophonic | 54 35 |
| | Other voices imitate, polyphonic | |
| { King of Kings, and Lord of Lords. <br> { for ever and ever, Hallelujah, <br> Hallelujah! | Long repeated tones against quick exclamations; phrases repeated at higher pitches | 55 36 |
| and He shall reign for ever and ever, | Polyphonic, imitation | |
| { King of Kings, and Lord of Lords, <br> { for ever and ever, Hallelujah, <br> Hallelujah! | Long repeated tones against quick exclamations | |
| and He shall reign for ever and ever, | Polyphonic | |
| King of Kings, and Lord of Lords. | Homophonic | |
| and He shall reign for ever and ever, | Polyphonic | |
| { King of Kings, and Lord of Lords, <br> { for ever and ever, for ever and ever, <br> Hallelujah, Hallelujah, Hallelujah, Hallelujah! | Quick exclamations | |
| | Pause | |
| Hallelujah! | Sustained chords, homophonic | |

# THE CLASSICAL PERIOD

Louis Carrogis de Carmontelle, *Misses Royer, Daughters of the Musician, Composer of "Zaide"* (1760).

# [ 1 ] THE CLASSICAL STYLE (1750–1820)

In the baroque era, the scientific methods and discoveries of geniuses like Galileo and Newton vastly changed people's view of the world. By the middle of the eighteenth century, the power of reason was so highly valued that it began to undermine the authority of the social and religious establishment. Philosophers and writers—especially Voltaire (1694–1778) and Denis Diderot (1713–1784)—saw their time as a great turning point in history and called it the "age of enlightenment." They believed in progress, holding that reason, not custom or tradition, was the best guide to human conduct. Their attacks on the privileges of the aristocracy and clergy reflected the outlook of the middle class, which was struggling for its rights. This new climate of opinion prepared the way for the American and French revolutions at the end of the eighteenth century.

Revolutions in thought and action were paralleled by shifts of style in the visual arts. During the early eighteenth century, the heavy, monumental baroque style gave way to the more intimate ròcoco style, with its light colors, curved lines, and graceful ornaments. The painters Antoine Watteau (1684–1721) and Jean Honoré Fragonard (1732–1806) depicted an enchanted world peopled by elegant men and women in constant pursuit of pleasure. But by the later eighteenth century there was yet another change in taste, and rococo art was thought frivolous, excessively ornamented, and lacking in ethical content. The rococo style was superseded by the neoclassical style, which attempted to recapture the "noble simplicity and calm grandeur" of ancient Greek and Roman art. Neoclassical artists emphasized firm lines, clear structures, and moralistic subject matter. The painter Jacques Louis David (1748–1825), who took part in the French Revolution, sought to inspire heroism and patriotism through his scenes of ancient Rome.

In music history, the transition from the baroque style to the full flowering of the classical (which parallels this trend in the visual arts) is called the *preclassical* period. It extends from roughly 1730 to 1770 and thus was developing even as Bach and Handel were creating baroque masterpieces. The preclassical composers—who included Bach's sons Carl Philipp Emanuel (1714–1788) and Johann Christian (1735–1782)—concentrated on simplicity and clarity, discarding much that had enriched late baroque music. They favored tuneful melody, simple harmony, and contrasts of mood and theme. The term *style galant (gallant style)* was applied to their light, graceful music.

The rococo painter Jean Honoré Fragonard showed the game of love in *The Pursuit*, 1771.

Most of Haydn's music was composed for a wealthy aristocratic family. Shown here is a performance of a Haydn comic opera in 1775 at the palace Esterháza.

The term *classical* is confusing because it has so many different meanings; it may refer to Greek or Roman antiquity, to any enduring creation or accomplishment (such as a *movie classic*), and—for many people—to any music that is *not* rock, jazz, folk, or popular. Music historians borrowed the term *classical* from art history, where it is more appropriate, since the painting, sculpture, and architecture of the late eighteenth and early nineteenth centuries were often influenced by Greek and Roman models. But the music of this period has little direct relationship to antiquity. The significant parallel between "classical" music and "neoclassical" art is a common stress on balance and clarity of structure. These traits can be found in the fully developed classical style in music, which flourished from about 1770 to 1820.

The master composers of the classical style were Joseph Haydn (1732–1809), Wolfgang Amadeus Mozart (1756–1791), and Ludwig van Beethoven (1770–1827). These three worked during a time that witnessed the American and French revolutions, the Napoleonic Wars, and a dramatic shift in power from the aristocracy and the church to the middle class. Like everyone else, musicians were strongly affected by these changes, and in the careers of Haydn, Mozart, and Beethoven we can trace the slow emancipation of the composer. Haydn, as we will see, was content to spend most of his life as a skilled servant to a wealthy aristocratic family. Mozart broke away from this pattern to try his luck as a free-lancer but died in financial need. Beethoven succeeded where Mozart failed—he was able to work independently. This was partly because his commanding personality (which prompted the nobility to give him gifts and treat him as an equal) allowed him to take advantage of the new social mobility, and partly because of the wider middle-class market for music.

During the classical period, in fact, though music was still an important part of court life (and many aristocrats were excellent musicians), the middle class had a great influence on music. Prosperous merchants, doctors, lawyers, and government officials not only organized public concerts (palace concerts usually being closed to townspeople) but also wanted to be surrounded by music at home. As a result, the demand for printed music, instruments, and music lessons vastly increased. Moreover, composers in the classical period took middle-class tastes into account; for example, their comic operas sometimes ridiculed the aristocracy. Composers were also influenced by folk and popular music. Haydn, Mozart, and Beethoven all wrote dance music for public balls in Vienna—one of the music centers of Europe and a city in which they were all active.

Let's now consider some characteristics of the classical style.

## CHARACTERISTICS OF THE CLASSICAL STYLE

### Contrast of Mood

Great variety and contrast of mood received new emphasis in classical music. While a late baroque piece may convey a single emotion, a classical composition will fluctuate in mood. Dramatic, turbulent music might lead into a carefree dance tune. Not only are there contrasting themes within a movement, but there also may be striking contrasts even within a single theme.

Mood in classical music may change gradually or suddenly, expressing conflicting surges of elation and depression. But such conflict and contrast are under the firm control of the classical composer. Masters like Haydn, Mozart, and Beethoven were able to impart unity and logic to music of wide emotional range.

## Rhythm

Flexibility of rhythm adds variety to classical music. A classical composition has a wealth of rhythmic patterns, while a baroque piece contains a few patterns that are reiterated throughout. Baroque works convey a sense of continuity and perpetual motion, so that after the first few bars one can predict pretty well the rhythmic character of an entire movement. But the classical style also includes unexpected pauses, syncopations, and frequent changes from long notes to shorter ones. And the change from one pattern of note lengths to another may be either sudden or gradual.

## Texture

In contrast to the polyphonic texture of late baroque music, classical music is basically homophonic. However, texture is treated as flexibly as rhythm. Pieces shift smoothly or suddenly from one texture to another. A work may begin homophonically with a melody and simple accompaniment but then change to a more complex polyphonic texture that features two simultaneous melodies or melodic fragments imitated among the various instruments.

## Melody

Classical melodies are among the most tuneful and easy to remember. The themes of even highly sophisticated compositions may have a folk or popular flavor. Occasionally, composers simply borrowed popular tunes. (Mozart did, in his variations on *Twinkle, Twinkle, Little Star*, which he knew as the French song *Ah, vous dirai-je, maman.*) More often, they wrote original themes with a popular character.

Classical melodies often sound balanced and symmetrical because they are frequently made up of two phrases of the same length. The second phrase, in such melodies, may begin like the first, but it ends more conclusively. Such a melodic type, which may be diagrammed a a', is easy to sing (it is frequently found in nursery tunes such as *Mary Had a Little Lamb*). Baroque melodies, on the contrary, tend to be less symmetrical, more elaborate, and harder to sing.

## Dynamics and the Piano

The classical composers' interest in expressing shades of emotion led to the widespread use of gradual dynamic change—crescendo and decrescendo. They did not restrict themselves to the terraced dynamics (abrupt shifts from loud to soft) characteristic of baroque music. Crescendos and decrescendos were an electrifying novelty; audiences sometimes rose excitedly from their seats.

During the classical period, the desire for gradual dynamic change led to the replacement of the harpsichord by the piano. By varying the finger pressure on the keys, a pianist can play more loudly or softly. Although the piano was invented around 1700, it began to replace the harpsichord only around 1775. Almost all the mature keyboard compositions of Haydn, Mozart, and Beethoven were written for the piano, rather than for harpsichord, clavichord, and organ, which were featured in baroque music.

### The End of the Basso Continuo

The basso continuo was gradually abandoned during the classical period. In Haydn's or Mozart's works, a harpsichordist did not need to improvise an accompaniment. One reason why the basso continuo became obsolete was that more and more music was written for amateurs, who could not master the difficult art of improvising from a figured bass. Also, classical composers wanted more control; they preferred to specify an accompaniment rather than trust the judgment of improvisers.

## THE CLASSICAL ORCHESTRA

A new orchestra evolved during the classical period. Unlike the baroque orchestra, which could vary from piece to piece, it was a standard group of four sections: strings, woodwinds, brass, and percussion. In the late instrumental works of Mozart and Haydn, an orchestra might consist of:

Strings—1st violins, 2d violins, violas, cellos, double basses
Woodwinds—2 flutes, 2 oboes, 2 clarinets, 2 bassoons
Brass—2 French horns, 2 trumpets
Percussion—2 timpani

Notice that woodwind and brass instruments are paired and that clarinets have been added. Trombones were also used by Haydn and Mozart, but only in opera and church music, not in solely instrumental works.

The number of musicians in a classical orchestra was greater than in a baroque group, but practice varied considerably from place to place. Haydn directed a private orchestra of only twenty-five players from 1761 to 1790. But for public concerts in London in 1795, he led a large orchestra of sixty musicians.

Classical composers exploited the individual tone colors of instruments. Unlike baroque composers, they did not treat instruments interchangeably. Classical composers would not let an oboe duplicate the violin melody for the entire length of a movement. A classical piece has greater variety and more rapid changes of tone color. A theme might begin in the full orchestra, shift to the strings, and then continue in the woodwinds.

Each section of the classical orchestra had a special role. The strings were the most important section, with the first violins taking the melody most of the time and the lower strings providing an accompaniment. The woodwinds added contrasting tone colors and were often given melodic solos. Horns and trumpets brought power to loud passages and filled out the harmony, but they did not usually play the main melody. Timpani were used for rhythmic bite and emphasis. As a whole, the classical orchestra had developed into a flexible and colorful instrument to which composers could entrust their most powerful and dramatic musical conceptions.

## CLASSICAL FORMS

Instrumental works of the classical period usually consist of several movements that contrast in tempo and character. There are often four movements, arranged as follows:

1. Fast movement
2. Slow movement
3. Dance-related movement
4. Fast movement

Classical symphonies and string quartets usually follow this four-movement pattern, while classical sonatas may consist of two, three, or four movements. A *symphony* is written for orchestra; a *string quartet* for two violins, viola, and cello; and a *sonata* for one or two instruments. (The classical symphony, string quartet, and sonata are more fully described in Sections 2 to 6 and 8.) In writing an individual movement of a symphony, string quartet, or sonata, a classical composer could choose from several different forms. One movement of a composition might be in A B A form, while another might be a theme and variations.

Classical movements often contrast themes vividly. A movement may contain two, three, or even four or more themes of different character. This use of contrasting themes distinguishes classical music from baroque music, which often uses only one main theme. The classical composer sometimes signals the arrival of a new theme with a brief pause.

Though we speak of a classical style, we must remember that Haydn, Mozart, and Beethoven were three individuals with different personalities. They employed similar musical procedures and forms, but their emotional statements bear the particular stamp of each.

# SONATA FORM

An astonishing amount of important music from the classical period to the twentieth century is composed in sonata form (sometimes called *sonata-allegro form*). The term **sonata form** refers to the form of a *single* movement. It should not be confused with the term *sonata*, which is used for a whole composition made up of *several* movements. The opening fast movement of a classical symphony, sonata, or string quartet is usually in sonata form. Sonata form is also used in slow movements and in fast concluding movements.

A sonata-form movement consists of three main sections: the exposition, where the themes are presented; the development, where themes are treated in new ways; and the recapitulation, where the themes return. These three main sections are often followed by a concluding section, the coda (Italian for *tail*). Remember that these sections are all within *one movement*.

A *single* sonata-form movement may be outlined as follows:

Exposition
First theme in tonic (home) key
Bridge containing modulation from home key to new key
Second theme in new key
Closing section in key of second theme

Development
New treatment of themes; modulations to different keys

Recapitulation
First theme in tonic key
Bridge
Second theme in tonic key
Closing section in tonic key

(Coda)
In tonic key

A fast movement in sonata form is sometimes preceded by a slow introduction that creates a strong feeling of expectancy.

On the following pages, we'll consider the exposition, development, recapitulation, and coda in more detail.

## EXPOSITION

The *exposition* sets up a strong conflict between the tonic key and the new key, between the first theme (or group of themes) and the second theme (or group of themes). It begins with the first theme in the tonic, or home, key. Then a *bridge,* or *transition,* leads to the second theme, in a new key. The modulation from the home key to a new key creates harmonic tension and forward motion. The second theme often contrasts in mood with the first. A closing section ends the exposition in the key of the second theme. At the end of a classical exposition there is usually a repeat sign (:‖) to indicate that the whole exposition is to be repeated.

## DEVELOPMENT

The *development* is often the most dramatic section of the movement. The listener may be kept off balance as the music moves restlessly through several different keys, heightening the harmonic tension. In this section, themes are *developed*, or treated in new ways. They are broken into fragments, or *motives*—short musical ideas developed within a composition. A motive may take on different and unexpected emotional meanings. A fragment of a comic theme, for example, may be made to sound aggressive and menacing through changes of melody, rhythm, or dynamics. Themes can be combined with new ideas or changed in texture. A complex polyphonic texture can be woven by shifting a motive rapidly among different instruments. The harmonic and thematic searching of the development builds a tension that demands resolution.

## RECAPITULATION

The beginning of the *recapitulation* brings resolution, as we again hear the first theme in the tonic key. In the recapitulation, the first theme, bridge, second theme, and concluding section are presented more or less as they were in the exposition, with one crucial difference: all the principal material is now in the tonic key. Earlier, in the exposition, there was strong contrast between the first theme in the home key and the second theme and closing section in a new key; that basis for tension is resolved in the recapitulation by presenting the first theme, second theme, and closing section all in the tonic key.

## CODA

An even stronger feeling of conclusion is attained by following the recapitulation with another section. The *coda* rounds off a movement by repeating themes or developing them further. It always ends in the tonic key.

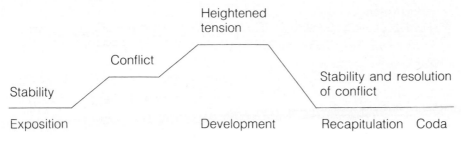

A movement in sonata form progresses from a stable situation toward conflict,
to heightened tension, and then back to stability.

The amazing durability and vitality of sonata form result from its capacity
for drama. The form moves from a stable situation toward conflict (in the
exposition), then to heightened tension (in the development), and then
back to stability and resolution of conflict. The illustration above shows a
diagram.

Sonata form is exceptionally flexible and subject to endless variation. It is
not a rigid mold into which musical ideas are poured. Rather, it may be
viewed as a set of principles that serve to shape and unify contrasts of
theme and key. Haydn, Mozart, and Beethoven repeatedly used sonata
form, yet each maintained individuality. Movements in sonata form may
differ radically in character, in length, and in the number and treatment of
themes. Sonata form is so versatile that it should be no surprise to find its
use spanning more than two centuries.

We'll now consider an excellent example of sonata form: the first movement of Mozart's Symphony No. 40.

## SYMPHONY NO. 40 IN G MINOR, K. 550,*
## BY WOLFGANG AMADEUS MOZART

### First Movement:

### Molto allegro

The rapid sonata-form opening movement of Mozart's Symphony No. 40
in G Minor, K. 550, conveys a feeling of controlled agitation. A throbbing
accompaniment in the violas contributes to the tension of the opening
theme, which begins softly in the violins. Dominating the violin melody is
the rhythmic pattern short-short-long, first heard in the opening three-
note motive.

**Brief sets:**
**Side 2, band 7**
**CD 1** 56

Basic sets:
Side 6, band 2
CD 3 28

---

*In the nineteenth century, Mozart's compositions (numbering more than 600) were cata-
logued chronologically by Ludwig von Köchel. Hence it is customary to refer to them by their
"K." numbers.

The persistence of this rhythmic pattern gives the music a sense of urgency. Yet the melody is balanced and symmetrical. Questioning upward leaps are answered by downward scales, and the second phrase of the melody is a sequential repetition of the first, one step lower. The exposition continues with a bridge section that presents a new staccato motive played loudly by the violins.

The lyrical second theme, in B flat major, contrasts completely with the agitated G minor opening. Mozart exploits the expressive resources of tone color by dividing the theme between strings and woodwinds. In the closing section of the exposition, he uses a fragment from the opening theme to achieve a different emotional effect. The three-note motive now sounds gentle and plaintive as it is passed between clarinet and bassoon against a sighing string background.

In the development, the movement becomes feverish. The opening theme is led into different keys and is cut into smaller and smaller pieces. The development begins mysteriously as the opening phrase ends in an unexpected way and sinks lower and lower. Then a sudden explosion of polyphonic texture increases the excitement and complexity. Mozart brusquely shifts the opening phrase between low and high strings while combining it with a furious staccato countermelody. Soon after, he demolishes the opening phrase: we hear the beginning of the theme without its upward leap.

Then the final note is lopped off.

Finally, we are left with the irreducible minimum of the original theme, the three-note motive.

First violins

The tension resolves only with the entrance of the entire opening theme in the tonic key.

In the recapitulation, exposition material is given new expressive meaning. The bridge is expanded and made more dramatic. The lyrical second theme, now in G minor, is touching and sad.

# Listening Outline To be read while music is heard

SYMPHONY NO. 40 IN G MINOR, K. 550 (1788), BY WOLFGANG AMADEUS MOZART

First Movement: Molto allegro

Sonata form, duple meter ($\frac{2}{2}$), G minor

Flute, 2 oboes, 2 clarinets, 2 bassoons, 2 French horns, 1st violins, 2d violins, violas, cellos, double basses

(Duration, 8:16)

EXPOSITION
First theme

[66] [20] 0.00      1. a. Main theme in violins, *p*, throbbing accompaniment in violas, minor key.

Molto allegro
Violins

                                     *b.* Full orchestra, *f.*

Bridge
[57] [29] 0:24      2. a. Violins, *p*, main theme takes new turn to
             *b.* Full orchestra, *f*, major key, staccato motive and insistent upward scales in violins. Pause.

3. *a.* Lyrical melody, *p,* major key, strings and woodwinds.

*p*

1:02     *b.* Woodwinds and strings, *p,* lyrical melody somewhat varied. Crescendo in full orchestra.
      *c.* Staccato phrase, *f,* downward scale to

4. *a.* String sighs, *p,* three-note motive in woodwinds, violins, *f.* Varied repetition of string sighs and three-note motive.
      *b.* Downward scales, *f,* full orchestra, cadence in major key.

Exposition is repeated.

## DEVELOPMENT
1. *a.* High woodwinds, *p,* lead to
      *b.* Violins, *p,* main-theme phrase repeated on lower pitches.
2. Sudden *f,* full orchestra, main-theme phrase combined with rapid countermelody.
3. *a.* Sudden *p,* high violins and woodwinds, three-note motive.
      *b.* Sudden *f,* full orchestra, three-note motive.
      *c.* Sudden *p,* high flutes and clarinets, three-note motive carried down to

## RECAPITULATION
1. *a.* Main theme in violins, *p,* throbbing accompaniment in violas, minor key.
      *b.* Full orchestra, *f.*

2. *a.* Violins, *p,* main theme takes new turn to
      *b.* Full orchestra, *f,* staccato motive in violins and cellos. Insistent upward scales in violins, *f.* Pause.

3. *a.* Lyrical melody, *p,* minor key, strings and woodwinds.
      *b.* Woodwinds and strings, *p,* lyrical melody somewhat varied. Crescendo in full orchestra.
      *c.* Staccato phrase, *f,* downward scale to

4. *a.* String sighs, *p,* three-note motive in woodwinds, violins, *f.* Varied repetition of string sighs and three-note motive.
      *b.* Downward scales, *f,* full orchestra.

## CODA
1. *a.* Sudden, *p,* main-theme motive in strings.
      *b.* Full orchestra, *f,* cadence in minor key.

# THEME AND VARIATIONS

The form called *theme and variations* is widely used in the classical period, either as an independent piece or as one movement of a symphony, a sonata, or a string quartet. In a **theme and variations**, a basic musical idea—the theme—is repeated over and over and is changed each time it is repeated. This form may be outlined as theme (A)–variation 1 (A')–variation 2 (A")–variation 3 (A"'), and so on; each prime mark indicates a variation of the basic idea. (Another way of indicating variations is $A^1$, $A^2$, etc.)

Each variation, though usually about the same length as the theme, is unique and may differ in mood from the theme. Changes of melody, rhythm, harmony, accompaniment, dynamics, or tone color may be used to give a variation its own identity. The core melody may appear in the bass, or it may be repeated in a minor key instead of a major one. It may be heard together with a new melody. The variations may be connected to each other or separated by pauses. For the theme itself, a composer may invent an original melody or borrow someone else's. Beethoven once borrowed a little waltz tune and put it through thirty-three brilliant variations. More modest examples of theme and variations may have as few as three variations.

## SYMPHONY NO. 94 IN G MAJOR *(SURPRISE)*, BY JOSEPH HAYDN

### Second Movement:

### Andante

The second movement (andante) of Haydn's *Surprise* Symphony (Symphony No. 94 in G Major) is a theme and variations. The folklike, staccato theme begins softly but is punctuated by a sudden loud chord. This is the "surprise" of the symphony. There are four variations, in which the theme is changed in tone color, dynamics, rhythm, and melody. Sometimes the original melody is accompanied by a new one called a *countermelody*. Such combinations of two distinctive melodies result in a polyphonic texture. In one variation the theme is presented in minor instead of major. The last variation is followed by a closing section in which a gently dissonant accompaniment momentarily darkens the mood of the carefree theme.

The theme is composed of two parts, sections a and b, which are each repeated. This pattern is usually retained in the variations.

Brief sets:
Side 2, band 8
CD 1 [65]

Basic sets:
Side 5, band 1
CD 3 [1]

# Listening Outline
To be read while music is heard

SYMPHONY NO. 94 IN G MAJOR *(SURPRISE;* 1791),
BY JOSEPH HAYDN (1732–1809)

Second Movement: Andante

Theme and variations, duple meter ($\frac{2}{4}$), C major

2 flutes, 2 oboes, 2 bassoons, 2 French horns, 2 trumpets, timpani, 1st violins, 2d violins, violas, cellos, double basses

(Duration, 6:12)

THEME
Section a

65 1 0:00     Violins, *p,* staccato theme.

Section b

       Section a repeated, *pp,* with pizzicato string accompaniment. Surprise chord, *ff.* Violins, *p,* continuation of theme.

       Section b repeated with flute and oboe.

VARIATION 1

66 2 1:07     *a.* Theme begins, *f,* higher countermelody in violins, *p.* Section a repeated.

       *b.* Violins, *p,* continuation of theme and higher countermelody. Section b repeated.

## VARIATION 2

`67` `3` 2:12    *a.* Theme in minor, *ff*, violin phrase in major, *p.* Section a repeated.

*b.* Violins, *f,* rapid downward scales, orchestra *f.* Violins alone, *p,* lead into

## VARIATION 3

`68` `4` 3:20    *a.* Oboe, *p,* theme in faster repeated notes, major key.

Flute and oboe, *p,* legato countermelody above staccato theme in violins, *p.*

*b.* Continuation of theme and countermelody. Section b repeated.

## VARIATION 4

`69` `5` 4:23    *a.* Theme in brasses and woodwinds, *ff,* fast notes in violins, *ff.* Violins, *p,* legato version of theme, dotted rhythm (long-short).

*b.* Violins, *p,* continuation of theme, dotted rhythm. Full orchestra, *ff,* triumphant continuation of theme leads to suspenseful chord, *ff,* sudden *p.*

## CLOSING SECTION

`70` `6` 5:45    Theme in oboe, *p,* gently dissonant chords in strings, flute joins, *pp* conclusion.

133

# MINUET AND TRIO

The form known as *minuet and trio,* or *minuet,* is typically employed as the third movement of classical symphonies, string quartets, and other works. Like the movements of the baroque suite, the minuet originated as a dance. It first appeared at the court of Louis XIV of France around 1650 and was danced by aristocrats throughout the eighteenth century. The minuet was a stately, dignified dance in which the dancing couple exchanged curtsies and bows.

The minuet movement of a symphony or string quartet is written for listening, not dancing. It is in triple meter ($\frac{3}{4}$ time) and usually in a moderate tempo. The movement is in A B A form: minuet (A), trio (B), minuet (A). The trio (B) is usually quieter than the minuet (A) section and requires fewer instruments. It often contains woodwind solos. The trio section got its name during the baroque period, when a set of two dances would be followed by a repetition of the first dance. The second dance was known as a "trio" because it was usually played by three instruments. Classical composers did not restrict themselves to three instruments in the B sections of their minuets, but the name *trio* remained.

The A (minuet) section includes smaller parts a, b, and a' (variation of a). In the opening A (minuet) section, all the smaller parts are repeated, as follows: a (repeated) ba' (repeated). (In the musical score, the repeat sign :‖ indicates each repetition.) The B (trio) section is similar in form: c (repeated) dc' (repeated). At the close of the B (trio) section, the repetition of the entire A (minuet) section is indicated by the words *da capo (from the beginning).* This time, however, the minuet is played straight through without the repetitions: a ba'. The whole movement can be outlined as follows:

| Minuet | Trio | Minuet |
|:---:|:---:|:---:|
| A | B | A |
| a (repeated) ba' (repeated) | c (repeated) dc' (repeated) | a ba' |

With its A B A form and its many repeated parts, the minuet is structurally the simplest movement of a symphony or string quartet.

In many of Beethoven's compositions, the third movement is not a minuet but, instead, a related form called a *scherzo.* Like a minuet, a **scherzo** is usually in A B A form and triple meter, but it moves more quickly, generating energy, rhythmic drive, and rough humor. (The word *scherzo* is Italian for *joke.*)

# THE CLASSICAL PERIOD

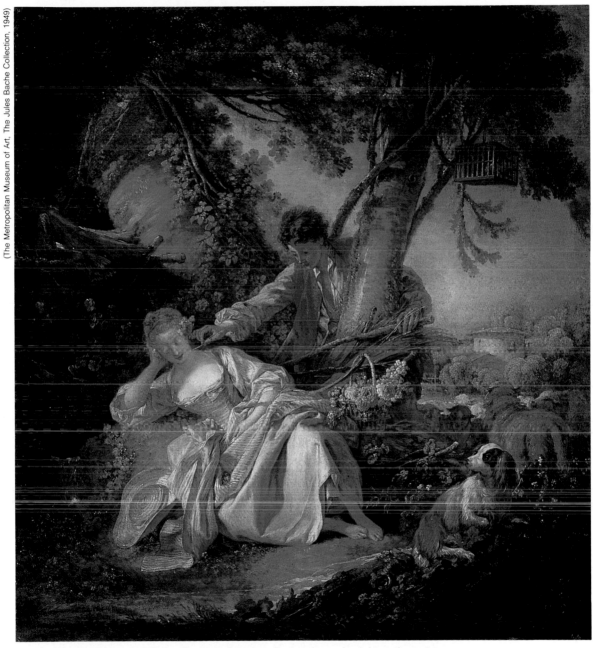

*The Interrupted Sleep* (1750), by François Boucher. During the early eighteenth century, the heavy monumental baroque style gave way to a more intimate style, the rococo, with light colors, curved lines, and graceful ornaments. The French rococo painter Boucher chose subjects that were decorative and sweetly sensuous.

Above: *Death of Socrates* (1787), by Jacques-Louis David. By the late eighteenth century, the rococo style had been superseded by the neoclassical style, which attempted to recapture the "noble simplicity and calm grandeur" of ancient Greek and Roman art. Neoclassical artists such as the French painter David emphasized firm lines, clear structures, and moralistic subjects.

Opposite page: *Napoleon at St. Bernard* (1800), by Jacques-Louis David. Beethoven originally planned to name his Third Symphony *(Eroica;* 1803–1804) "Bonaparte," because he saw Napoleon as the embodiment of heroism; but when he learned that Napoleon had proclaimed himself emperor, he tore out the title page and later renamed the symphony "Heroic Symphony composed to celebrate the memory of a great man."

MINUET (A)
73 9 1:37

Climbing legato phrase, *f*, leads to legato melody, *p*. Repeated.

3. Stately melody, *f*, predominantly staccato.
   Legato phrase, *p*, leads to stately staccato phrase, *f*.

# CLASSICAL 5 RONDO

Many classical movements are in rondo form. A *rondo* features a tuneful main theme (A) which returns several times in alternation with other themes. Common rondo patterns are A B A C A and A B A C A B A. The main theme is usually lively, pleasing, and simple to remember, and the listener can easily recognize its return. Because the main theme is usually stated in the tonic key, its return is all the more welcome. The rondo can be used either as an independent piece or as one movement of a symphony, string quartet, or sonata. It often serves as a finale, because its liveliness, regularity, and buoyancy bring a happy sense of conclusion.

Rondo form is often combined with elements of sonata form to produce the sonata-rondo. The *sonata-rondo* has a development section similar to that in sonata form and is outlined A B A–development section–A B A.

The popularity of the rondo did not end with the classical period. It has been used by twentieth-century composers such as Igor Stravinsky and Arnold Schoenberg.

## STRING QUARTET IN C MINOR, OP. 18, NO. 4, BY LUDWIG VAN BEETHOVEN

**Fourth Movement:**

**Rondo (Allegro)**

Brief sets:
Side 3, band 1
CD 2 1

Basic sets:
Side 8, band 1
CD 4 26

The exciting rondo movement from Beethoven's String Quartet in C Minor, Op. 18, No. 4, may be outlined A B A C A B A. Its main theme, A, is a lively gypsy dance made up of two repeated parts: a a b b. An unexpected held tone in part b suggests the improvisatory playing of a gypsy fiddler. The main theme, in minor, contrasts with the other themes, which are in major. Theme B is a lyrical legato melody; theme C is playful, with quick upward rushes. At its final return, the main theme (A) has a faster tempo, prestissimo, and leads into a frenzied concluding section.

# Listening Outline To be read while music is heard

STRING QUARTET IN C MINOR, OP. 18, NO. 4 (1798–1800),
BY LUDWIG VAN BEETHOVEN

Fourth Movement: Rondo (Allegro)

Duple meter ($\frac{2}{2}$), C minor

1st violin, 2d violin, viola, cello

(Duration, 4:14)

A

1 26 0:00      1. Lively main theme in 1st violin, minor key.

B

2 27 0:32      2. Lyrical melody, legato, major key.

A

3 28 1:16      3. Lively main theme, minor key. Theme becomes more agitated.

C

4 29 1:46      4. Upward rushes in each instrument, playful downward phrase in 1st violin, major key.

A

2:10      5. Lively main theme, minor key. Crescendo to held chord, ff.

B

2:48      6. Lyrical melody, legato, major key. Melody repeated an octave higher. Playful phrases in violins, crescendo to f, sustained tones in 1st violin.

A

3:31      7. Lively main theme, ff, faster tempo (prestissimo), minor key. Concluding section builds, downward staccato scale, high repeated tones, p. Upward rushes, ff, at end.

# [ 6 ] THE CLASSICAL SYMPHONY

The great contribution of the classical period to orchestral music is the symphony. Haydn wrote at least 104 symphonies, Mozart over forty, and Beethoven nine. Most of Haydn's symphonies were composed for his employers, who required a steady flow of works for their palace concerts. Beethoven, on the other hand, wrote a symphony only when inspired. His symphonies are longer than Haydn's or Mozart's and were conceived for performance in large concert halls.

A *symphony* is an extended, ambitious composition typically lasting between 20 and 45 minutes, exploiting the expanded range of tone color and dynamics of the classical orchestra. A classical symphony usually consists of four movements which evoke a wide range of emotions through contrasts of tempo and mood. A typical sequence in a classical symphony is (1) a vigorous, dramatic fast movement; (2) a lyrical slow movement; (3) a dancelike movement (minuet or scherzo); and (4) a brilliant or heroic fast movement.

The opening movement is almost always fast and in sonata form. It is usually the most dramatic movement and stresses an exciting development of short motives. Sometimes a slow introduction leads to the opening fast movement and creates a feeling of anticipation.

It is in the slow second movement that we are most likely to find broad, songlike melodies. This movement, by and large, is in sonata form, A B A form, or theme-and-variations form. Unlike the other movements in the symphony, the slow movement is generally *not* in the tonic key. For example, if the first, third, and fourth movements are in the tonic key of C major, the second movement may be in F major. The new key points up the expressive contrast of the slow movement.

In the symphonies of Haydn and Mozart, the third movement is generally a minuet and trio, which may be in a moderate or fairly quick tempo. This movement varies in character from a courtly dance to a peasant romp or a vigorous piece that is hardly dancelike. Beethoven liked fast, energetic scherzos for his third movements.

The fourth, concluding movement of a Haydn or Mozart symphony is fast, lively, and brilliant, but somewhat lighter in mood than the opening movement. (The agitated final movement of Mozart's Symphony No. 40 in G Minor is not typical.) Beethoven's concluding movement tends to be more triumphant and heroic in character and sometimes is meant as the climax of the whole symphony. The final movement of a classical symphony is most often in sonata or sonata-rondo form.

In most classical symphonies, each movement is a self-contained composition with its own set of themes. A theme in one movement will only rarely reappear in a later movement. (Beethoven's Fifth and Ninth Symphonies are exceptions.) But a symphony is unified partly by the use of the same key in three of its movements. More important, the movements balance and complement each other both musically and emotionally.

The importance of the symphony has lasted into the middle of the twentieth century. Its great significance is reflected in such familiar terms as *symphonic music, symphony hall,* and *symphony orchestra.*

# THE CLASSICAL CONCERTO

CLASSICAL

7

A classical *concerto* is a three-movement work for an instrumental soloist and orchestra. It combines the soloist's virtuosity and interpretive abilities with the orchestra's wide range of tone color and dynamics. Emerging from this encounter is a contrast of ideas and sound that is dramatic and satisfying. The soloist is very much the star, and all of his or her musical talents are needed in this challenging dialogue.

The classical love of balance can be seen in the concerto, where soloist and orchestra are equally important. Between them, there is an interplay of melodic lines and a spirit of give-and-take. One moment the soloist plays the melody while the orchestra accompanies. Then the woodwinds may unfold the main theme against rippling arpeggios (broken chords) played by the soloist. Mozart and Beethoven—the greatest masters of the classical concerto—often wrote concertos for themselves to play as piano soloists; the piano is their favored solo instrument. Other solo instruments in classical concertos include violin, cello, clarinet, bassoon, trumpet, and horn.

Like symphonies, concertos can last anywhere from 20 to 45 minutes. But instead of the symphony's four movements, a concerto has three: (1) fast, (2) slow, and (3) fast. A concerto has no minuet or scherzo.

In the first movement and sometimes in the last movement, there is a special unaccompanied showpiece for the soloist, the *cadenza* (Italian for *cadence*). Near the end of the movement, the orchestra suspends forward motion by briefly sustaining a dissonant chord. This is indicated in the score by a *fermata* (⌢), a sign meaning *pause*, placed over the chord. The suspense announces the soloist's cadenza. For several minutes, the soloist, *without orchestra*, displays virtuosity by playing dazzling scale passages and broken chords. Themes of the movement are varied and presented in new keys. At the end of a cadenza, the soloist plays a long trill followed by a chord that meshes with the reentrance of the orchestra.

In the classical era, the soloist, who was often the composer, generally improvised the cadenzas. In this case, the score contained only the fermata, indicating where the cadenza should be inserted. But after the eighteenth century, the art of improvisation declined, and composers began to write cadenzas directly into the score. This gave them more control over their compositions.

A classical concerto begins with a movement in sonata form of a special kind, containing *two* expositions. The first is played by the orchestra, which presents several themes in the home key. This opening section sets the mood for the movement and leads us to expect the soloist's entrance. The second exposition begins with the soloist's first notes. Music for the solo entry may be powerful or quiet, but its effect is dramatic because suspense has been built. Together with the orchestra, the soloist explores themes from the first exposition and introduces new ones. After a modulation from the home key to a new key, the second exposition then moves to a development section, followed by the recapitulation, cadenza, and coda. The slow middle movement may take any one of several forms, but the finale is usually a quick rondo or sonata-rondo.

# CLASSICAL CHAMBER MUSIC

Classical *chamber music* is designed for the intimate setting of a room (chamber) in a home or palace, rather than for a public concert hall. It is performed by a small group of two to nine musicians, with one player to a part. Chamber music is lighter in sound than classical orchestral music. During the classical period, it was fashionable for an aristocrat or a member of the well-to-do middle class to play chamber music with friends and to hire professional musicians to entertain guests after dinner.

Chamber music is subtle and intimate, intended to please the performer as much as the listener. A chamber music group is a team. Each member is essential, and each may have an important share of the thematic material. Therefore much give-and-take is called for among the instruments. Classical chamber music does not need a conductor; instead, each musician must be sensitive to what goes on and coordinate dynamics and phrasing with the other musicians.

The most important form in classical chamber music is the *string quartet,* written for two violins, a viola, and a cello. Haydn, Mozart, and Beethoven wrote some of their most important music in this form. The string quartet can be compared to a conversation among four lively, sensitive, and intelligent people. And it's not surprising that the string quartet evolved when conversation was cultivated as a fine art.

Like the symphony, the string quartet usually consists of four movements: (1) fast, (2) slow, (3) minuet or scherzo, (4) fast. (Sometimes the second movement is a minuet or a scherzo and the slow movement is third.)

Other popular forms of classical chamber music are the sonata for violin and piano, the piano trio (violin, cello, and piano), and the string quintet (two violins, two violas, and cello).

# JOSEPH HAYDN

Joseph Haydn (1732–1809) was born in Rohrau, a tiny Austrian village. Until he was six, his musical background consisted of folk songs and peasant dances (which later had an influence on his style); but then his eager response to music was recognized and he was given training. At eight, he went to Vienna to serve as a choirboy in the Cathedral of St. Stephen.

When his voice changed, Haydn was dismissed, penniless, from St. Stephen's; he gave music lessons to children, struggled to teach himself composition, and took odd jobs (including playing violin in street bands). But gradually, aristocratic patrons of music began to notice his talent; and in 1761, when he was twenty-nine, his life changed for the better, permanently: he entered the service of the Esterházys, the richest and most powerful of the Hungarian noble families. For nearly thirty years, most of his music was composed for performances in the palaces of the family, especially Esterháza—which contained an opera house, a theater, two concert halls, and 126 guest rooms.

As a highly skilled servant, Haydn was to compose all the music requested by his patron, conduct the orchestra, coach singers, and oversee the instruments and the music library. This entailed a staggering amount of work; there were usually two concerts and two opera performances weekly, as well as daily chamber music. Though today this sort of patronage seems degrading, it was taken for granted at the time and had definite advantages for composers: they received a steady income and their works were performed. Haydn was conscientious about his professional duties, concerned about his musicians' interests, and—despite an unhappy marriage—good-humored and unselfish.

Word spread about the Esterházys' composer, and Haydn's music became immensely popular all over Europe. In 1791–1792 and again in 1794–1795, Haydn went to London, and reports of the time say that his appearances there were triumphs. (The twelve symphonies he composed for these visits are now known as the *London symphonies.*) A servant had become a celebrity; Haydn was wined and dined by the aristocracy, given an honorary doctorate at Oxford, and received by the royal family.

(Royal College of Music)

Joseph Haydn.

In 1795, he returned to Vienna rich and honored. In his late sixties, he composed six masses and two oratorios, *The Creation* (1798) and *The Seasons* (1801), which were so popular that choruses and orchestras were formed solely to present them. He died in 1809, at seventy-seven.

## HAYDN'S MUSIC

Haydn was a pathfinder for the classical style, a pioneer in the development of the symphony and the string quartet. Both Mozart and Beethoven were influenced by his style. His music, like his personality, is robust and direct; it radiates healthy optimism. Much of it has a folk flavor, and *The Creation* and *The Seasons* reflect his love of nature. Haydn was a master at developing themes; he could build a whole movement out of a single main theme, creating contrasts of mood through changes in texture, rhythm, dynamics, and orchestration. The contagious joy that springs from his lively rhythms and vivid contrasts makes it clear why London went wild.

Haydn's 104 symphonies—along with his 68 string quartets—are considered the most important part of his enormous output. Many of them have nicknames, such as *Surprise* (No. 94), *Military* (No. 100), *Clock* (No. 101), and *Drum Roll* (No. 103).

Some scholars believe that Haydn invented the string quartet form. He began writing the first of his lifelong series of string quartets for good reason—only three other musicians (two violinists and a cellist, in addition to Haydn as violist) were on hand during the summer of 1757, when he was invited to take part in chamber music performances at a castle.

Haydn's output also includes piano sonatas, piano trios, divertimentos, concertos, operas, and masses. The variety in his works is astounding. He was a great innovator and experimenter who hated arbitrary "rules" of composition. "Art is free," he said. "The educated ear is the sole authority, . . . and I think that I have as much right to lay down the law as anyone."

## TRUMPET CONCERTO IN E FLAT MAJOR (1796)

Haydn's Trumpet Concerto in E Flat Major has a remarkable history. After its premiere in 1800, it was forgotten for almost 130 years. It was first published only in 1929, but in the 1930s a phonograph recording brought it to a wide audience. Now, it may well be Haydn's most popular work.

Haydn wrote the concerto in 1796 for a friend, a trumpeter at the Viennese court who had recently invented a keyed trumpet that could produce a complete chromatic scale. The keyed trumpet was intended to replace the natural trumpet, which could produce only a restricted number of tones. But the keyed trumpet had a dull sound and was supplanted by the valve trumpet around 1840. Today, the concerto is performed on a valve trumpet. Like most concertos, it has three movements: (1) fast, (2) slow, (3) fast. We'll examine the third movement.

### Third Movement:
### Allegro

The third movement is a dazzling sonata-rondo in which Haydn gives the trumpeter's virtuosity free rein. The movement combines the recurring main theme characteristic of rondo form with the development section found in sonata form. It may be outlined as A B A B' A–development section–A B"–coda. Themes A and B are introduced by the orchestra and are then presented mainly by the trumpet, with orchestral support. The main theme, A, is a high-spirited melody that is well suited to the trumpet.

Basic sets.
Side 4, band 9
CD 2 37

37 0:00

Theme B is playful; it contains a short, downward-moving phrase that is repeated several times.

38 0:22

Haydn's fondness for musical surprises is reflected in the coda, which contains sudden changes of dynamics, unexpected harmonic twists, and a suspenseful long pause.

# 10 WOLFGANG AMADEUS MOZART

Wolfgang Amadeus Mozart (1756–1791), one of the most amazing child prodigies in history, was born in Salzburg, Austria. By the age of six, he could play the harpsichord and violin, improvise fugues, write minuets, and read music perfectly at first sight. At age eight, he wrote a symphony; at eleven, an oratorio; at twelve, an opera.

Mozart's father, Leopold, a court musician, was eager to show him off. Between the ages of six and fifteen Mozart was continually on tour; he played for Empress Maria Theresa in Vienna, Louis XV at Versailles, George III in London, and innumerable aristocrats. On his trips to Italy he was able to master the current operatic style, which he later put to superb use.

When he was fifteen, Mozart returned to Salzburg—then ruled by a prince-archbishop. The archbishop was a tyrant who did not appreciate Mozart's music and refused to grant him more than a subordinate seat in the court orchestra. With his father's help, Mozart tried repeatedly but unsuccessfully over the next decade to find a position elsewhere.

Ironically, and tragically, Mozart won more acclaim as a boy wonder than as an adult musician. Having begun his professional life as an international celebrity, he could not tolerate being treated like a servant; he became insubordinate when the archbishop forbade him to give concerts or to perform at the houses of the aristocracy, and his relations with his patron went from bad to worse. Moreover, his complete dependence on his father had given him little opportunity to develop initiative; and a contemporary observed that he was "too good-natured, not active enough, too easily taken in, too little concerned with the means that may lead him to good fortune."

When he was twenty-five, Mozart could stand it no more: he broke free of provincial Salzburg and became a free-lance musician in Vienna. His first few years there were very successful. His German opera *Die Entführung aus dem Serail* (*The Abduction from the Seraglio,* 1782) was acclaimed; concerts of his own music were attended by the emperor and nobility; his compositions were published; pupils paid him high fees; and he formed a friendship with Haydn, who told Mozart's father, "Your son is the greatest composer that I know; he has taste and, what is more, the most profound knowledge of composition." In 1786 came his opera *Le Nozze di Figaro (The Marriage of Figaro).* Vienna loved it, and Prague was even more enthusiastic; "they talk of nothing but *Figaro,*" Mozart joyfully wrote. This success led an opera company in Prague to commission *Don Giovanni* the next year.

Although *Don Giovanni* was a triumph in Prague, its dark qualities and dissonance did not appeal to the Viennese, and Mozart's popularity in Vienna began to decline. Vienna was a fickle city in any case, and it found Mozart's music complicated and hard to follow. His pupils dwindled; the elite snubbed his concerts.

During the last year of his life—1791—Mozart was more successful. He received a commission for a comic opera, *Die Zauberflöte (The Magic Flute)*, and while working on it was visited by a mysterious stranger who carried an anonymous letter commissioning a requiem, a mass for the dead. As Mozart's health grew worse, he came to believe that the requiem was for himself and rushed to finish it while on his deathbed. (In fact, the stranger was the servant of a nobleman who intended to claim the requiem as his own composition.) *The Magic Flute* was premiered to resounding praise in Vienna, but its success came too late. Mozart died shortly before his thirty-sixth birthday, leaving the Requiem unfinished. (It was completed by his friend and pupil Franz Süssmayer.)

## MOZART'S MUSIC

Mozart was among the most versatile of composers and wrote master-pieces in all the musical forms of his time—symphonies, concertos, chamber music, operas. His music sings and conveys ease, grace, and spontaneity as well as balance, restraint, and proportion. Yet mysterious harmonies contrast with its lyricism, and it fuses elegance with power. His compositions sound effortless and were created with miraculous rapidity—for example, he completed his last three symphonies in six weeks.

Many of Mozart's concertos are among his greatest works. His piano concertos—composed mainly for his own performances—are particularly important; but he also wrote concertos for violin, horn, flute, bassoon, oboe, and clarinet.

Mozart was also a master of opera, with a supreme ability to coordinate music and stage action, a keen sense of theater, an inexhaustible gift of melody, and a genius for creating characters through tone. Most of his operas are comedies, composed to German or Italian librettos. His three masterpieces of Italian comic opera (all composed to librettos by Lorenzo da Ponte) are *The Marriage of Figaro* (1786), *Don Giovanni* (1787), and *Così fan tutte* (1790); his finest opera in German is *The Magic Flute* (1791). The comic operas have both humorous and serious characters—not mere stereotypes but individual human beings who think and feel. Emotions in his arias and ensembles continually evolve and change.

"I am never happier," Mozart once wrote, "than when I have something to compose, for that, after all, is my sole delight and passion." His delight and passion are communicated in his works, which represent late eighteenth-century musical style at its highest level of perfection.

(Austrian Information Service, New York)

Wolfgang Amadeus Mozart.

## DON GIOVANNI (1787)

*Don Giovanni (Don Juan)* is a unique blend of comic and serious opera, combining seduction and slapstick with violence and the supernatural. The old tale of Don Juan, the legendary Spanish lover, had attracted many playwrights and composers before Mozart. In Mozart's opera, Don Giovanni is an extremely charming but ruthless nobleman who will stop at nothing to satisfy his sexual appetite. Don Giovanni's comic servant, Leporello, is a grumbling accomplice who dreams of being in his master's place.

The Don attempts to rape a young noblewoman, Donna Anna; her father, the Commendatore (Commandant), challenges him to a duel. Don Giovanni kills the old man, causing Donna Anna and her fiancé, Don Ottavio, to swear revenge. Pursued by his enemies, the Don deftly engages in new amorous adventures. During one of them, he hides in a cemetery, where he sees a marble statue of the dead Commandant. The unearthly statue utters threatening words, but Don Giovanni brazenly invites it to dinner. When the statue appears at the banquet hall, it orders the Don to repent his sins. Don Giovanni defiantly refuses and is dragged down to hell.

## Act I:

## Introduction

The overture leads directly into the action-packed opening scene. In breathless succession we witness Leporello keeping guard, Don Giovanni struggling with Donna Anna, the Commandant dueling with the Don, and the Commandant's agonized last gasps. Mozart's music vividly depicts the characters and pushes the action forward. (In the excerpt from the libretto that follows, braces indicate that characters sing at the same time. *Etc.* indicates that previous lines of text are repeated.)

(Late evening outside the Commandant's palace in Seville. Don Giovanni, concealing his identity, has stolen into Donna Anna's room for an amorous adventure. Leporello paces back and forth.)

Brief sets:
Side 3, band 2
CD 2 [5]

Basic sets:
Side 5, band 4
CD 3 [17]

[5] [17] 0:00
Orchestral introduction, molto allegro; sudden fortes suggest pacing and abrupt turns.

### Leporello

| | |
|---|---|
| *Notte e giorno faticar,* | Night and day I slave |
| *Per chi nulla sa gradir;* | For one who does not appreciate it. |
| *Piova e vento sopportar,* | I put up with wind and rain, |
| *Mangiar male e mal dormir!* | Eat and sleep badly. |
| *Voglio far il gentiluomo,* | I want to be a gentleman |
| *E non voglio più servir,* | And to give up my servitude. |
| *No, no, no, no, no, no,* | No, no, no, no, no, no, |
| *Non voglio più servir!* | I want to give up my servitude. |
| *O che caro galantuomo!* | Oh, what a fine gentleman! |
| *Voi star dentro colla bella* | You stay inside with your lady |
| *Ed io far la sentinella!* | And I must play the sentinel! |
| *Voglio far il gentiluomo, ecc.* | Oh, what a fine gentleman, etc. |
| *Ma mi par che venga gente . . .* | But I think someone is coming! |
| *Non mi voglio far sentir, ecc.* | I don't want them to hear me, etc. |

(Leporello hides to one side. Don Giovanni and Donna Anna come down the palace stairs struggling. The Don hides his face to prevent her from recognizing him.)

1:39
Orchestral crescendo.

### Donna Anna

| | |
|---|---|
| *Non sperar, se non m'uccidi.* | There's no hope, unless you kill me |
| *Ch'io ti lasci fuggir mai!* | That I'll ever let you go! |

### Don Giovanni

| | |
|---|---|
| *Donna folle, indarno gridi:* | Idiot! You scream in vain. |
| *Chi son io tu non saprai.* | Who I am you'll never know! |

### Donna Anna

| | |
|---|---|
| *Non sperar, ecc.* | There's no hope, etc. |

|  |  |
|---|---|
| **Don Giovanni** | |
| *Donna folle! ecc.* | Idiot! etc. |
| | |
| **Leporello** | |
| *Che tumulto! Oh ciel, che gridi!* | What a racket! Heaven, what screams! |
| *Il padron in nuovi guai.* | My master in another scrape. |
| | |
| **Donna Anna** | |
| *Gente! Servi! Al traditore!* | Help! Everyone! The betrayer! |
| | |
| **Don Giovanni** | |
| *Taci, e trema al mio furore!* | Keep quiet! Beware my wrath! |
| | |
| **Donna Anna** | |
| *Scellerato!* | Scoundrel! |
| | |
| **Don Giovanni** | |
| *Sconsigliata!* | Fool! |
| | |
| **Donna Anna** | |
| *Scellerato!* | Scoundrel! |
| | |
| **Don Giovanni** | |
| *Sconsigliata!* | Fool! |
| | |
| **Leporello** | |
| *Sta a veder che il malandrino* | We will see if this rascal |
| *Mi farà precipitar.* | Will be the ruin of me! |
| | |
| **Donna Anna** | |
| *Gente! Servi!* | Help! Everyone! |
| | |
| **Don Giovanni** | |
| *Taci, e trema!* | Keep quiet! |
| | |
| **Donna Anna** | |
| *Come furia disperata* | Like a desperate fury |
| *Ti saprò perseguitar! ecc.* | I'll know how to pursue you! etc. |
| *Scellerato! Gente! Servi!* | Scoundrel! Help! Everyone! |
| *Come furia disperata, ecc.* | Like a desperate fury, etc. |
| | |
| **Don Giovanni** | |
| *Questa furia disperata* | This desperate fury |
| *Mi vuol far precipitar! ecc.* | Is aimed at destroying me! |
| *Sconsigliata! Taci, e trema!* | Fool! Keep quiet! |
| *Questa furia disperata, ecc.* | This desperate fury, etc. |
| | |
| **Leporello** | |
| *Che tumulto! Oh ciel, che gridi!* | What a racket! Heavens, what screams! |
| *Sta a veder che il malandrino, ecc.* | We will see if this rascal, etc. |

(Donna Anna hears the Commandant: she leaves Don Giovanni and goes into the house. The Commandant appears.)

6 18 3:05
String tremolo, *ff*, shift to minor key.

**Commandant**

*Lasciala, indegno! Battiti meco!*     Leave her alone, wretch, and defend yourself.

**Don Giovanni**

*Va, non mi degno di pugnar teco.*     Go away! I disdain to fight with you.

**Commandant**

*Così pretendi da me fuggir?*     Thus you think to escape me?

**Leporello**

*Potessi almeno di qua partir.*     If I could only get out of here!

**Don Giovanni**

*Va, non mi degno, no!*     Go away! I disdain you!

**Commandant**

*Così pretendi da me fuggir?*     Thus you think to escape me!

**Leporello**

*Potessi almeno di qua partir!*     If I could only get out of here!

**Commandant**

*Battiti!*     Fight!

**Don Giovanni**

*Misero! Attendi, se vuoi morir!*     So be it, if you want to die!

(They duel. The Commandant is fatally wounded.)

Dueling music, upward sweeps in strings.
Death blow, suspenseful, held chord.

**Commandant**

7 19 4:09
Andante, *pp*, pathetic minor phrases.

*Ah, soccorso! son tradito!*     Help! I've been betrayed!
*L'assassino m'ha ferito,*     The assassin has wounded me!
*E dal seno palpitante*     And from my heaving breast
*Sento l'anima partir.*     I feel my soul escaping!

**Don Giovanni**

*Ah! già cade il sciagurato!*     Ah, already the wretch has fallen,
*Affannosa e agonizzante*     And he gasps for air.
*Già dal seno palpitante*     From his heaving breast I already
*Veggo l'anima partir, ecc.*     See his soul escaping, etc.

149

**Leporello**

*Qual misfatto! Qual eccesso!*      What a misdeed! What a crime!
*Entro il sen dallo spavento*      I can feel my heart
*Palpitar il cor mi sento!*      Beating hard from fright!
*Io non sò che far, che dir, ecc.*      I don't know what to do or say, etc.

(The Commandant dies.)

8  20  5:19
Recitative,
harpsichord
accompanies.

**Don Giovanni**

*Leporello, ove sei?*      Leporello, where are you?

**Leporello**

*Son qui, per mia disgrazia. E voi?*      I'm here, unfortunately, and you?

**Don Giovanni**

*Son qui.*      Over here.

**Leporello**

*Chi è morto, voi, o il vecchio?*      Who's dead, you or the old man?

**Don Giovanni**

*Che domanda da bestia! Il vecchio.*      What an idiotic question! The old
      man.

**Leporello**

*Bravo! Due imprese leggiadre,*      Well done! Two misdeeds!
*Storzar la figlia, ed ammazzar il padre!*      First you raped the daughter then
      murdered the father!

**Don Giovanni**

*L'ha voluto, suo danno.*      It was his own doing: too bad for
      him.

**Leporello**

*Ma Donn'Anna cosa ha voluto?*      And Donna Anna, did she ask for it
      too?

**Don Giovanni**

*Taci, non mi seccar!*      Keep quiet and don't bother me.
*Vien meco, se non vuoi qualche cosa*      Now come along, unless you're
*ancor tu.*      anxious for something for yourself.

**Leporello**

*Non vo' nulla, signor, non parlo più.*      I have no desires, sir, and no more to
      say.

## Act I:

### Leporello's catalog aria (*Madamina*)

Not long after the opening scene, Leporello sings his famous "catalog" aria (*Madamina*) to Donna Elvira, a woman whom Don Giovanni had earlier seduced and deserted and who has now appeared on the scene. In mocking "consolation," Leporello tells her that she is but one of many and displays a fat catalog of his master's conquests. The music bubbles with Leporello's delight as he reels off the amazing totals: 640 in Italy, 231 in Germany, 100 in France, 91 in Turkey, and in Spain, 1,003! Mozart makes the most of comic description as Leporello proceeds to list the Don's seduction techniques for different women:

Basic sets:
Side 5, band 5
CD 3 [21]

| | | |
|---|---|---|
| *Madamina, il catalogo è questo*<br>*Delle belle, che amò il padron mio;* | My dear lady, this is a list<br>Of the beauties my master has loved, | [21] 0:00<br>Allegro |
| *Un catalogo egli è, che ho fatt'io,*<br>*Osservate, leggete con me.* | A list which I have compiled.<br>Observe, read along with me. | |
| *In Italia seicento e quaranta,* | In Italy, six hundred and forty; | 0:22<br>Staccato woodwind chuckles. |
| *In Almagna duecento a trentuna,* | In Germany, two hundred and thirty-one; | |
| *Cento in Francia, in Turchia novantuna,* | A hundred in France; in Turkey ninety-one. | |
| *Ma in Ispagna son già mille e tre!* | In Spain already one thousand and three! | 0:39<br>Longer notes. |
| *V'han fra queste contadine,*<br>*Cameriere, cittadine,*<br>*V'han contesse, baronesse,*<br>*Marchesine, principesse,*<br>*E v'han donne d'ogni grado,*<br>*D'ogni forma, d'ogni età!*<br>*In Italia seicento e quaranta, ecc.* | Among these are peasant girls<br>Maidservants, city girls,<br>Countesses, baronesses,<br>Marchionesses, princesses,<br>Women of every rank,<br>Every shape, every age.<br>In Italy six hundred and forty, etc. | 0:57<br>Shorter notes. |
| *Nella bionda egli ha l'usanza*<br>*Di lodar la gentilezza;* | With blondes it is his habit<br>To praise their kindness; | [22] 2:12<br>Andante con moto, courtly minuet. |
| *Nella bruna, la costanza;* | In brunettes, their faithfulness; | 2:32<br>Mock-heroic flourish. |
| *Nella bianca la dolcezza;* | In the very blonde, their sweetness. | 2:42<br>Suave melodic phrase |

3:05
Crescendo,
melody slowly
rises to high held
tone.

3:28
Sprightly quick
notes

| | |
|---|---|
| *Vuol d'inverno la grassotta,* | In winter he likes fat ones, |
| *Vuol d'estate la magrotta;* | In summer he likes thin ones. |
| | |
| *È la grande maestosa,* | He calls the tall ones majestic. |

| | |
|---|---|
| *La piccina è ognor vezzosa;* | The little ones are always charming. |
| *Delle vecchie fa conquista* | He seduces the old ones |
| *Pel piacer di porle in lista.* | For the pleasure of adding to the list. |
| *Sua passion predominante* | His greatest favorite |
| *È la giovin principiante.* | Is the young beginner. |
| *Non si picca se sia ricca,* | It doesn't matter if she's rich, |
| *Se sia brutta, se sia bella,* | Ugly or beautiful; |
| *Se sia ricca, brutta, se sia bella;* | If she is rich, ugly or beautiful. |
| *Purchè porti la gonnella,* | If she wears a petticoat, |
| *Voi sapete quel che fa!* | *You* know what he does. |
| *Purchè porti la gonnella, ecc.* | If she wears a petticoat, etc. |

## SYMPHONY NO. 40 IN G MINOR, K. 550 (1788)

Symphony No. 40 in G Minor is the most passionate and dramatic of Mozart's symphonies. Although the work is classical in form and technique, it is almost romantic in emotional intensity. It staggers the imagination that Mozart could compose the G minor and two other great symphonies—No. 39 in E Flat and No. 41 in C *(Jupiter)*—during the short period of six weeks. They are his last three symphonies.

Like most classical symphonies, Symphony No. 40 in G minor has four movements: (1) fast, (2) slow, (3) minuet, (4) fast.

Brief sets:
Side 2, band 7
CD 1 56

Basic sets:
Side 6, band 2
CD 3 28

### First Movement:
### Molto allegro
Mozart opens his Symphony No. 40 in G Minor with the agitated movement already described in section 2.

Basic sets:
Side 6, band 3
CD 3 37

Exposition
37 0:00
Development
38 3:21
Recapitulation
39 4:37

### Second Movement:
### Andante
The mood of the andante hovers between gentleness and longing. The andante is written in sonata form and is the only movement of this symphony in major (it is in E flat). This movement develops from a series of gently pulsating notes in the opening theme.

152

As the theme continues, the violins introduce an airy two-note rhythmic figure that will appear—with changes of dynamics and orchestration—in almost every section of the andante. The rhythmic figure will be, at different times, graceful, insistent, and forceful.

Later, Mozart uses the airy figures as a delicate countermelody to the repeated-note idea. Floating woodwinds interwoven with strings reveal Mozart's sensitivity to tone color as an expressive resource.

## Third Movement:

### Menuetto (Allegretto)

The minuet, in G minor, is serious and intense; it does not sound like an aristocratic dance. The form of the minuet is A B A:

Basic sets:
Side 6, band 4
CD 3 40

| Minuet | Trio | Minuet |
|--------|------|--------|
| A | B | A |
| A (repeated)  ba' (repeated) | c (repeated)  dc' (repeated) | a ba' |

Powerful syncopations give a fierce character to the A section (the minuet), which is predominantly loud and in minor.

Section A
40 0:00

Later, Mozart increases the tension through polyphonic texture and striking dissonances. At the end of the A section, there is a sudden drop in dynamics; the flute, supported by oboes and a bassoon, softly recalls the opening melody of the minuet.

The trio section (B) brings a shift from minor to major, from fierce energy to graceful relaxation.

Section B
41 1:51

This change of mood is underscored by a soft dynamic level and pastoral woodwind interludes. After the trio, a sudden forte announces the return of the fierce A section.

Return of section A
42 3:48

## Fourth Movement:

### Allegro assai (very fast)

Basic sets:
Side 6, band 5
CD 3 43
First theme
43 0:00

The very fast finale, in sonata form, is unusually tense. Its opening theme, in the tonic key of G minor, offers brusque contrasts of dynamics and rhythm. A soft upward arpeggio (broken chord) alternates repeatedly with a loud rushing phrase.

Bridge
44 0:28

Excitement is maintained throughout the long bridge, which is based on the loud rushing phrase of the first theme. The bridge ends clearly with a brief pause, as do other sections in this movement.

Second theme:
45 1:05

The tender second theme, in the new key of B flat major, is a lyrical contrast to the brusque opening theme. It is softer, flows more smoothly, and uses longer notes.

Closing section:
46 1:35

Development
47 1:57

The exposition closes with a loud passage of continuously rushing notes in the strings.

Mozart weaves almost the entire development section from the upward arpeggio of the first theme. During the opening few seconds, there is an eruption of violence as the orchestra in unison plays a variation of the arpeggio and a series of jagged downward leaps.

As the development continues, the texture becomes polyphonic and contrasts with the homophony of the exposition. Arpeggios press upon each other in quick imitation. Rapid shifts of key create restless intensity.

In the recapitulation, both the first and the second theme are in the tonic key, G minor. This minor key now adds a touch of melancholy to the tender second theme, which was heard in major before. The passion and violence of this movement foreshadow the romantic expression to come during the nineteenth century.

Recapitulation
First theme
48  3:14

Second theme
49  3:52

## PIANO CONCERTO NO. 23 IN A MAJOR, K. 488

The Piano Concerto in A Major—completed on March 2, 1786—dates from a very productive and successful period in Mozart's life. Between October 1785 and May 1786, he taught piano and composition, conducted operas, performed in concerts, and composed *The Marriage of Figaro*, the comic one-act opera *The Impressario*, two other great piano concertos (K. 482 in E Flat and K. 491 in C Minor), a Quartet for Piano and Strings (K. 478), and the *Masonic Funeral Music* (K. 477).

Mozart thought highly of the A Major concerto. In a letter to the court chamberlain of a prospective patron, he included it among "the compositions which I keep for myself or for a small circle of music-lovers and connoisseurs." Today, it is one of the best known of his piano concertos.

Like all classical concertos, this one has three movements. The grace of the opening movement (which we'll study) and the high spirits of the finale contrast with the melancholy of the middle movement. This concerto stresses poetry and delicacy rather than pianistic virtuosity or orchestral power. It is scored for an orchestra without trumpets or timpani and highlights the clarinets, flute, and bassoon. Mozart associated its key—A major—with tenderness, lyricism, and elegance. (He also used this key for the Clarinet Concerto and the duet between Don Giovanni and Zerlina in *Don Giovanni*.)

In our recording the soloist Malcolm Bilson plays a modern replica of Mozart's concert fortepiano. The late-eighteenth-century *fortepiano*—an early piano—weighed much less than the modern piano and had thinner strings held by a frame made of wood, rather than metal. Its pitch range was smaller, and its tone was softer and lasted a shorter time.

### First Movement:

### Allegro

The gentle opening movement blends lyricism with a touch of sadness owing to many shifts between major and minor. Two main lyrical themes introduced by the orchestra in the first exposition are restated by the piano and orchestra in the second exposition. The development section is based on a new legato theme that is unexpectedly introduced by the orchestra after a dramatic pause. (In the listening outline, this is called the *development theme*.) Mozart creates a dramatic confrontation by juxtaposing fragments of this new theme, played by the woodwinds, with restless ideas in the piano and orchestra.

Toward the end of the allegro is a cadenza—an unaccompanied showpiece for the soloist. Exceptionally, Mozart notated the cadenza directly into the score, instead of leaving it to be improvised by the soloist. With its rapid sweeps up and down the keyboard, its alternation between brilliant and tender passages, and its concluding trill, this cadenza gives us some idea of how Mozart himself must have improvised.

**Brief sets:**
**Side 3, band 3**
**CD 2** 9

Basic sets:
Side 5, band 3
CD 3 10

# Listening Outline  To be read while music is heard

PIANO CONCERTO NO. 23 IN A MAJOR, K. 488 (1786),
BY WOLFGANG AMADEUS MOZART

First Movement: Allegro

Sonata form, quadruple meter ($\frac{4}{4}$), A major

Solo piano, flute, 2 clarinets, 2 bassoons, 2 French horns, 1st violins, 2d violins, violas, cellos, double basses

(Duration, 10:33)

FIRST
EXPOSITION
First theme
9 10 0:00

1. *a.* Strings, *p,* gracious main melody, legato, major key,

staccato ascent.

*b.* Winds, *p,* repeat opening of main melody an octave higher. Strings, *f,* answered by winds; cadence to

156

Bridge
10 11 0:32
2. *a.* Full orchestra, *f,* vigorous bridge theme,

running notes in violins, *f.* Brief pause.

Second
theme
group
11 12 0:55
3. *a.* Violins, *p,* tender second theme, repeated notes in dotted rhythm.

1:25
  *b.* Violins and bassoon, *p,* repeat second theme, flute joins.
  *c.* Agitated rhythms in minor lead to
  *d.* Full orchestra, *f,* major; sudden *p,* winds alternate with violins, minor, crescendo to
  *e.* Full orchestra, *f,* major, cadence. Brief pause.
  *f.* High woodwind phrase, *p,* orchestral chords, *f.* Brief pause.

**SECOND
EXPOSITION**
First theme
12 13 2:03
1. *a.* Piano solo, main melody, low strings join, violins introduce
  *b.* Piano, varied repetition of main melody, rapid downward and upward scales.

Bridge
2:31
2. *a.* Full orchestra, *f,* bridge theme.
  *b.* Piano, running notes, with string accompaniment. High staccato violins, high staccato winds, downward scale in piano. Brief pause.

Second
theme
group
2:59
3. *a.* Piano solo, second theme, dolce.
  *b.* Violins and flute repeat second theme, piano joins.
3:29
  *c.* Piano and orchestra, minor; sudden *f,* in piano, major.
3:39
  *d.* Sudden *p,* violins and piano, repeated figure, minor.
3:46
  *e.* Sudden *f* in piano, major. Long passage of running notes in piano culminating in short trill closing into
4.09
4. Full orchestra, opening of bridge theme. Sudden pause.

13 14 4:22

1. *a.* Strings, *p,* legato development theme.

*p*

        *b.* Piano solo, development theme embellished by rapid notes.

4:44   2. *a.* Clarinet, fragment of development theme in minor, answered by piano and staccato strings.

4:52        *b.* Flute, fragment of development theme in major, answered by piano and staccato strings.

4:59        *c.* High woodwinds, development theme fragment in minor answered by piano, strings join with development theme fragment.

5:10   3. Piano continues with running notes; clarinet and flute, imitations of development theme fragment.

5:25   4. Strings, minor, repeatedly alternate with piano and woodwinds.

5:39   5. Piano solo, orchestra joins. Long descents and ascents, rising chromatic scale leads into

## RECAPITULATION
### First theme

14 15 6:02

1. *a.* Strings, *p,* main melody, woodwinds join.

       *b.* Piano *p,* with woodwinds, ornamented repeat of main melody in higher octave; piano scales lead to

### Bridge

6:29   2. *a.* Full orchestra, *f,* bridge theme.

       *b.* Piano, running notes, strings accompany; staccato violins, high staccato winds, upward scale in piano. Brief pause.

### Second theme group

6:56   3. *a.* Piano solo, second theme.

       *b.* Winds repeat second theme an octave higher, piano joins.

7:24        *c.* Piano and orchestra, minor; sudden *f* in piano, major.

7:35        *d.* Sudden *p,* violins and piano, repeated figure, minor.

7:42        *e.* Sudden *f* in piano, major, running-note passage interrupted by brief pause.

7:56   4. *a.* Piano alone, development theme.

       *b.* Clarinets and bassoons repeat development theme, accompanied by running notes in piano, staccato winds join, piano trill meshes with entrance of

8:36   5. *a.* Full orchestra, *f,* bridge theme; sudden brief pause.

8:49        *b.* Strings and winds, *p,* development theme. Full orchestra, *f,* dotted rhythm, briefly held chord.

## CADENZA

15 16 9:03

       *c.* Extended piano solo; long trill closes into

## CODA

10:02   6. *a.* Full orchestra, *f,* cadence.

       *b.* High woodwind phrase, *p*; sudden *f,* full orchestra; sudden *p* ending, trills in flutes and violins.

# LUDWIG VAN BEETHOVEN

For many people, Ludwig van Beethoven (1770–1827) represents the highest level of musical genius. He opened new realms of musical expression and profoundly influenced composers throughout the nineteenth century.

Beethoven was born in Bonn, Germany, into a family of musicians. By the age of eleven, he was serving as assistant to the court organist, and at age twelve he had several compositions published. When he was sixteen, he played for Mozart, who reportedly said, "Keep your eyes on him; some day he will give the world something to talk about." Shortly before his twenty-second birthday, he left Bonn to study with Haydn in Vienna, where he spent the rest of his life.

Beethoven's first years in Vienna brought hard work, growing confidence, and public praise (although his studies with Haydn were not entirely successful and he went secretly to another teacher). This music loving city was dazzled by his virtuosity and moved by his improvisations. And although he rebelled against social convention, asserting that an artist deserved as much respect as the nobility, the same aristocrats who had allowed Mozart to die in poverty showered Beethoven with gifts. In 1809, three noblemen obligated themselves to give him an annual income, their only condition being that he remain in Vienna—an arrangement unprecedented in music history. Unlike earlier composers, Beethoven was never actually in the service of the Viennese aristocracy. He earned good fees from piano lessons and concerts, and publishers were quick to buy his compositions.

But during his twenty-ninth year, disaster struck: he felt the first symptoms of deafness, which his doctors could do nothing to halt. On October 6, 1802, Beethoven wrote an agonized letter addressed to his brothers from Heiligenstadt, a village outside Vienna. In the letter (now known as the *Heiligenstadt testament*), he said, "I would have ended my life—it was only my art that held me back." This victory over despair coincided with an important change in his musical style; works that he created after his emotional crisis—perhaps most significantly the gigantic Third Symphony, the *Eroica*, composed from 1803 to 1804—have a new power and heroism. (He planned to name the Third Symphony *Bonaparte*, after Napoleon; but when Napoleon proclaimed himself emperor, Beethoven struck out the dedication and later wrote on the new title page, "Heroic Symphony composed to celebrate the memory of a great man.")

As a man, Beethoven remains something of a mystery. He was self-educated and had read widely, but he was weak in elementary arithmetic. He claimed the highest moral principles, but was often unscrupulous in dealing with publishers. He was orderly and methodical when composing but dressed sloppily and lived in incredibly messy apartments. He fell in love with several women but never formed a lasting relationship. The contradictions in his personality are especially evident in his disastrous guardianship of his young nephew Karl, who eventually attempted suicide. Beethoven took consolation from nature for disappointments in his personal life, and ideas came to him as he walked in the countryside. His Sixth Symphony, the *Pastoral,* expresses his recollections of life in the country.

As Beethoven's hearing weakened, this once brilliant pianist was forced to stop performing in public—though he insisted on conducting his orchestral works long after he could do it efficiently. His sense of isolation grew with his deafness. Friends had to communicate with him through an ear trumpet and, during his last years, by writing in notebooks which he carried.

Despite this, and despite mounting personal problems, Beethoven had a creative outburst after 1818 that produced some of his greatest works: the late piano sonatas and string quartets, the *Missa solemnis,* and the Ninth Symphony—out of total deafness, new realms of sound.

## BEETHOVEN'S MUSIC

For Beethoven, music was not mere entertainment, but a moral force, "a higher revelation than all wisdom and philosophy." His music directly reflects his powerful, tortured personality.

Beethoven's demand for perfection meant long and hard work—sometimes he worked for years on a single symphony while also writing other compositions. He carried musical sketchbooks everywhere, jotting down and revising ideas; the final versions of his works were often hammered out laboriously.

Beethoven mostly used classical forms and techniques, but he gave them new power and intensity. The musical heir of Haydn and Mozart, he bridged the classical and romantic eras; many of his innovations were used by later composers. In his works, tension and excitement are built up through syncopations and dissonances. The range of pitch and dynamics is greater than ever before, so that contrasts of mood are more pronounced. Accents and climaxes seem titanic. Greater tension called for a larger musical framework, and so he expanded his forms; he was a musical architect who could create large-scale structures in which every note seems inevitable. But his music is not all stormy and powerful; much of it is gentle, humorous, noble, or lyrical.

More than his predecessors, he tried to unify contrasting movements by means of musical continuity. Sometimes one movement leads directly into the next, without the traditional pause; sometimes a musical bond is created by similar themes. He also greatly expanded the development section

(Granger Collection)

Ludwig van Beethoven.

and coda of sonata-form movements and made them more dramatic. His works often have climactic, triumphant finales toward which the previous movements seem to build—an important departure from the light, relaxed endings of Haydn and Mozart.

Beethoven's most popular works are the nine symphonies, written for larger orchestras than Haydn's or Mozart's. Each of them is unique in character and style, though the odd-numbered symphonies tend to be more forceful and the even-numbered ones calmer and more lyrical. In the finale of the Ninth Symphony *(Choral)*, Beethoven took the unprecedented step of using a chorus and four vocal soloists, who sing the text of Schiller's *Ode to Joy*.

His thirty-two piano sonatas are far more difficult than those of Haydn and Mozart and exploit the improved piano of his time, drawing many new effects from it. In these sonatas, he experimented with compositional techniques which he later expanded in the symphonies and string quartets. The sixteen string quartets are among the greatest music ever composed; and each of the five superb piano concertos is remarkable for its individuality.

While most of Beethoven's important works are for instruments, his sense of drama was also expressed in vocal music, including two masses and his only opera, *Fidelio*.

Beethoven's work is usually divided into three periods: early (up to 1802), middle (1803–1814), and late (1815–1827). Some works of the early period show the influence of Haydn and Mozart, but others clearly show Beethoven's personal style. The works of the middle period tend to be longer and more heroic; the sublime works of the late period often contain fugues as well as passages that sound surprisingly harsh and "modern." When a violinist complained that the music was very difficult to play, Beethoven reportedly replied, "Do you believe that I think of a wretched fiddle when the spirit speaks to me?"

## PIANO SONATA IN C MINOR, OP. 13 *(PATHÉTIQUE;* 1798)

The title *Pathétique*, coined by Beethoven, suggests the tragically passionate character of his famous Piano Sonata in C Minor, Op. 13 (we'll focus on the first of its three movements). Beethoven's impetuous playing and masterful improvisational powers are mirrored in the sonata's extreme dynamic contrasts, explosive accents, and crashing chords. At the age of twenty-seven, during his early period, Beethoven had already created a powerful and original piano style that foreshadowed nineteenth-century romanticism.

### First Movement:
### Grave (solemn, slow introduction);
### Allegro molto e con brio (very fast and brilliant allegro)
The *Pathétique* begins in C minor with an intense, slow introduction, dominated by an opening motive in dotted rhythm: long-short-long-short-long-long.

Basic sets:
Side 8, band 2
CD 4  30

30  0:00

This six-note idea seems to pose a series of unresolved questions as it is repeated on higher and higher pitch levels. The tragic mood is intensified by dissonant chords, sudden contrasts of dynamics and register, and pauses filled with expectancy. The slow introduction is integrated into the allegro that follows it in imaginative and dramatic ways.

The tension of the introduction is maintained in the allegro con brio, a breathless, fast movement in sonata form. The opening theme, in C minor, begins with a staccato idea that rapidly rises up a 2-octave scale. It is accompanied by low broken octaves, the rapid alternation of two tones an octave apart. 31 1:34

Growing directly out of the opening theme is a bridge that is also built from a climbing staccato motive. 1:54

This bridge motive has an important role later in the movement.

The contrasting second theme, which enters without a pause, is spun out of a short motive that is repeatedly shifted between low and high registers. 32 2:08

This restless idea begins in E flat minor but then moves through different keys. The exposition is rounded off by several themes, including a high running passage and a return of the opening staccato idea in E flat major. 33 3:03

The development section begins with a dramatic surprise: Beethoven brings back the opening bars of the slow introduction. This reappearance creates an enormous contrast of tempo, rhythm, and mood. After four bars of slow music, the fast tempo resumes as Beethoven combines two different ideas: the staccato bridge motive and a quickened version of the introduction motive. The introduction motive is presented in a rhythmically altered form: short-short-short-long-long.

The bridge motive is then developed in the bass, played by the pianist's left hand while the right hand has high broken octaves. After several high accented notes, the brief development concludes with a running passage that leads down to the recapitulation.

For a while, the recapitulation runs its usual course as themes from the exposition are presented in the tonic key of C minor. But Beethoven has one more surprise for the coda—after a loud dissonant chord and a brief pause, he again brings back the opening of the slow introduction. This time the slow music is even more moving, as it is punctuated by moments of silence. Then the fast tempo resumes, and the opening staccato idea and powerful chords bring the movement to a decisive close.

## SYMPHONY NO. 5 IN C MINOR, OP. 67 (1808)

The Fifth Symphony opens with one of the most famous rhythmic ideas in all music, a short-short-short-long motive. Beethoven reportedly interpreted this four-note motive as "fate knocking at the door." It dominates the first movement and plays an important role later in the symphony, too.

34  3:25

4:01

Recapitulation
35  4:50

36  6:25

The entire work can be seen as an emotional progression from the conflict and struggle of the first movement, in C minor, to the exultation and victory of the final movement, in C major. The finale is the climax of the symphony; it is longer than the first movement and more powerful in sound.

Through several different techniques, Beethoven brilliantly welds four contrasting movements into a unified work. The basic rhythmic motive of the first movement (short-short-short-long) is used in a marchlike theme in the third movement. And this third-movement theme is later quoted dramatically within the finale. The last two movements are also connected by a bridge passage.

Beethoven jotted down a few themes for the Fifth Symphony in 1804, but mainly worked on it during 1807 and 1808, an amazingly productive period when he also composed the Mass in C Major; the Sonata for Cello and Piano, Op. 69; and the Sixth Symphony.

## First Movement:

### Allegro con brio (allegro with vigor)

The allegro con brio is an enormously powerful and concentrated movement in sonata form. Its character is determined by a single rhythmic motive, short-short-short-long, from which Beethoven creates an astonishing variety of musical ideas. Tension and expectation are generated from the very beginning of the movement. Three rapid notes of the same pitch are followed by a downward leap to a held, suspenseful tone. This powerful idea is hammered out twice by all the strings in unison; the second time, it is a step lower in pitch.

Brief sets:
Side 3, band 4
CD 2 ⟦16⟧

Basic sets:
Side 7, band 1
CD 4 ⟦1⟧

As the opening theme continues in C minor, Beethoven maintains excitement by quickly developing his basic idea. He crowds varied repetitions of the motive together and rapidly shifts the motive to different pitches and instruments.

The second theme, in E flat major, dramatically combines different ideas. It begins with an unaccompanied horn call that asserts the basic motive in a varied form (short-short-short-long-long-long).

This horn-call motive announces a new legato melody which is calm and contrasts with the preceding agitation. Yet even during this lyrical moment, we are not allowed to forget the basic motive; now it is muttered in the background by cellos and double basses.

Beethoven generates tension in the development section by breaking the horn-call motive into smaller and smaller fragments until it is represented by only a single tone. Supported by a chord, this tone is echoed between woodwinds and strings in a breathtaking decrescendo. The recapitulation comes as a tremendous climax as the full orchestra thunders the basic motive. The recapitulation also brings a new expressive oboe solo at the end of the first theme. The heroic closing section of the recapitulation, in C major, moves without a break into a long and exciting coda in C minor. This coda is like a second development section in which the basic motive creates still greater power and energy.

# Listening Outline   To be read while music is heard

SYMPHONY NO. 5 IN C MINOR, OP. 67 (1808),
BY LUDWIG VAN BEETHOVEN

First Movement: Allegro con brio

Sonata form, duple meter ($\frac{2}{4}$), C minor

2 flutes, 2 oboes, 2 clarinets, 2 bassoons, 2 French horns, 2 trumpets, timpani, 1st violins, 2d violins, violas, cellos, double basses

(Duration, 7:35)

EXPOSITION
  First theme
  16  1  0:00      1.  *a.*  Basic motive, *ff*, repeated a step lower, strings in unison.

        0:08           *b.*  Sudden *p,* strings quickly develop basic motive, minor key, powerful chords, high held tone.

17 2 0:21    2. *a.* Basic motive, *ff*, orchestra in unison.
   0:25       *b.* Sudden *p,* strings quickly develop basic motive, crescendo, *ff*, powerful chords.

Second
theme
18 3 0:46    3. *a.* Solo French horns, *ff*, horn-call motive.

   0:49       *b.* Violins, *p,* lyrical melody in major. Basic motive accompanies in low strings.

         Crescendo to
19 4 1.09    4. *a.* Triumphant melody, *ff*, violins

   1:19       *b.* Woodwinds and horns, basic motive rushes downward. Cadences in basic rhythm. Pause.
20 5 1:28    Exposition is repeated.

DEVELOPMENT
21 6 2:57    1. *a.* Basic motive, *ff*, horns, strings.
            *b.* Sudden *p,* strings and woodwinds, basic motive quickly developed. Motive climbs to rapidly repeated chords, *ff*.
   3:33    2. *a.* Violins, *ff*, horn-call motive, low strings, descending line.

Cellos and basses

167

3:43　　　*b.* High woodwinds, *ff,* in dialogue with lower strings, *ff.* Horn-call motive broken into tiny fragments. Decrescendo to *pp*.

4:05　　　*c.* Sudden *ff,* horn-call rhythm.
　　　　　*d.* Sudden *pp,* woodwinds echoed by strings.
　　　　　*e.* Sudden *ff,* repeated motive drives into

## RECAPITULATION
### First theme
22 7 4:18　　1. *a.* Climactic basic motive, full orchestra, *ff,* repeated a step lower.
　　　　　　　*b.* Sudden *p,* strings quickly develop basic motive, minor key, chords lead to
4:38　　　　　*c.* Oboe solo.

### Bridge
4:50　　　2. Basic motive quickly developed in strings, crescendo to *ff,* full orchestra.

### Second theme
5:12　　　3. *a.* Horn-call motive, solo bassoons, *ff.*
　　　　　　　*b.* Lyrical major melody, *p,* violins and flutes alternate. Basic motive accompanies in timpani, *p.* Crescendo to
5:39　　　4. *a.* Triumphant melody, *ff,* violins.
　　　　　　　*b.* Woodwinds, basic motive rushes downward.
　　　　　　　　 Cadences in basic rhythm.

## CODA
23 8 5:54　　1. *a.* Rapidly repeated chords, *ff.*
6:13　　　　　*b.* Horn-call motive, lower strings, *f,* with higher violin melody, minor.

Descending violin melody, staccato, leads to

6:29     2. *a.* New, rising theme in strings, legato and staccato.

6:39     *b.* High woodwinds, *ff*, answered by lower strings in powerful interchange. Rapidly repeated notes lead to

7:05     3. *a.* Basic motive, *ff*, repeated a step lower, full orchestra.
        *b.* Sudden *p*, basic motive quickly developed in strings and woodwinds.
        *c.* Sudden *ff*, powerful concluding chords.

## Second Movement:

### Andante con moto (moderately slow, with movement)

The second movement, in A flat major, is mostly relaxed and lyrical, but it includes moments of tension and heroism. It is an extended set of variations based on two themes and may be outlined as A—B—A¹—B¹— middle section—A³—coda.

Basic sets:
Side 7, band 2
CD 4 [9]

The main theme (A), softly introduced by the cellos and violas, is a long, legato melody of great nobility.    [9] 0:00

The second theme (B) begins very gently in the clarinets.    [10] 0:56

But soon there is a startling contrast of mood as the full orchestra bursts in,   1:18
and the clarinet melody is transformed into a triumphant trumpet fanfare.

169

11 2:03

A hushed transitional passage then leads back to variation A$^1$, in which the theme is presented in even-flowing rhythm.

*p*

12 4:05

In variation A$^2$ the theme appears in quicker even-flowing notes.

*p*

13 5:09
14 7:36

In the middle section, fragments of A and B are treated in new ways. Woodwind instruments are featured, and there is a brief episode in minor. The movement concludes with a final variation of the main melody (A$^3$)—now majestically proclaimed by the full orchestra—and a coda that poetically recalls what has come before.

### Third Movement:

### Allegro (scherzo)

Basic sets:
Side 7, band 3
CD 4 15
Section A
15 0:00

The rapid third movement is a scherzo, in C minor, with three sections: A (scherzo) B (trio) A' (scherzo). The scherzo opens with a hushed, mysterious theme played by cellos and double basses in a low register.

Allegro

*pp*

Soon, in sharp contrast, a bold repeated-note theme is hammered out loudly by the horns.

*ff*

This theme is dominated by the rhythmic pattern short-short-short-long and recalls the basic motive of the first movement.

170

The B section (trio), in major, brings a gruff, hurried theme, played by cellos and double basses.

Section B
16  1:44

This theme is imitated, in the style of a fugue, by each of the higher strings. The bustling rhythmic motion of the B section has a feeling of energy and rough humor.

When the scherzo section (A') returns, it is hushed and ominous throughout, sounding like a ghost of its former self. The mysterious opening theme is now played pizzicato rather than legato. The repeated-note theme is completely transformed in mood; it is no longer proclaimed by horns but is whispered by clarinets, plucked violins, and oboe.

Section A'
17  3:08

One of the most extraordinary passages in the symphony follows the scherzo section (A'): a bridge leading from the dark, mysterious world of the scherzo to the bright sunlight of the finale. It opens with a feeling of suspended animation as the timpani softly repeat a single tone against a sustained chord in the strings. Over the timpani pulsation, the violins hesitantly play a fragment of the mysterious scherzo theme. Tension mounts as this fragment is carried higher and higher, until a sudden crescendo climaxes with the heroic opening of the finale.

Bridge
18  4:10

## Fourth Movement:

### Allegro

The fourth movement, in sonata form, is the climax of the symphony. It brings the victory of C major over C minor, of optimism and exultation over struggle and uncertainty. For greater power and brilliance, Beethoven enlarged the orchestra in the finale to include three trombones, a piccolo, and a contrabassoon. Brass instruments are especially prominent and give a marchlike character to much of the movement.

Basic sets:
Side 7, band 3
(continued)
CD 4  19

The exposition is rich in melodic ideas; even the bridge has a theme of its own, and there is also a distinctive closing theme. The triumphant opening theme begins with the three tones of the C major triad, brilliantly proclaimed by the trumpets.

19  0:00

20 0:36
A bridge theme, similar in mood to the opening theme, is announced by the horns and continued by the violins.

21 1:04
Triplets lend a joyous quality to the second theme, which contrasts loud and soft phrases.

22 1:33
Two powerful chords and a brief pause announce the closing theme of the exposition. This melody, consisting of descending phrases, is first played by the strings and woodwinds and then forcefully repeated by the entire orchestra.

23 2:05
24 4:17
The exposition is repeated.

The development focuses mainly on the second theme and its triplet rhythm. A huge climax at the end of the development is followed by one of the most marvelous surprises in all music. Beethoven dramatically quotes

25 5:54
the whispered repeated-note theme (short-short-short-long) of the preceding scherzo movement. This ominous quotation is like a sudden recollection of past anxiety, and it creates a connection between the last two movements. Leading into the powerful recapitulation of the fourth movement, it

Recapitulation
6:25
prepares the renewal of the victory over uncertainty.

Coda
9:09
During the long coda of the finale, earlier themes are heard in altered and quickened versions. Several times, the music keeps going even though the listener thinks it is coming to an end. Over and over, Beethoven affirms the tonic key and resolves the frenzied tensions built up during the symphony. Such control over tension is an essential element of Beethoven's genius.

V

# THE ROMANTIC PERIOD

# V

Emotional subjectivity was a basic quality of romanticism. The artist's suffering and isolation are depicted in *Portrait of a Young Man in an Artist's Studio*, an anonymous painting of the early nineteenth century (formerly attributed to Théodore Géricault).

# [ 1 ] ROMANTICISM IN MUSIC (1820–1900)

The early nineteenth century brought the flowering of romanticism, a cultural movement that stressed emotion, imagination, and individualism. In part, romanticism was a rebellion against the neoclassicism of the eighteenth century and the age of reason. Romantic writers broke away from time-honored conventions and emphasized freedom of expression. Romantic painters used bolder, more brilliant colors and preferred dynamic motion to gracefully balanced poses.

But romanticism was too diverse and complex to be defined by any single formula. It aimed to broaden all human horizons and encompass the totality of human experience. The romantic movement was international in scope and influenced all the arts.

Emotional subjectivity was a basic quality of romanticism in art. "All good poetry is the spontaneous overflow of powerful feelings," wrote William Wordsworth, the English romantic poet. And "spontaneous overflow" made much romantic literature autobiographical; authors projected their personalities in their work. Walt Whitman, the American poet, expressed this subjective attitude beautifully when he began a poem, "I celebrate myself, and sing myself."

In exploring their inner lives, the romantics were especially drawn to the realm of fantasy: the unconscious, the irrational, the world of dreams. Romantic literature includes tales of horror and the supernatural such as Edgar Allan Poe's stories and Mary Wollstonecraft Shelley's *Frankenstein*, and Thomas De Quincy's descriptions of his drug-induced dreams. The visual arts include the nightmarish etchings of the Spanish painter Francisco Goya.

The romantic fascination with fantasy was paired with interest in exoticism and the past—the far-away and the long-ago. For example, the French artist Eugène Delacroix often depicted violent scenes in far-off lands; and the romantics cherished the Middle Ages and found inspiration in medieval folk ballads and tales. (In contrast, the neoclassicists had considered the medieval period the "dark ages.") Romantic novels set in the Middle Ages include Sir Walter Scott's *Ivanhoe* (1819) and Victor Hugo's *Hunchback of Notre Dame* (1831). There was a "gothic revival" in architecture, and a new appreciation of the gothic cathedrals.

Of all the inspirations for romantic art, none was more important than nature, which was seen as a source of consolation and a mirror of the human heart—Wordsworth, for instance, thought of nature as "the nurse,/the guide, the guardian of my heart and soul."

176

Eugène Delacroix's painting *The Bark of Dante* (1822) depicts the agony of the damned in hell. The romantics were drawn to the realm of the supernatural and drew inspiration from medieval literary works such as Dante's *Inferno*.

The romantic sensitivity to nature is revealed in landscape painting, which attained new importance. Artists like John Constable and J. M. W. Turner in England were masters at conveying the movement of nature: rippling brooks, drifting clouds, stormy seas. In Turner's seascapes, the sweep of waves expresses not only the grandeur of nature, but human passion as well.

Romanticism coincided with the industrial revolution, which caused vast social and economic changes. Many writers and painters recorded the new social realities of their time. The novels of Charles Dickens and the paintings of Honoré Daumier reflect an interest in the working class and the poor.

(National Gallery, London)

*The Hay Wain* (1821), by John Constable. Of all the sources of inspiration for romantic art, none was more important than nature.

## THE ROMANTIC PERIOD IN MUSIC

The romantic period in music extended from about 1820 to 1900. Among the most significant romantic musicians were Franz Schubert, Robert Schumann, Clara Wieck Schumann, Frédéric Chopin, Franz Liszt, Felix Mendelssohn, Hector Berlioz, Bedřich Smetana, Peter Ilyich Tchaikovsky, Johannes Brahms, Giuseppe Verdi, Giacomo Puccini, and Richard Wagner. The length of this list—even though some important musicians have been omitted from it—testifies to the richness, variety, and continuing importance of romantic music.

Romantic musicians, inspired by the image of Beethoven as a "free artist," often composed to fulfill an inner need rather than to execute a commission or meet the demands of an aristocratic or church patron; and they also thought in terms of creating something for posterity. Sometimes, however, they were "free artists" by necessity rather than choice, since most aristocrats could no longer afford private opera houses, orchestras, and "composers in residence." Romantic composers came from the middle class, wrote primarily for a middle-class audience, and had to sell their wares in the marketplace. Because few could support themselves through composition alone, they also worked as conductors (like Wagner), music teachers (like Chopin), and music critics (like Berlioz). Some were touring virtuosos, like the Hungarian Franz Liszt (1811–1886). Liszt, the composer who invented the tone poem, was one of the most dazzling and charismatic pianists of all time.

The rise of the urban middle class led to the formation of many orchestras and opera groups, and the development of regular subscription concerts. Private music making increased, too—the piano became a fixture in every middle-class home. The nineteenth century also saw the founding of music conservatories in Europe and the United States.

Another influence on romantic music was audiences' fascination with virtuosity. Liszt and the violinist Niccolò Paganini were musical heroes; and following Liszt's example, performers like the pianist Clara Wieck Schumann began to give solo recitals in addition to their customary appearances with orchestras.

## CHARACTERISTICS OF ROMANTIC MUSIC

Composers of the romantic period continued to use the musical forms of the preceding classical era. The emotional intensity associated with romanticism had already been present in the work of Mozart and, particularly, of Beethoven, who greatly influenced composers after him. The romantic preference for expressive, songlike melody also grew out of the classical style.

Romantic composers wrote primarily for a middle-class audience. In this picture by Moritz von Schwind, Franz Schubert is shown at the piano accompanying the singer Johann Michael Vogl.

(Bettmann Archive)

Nonetheless, there are many differences between romantic and classical music. Romantic works tend to have greater ranges of tone color, dynamics, and pitch. Also, the romantic harmonic vocabulary is broader, with more emphasis on colorful, unstable chords. Romantic music is linked more closely to the other arts, particularly to literature. New forms developed, and in all forms there was greater tension and less emphasis on balance and resolution. But romantic music is so diverse that generalizations are apt to mislead. Some romantic composers, such as Mendelssohn and Brahms, created works that were deeply rooted in classical tradition; others, such as Berlioz, Liszt, and Wagner, were more revolutionary.

## Individuality of Style

Romantic music puts unprecedented emphasis on self-expression and individuality of style. There is "not a bar which I have not truly felt and which is not an echo of my innermost feelings," wrote Tchaikovsky of his Fourth Symphony. "A new world of music" was the goal of the young Chopin. Many romantics created music that sounds unique and reflects their personalities. Robert Schumann observed that "Chopin will soon be unable to write anything without people crying out at the seventh or eighth bar, 'That is indeed by him.'" And today, with some listening experience, a music lover can tell within a few minutes—sometimes within a few seconds—whether a piece is by Schumann or Chopin, Tchaikovsky or Brahms.

## Expressive Aims and Subjects

The romantics explored a universe of feeling that included flamboyance and intimacy, unpredictability and melancholy, rapture and longing. Countless songs and operas glorify romantic love. Often the lovers are unhappy and face overwhelming obstacles. Fascination with the fantastic and diabolical is expressed in music like the *Dream of a Witches' Sabbath* from Berlioz's *Symphonie fantastique (Fantastic Symphony)*. All aspects of nature attracted romantic musicians. In different sections of Part V we'll study music that depicts a wild horseback ride on a stormy night (Schubert's *Erlkönig*, or *Erlking*) and the flow of a river (Smetana's *Moldau*). Romantic composers also dealt with subjects drawn from the Middle Ages and from Shakespeare's plays.

## Nationalism and Exoticism

Nationalism was an important political movement that influenced nineteenth-century music. Musical *nationalism* was expressed when romantic composers deliberately created music with a specific national identity, using the folk songs, dances, legends, and history of their homelands. This national flavor of romantic music—whether Polish, Russian, Bohemian (Czech), or German—contrasts with the more universal character of classical music.

Fascination with national identity also led composers to draw on colorful materials from foreign lands, a trend known as musical *exoticism.* For instance, some wrote melodies in an Asian style or used rhythms and instruments associated with distant lands. The French composer Georges Bizet wrote *Carmen,* an opera set in Spain; the Italian Giacomo Puccini evoked Japan in his opera *Madame Butterfly;* and the Russian Rimsky-Korsakov suggested an Arabian atmosphere in his orchestral work *Scheherazade.* Musical exoticism was in keeping with the romantics' attraction to things remote, picturesque, and mysterious.

## Program Music

The nineteenth century was the great age of *program music,* instrumental music associated with a story, poem, idea, or scene. Usually the nonmusical element is specified by a title or by explanatory comments called a *program.* A programmatic instrumental piece can represent the emotions, characters, and events of a particular story, or it can evoke the sounds and motions of nature. For example, in Tchaikovsky's *Romeo and Juliet,* an orchestral work inspired by Shakespeare's play, agitated music depicts the feud between the rival families, a tender melody conveys young love, and a funeral-march rhythm suggests the lovers' tragic fate. And in *The Moldau,* an orchestral work glorifying the main river of Bohemia, Smetana uses musical effects that call to mind a flowing stream, a hunting scene, a peasant wedding, and the crash of waves.

Program music in some form or another has existed for centuries, but it became particularly prominent in the romantic period, when music was closely associated with literature. Many composers—Berlioz, Schumann, Liszt, and Wagner, for example—were prolific authors as well. Artists in all fields were intoxicated by the idea of a "union of the arts." Poets wanted their poetry to be musical, and musicians wanted their music to be poetic.

## Expressive Tone Color

Romantic composers reveled in rich and sensuous sound, using tone color to obtain variety of mood and atmosphere. Never before had timbre been so important.

In both symphonic and operatic works, the romantic orchestra was larger and more varied in tone color than the classical orchestra. Toward the end of the romantic era, an orchestra might include close to 100 musicians. (There were twenty to sixty players in the classical ensemble.) The constant expansion of the orchestra reflected composers' changing needs as well as the growing size of concert halls and opera houses. The brass, woodwind, and percussion sections of the orchestra took on a more active role. Romantic composers increased the power of the brass section to something spectacular, calling for trombones, tubas, and more horns and trumpets. In 1824, Beethoven broke precedent by asking for nine brasses in the Ninth Symphony; and in 1894, the Austrian composer Gustav Mahler (1860–1911) demanded twenty-five brass instruments for his Second Symphony. The addition of valves had made it easier for horns and trumpets to cope with intricate melodies.

The woodwind section took on new tone colors as the contrabassoon, bass clarinet, English horn, and piccolo became regular members of the orchestra. Improvements in the construction of instruments allowed woodwind players to perform more flexibly and accurately. Orchestral sounds became more brilliant and sensuously appealing through increased use of cymbals, the triangle, and the harp.

New sounds were drawn from all instruments of the nineteenth-century orchestra. Flutists were asked to play in the breathy low register, and violinists to strike the strings with the wood of their bows. These demands compelled performers to attain a higher level of technical virtuosity.

New ways of blending and combining tone colors were sought to achieve the most poignant and intense sound. In 1844, Hector Berlioz's *Treatise on Modern Instrumentation and Orchestration* signaled the recognition of orchestration as an art in itself.

The piano, the favorite instrument of the romantic age, was improved vastly during the 1820s and 1830s. A cast-iron frame was introduced to hold the strings under greater tension, and the hammers were covered with felt. Thus the piano's tone became more "singing." Its range was also extended. With a stronger instrument, the pianist could produce more sound. And use of the damper ("loud") pedal allowed a sonorous blend of tones from all registers of the piano.

## Colorful Harmony

In addition to exploiting new tone colors, the romantics explored new chords and novel ways of using familiar chords. Seeking greater emotional intensity, composers emphasized rich, colorful, and complex harmonies. There was more prominent use of **chromatic harmony,** which employs chords containing tones not found in the prevailing major or minor scale. Such chord tones come from the chromatic scale (which has twelve tones), rather than from the major or minor scales (which have seven different tones). Chromatic chords add color and motion to romantic music. Dissonant, or unstable, chords were also used more freely than during the classical era. By deliberately delaying the resolution of dissonance to a consonant, or stable, chord, romantic composers created feelings of yearning, tension, and mystery.

A romantic piece tends to have a wide variety of keys and rapid modulations, or changes from one key to another. Because of the nature and frequency of these key shifts, the tonic key is somewhat less clear than in classical works. The feeling of tonal gravity tends to be less strong. By the end of the romantic period, even more emphasis was given to harmonic instability and less to stability and resolution.

## Expanded Range of Dynamics, Pitch, and Tempo

Romantic music also calls for a wide range of dynamics. It includes sharp contrasts between faint whispers and sonorities of unprecedented power. The classical dynamic extremes of *ff* and *pp* did not meet the needs of romantics, who sometimes demanded *ffff* and *pppp*. Seeking more and more expressiveness, nineteenth-century composers used frequent crescendos and decrescendos, as well as sudden dynamic changes.

The range of pitch was expanded, too, as composers reached for extremely high or low sounds. In search of increased brilliance and depth of sound, the romantics exploited instruments like the piccolo and contrabassoon, as well as the expanded keyboard of the piano.

Mood changes in romantic music are often underlined by accelerandos, ritardandos, and subtle variations of pace: there are many more fluctuations in tempo than there are in classical music. To intensify the expression of the music, romantic performers made use of *rubato*, a slight holding back or pressing forward of tempo.

## Form: Miniature and Monumental

The nineteenth century was very much an age of contradictions. Romantic composers characteristically expressed themselves both in musical miniatures and in monumental compositions. On the one hand are piano pieces by Chopin and songs by Schubert that last but a few minutes. Such short forms were meant to be heard in the intimate surroundings of a home; they met the needs of the growing number of people who owned pianos. These miniatures were a perfect outlet for the romantic genius at creating an intense mood through a melody, a few chords, or an unusual tone color. On the other hand, there are gigantic works by Berlioz and Wagner that call for a huge number of performers and last for several hours. Mammoth compositions, of course, were designed for large opera houses or concert halls.

Romantic composers continued to write symphonies, sonatas, string quartets, concertos, operas, and choral works, but their individual movements tended to be longer than Haydn's and Mozart's. For example, a typical nineteenth-century symphony might last about 45 minutes, as opposed to 25 minutes for an eighteenth-century symphony. And as the romantic period drew to a close, compositions tended to become even longer, more richly orchestrated, and more complex in harmony. For example, Mahler's Eighth Symphony (*Symphony of a Thousand*, 1907) lasts about an hour and a half and calls for eight vocal soloists, a boys' choir, two choruses, and a gigantic orchestra.

New techniques were used to unify such long works. Following the example of Beethoven's Fifth Symphony, the same theme or themes might occur in several movements. When a melody returns in a later movement or section of a romantic work, its character may be changed by use of different dynamics, orchestration, or rhythm—a technique known as **thematic transformation.** A striking use of thematic transformation occurs in Berlioz's *Symphonie fantastique (Fantastic Symphony*, 1830), where a lyrical melody from the opening movement becomes a grotesque dance tune in the finale.

Different movements or sections of a romantic work may also be linked through transitional passages; one movement of a symphony or concerto may lead directly into the next. Here, again, Beethoven was the pioneer. And nineteenth-century operas are unified by melodic ideas that reappear in different acts or scenes, some of which may be tied together by connecting passages.

In dealing with an age that so prized individuality, generalizations are especially difficult. The great diversity found in romantic music can best be appreciated, perhaps, by approaching each piece as its composer did—with an open mind and heart.

# ROMANTIC 2

# THE ART SONG

One of the most distinctive forms in romantic music is the **art song,** a composition for solo voice and piano. Here, the accompaniment is an integral part of the composer's conception, and it serves as an interpretive partner to the voice. Although they are now performed in concert halls, romantic songs were written to be sung and enjoyed at home.

Poetry and music are intimately fused in the art song. It is no accident that this form flowered with the emergence of a rich body of romantic poetry in the early nineteenth century. Many of the finest song composers—Schubert, Schumann, and Brahms, for example—were German or Austrian and set poems in their native language. Among the poets favored by these composers were Johann Wolfgang von Goethe (1749–1832) and Heinrich Heine (1797–1856). The German word *Lied (song)* is commonly used for a song with German text. (*Lied* is pronounced *leet;* its plural, *Lieder,* is pronounced *leader*.)

Yearning—inspired by a lost love, nature, a legend, or other times and places—haunted the imagination of romantic poets. Thus art songs are filled with the despair of unrequited love; the beauty of flowers, trees, and brooks; and the supernatural happenings of folk tales. There are also songs of joy, wit, and humor. But by and large, romantic song was a reaching out of the soul.

Song composers would interpret a poem, translating its mood, atmosphere, and imagery into music. They created a vocal melody that was musically satisfying and perfectly molded to the text. Important words were emphasized by stressed tones or melodic climaxes.

The voice shares the interpretive task with the piano. Emotions and images of the text are given an added dimension from the keyboard commentary. Arpeggios in the piano might suggest the splashing of oars or the motion of a mill wheel. Chords in a low register might depict darkness or a lover's torment. The mood is often set by a brief piano introduction and summed up at the end by a piano section called a *postlude.*

## STROPHIC AND THROUGH-COMPOSED FORM

When a poem has several stanzas, the musical setting must accommodate their total emotional impact. Composers can use *strophic form,* repeating the same music for each stanza of the poem. Strophic form makes a song easy to remember and is used in almost all folk songs. Or composers might use *through-composed form,* writing new music for each stanza. (*Through-composed* is a translation of the German term *durchkomponiert.*) Through-composed form allows music to reflect a poem's changing moods.

The art song is not restricted to strophic or through-composed form. There are many ways that music can be molded to the structure and feeling of a poem. A three-stanza poem is frequently set as follows: A (stanza 1) B (stanza 2) A (stanza 3). This might be called a *modified strophic form,* since two of the three stanzas are set to the same music.

## THE SONG CYCLE

Romantic art songs are sometimes grouped in a set, or *song cycle.* A cycle may be unified by a story line that runs through the poems, or by musical ideas linking the songs. Among the great romantic song cycles are *Die Winterreise* (*The Winter Journey,* 1827), by Schubert; and *Dichterliebe* (*Poet's Love,* 1840) by Schumann.

In their art songs, romantic composers achieved a perfect union of music and poetry. They created an intensely personal world with a tremendous variety of moods. These miniatures contain some of the most haunting melodies and harmonies in all music.

# FRANZ SCHUBERT

Franz Schubert (1797–1828), the earliest master of the romantic art song, was unlike any great composer before him: he never held an official musical position and was neither a conductor nor a virtuoso; his income came entirely from composition. ''I have come into the world for no other purpose than to compose,'' he said. The full measure of his genius was recognized only years after his tragically early death.

Schubert was born in Vienna, the son of a schoolmaster. Even as a child, he had astounding musical gifts. ''If I wanted to instruct him in anything new,'' recalled his amazed teacher, ''he knew it already.'' At eleven, he became a choirboy in the court chapel and won a scholarship to the Imperial Seminary.

Schubert managed to compose an extraordinary number of masterpieces in his late teens while teaching at his father's school, a job he hated. His love of poetry led him to the art song; he composed his first great song, *Gretchen am Spinnrade (Gretchen at the Spinning Wheel)*, when he was seventeen, and the next year he composed 143 songs, including *The Erlking*.

When he was nineteen, Schubert's productivity rose to a peak; he composed 179 works, including two symphonies, an opera, and a mass. At twenty-one, he gave up teaching school to devote himself to music. He associated with a group of Viennese poets and artists who led a bohemian existence; often, he lived with friends because he had no money to rent a room of his own. Working incredibly fast, from seven in the morning until early afternoon, he turned out one piece after another. He spent his afternoons in cafes and many of his evenings at ''Schubertiads,'' parties where only his music was played. Most of his works were composed for performances in the homes of Vienna's cultivated middle class; unlike Beethoven, he did not mingle with the aristocracy. The publication and performance of his songs brought him some recognition, but his two most important symphonies—the *Unfinished* and the *Great C* Major—were not performed in public during his lifetime.

Schubert died in 1828, age thirty-one. He was thought of mainly as a fine song composer, until the *Unfinished* Symphony was performed nearly forty years later and the world could recognize his comprehensive greatness.

## SCHUBERT'S MUSIC

Along with over 600 songs, Schubert composed symphonies, string quartets, and other chamber music, sonatas and short pieces for piano, masses, and operas. The songs embrace an enormous variety of moods and types;

their melodies range from simple, folklike tunes to complex lines that suggest impassioned speech, and their piano accompaniments are equally rich and evocative. Schubert's imaginative harmonies and dissonances provide some of the most poetic moments in music.

The spirit of song pervades his instrumental music, too, and his longer works often include variation movements based on his own songs; his famous *Trout* Quintet in A Major (1819) is an example. Many of the symphonies and chamber works have long, lyrical melodies, and some—especially the *Unfinished* Symphony (1822) and the *Great* C Major Symphony (1825–1826)—are comparable in power and intensity to Beethoven's. The *Unfinished* was written six years before Schubert's death; no one knows why it has only two (rather than four) movements. The *Great* C Major Symphony was discovered ten years after his death by Robert Schumann.

Franz Schubert.

## ERLKÖNIG (THE ERLKING; 1815)

Schubert's song *Erlkönig (The Erlking)* is one of the earliest and finest examples of musical romanticism. It is a musical setting of a narrative ballad of the supernatural by Goethe. A friend of Schubert's tells how he saw the eighteen-year-old composer reading Goethe's poem. "He paced up and down several times with the book; suddenly he sat down, and in no time at all (just as quickly as he could write) there was the glorious ballad finished on the paper." Goethe's ballad, in dialogue almost throughout, tells of a father riding on horseback through a storm with his sick child in his arms. The delirious boy has visions of the legendary Erlking, the king of the elves who symbolizes death.

Schubert employs a through-composed setting to capture the mounting excitement of the poem. The piano part, with its rapid octaves and menacing bass motive, conveys the tension of the wild ride.

**Brief sets:**
**Side 3, band 5**
**CD 2** 24

Basic sets:
Side 8, band 5
CD 4 45

187

The piano's relentless triplet rhythm unifies the episodes of the song and suggests the horse's gallop.

By imaginatively varying the music, Schubert makes one singer sound like several characters in a miniature drama. The terrified boy sings in a high register in minor. Three times during the poem, he cries out, "My father, my father." Each time, the boy sings a musical outcry that is intensified through dissonant harmonies.

Mein Va - ter, mein Va - ter,

To convey mounting fear, Schubert pitches the boy's outcry higher and higher each time. The reassuring father sings in a low register that contrasts with the high-pitched outcries of his child. The Erlking, who tries to entice the boy, has coy melodies in major keys.

"Du lie - bes Kind, komm, geh mit mir! gar schö - ne Spie - le spiel' - ich mit dir;

The deeply moving climax of *The Erlking* comes when father and son arrive home and the galloping accompaniment gradually comes to a halt. In a bleak, heartbreaking recitative that allows every word to make its impact, the narrator tells us, "In his arms the child was dead!"

24 45 0:00
Piano introduction, rapid octaves, *f*, bass motive, minor key.

**Narrator**

| | |
|---|---|
| *Wer reitet so spät durch Nacht und Wind?* | Who rides so late through the night and the wind? |
| *Es ist der Vater mit seinem Kind;* | It is the father with his child; |
| *Er hat den Knaben wohl in dem Arm,* | he folds the boy close in his arms, |
| *Er fasst ihn sicher, er hält ihn warm.* | he clasps him securely, he holds him warmly. |

25 46 0:56
Low register.

**Father**

| | |
|---|---|
| *"Mein Sohn, was birgst du so bang dein Gesicht?"* | "My son, why do you hide your face so anxiously?" |

"Siehst, Vater, du den Erlkönig nicht?

"Father, don't you see the Erlking?

Den Erlenkönig mit Kron' und Schweif?"

The Erlking with his crown and his train?"

**Father**

1:20
Low register.

"Mein Sohn, es ist ein Nebelstreif."

"My son, it is a streak of mist."

**Erlking**

27 48 1:29
Coaxing tune, *pp*, higher register, major.

"Du liebes Kind, komm, geh mit mir!

"Dear child, come, go with me!

Gar schöne Spiele spiel' ich mit dir,

I'll play the prettiest games with you.

Manch bunte Blumen sind an dem Strand,

Many colored flowers grow along the shore;

Meine Mutter hat manch gülden Gewand."

My mother has many golden garments."

**Son**

28 49 1:54
Outcry, *f*, minor

"Mein Vater, mein Vater, und hörest du nicht,

"My father, my father, and don't you hear

Was Erlenkönig mir leise verspricht?"

the Erlking whispering promises to me?"

**Father**

2:07
Low register.

"Sei ruhig, bleibe ruhig, mein Kind:

"Be quiet, stay quiet, my child;

In dürren Blättern säuselt der Wind"

the wind is rustling in the dead leaves."

**Erlking**

2:17
Playful tune, *pp*, major.

"Willst, feiner Knabe, du mit mir gehn?

"My handsome boy, will you come with me?

Meine Töchter sollen dich warten schön;

My daughters shall wait upon you;

Meine Töchter führen den nächtlichen Reihn

my daughters lead off in the dance every night,

Und wiegen und tanzen und singen dich ein."

and cradle and dance and sing you to sleep."

**Son**

29 50 2:36
Outcry, *f*, higher than before, minor.

"Mein Vater, mein Vater, und siehst du nicht dort.

"My father, my father, and don't you see there

Erlkönigs Töchter am düstern Ort?"

the Erlking's daughters in the shadows?"

| | | **Father** | |
|---|---|---|---|
| 2:48 Lower register. | *"Mein Sohn, mein Sohn, ich seh' es genau:* | | "My son, my son, I see it clearly; |
| | *Es scheinen die alten Weiden so grau."* | | the old willows look so gray." |

**Erlking**

*"Ich liebe dich, mich reizt deine schöne Gestalt;*      "I love you, your beautiful figure delights me!

*Und bist du nicht willig, so brauch' ich Gewalt."*      And if you are not willing, then I shall use force!"

**Son**

3:18
Outcry, *f*, highest yet.      *"Mein Vater, mein Vater, jetzt fasst er mich an!*      "My father, my father, now he is taking hold of me!

*Erlkönig hat mir ein Leids getan!"*      The Erlking has hurt me!"

**Narrator**

3:31      *Dem Vater grauset's, er reitet geschwind,*      The father shudders, he rides swiftly on;

*Er hält in Armen das ächzende Kind,*      he holds in his arms the groaning child,

*Erreicht den Hof mit Mühe und Not;*      he reaches the courtyard weary and anxious:

Piano stops.
Recitative.      *In seinen Armen das Kind war tot.*      in his arms the child was dead.

---

ROMANTIC

# 4 ROBERT SCHUMANN

Robert Schumann (1810–1856) in many ways embodied musical romanticism. His works are intensely autobiographical and usually have descriptive titles, texts, or programs. He expressed his essentially lyrical nature in startlingly original piano pieces and songs. And as a writer and critic, he also discovered and made famous some of the leading composers of his day.

Schumann was born in Zwickau, Germany. He studied law at Leipzig University but actually devoted himself to literature and music. At twenty, he decided to become a piano virtuoso, but this goal became impossible

(Bettmann Archive)

Robert Schumann.

when he developed serious problems with his right hand which were not helped by medical treatments or by a gadget he used to stretch and strengthen the fingers. "Don't worry about my finger," he wrote to his mother; "I can compose without it"—and in his twenties he did compose many piano works which remain a basic part of the repertory, although at the time they were often considered too unconventional and personal. During his twenties, too, he founded and edited the influential *New Journal of Music*, which contained his appreciative reviews of young "radical" composers like Chopin and Berlioz.

While studying piano, Schumann met his teacher's daughter and pupil, Clara Wieck, then a nine-year-old prodigy. The two were engaged when Clara was seventeen; but her father was bitterly opposed, and the couple had to fight against him in court before they could be married. Their marriage was a happy one. Clara—herself a composer—was also the ideal interpreter of Robert's works and introduced many of them to the public.

Schumann held some musical positions but was temperamentally unsuited for them, and during his later years, his mental and physical health deteriorated. In 1854 he tried to drown himself and was committed to an asylum, where he died two years later.

## ROBERT SCHUMANN'S MUSIC

During his first ten years as a composer, Schumann published only piano pieces, and his musical style seemed to grow out of piano improvisation. His short pieces often express a single mood through a sensitive melody; dance rhythms, dotted rhythms, and syncopations are also prominent.

In 1840, the year of his marriage, he composed many art songs which also reveal his gift for melody. Both the songs and the short piano pieces are usually organized in sets or cycles, whose titles—*Carnaval (Carnival)*, *Kinderscenen (Scenes of Childhood)*, *Nachtstücke (Night Pieces)*, *Dichterliebe (Poet's Love)*, *Fantasiestücke (Fantasy Pieces)*—give insight into his imagination. Schumann thought of music in emotional, literary, and autobiographical terms; his work is full of extramusical references.

After 1840, possibly as a result of Clara's influence, he turned to symphonies and chamber music. The symphonies are romantic in their emphasis on lyrical second themes, use of thematic transformation, and connections between movements.

### IM WUNDERSCHÖNEN MONAT MAI (IN THE LOVELY MONTH OF MAY), FROM *DICHTERLIEBE (POET'S LOVE)*, OP. 48 (1840)

Basic sets:
Side 9, band 1
CD 5 ⬚1

*Im wunderschönen Monat Mai (In the lovely month of May)* opens *Dichterliebe (Poet's Love)*, a cycle of sixteen songs set to poems by the great German romantic poet Heinrich Heine. Schumann composed the cycle in 1840, his "song year," during a difficult period of separation from Clara and legal battles against her father. The title *Poet's Love* doubtless refers to Schumann's own feelings for his bride-to-be.

A mood of tenderness and longing is beautifully conveyed in *Im wunderschönen Monat Mai*, which is just 1½ minutes long. The song is in strophic form, with each of its two stanzas sung to the same melody (A A). Schumann probably decided on a strophic setting because of the similarity between the two stanzas, which open with the same words *(In the lovely month of May, when all . . . "*). A piano introduction reappears as an interlude between stanzas and as a postlude at the end.

Schumann creates a sense of longing by wavering between several different keys and by avoiding a feeling of conclusion. The piano introduction sounds as though it will lead to a cadence in a minor key, yet the vocal melody that follows it is in major. The melodic ascent (from *da ist*) to the voice's concluding high note expresses love breaking forth. Dissonances on the accented syllables of *Herzen (heart)* and *aufgegangen (broke forth)* contribute to the emotional intensity of this phrase. Most remarkably, the piano postlude ends the song inconclusively on an unstable chord that remains unresolved, a poignant expression of "longing and desire."

Im wun - der-schö-nen Mo - nat Mai, als al - le Knos - pen

sprang-gen, da ist in mei-nem Her-zen die Lie - be auf - ge - gan-gen.

1 0:00
Piano introduction
A

Piano interlude

A

Piano postlude,
ends on unstable
chord

| | |
|---|---|
| *Im wunderschönen Monat Mai,* | In the lovely month of May, |
| *Als alle Knospen sprangen,* | when all the buds were bursting, |
| *Da ist in meinem Herzen* | then within my heart |
| *Die Liebe aufgegangen.* | love broke forth. |
| | |
| *Im wunderschönen Monat Mai,* | In the lovely month of May, |
| *Als alle Vögel sangen,* | when all the birds were singing, |
| *Da hab' ich ihr gestanden* | then I confessed to her |
| *Mein Sehnen und Verlangen.* | my longing and desire. |

# CLARA WIECK SCHUMANN

ROMANTIC

**5**

Clara Wieck Schumann (1819–1896), a leading nineteenth-century pianist, premiered many works of her husband Robert and her close friend Johannes Brahms. She was born in Leipzig, Germany, and was an acclaimed child prodigy, taught by her father, the well-known piano pedagogue Friedrich Wieck.

She married Robert Schumann despite her father's opposition and continued to concertize and compose while caring for him and their seven children. In 1853 the twenty-year-old composer Johannes Brahms came to play his works for the Schumanns, beginning a friendship with Clara that lasted until her death; that same year, she met the violinist Joseph Joachim, with whom she would often perform. After her husband's death, she also became renowned as a teacher and edited his collected works. She helped refine the tastes of audiences by presenting works of earlier composers like Bach, Mozart, and Beethoven as well as works by Robert Schumann and Brahms.

## CLARA WIECK SCHUMANN'S MUSIC

Clara Schumann considered herself primarily a performing artist ("I feel I have a mission to perform beautiful works. Robert's above all," she once wrote) and stopped composing when she was thirty-six. Her doubts about composing were perhaps influenced by the negative attitude toward woman composers that predominated during her lifetime, and by her relationship with overwhelming geniuses like her husband and Brahms. Until recently, she was known primarily as a famous pianist who had been the wife of one great composer and the close friend of another. But her compositions are now being increasingly performed and recorded. They include songs; piano pieces; a piano concerto; a trio for piano, violin, and cello; and three Romances for violin and piano, one of which will be studied here.

## ROMANCE IN G MINOR FOR VIOLIN AND PIANO, OP. 22, NO. 2 (1853)

Brief sets:
Side 3, band 6
CD 2 30

Basic sets:
Side 9, band 3
CD 5 5

Clara Schumann composed her three Romances for Violin and Piano in 1853, during a creative spurt that was inspired by her husband's forty-third birthday. The Romances were dedicated to Joseph Joachim, who performed them for his employer, King George V of Hannover, Germany. The music-loving king was reportedly "completely ecstatic" about the Romances and was eager to experience such "marvelous, heavenly pleasure" again.

In the nineteenth century, the term *romance* (*Romanze* in German) was often used for short, lyrical pieces for piano or solo instrument with piano accompaniment. The Romance in G Minor displays Clara Schumann's gifts as a melodist. Marked *Allegretto, to be performed tenderly*, it is in A B A' form. Sweet melancholy is created in the outer (A) sections by the minor key and by a violin melody that repeatedly leaps upward an octave to a syncopated tone. A transition smoothly links section A to the middle section. It uses a two-note figure, which is repeated in gradually quickening rhythms until it blossoms into the trill and the soaring phrase that open section B.

The more extended middle section (B) brings a shift from minor to major, from sweet melancholy to relaxed playfulness. Its mood is lightened by a staccato "chirping" idea that is tossed between violin and piano. As in the opening section, a transition using the two-note figure smoothly links B with the concluding A' section, which is in minor. At the end of A', we hear a very brief recollection of the opening phrase of B, now sounding melancholy because it is minor instead of major. The Romance ends unexpectedly on a pizzicato major chord, perhaps to recall the playfulness of its middle section.

Clara Wieck Schumann.

---

# Listening Outline   To be read while music is heard

ROMANCE IN G MINOR FOR VIOLIN AND PIANO, OP. 22, NO. 2 (1853), BY CLARA WIECK SCHUMANN

Allegretto, duple meter ($\frac{2}{4}$), ABA′ form

Violin, piano

(Duration, 2:46)

A (minor)

| 30 | 5 | 0:00 |

1. *a.* Main violin melody, *p*, minor, syncopated upward octave leap.

Melody descends from high tone.

0:18        *b.* Main melody repeated, syncopated leaps in violin, tempo slows slightly.

[31] [6] 0:37  *c.* Long trills in violin, melody in piano; two-note figure, repeated in
            ever-quicker rhythms,

introduces

B (major)

[32] [7] 0:47  2. *a.* New soaring phrase in major, beginning with short trill, *p.*

[33] [8] 0:56  *b.* Playful phrase with trill; staccato "chirping" idea tossed from violin to piano.

1:04        *c.* Violin trill, soaring phrase returns, shift from major to minor, melody in low
            register in violin and piano, *mf.* Staccato "chirping" idea and trill bring return
            to major.

1:33        *d.* Violin trill, soaring phrase, *p*, playful phrase with trills.

1:46        *e.* Two-note figure repeated in ever-quicker rhythms introduces

A′ (minor)

[34] [9] 1:53  3. *a.* Main violin melody, minor; piano immediately imitates violin. Melody
            descends from high tone.

2:10        *b.* Main melody repeated, syncopated leaps in violin, tempo slows slightly.

2:30        *c.* Long trills in violin; melody in piano leads to soaring phrase, now in minor;

ascent from low register to high; pizzicato major ending, *p.*

196

# FRÉDÉRIC CHOPIN

Frédéric Chopin (1810–1849) was the only great composer who wrote almost exclusively for the piano. The son of a Polish mother and a French father, he was brought up in Warsaw and graduated from the Warsaw Conservatory. At twenty-one, he arrived in Paris, then the center of romanticism and the artistic capital of Europe.

In Paris, he met such writers as Victor Hugo, Balzac, and Heine and became close friends with the painter Delacroix and with Liszt and Berlioz. His playing soon gained him access to aristocratic salons; he was a shy, reserved man who preferred salons to concert halls, and it was for such intimate gatherings that he conceived his short pieces like the nocturnes, waltzes, and preludes. He earned a good living teaching piano to the daughters of the rich and lived in luxury.

Chopin had a well-known love affair with Aurore Dudevant, a novelist whose pen name was George Sand; a frail man, he thrived on her care and composed many of his greatest works during the years they lived together. After they separated, his health declined rapidly and he composed very little. He died of tuberculosis at thirty-nine.

## CHOPIN'S MUSIC

By the age of eighteen, Chopin had evolved an utterly personal and original style. Most of his pieces are exquisite miniatures; they evoke an infinite variety of moods and are always elegant, graceful, and melodic. Unlike Schumann's works, they do not have literary programs or titles. The mazurkas and polonaises—stylized dances—capture a Polish spirit without actually using folk tunes.

No other composer has made the piano sound as beautiful as Chopin, who creates the illusion that the piano sings. He uses graceful and delicate ornamentation and exploits the pedals sensitively. His colorful treatment of harmony was highly original and influenced later composers.

## NOCTURNE IN E FLAT MAJOR, OP. 9, NO. 2 (1830–1831)

Chopin composed his popular Nocturne in E Flat Major, Op. 9, No. 2, when he was about twenty. A ***nocturne,*** or *night piece,* is a slow, lyrical, intimate composition for piano. Like much of Chopin's music, this Nocturne is tinged with sweet melancholy.

Brief sets:
Side 4, band 1
CD 2 35

Basic sets:
Side 9, band 5
CD 5 14

Frédéric Chopin, in a portrait by Eugène Delacroix.

The Nocturne in E Flat Major opens with a legato melody containing graceful upward leaps which become increasingly wide as the line unfolds. This melody is heard again three times during the piece. With each repetition, it is varied by ever more elaborate decorative tones and trills. The nocturne also includes a subordinate melody, which is played with rubato— slight fluctuations of tempo.

A sonorous foundation for the melodic line is provided by the widely spaced notes in the accompaniment, connected by the damper ("loud") pedal. The waltz-like accompaniment gently emphasizes the $\frac{12}{8}$ meter, twelve beats to the measure subdivided into four groups of 3 beats each.

The nocturne is reflective in mood until it suddenly becomes passionate near the end. The new concluding melody begins softly but then ascends to a high register and is played forcefully in octaves. After a brilliant trill-like passage, the excitement subsides; the nocturne ends calmly.

# Listening Outline   To be read while music is heard

NOCTURNE IN E FLAT MAJOR, OP. 9, NO. 2 (1830–1831),
BY FRÉDÉRIC CHOPIN

Andante, $\frac{12}{8}$ meter

Piano

(Duration, 4:05)

35  14  0:00      1. *a.* Main melody, dolce, espressivo, waltzlike accompaniment.

36 15 0:25

*b.* Main melody, *p,* embellished with decorative notes and trills.

37 16 0:51

2. *a.* Subordinate melody, *p,* played with rubato;

crescendo to

1:18  *b.* Main melody, with more elaborate decorative notes and trills; chromatic descent leads to cadence.

1:45  *c.* Subordinate melody, *p,* played with rubato; crescendo to

2:11  *d.* Main melody, with more elaborate decorative notes and trills; chromatic descent leads to cadence.

2:39  3. *a.* Concluding melody, *p.* then *pp.*

3:10  *b.* Concluding melody varied, crescendo with ascent to high register, melody played forcefully in octaves, *ff;* high trill-like figure, decrescendo and descent to gentle, rocking close, *pp,* then *ppp.*

## ÉTUDE IN C MINOR, OP. 10, NO. 12
## (*REVOLUTIONARY;* 1831?)

Supplementary sets:
Side 4, band 2
CD 2 [31]

The Russian takeover of Warsaw in 1831 may have inspired Chopin to compose the blazing and furious *Revolutionary* Étude in C Minor, Op. 10, No. 12. An *étude* is a study piece designed to help a performer master specific technical difficulties. The *Revolutionary* Étude, for example, develops speed and endurance in a pianist's left hand, which must play rapid passages throughout. Chopin's études reach beyond mere exercises in technique to become masterpieces of music, exciting to hear as well as to master.

The *Revolutionary* Étude begins with a dramatic outburst. High, dissonant chords and downward-rushing passages lead to the main melody, marked *appassionato (impassioned),* which is played in octaves by the right hand. Tension mounts because of the melody's dotted rhythms and its tempestuous accompaniment. Toward the end of the piece, after a climax, the tension momentarily subsides. Then a torrential passage sweeps down the keyboard to come to rest in powerful closing chords.

## POLONAISE IN A FLAT MAJOR, OP. 53 (1842)

Basic sets:
Side 9, band 4
CD 5 [10]

Introduction
[10] 0:00
Section A
[11] 0:32

Section B
[12] 3:02

Section A'
[13] 5:20

The *polonaise,* a piece in triple meter, originated as a stately processional dance for the Polish nobility. Chopin's heroic polonaises evoke the ancient splendor of the Polish people.

The Polonaise in A Flat Major is majestic and powerful, with moments of lyrical contrast. It may be outlined as follows: introduction–A B A'–coda. Its main theme makes a grand entrance. The majesty of this theme is enhanced by intervals of thirds in the right hand and by the resonant, wide-ranging accompaniment.

After the main theme is repeated twice with an even richer texture, Chopin offers the contrasting middle section (B). This is a marchlike melody accompanied by relentlessly repeated rapid octaves in the left hand. This section tests a pianist's strength and endurance. Powerful crescendos bring mounting excitement. Then Chopin gradually relaxes the mood to prepare for the final return of the heroic main theme (A').

# FRANZ LISZT

Franz Liszt (1811–1886) was handsome, magnetic, irresistible to women, an incredible showman, and a pacesetter in musical history. During the 1840s, he performed superhuman feats at the piano, overwhelming the European public and impressing musicians as much as concertgoers. Chopin wished that he could play his own piano études the way Liszt did. Schumann wrote that Liszt "enmeshed every member of the audience with his art and did with them as he willed." Brahms later said, "Whoever has not heard Liszt cannot speak of piano playing."

Liszt was born in Hungary; his father was an administrator for the Esterházy family (which Haydn had also served). At age eleven, Liszt studied in Vienna, where he met Schubert and Beethoven; during his teens and twenties, he lived in Paris, a city where romanticism flourished and a mecca for virtuosos. When he was nineteen and already acclaimed, Liszt was awed by the great violinist Paganini, who drove audiences into a frenzy and was half suspected of being in league with the devil. Young Liszt was determined to become the Paganini of the piano. He withdrew from the concert stage for a few years, practiced from eight to twelve hours a day, and emerged as probably the greatest pianist of his time.

To display his incomparable mastery, Liszt composed his *Transcendental Études* and made piano transcriptions of Paganini's violin pieces. "My piano," he wrote, "is my very self. . . . Ten fingers have the power to reproduce the harmonies which are created by hundreds of performers." Once, after an orchestral performance of a movement from Berlioz's *Fantastic Symphony*, Liszt played his own piano arrangement and made a more powerful effect than the entire orchestra. He toured Europe tirelessly between 1839 and 1847, playing mainly his own piano music and receiving unprecedented adulation.

But Liszt also wanted recognition as a serious composer. At thirty-six, he abandoned his career as a traveling virtuoso to become court conductor in Weimar, where he composed many orchestral pieces (developing a new and influential form of program music) and conducted works by such contemporaries as Berlioz, Schumann, and Wagner. Unselfish and generous, he taught hundreds of gifted pianists free of charge and provided musical and financial support crucial to Wagner's success. He also wrote music criticism and books on Chopin and on gypsy music. His literary efforts were aided by two aristocratic women writers: Countess Marie d'Agoult and, later, the Russian Princess Carolyne Sayn-Wittgenstein. (Marie d'Agoult left her husband to live with Liszt; she and Liszt had three children, one of whom, Cosima, later left her own husband to marry Richard Wagner.).

201

Liszt went to Rome for religious studies in 1861, and in 1865 he took minor holy orders, becoming Abbé Liszt. This seeming incongruity—a notorious Don Juan and diabolical virtuoso as churchman—stunned his contemporaries. In Rome, he composed oratorios and masses.

During his last years, Liszt traveled between Rome, Weimar, and Budapest, where he was president of the new Academy of Music. Now he began to write curious, experimental piano pieces that foreshadowed features of twentieth-century music. Though these late works went unappreciated, Liszt had become a living legend. The grand duke of Weimar said, "Liszt *was* what a prince *ought* to be."

## LISZT'S MUSIC

Liszt's music is controversial. Some consider it vulgar and bombastic; others revel in its extroverted romantic rhetoric. Yet few would deny Liszt's originality, his influence, or his importance as the creator of the symphonic poem.

Liszt found new ways to exploit the piano; his melodies are sometimes surrounded by arpeggios that create the impression of three hands playing; and in the *Hungarian Rhapsodies*, which influenced a generation of nationalist composers, he makes the piano sound at times like an entire gypsy band. His piano works contain daring leaps, rapid octaves and runs, and an unprecedented range of dynamics. Before the age of recordings and frequent concerts, Liszt's transcriptions made it possible for people to play operas and symphonies on their own pianos.

Breaking away from classical sonata form and the standard four-movement symphony, Liszt created the **symphonic poem,** or **tone poem,** a one-movement orchestral composition based to some extent on literary or pictorial ideas (see Section 9). Among his favorite inspirations were the works of Goethe, on which he based his *Faust* Symphony (1854); and those of Dante, which inspired the *Dante* Symphony (1856). Many of his compositions are concerned with the devil or death and bear titles like *Mephisto Waltz, Totentanz (Dance of Death),* and *Funérailles.* Constant changes of tempo and mood and alternations between diabolical fury and semireligious meditation contribute to a feeling of improvisation; but in his symphonic poems and other orchestral works, contrasting moods are often unified through thematic transformations of a single, recurring musical idea.

Liszt's music influenced many composers, including Wagner, who admitted to him: "When I compose and orchestrate, I always think only of you." As a stupendous performer, innovative composer, and charismatic personality, Liszt typified the romantic movement.

(Omikron/Photo Researchers)

Franz Liszt.

## TRANSCENDENTAL ÉTUDE NO. 10 IN F MINOR

As dazzling, passionate, and poetic as Liszt himself, the *Transcendental Étude* No. 10 in F Minor is one of the finest virtuoso pieces of the romantic era. Liszt had written an early, simpler version of this piece in 1824, when he was only thirteen, and included it in a group of twelve studies. Fifteen years later, at the peak of his career as a virtuoso, he published a revised version that demanded transcendent, almost superhuman technical skill from the pianist. (Schumann was so overwhelmed by Liszt's études that he described them as "studies in storm and dread meant to be played by, at most, ten or twelve players in the world.") In 1851, after retiring from the concert stage, Liszt dedicated a third and final version—which we'll study— to his piano teacher Carl Czerny "as a token of esteem, gratitude and friendship."

The étude taxes the player with left-hand passages that require rapid skips and changes of hand position. Though written in A–B–A'–coda form, it almost seems like an improvisation, owing to its frequent alterna- tions between brilliant, virtuoso passages and more melodic ideas. The A section contains three themes: the first, in minor, is fragmentary and syn- copated. The second, in major, is more lyrical and in a high register, with

Brief sets:
Side 4, band 2
CD 2 38

Basic sets:
Side 9, band 6
CD 5 17

dotted rhythms, and rapid notes in the accompaniment. The third, which has a processional character, is a transformation of the second. (In the listening outline, this is called the *processional theme*.) A melody that was introduced in major in a high register is now presented in minor, in a low register set against higher arpeggios. Yet another thematic transformation takes place in the coda, which is based on a speeded-up variant of the syncopated main theme.

# Listening Outline    To be read while music is heard

*TRANSCENDENTAL ÉTUDE* NO. 10 IN F MINOR (1851), BY FRANZ LISZT

Allegro agitato molto (very agitated allegro), duple meter ($\frac{2}{4}$), ABA′-coda form, F minor

Piano

(Duration, 4:42)

A

|38| |17| 0:00

1. *a.* Rapid falling chords and syncopated fragment, *p;* rapid falling chords, syncopated main theme.

Gradual ascent and crescendo to

0:17    *b.* Abrupt outbursts, *f,* alternating with upward sweeps; descent to rapid falling chords, decrescendo, slight ritard.

0:29    *c.* Syncopated main theme, ascent and crescendo to

|39| |18| 0:42

2. *a.* Very high lyrical theme in octaves, *ff,* major, dotted rhythm, rapid accompaniment.

High syncopated octaves in melody, close into

1:00    *b.* Abrupt outbursts, *f,* alternating with upward sweeps, *ff,* slight ritard.

3. Low "processional theme," *ff,* in minor, against higher rapid arpeggios.

**B**
4. *a.* Sudden *p,* syncopated main theme varied, crescendo, ascending phrases lead to *ff* climax, downward sweeps, slight ritard.

1:49      *b.* Breathless staccato syncopated chords, ascent with crescendo and accelerando to high chord, *ff.* Rapid falling chords, decrescendo, and ritard introduce

**A′**
5. Syncopated main theme, *p,* gradual ascent, crescendo and ritard to high octaves.

2:22   6. *a.* Very high lyrical theme in minor, *p,* accompanied by rapid arpeggios; gradual crescendo builds to high repeated octaves, *ff,* climax on

3:04      *b.* Syncopated octave descending melody in minor, *ff,* ritard; cadence to

3:22      *c.* Abrupt outbursts, *f,* alternating with upward sweeps, *ff;* high broken octaves descend to

3:36   7. *a.* Low minor "processional theme," *ff,* against higher rapid arpeggios; ascent to dissonant held chord.

     *b.* High broken chords ascend chromatically. Brief pause.

**Coda**
8. *a.* Faster tempo, furiously syncopated octaves,

crescendo, close into

*b.* Rising octave leaps, concluding massive chords.

# FELIX MENDELSSOHN ⎡ ROMANTIC **8** ⎤

Felix Mendelssohn (1809–1847), a romantic whose music was rooted in classicism, was born in Hamburg, Germany, to a wealthy and distinguished Jewish family. (He was, however, raised as a Protestant.) By the age of nine, he was a brilliant pianist; by thirteen, he had written symphonies, concertos, sonatas, and vocal works of astounding quality. As a teenager, he performed his works at home with a private orchestra for the intellectual and artistic elite of Berlin, where the Mendelssohns had settled.

Felix Mendelssohn.

In 1829, at age twenty, he conducted Bach's *St. Matthew Passion* in its first performance since the composer's death. This historic concert rekindled interest in Bach and earned Mendelssohn an international reputation. He performed as a pianist, organist, and conductor in Germany and in England, where his music was especially popular. He often visited and played for Queen Victoria, and the high point of his career was the triumphant premiere of his oratorio *Elijah* in Birmingham in 1846. When only twenty-six, he became conductor of the Leipzig Gewandhaus Orchestra; and he founded the Leipzig Conservatory at age thirty-three.

Mendelssohn's personal life was more conventional than that of many romantics; he was happily married and had four children. But constant travel and work sapped his strength, and he died, after a stroke, at the age of thirty-eight.

## MENDELSSOHN'S MUSIC

Mendelssohn's music radiates the elegance and balance of his personality; it evokes many moods but avoids emotional extremes and typically conveys an elfin quality through rapid movement, lightness, and transparent orchestral texture. He wrote an enormous amount of music in all the forms of his day except opera; today, only a few of his works are in the concert repertory, but these are very popular. They include the Violin Concerto— which we'll study—the *Midsummer Night's Dream* and *Hebrides* overtures; the *Italian* (1833) and *Scotch* (1842) symphonies; the oratorio *Elijah;* and a number of chamber works.

### CONCERTO FOR VIOLIN AND ORCHESTRA IN E MINOR, OP. 64

The Violin Concerto in E Minor, Op. 64, was inspired by Mendelssohn's friendship with the concertmaster of his orchestra, the famous violinist Ferdinand David. "I should like to make a violin concerto for you next winter," Mendelssohn wrote. "One in E minor runs in my head and its beginning gives me no rest." With David as soloist, Mendelssohn's Violin Concerto met great success at its premiere in 1845, and its unique fusion of lyricism and virtuosity has made it one of the best-loved concertos.

The concerto's three movements are played without pause, in a characteristic linking technique used by romantic composers. Mendelssohn's love of balance is reflected in the cooperation and interplay between soloist and orchestra. Themes pass from one to the other, producing a beautiful contrast of tone color and expression. At one moment, the violinist plays a melody while the orchestra discreetly accompanies; at another, the woodwinds present thematic fragments while the soloist has dazzling running passages. We'll now consider the first movement.

## First Movement:

## Allegro molto appassionato (very impassioned allegro)

Though Mendelssohn is usually considered a conservative composer, a "classical romantic," his opening movement departs from classical concerto form. Traditionally, the opening movement of a concerto began with an extended section for orchestra. But Mendelssohn's first movement begins with the soloist, who presents the main theme.

Basic sets:
Side 9, band 7
CD 5 [23]

First
theme
[23] 0:00

This ardent, expansive melody is heard high above a murmuring string accompaniment. The orchestra then expands the violin's theme and introduces a new, flowing melody that begins the bridge section of this sonata-form movement.

Bridge
[24] 1:27

Toward the end of the bridge the excitement is gradually relaxed to prepare for the second theme, a tranquil woodwind melody which the soloist accompanies with a single sustained tone.

Second
theme
[25] 2:47

This unusual combination of instruments produces a delicate, intimate sound. Following this, the violin reclaims the spotlight and sings the tranquil theme while the woodwinds support.

Development
[26] 5:09

207

Cadenza
27 6:40

The cadenza has a new function in this movement. In classical concertos, the cadenza was improvised by the soloist and played near the end of the movement. Here, the composer has written it out and placed it at the end of the development section as a transition to the recapitulation. Mendelssohn wanted the cadenza to be an integral part of the movement, not merely something tacked on to display the soloist's virtuosity. Listen for the magical moment when the violinist's rapid arpeggios are joined by the orchestra softly playing the first theme of the recapitulation.

Recapitulation
8:02

# [ 9 ] PROGRAM MUSIC

Romantic composers were particularly attracted to *program music*—instrumental music associated with a story, poem, idea, or scene. Programmatic works such as Berlioz's *Fantastic Symphony*, Tchaikovsky's *Romeo and Juliet*, and Smetana's *Moldau* depict emotions, characters, and events, or the sounds and motions of nature; these nonmusical ideas are usually specified by the title or by the composer's explanatory comments (the *program*).

Program compositions draw on music's capacity to suggest and evoke. Music can, of course, imitate certain sounds (bird songs, bells, thunder, wind), and composers sometimes exploit the correspondence between musical rhythm and objects in motion (continuous rapid notes, for example, can evoke waves or a stream). Most important is the ability of music to create mood, emotion, and atmosphere: an agitated theme may represent conflict; a lyrical melody may symbolize love. However, music alone makes no definite reference to ideas, emotions, and objects; it cannot identify anything. What lets us fully grasp a composer's source or inspiration is the title or a verbal explanation.

The aim of most program music is expression more than mere description; Beethoven, for example, referred to his Sixth Symphony (the *Pastoral*) as "an expression of feeling rather than painting." Even the most "realistic" episodes in program music can also serve a purely musical function; and one can generally appreciate a descriptive piece as pure music, without knowing its title or program. (We can enjoy the lyrical theme of Tchaikovsky's *Romeo and Juliet* without associating it with young love.) The forms used for program music are similar to those used for nonprogram music, or *absolute music;* thus a programmatic work can be heard simply as a rondo, fugue, sonata form, or theme and variations. But our pleasure may be greater when we can relate music to literary or pictorial ideas, and romantic composers were well aware of this. Occasionally, they even added programs or titles to finished works; and both musicians and audiences in the romantic era liked to read stories into all music, whether intended by the composer or not.

Most romantic program music was written for piano or orchestra. The main forms of orchestral program music are the program symphony, the concert overture, the symphonic poem (tone poem), and incidental music.

A *program symphony* is a composition in several movements—as its name implies, a symphony with a program. Usually, each movement has a descriptive title. For example, Berlioz's *Fantastic Symphony* has five movements: (1) *Reveries, Passions,* (2) *A Ball,* (3) *Scene in the Country,* (4) *March to the Scaffold,* and (5) *Dream of a Witches' Sabbath.* (This work is discussed in Section 10.)

A *concert overture* has one movement, usually in sonata form. The romantic concert overture was modeled after the opera overture, a one-movement composition that establishes the mood of an opera. But the concert overture is *not* intended to usher in a stage work; it is an independent composition. Well-known concert overtures include Mendelssohn's *Hebrides* Overture and Tchaikovsky's *Overture 1812* and *Romeo and Juliet* Overture-Fantasy, which is studied in Section 12.

A *symphonic poem,* or *tone poem,* is also in one movement. Symphonic poems take many traditional forms—sonata form, rondo, or theme and variations—as well as irregular forms. This flexibility of form separates the symphonic poem from the concert overture, which is usually in sonata form. Franz Liszt developed the symphonic poem in the late 1840s and 1850s, and it became the most important type of program music after 1860. Well-known tone poems include *Les Préludes* (1854), by Liszt; *Don Juan* (1888) and *Till Eulenspiegel* (1895), by Richard Strauss (1864–1949); and *The Sorcerer's Apprentice* (1897), by Paul Dukas (1865–1935). In the late nineteenth century, symphonic poems became an important form for nationalism in music. In Section 11, we'll consider a nationalistic tone poem, Smetana's *Moldau,* which depicts a river of Bohemia (in the former Czechoslovakia) as it winds through the countryside.

*Incidental music* is music to be performed before and during a play. It is "incidental" to the staged drama, but it sets the mood for certain scenes. Interludes, background music, marches, and dances are all incidental music (as are today's movie scores). Mendelssohn's incidental music for *A Midsummer Night's Dream* includes his famous *Wedding March.*

# HECTOR BERLIOZ

ROMANTIC
**10**

Hector Berlioz (1803–1869), one of the first French romantic composers and a daring creator of new orchestral sounds, was born in a small town near Grenoble. His father, a physician, sent him to Paris to study medicine, but he was "filled with horror" by the dissecting room and shocked his parents by abandoning medicine to pursue a career in music. He studied at the Paris Conservatory, haunted the opera house, and composed.

(Snark/Art Resource)

Hector Berlioz.

When he was twenty-three, Berlioz was overwhelmed by the works of Shakespeare and also fell madly in love with a Shakespearean actress, Harriet Smithson, to whom he wrote such wild, impassioned letters that she considered him a lunatic and refused to see him. To depict his "endless and unquenchable passion," Berlioz wrote the *Symphonie fantastique (Fantastic Symphony)* in 1830, which startled Parisians by its sensationally autobiographical program, its amazingly novel orchestration, and its vivid depiction of the weird and diabolical.

In 1830, too, Berlioz won the Prix de Rome (the Rome Prize), subsidizing two years' study in Rome; when he returned to Paris, he finally met and married Harriet Smithson—after she had attended a performance of the *Fantastic Symphony* and realized that it depicted her. (They separated, however, after only a few years.)

Berlioz's unconventional music irritated the opera and concert establishment. To get a hearing for his works, he had to arrange concerts at his own expense—an enormous undertaking which drained him financially, physically, and emotionally. Although he had a following of about 1,200 who faithfully bought tickets to his concerts, this was not enough support for a composer of difficult, monumental works requiring hundreds of performers. Berlioz turned to musical journalism, becoming a brilliant and witty music critic who tried to convince the Parisians that music was not merely entertainment but dramatic emotional expression.

Outside France, Berlioz's stock was higher. After 1840, he was in demand throughout Europe, conducting his own and others' music. As one of the first great conductors, he influenced a whole generation of musicians. But his last years were bitter; he was passed over for important positions and honors and composed very little during the six years before his death at sixty-five.

## BERLIOZ'S MUSIC

"The prevailing qualities of my music," wrote Berlioz, "are passionate expressiveness, inner fire, rhythmic drive, and unexpectedness." Above all, Berlioz's music sounds unique. It includes abrupt contrasts, fluctuating dynamics, and many changes in tempo.

As an orchestrator, Berlioz was extraordinarily imaginative and innovative. At a time when the average orchestra had about sixty players, he often assembled hundreds of musicians to achieve new power, tone colors, and timbres. His melodies are often long, irregular, and asymmetrical, taking unexpected turns. Most of his works are for orchestra, or orchestra with chorus and vocal soloists; all are dramatic and programmatic. He invented new forms: his "dramatic symphony" *Romeo and Juliet* (1839) is for orchestra, chorus, and vocal soloists; and his "dramatic legend" *The Damnation of Faust* combines opera and oratorio. He also wrote three operas and a grandiose, monumental Requiem.

Berlioz knew he was a pioneer; he wrote of the Requiem, "I have seen one man listening in terror, shaken to the depths of his soul, while his next neighbor could not catch an idea, though trying with all his might to do so."

## SYMPHONIE FANTASTIQUE (*FANTASTIC SYMPHONY*; 1830)

The astonishing *Symphonie fantastique (Fantastic Symphony)*, a five-movement program symphony (we'll study its fourth and fifth movements), is a romantic manifesto. Both the music and Berlioz's program reflect the twenty-six-year-old composer's unrequited passion for the actress Harriet Smithson:

A young musician of extraordinary sensibility and abundant imagination, in the depths of despair because of hopeless love, has poisoned himself with opium. The drug is too feeble to kill him but plunges him into a heavy sleep accompanied by weird visions. His sensations, emotions, and memories, as they pass through his affected mind, are transformed into musical images and ideas. The beloved one herself becomes to him a melody, a recurrent theme (*idée fixe*) which haunts him continually.

A single melody, which Berlioz called the **idée fixe,** or *fixed idea*, is used to represent the beloved. When introduced in the first movement—*Reveries, Passions*—it sounds, in Berlioz's description, "passionate but at the same time noble and shy."

It appears in all five movements and unifies the contrasting episodes of the symphony. This recurrence of the same theme in every movement of a symphony was a striking novelty in Berlioz's day. The theme changes in character during the work. For example, in the second movement—*A Ball*—it is transformed into a waltz, and in the third movement—*Scene in the Country*—it is played against an agitated countermelody.

Another innovation in the symphony is its use of a very large and colorful orchestra: piccolo, 2 flutes, 2 oboes, English horn, 2 clarinets, 4 bassoons, 4 French horns, 2 cornets, 2 trumpets, 3 trombones, 2 tubas, 4 timpani, bass drum, snare drum, cymbals, bells, 2 harps, and strings. Beethoven had not used the English horn, tuba, bells (chimes), cornet, or harp in his symphonies. Berlioz saves the heaviest orchestration for the last two movements, where he depicts the fantastic and diabolical. Though the macabre and supernatural had long been dealt with in opera (in Mozart's *Don Giovanni*, for example), this is their first expression in an important symphony.

## Fourth Movement: *March to the Scaffold*
## Allegretto non troppo

> He dreams that he has murdered his beloved, that he has been condemned to death and is being led to execution. A march that is alternately somber and wild, brilliant and solemn, accompanies the procession. . . . The tumultuous outbursts are followed without transition by the muffled sound of heavy steps. At the end, the fixed idea returns for a moment, like a last thought of love interrupted by the death blow.

> "The *March to the Scaffold* is fifty times more frightening than I expected," Berlioz gleefully observed after the first rehearsals of the *Fantastic Symphony*. It is not until this fiendish fourth movement that all the brass and percussion instruments enter the action.

Berlioz creates a menacing atmosphere with the opening orchestral sound, a unique combination of muted French horns, timpani tuned a third apart, and basses playing pizzicato chords. The first theme, stated by the cellos and basses, moves steadily downward for two octaves.

Introduction
28 0:00

First theme
29 0:27

This idea is repeated several times with countermelodies in the bassoons. Then we hear a syncopated march tune blared by the brasses and wood-winds.

March tune
30 1:36

At the end of the march a solo clarinet begins to play the *idée fixe* but is savagely interrupted by a very loud chord representing the fall of the guil-lotine's blade.

Idée fixe
31 6:19

## Fifth Movement: *Dream of a Witches' Sabbath*
## Larghetto; Allegro

> He sees himself at a witches' sabbath in the midst of a hideous crowd of ghouls, sorcerers, and monsters of every description, united for his funeral. Strange noises, groans, shrieks of laughter, distant cries, which other cries seem to answer. The melody of the loved one is heard, but it has lost its character of nobleness and timidity; it is no more than a dance tune, ignoble, trivial, and grotesque. It is she who comes to the sabbath! . . . . A howl of joy greets her arrival. . . . She participates in the diabolical orgy. . . . The funeral knell, burlesque of the *Dies irae*. Witches' dance. The dance and the *Dies irae* combined.

The *Dream of a Witches' Sabbath* is the most "fantastic" movement of the symphony; it depicts a series of grotesque events. Its slow, hushed intro-duction (larghetto) immediately draws the listener into the realm of the macabre and supernatural, evoking "strange noises, groans, shrieks of laughter" and "distant cries." Eerie tremolos in high muted strings and menacing low tones of cellos and basses begin a succession of fragmentary ideas in starkly contrasting tone colors, registers, and dynamics. In the exploratory spirit of the romantic age, Berlioz dared to create sounds that are weird rather than conventionally pleasing.

Brief sets:
Side 4, band 3
CD 2 44

Basic sets:
Side 10, band 2
CD 5 32

213

In the allegro section, the beloved is revealed to be a witch. Her theme, the once "noble and timid" *idée fixe*, is transformed into a dance tune that is "trivial and grotesque." Played shrilly by a high-pitched clarinet, the tune moves in quick notes decorated by trills.

A "funeral knell" of sonorous bells (chimes) lends an awesome atmosphere to the next part of the movement. Tubas and bassoons intone a solemn low melody in long, even notes. This melody is the medieval chant *Dies irae (Day of wrath)*, traditionally sung in the mass for the dead. Berlioz quotes it here as a symbol of eternal damnation. Soon the chant melody is shifted up to a high register and played by woodwinds and pizzicato strings in a quick dancelike rhythm. Thus Berlioz dared to parody a sacred chant by transforming it into a trivial tune, as he had just done moments earlier with the *idée fixe*.

Berlioz conveys the frenzy of a witches' dance in a fuguelike section. The fugue subject (the witches' dance) is introduced by the lower strings and then imitated by other instruments. A crescendo builds to a powerful climax in which the rapid witches' dance, played in the strings, is set against the slower-moving *Dies irae*, proclaimed by the brasses and woodwinds. This musical nightmare ends in an orgy of orchestral power.

# Listening Outline   To be read while music is heard

*SYMPHONIE FANTASTIQUE (FANTASTIC SYMPHONY; 1830),*
BY HECTOR BERLIOZ

Fifth Movement: *Dream of a Witches' Sabbath*

Larghetto; Allegro

Piccolo, flute, 2 oboes, 2 clarinets, 4 bassoons, 2 trumpets, 2 cornets, 4 French horns, 3 trombones, 2 tubas, timpani, bass drum, bells (chimes), 1st violins, 2d violins, violas, cellos, double basses

(Duration, 9:51)

Larghetto

Strange noises
| 44 32 0:00 | 1. *a.* | High string tremolo, *pp*, joined by low repeated figure in cellos and basses; high descending staccato strings, *ppp*; staccato brasses, *f*; sudden low chord. |
| 0:27 | *b.* | High woodwinds, short repeated notes, *mf*, echoed in lower register by muted horn, *ppp*, ascent to |
| 0:47 | *c.* | High string tremolo, *pp*, joined by low repeated figure in cellos and basses; high staccato strings descend to rumble in low strings; sudden loud chord. |
| 1:11 | *d.* | High woodwinds, short repeated notes, *mf*, echoed in lower register by muted horn, *pppp*. |

2. *a.* Clarinet, part of *idée fixe* as dance tune, timpani accompany, full orchestra interrupts, *ff.*
   *b.* High clarinet, joined by piccolo, *idée fixe* as dance tune, woodwinds accompany; high violins join, leading to

high repeated figure in strings, *ff;* orchestral chord *ff,* staccato chromatic descent; repeated chords and string descent lead to

   *c.* Violins, *p,* rapid ascent and crescendo, cellos and basses, *p,* descend; long low tones introduce

3. Bell tolls (chimes) alternating with violas, beginning of witches' dance.
4. *a.* Low tubas and bassoons, *f,* beginning of *Dies irae* in long even notes, bells (chimes) accompany.

   *b.* Higher horns and trumpets, beginning of *Dies irae* played faster.

   *c.* High woodwinds, beginning of *Dies irae* as fast staccato dance tune.

215

4:04    5. *a.* Low tubas and bassoons, continuation of *Dies irae* in long even notes, bells (chimes) accompany.

4:18       *b.* Higher horns and trumpets, continuation of *Dies irae* played faster.

4:24       *c.* High woodwinds, continuation of *Dies irae* as fast dance tune.

4:29    6. *a.* Low tubas and bassoons, *f,* conclusion of *Dies irae* in long even notes.

4:48       *b.* Higher horns and trumpets, conclusion of *Dies irae* played faster.

4:58       *c.* High woodwinds, conclusion of *Dies irae* as fast dance tune.

5:05       *d.* Strings, beginning of witches' dance with brass interruptions; crescendo to *ff,* full orchestra.

Witches' dance (fuguelike section)

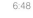 5:21    7. *a.* Witches' dance introduced by cellos and double basses, imitated in violins, then high woodwinds.

5:49       *b.* Violin syncopations, *ff,* piccolo; strings alternate between *ff* and *p;* crescendo to *ff* repeated chords.

6:07       *c.* Witches' dance introduced in woodwinds, imitated in low strings, then violins.

6:22       *d.* Rapid brass chords, *ff,* bass drum, repeatedly answered by descending high woodwinds; decrescendo to

6:48       *e.* Pizzicato cellos and basses, varied witches' dance, imitations by bassoon, horn punctuations.

7:05       *f.* Low strings, *mf, Dies irae* phrases.

7:20       *g.* Very soft, witches' dance rhythm passed from low to high strings, long crescendo; orchestra, *ff,* repeated syncopated chords.

49 37 8:00    8. *a.* Witches' dance, strings in unison, *ff,* joined by *Dies irae* in brasses and woodwinds, *ff.*

8:27       *b.* Sudden *p; ff* repeated figure in strings and woodwinds, high strings struck with wood of bow joined by

8:39       *c.* Woodwinds, *mf,* varied witches' dance with trills.

8:50       *d.* Staccato woodwinds, *pp;* full orchestral chords, *ff,* alternate with high woodwind trills; sudden *pp,* crescendo to *ff.*

9:13       *e.* Bass drum, *Dies irae* phrase in tubas, played faster by higher brasses and woodwinds; fast and powerful orchestral conclusion.

# NATIONALISM IN NINETEENTH-CENTURY MUSIC

During the nineteenth century, nationalism—awakened partly by resistance to Napoleon's invading armies—was a dominant force in Europe. Patriotic feelings and common bonds of language, culture, and history were also strengthened by romanticism, which glorified love for one's national heritage. As a revolutionary political movement, nationalism led to the unification of some countries (like Germany and Italy) that had been divided into tiny states, and it spurred revolts in countries under foreign rule (like Poland and Bohemia). As a potent cultural movement, it led to the revival of national languages (such as Czech) and to a new interest in the peasantry and folk art—songs, dances, poetry, legends.

*Nationalism* also influenced romantic music, as composers deliberately gave their works a distinctive national identity. They used folk songs and dances, created original melodies with a folk flavor, and wrote operas and program music inspired by their countries' history, legends, and land scapes. Their works bear titles like *Russian Easter* Overture (by Rimsky-Korsakov), *Finlandia* (by Sibelius), and *Slavonic Dances* (by Dvořák). But, beyond their use of folk songs and patriotic elements, their music often *sounds* Scandinavian, Slavic, or Russian because its rhythm, tone color, and melody spring from national tradition.

The strongest impact of nationalism was felt in countries whose own musical heritage had been dominated by the music of Italy, France, Germany, or Austria. Early in the nineteenth century, Chopin transformed the dances of his native Poland into great art. After about 1860, groups or "schools" of composers consciously declared their musical independence and established national styles. The Scandinavian countries produced Edvard Grieg (Norwegian, 1843–1907) and Jean Sibelius (Finnish, 1865–1957). Bohemia (which became part of Czechoslovakia) produced Bedřich Smetana (1824–1887; we'll study his symphonic poem *The Moldau*) and Antonin Dvořák (1841–1904). Dvořák's Symphony No. 9 (*From the New World;* 1893)—his most famous work, written while he was living in the United States—glorifies both the Czech and the American folk spirit. An important national school is the Russian, which created highly distinctive music. Mikhail Glinka's opera *A Life for the Tsar* (1836) laid the groundwork for a national style, and in the 1860s five young men—now known as the *Russian five*—formed a true national school. They were Mily Balakirev (1837–1910), César Cui (1835–1918), Alexander Borodin (1833–1887), Nikolai Rimsky-Korsakov (1844–1908), and Modest Mussorgsky (1839–1881).

Remarkably, all but Balakirev began as amateurs, and most of them held nonmusical jobs. Mussorgsky was the most original of the Russian five, and his opera *Boris Godunov* is a masterpiece of musical nationalism.

We'll turn now to a famous nationalistic work, *The Moldau*.

## THE MOLDAU (1874), BY BEDŘICH SMETANA

**Brief sets:**
**Side 4, band 4**
**CD 2 ⟨50⟩**

Basic sets:
Side 11, band 1
CD 6 ⟨1⟩

Bedřich Smetana (1824–1884) was the founder of Czech national music. His works are steeped in the folk music and legends of his native Bohemia. But he grew up when Bohemia was under Austrian domination, and in this repressive atmosphere his musical nationalism could make little headway; he emigrated to Sweden in 1856.

In 1862, when Austria had made some liberal concessions, Smetana returned to Prague. He was active as a composer, pianist, conductor, and teacher and wrote *The Bartered Bride*, his most famous opera. At age fifty, he became completely deaf, but some of his finest works followed, including *Má Vlast (My Country, 1874–1879)*, a cycle of six symphonic poems. His last years were blighted by syphilis, and he died at sixty in an asylum.

"Today I took an excursion to the St. John Rapids where I sailed in a boat through huge waves. . . . The view of the landscape was both beautiful and grand." Smetana's trip inspired his symphonic poem *The Moldau*, which depicts Bohemia's main river as it flows through the countryside. This orchestral work, part of the cycle *Má Vlast (My Country)*, is both a romantic representation of nature and a display of Czech nationalism. It was written in three weeks shortly after Smetana became deaf. *The Moldau*'s fresh, optimistic mood gives no hint of the composer's anguish and despair. Smetana wrote the following program to preface his score:

> The composition depicts the course of the river, beginning from its two small sources, one cold the other warm, the joining of both streams into one, then the flow of the Moldau through forests and across meadows, through the countryside where merry feasts are celebrated; water nymphs dance in the moonlight; on nearby rocks can be seen the outline of ruined castles, proudly soaring into the sky. The Moldau swirls through the St. John Rapids and flows in a broad stream toward Prague. It passes Vyšehrad [where an ancient royal castle once stood], and finally the river disappears in the distance as it flows majestically into the Elbe.

*The Moldau* falls into contrasting musical sections that represent different scenes and episodes described in the program. Hunting at the river bank is suggested by horn fanfares, a peasant wedding by a rustic polka—the Bohemian dance—and a moonlit night by shimmering woodwinds and a serene melody in high muted strings. An expansive folklike theme that recurs several times symbolizes the river. Smetana unifies the symphonic poem by running notes evoking the movement of water, sometimes rippling, sometimes turbulent.

# Listening Outline To be read while music is heard

*THE MOLDAU* (1874), BY BEDŘICH SMETANA

Allegro commodo non agitato (unhurried allegro, not agitated), sextuple meter ($^6_8$), E minor

Piccolo, 2 flutes, 2 oboes, 2 clarinets, 2 bassoons, 4 French horns, 2 trumpets, 3 trombones, tuba, timpani, bass drum, triangle, cymbals, harp, 1st violins, 2d violins, violas, cellos, double basses

(Duration, 11:53)

**Two springs**
50 1 0:00     1. *a.* Flutes, *p*, running notes. Harp, pizzicato violins.

         Clarinets, *p*, join, running notes.
         *b.* Lower strings, *p*, running notes lead to

**The river**
51 2 1:00     2. Violins, songlike river theme, minor key. Running-note accompaniment in strings.

         River theme extended.

**Forest hunt**
52 3 2:50     3. *a.* French horns and trumpets, *f*, hunting calls. Strings, running notes. Crescendo to *ff*.
         *b.* Decrescendo to *ppp*.

**Peasant wedding**
53 4 3:54     4. *a.* Strings, *p*, polka.

         Crescendo to *f*, triangle strokes.
         *b.* Decrescendo to *ppp*, melody descends.

219

5. *a.* Woodwinds, *pp,* sustained tones. Flutes, *p,* running notes lead to
   *b.* High muted violins, *pp,* serene legato melody. Harp, *p.*
   *c.* Brasses, *pp.* Staccato chords join accompaniment to violin melody.
   *d.* Crescendo. Woodwinds, running notes lead to

6. Violins, river theme. Running-note accompaniment in strings.

7. *a.* Full orchestra, *ff.* Brasses, timpani roll, piccolo, cymbal crashes.
   *b.* Strings, *pp.* Quick crescendo.

8. Full orchestra, *ff,* river theme in major key. Faster tempo.

9. *a.* Brasses and woodwinds, *ff,* hymnlike melody. Cymbal crashes.
   *b.* Decrescendo. Violins, *ppp.* Full orchestra, *ff,* closing chords.

<br>

[ ROMANTIC ]
# 12 PETER ILYICH TCHAIKOVSKY

Peter Ilyich Tchaikovsky (1840–1893), the most famous Russian composer, started his career as a government clerk and began to study music theory at the relatively late age of twenty-one. His progress in music was rapid, however. After graduating from the St. Petersburg Conservatory, he became a professor of harmony at the Moscow Conservatory and composed furiously: a symphony, an opera, a tone poem, and—by the age of thirty—his first great orchestral work, *Romeo and Juliet*.

The year 1877 was dramatic for Tchaikovsky. He married, disastrously and apparently only to conceal his homosexuality; attempted suicide two weeks after the wedding; and had a nervous collapse. (He and his wife separated and never saw each other again.) But in 1877 he also acquired a wealthy benefactress, Nadezhda von Meck, with whom he had a curious but intimate friendship—they corresponded but did not meet. Madame von Meck gave him an annuity that allowed him to leave the conservatory and devote himself to composition; fourteen years later, he was deeply hurt when she cut off the annuity and stopped writing to him.

(Bertarelli/SFF/Art Resource)

Peter Ilyich Tchaikovsky.

During these years, Tchaikovsky achieved success conducting his own works throughout Europe (and, in 1891, in the United States), but he always remained a spiritually troubled man. In 1893, nine days after conducting the premiere of his Symphony No. 6 *(Pathétique)*—which ends unconventionally with a slow, despairing finale—he died at the age of fifty-three.

## TCHAIKOVSKY'S MUSIC

Tchaikovsky thought of himself as *"Russian in the fullest sense of the word,"* but his style was influenced by French, Italian, and German music as well as Russian folk song. His works are much more in the western tradition than those of his contemporaries, the "Russian five." He fused national and international elements to produce intensely subjective and passionate music.

Among his most popular orchestral compositions are Symphonies No. 4 (1877), No. 5 (1888), and No. 6 (*Pathétique*, 1893); the Piano Concerto No. 1 in B Flat Minor (1875); the Violin Concerto (1878); and the overture-fantasy *Romeo and Juliet*, which we'll study. He wrote some of the best scores for ballet—*Swan Lake* (1876), *The Sleeping Beauty* (1889), and *The Nutcracker* (1892)—and the spirit of ballet permeates much of his music. He also wrote eight operas and the orchestral showpieces *Marche slave* and *Overture 1812.*

## ROMEO AND JULIET, OVERTURE-FANTASY

Basic sets:
Side 10, band 3
CD 5 [38]

Romantic composers felt an artistic kinship to Shakespeare because of his passionate poetry, dramatic contrasts, and profound knowledge of the human heart. Some of Shakespeare's plays inspired many of the finest nineteenth-century compositions. Among these were *Macbeth* and *Othello*, set as operas by Verdi; and *A Midsummer Night's Dream,* depicted in incidental music by Mendelssohn. *Romeo and Juliet* inspired both a ''dramatic symphony'' by Berlioz and a concert overture by Tchaikovsky.

Tchaikovsky composed *Romeo and Juliet* at twenty-nine, near the beginning of his musical career. Now one of the best-loved orchestral works, *Romeo and Juliet* was a dismal failure at its premiere in 1870. ''After the concert we dined. . . . No one said a single word to me about the overture the whole evening. And yet I yearned so for appreciation and kindness.'' Tchaikovsky decided to revise the overture. He composed a new theme to represent Friar Laurence, adopting a suggestion of his friend Balakirev. Despite this, the work remained unappreciated. Only about twenty years later, after further revisions, did *Romeo and Juliet* achieve worldwide popularity.

Like Shakespeare's play, Tchaikovsky's *Romeo and Juliet* glorifies a romantic love powerful enough to triumph over death. Tchaikovsky captures the essential emotions of Shakespeare's play without defining each character or the exact course of events. Highly contrasted themes are used to express the conflict between family hatred and youthful love. Tchaikovsky also depicts the gentle and philosophical Friar Laurence, intermediary between the lovers and the harsh outside world.

*Romeo and Juliet* is a concert overture consisting of a slow introduction and a fast movement in sonata form. (Tchaikovsky's title—*Overture-Fantasy*—implies that he treated the musical material in a free and imaginative way.) We can enjoy *Romeo and Juliet* as an exciting orchestral piece without knowing the play. However, a new dimension is added to our listening experience when we associate the music with the drama.

Introduction
[38] 0:00

Tchaikovsky opens the overture with the Friar Laurence theme, a solemn, hymnlike melody.

As the slow introduction unfolds, brooding strings set an atmosphere of impending tragedy. The clash of swords and the anger of the feud between the Montagues and the Capulets is suggested by the violent first theme of the allegro.

First theme
[39] 5:01

Syncopations, rushing strings, and massive sounds create enormous excitement. The exposition continues with a bridge section that brings a sudden *p*, a calmer mood, and a slower rhythm.

Bridge
40  6:19

The second theme of the exposition, a tender love theme, is expressively scored for English horn and muted violas.

Second theme
41  6:58

It is followed by a gently pulsating melody in the muted violins,

Pulsating melody
42  7:13

The development section focuses mainly on the feud theme and the Friar Laurence theme. In the recapitulation, the gently pulsating melody precedes the love theme, which now has a new exultant character as Tchaikovsky envelops the listener in opulent sound. There are long crescendos as the melody is led higher and higher to ever more passionate orchestral climaxes.

Development
43  9:52

Recapitulation
44  11:58

In the coda, Tchaikovsky transforms the love theme into a song of mourning, while timpani softly beat the rhythm of a funeral march.

Coda
47  15:53

Then, a new hymn and a tender reminiscence of the love theme suggest that Romeo and Juliet are reunited in death.

223

# [13] JOHANNES BRAHMS

Johannes Brahms (1833–1897) was a romantic who breathed new life into classical forms. He was born in Hamburg, Germany, where his father made a precarious living as a bass player. At thirteen, Brahms led a double life: during the day he studied piano, music theory, and composition; at night he played dance music for prostitutes and their clients in waterfront bars.

On his first concert tour, when he was twenty, Brahms met Robert Schumann and Schumann's wife Clara, who were to shape the course of his artistic and personal life. The Schumanns listened enthusiastically to Brahms's music, and Robert published an article hailing young Brahms as a musical messiah.

As Brahms was preparing new works for an eager publisher, Schumann had a nervous collapse and tried to drown himself. When Schumann was committed to an asylum, leaving Clara with seven children to support, Brahms came to live in the Schumann home. He stayed for two years, helping to care for the children when Clara was on tour and becoming increas-

(Bettmann Archive)

Johannes Brahms.

ingly involved with Clara, who was fourteen years older than he. It is not known what passed between them (they destroyed many of their letters). Afterward, they remained lifelong friends, and Brahms never married.

Brahms desperately wanted to become conductor of the Philharmonic Orchestra in Hamburg. When he was passed over for the post in 1862, he left Hamburg for Vienna, where he spent the rest of his life. He conducted a Viennese musical society and introduced many forgotten works of Bach, Handel, and Mozart. He had a wide knowledge of older music (which made him extremely critical of his own work), edited baroque and classical compositions, and collected music manuscripts.

Brahms always lived frugally, though he earned a good income from publishers and from playing and conducting his works. He hid a shy, sensitive nature behind a mask of sarcasm and rudeness; yet he could be very generous to talented young musicians (Dvořák was one).

When Clara Schumann lay dying in 1896, his grief found expression in the haunting *Four Serious Songs*; not long after, it was discovered that he had cancer. On March 7, 1897, he dragged himself to hear a performance of his Fourth Symphony; the audience and orchestra gave him a tremendous ovation. Less than a month later, at age sixty-four, he died.

## BRAHMS'S MUSIC

Brahms created masterpieces in all the traditional forms (except opera): four symphonies; two concertos for piano, one for violin, and one for violin and cello; piano pieces; over 200 songs; some magnificent choral music, such as the *German Requiem* (1868); and numerous chamber pieces. His work is personal in style but rooted in the music of Haydn, Mozart, and Beethoven. Brahms reinterpreted classical forms using the harmonic and instrumental resources of his own time. We'll study his masterful treatment of theme and variations in the last movement of his Fourth Symphony.

Brahms's music has a range of moods, but particularly an autumnal feeling and lyrical warmth. Lyricism pervades even the rich polyphonic textures he was so fond of, and he was always able to make them sound natural and spontaneous. One scholar has observed, "It is possible to sing every Brahms movement from beginning to end as though it were a single, uninterrupted melody." His music is rhythmically exciting, with contrasting patterns and syncopations (the use of "2 against 3"—one instrument playing two even notes to a beat while another plays three—is one of his trademarks). It also has a special quality of sound: rich, dark tone colors and, in the orchestral works, a blending of the instrumental choirs that favor mellow instruments like the viola, clarinet, and French horn.

All of his music radiates the security and solidity of a complete master who fully justified Schumann's prediction of greatness.

## SYMPHONY NO. 4 IN E MINOR, OP. 98

Brahms composed his Fourth Symphony during the summers of 1884 and 1885 in the tiny Austrian town of Mürzzuschlag. At its premiere in Vienna in 1886, the Fourth Symphony bewildered the audience; some even hissed. Yet this work grew on the Viennese and was responsible for Brahms's greatest triumph in Vienna, less than a month before his death. At a concert of the Vienna Philharmonic Orchestra on March 7, 1897, tremendous applause broke out after every movement of the symphony. "Tears ran down his cheeks," a biographer of Brahms writes, "as he stood there, shrunken in form, with lined countenance, strained expression, white hair hanging lank, and through the audience there was a feeling as of a stifled sob, for each knew that he was saying farewell. Another outburst of applause and yet another; one more acknowledgment from the master; and Brahms and his Vienna had parted forever."

The Fourth Symphony combines strength and lyricism with the autumnal melancholy that is so typical of Brahms's music. The first movement, in sonata form, is dominated by its expansive opening theme. Listen for the magical moment when the first two phrases of the theme are presented in long notes to usher in the recapitulation. The slow second movement is based upon a pair of songlike themes that are stated and then recapitulated with imaginative changes in orchestration. The rapid third movement is a scherzo in sonata form. Let's now examine the fourth movement.

### Fourth Movement

**Brief sets:**
**Side 4, band 5**
**CD 2** 57

Basic sets:
Side 11, band 2
CD 6 8

The monumental fourth movement, marked *allegro energico e passionato (energetic and impassioned allegro),* is the climax of the symphony. It is a type of theme and variations related to the baroque ground-bass form (also called *passacaglia*). Brahms's use of a baroque variation form is unique in the romantic symphonic literature and reflects his strong attachment to the musical past.

The movement, which is in E minor, consists of a theme, thirty variations, and an extended coda. Brasses and woodwinds introduce the theme, a solemn eight-note melody that steadily ascends by step before coming to a cadence.

Brahms borrowed the theme from Bach's Cantata No. 150, *Unto Thee, O Lord, I Lift Up My Soul,* but enhanced it harmonically and dramatically by inserting a new chromatic note into the original melody.

The variations embrace a wide range of moods: some are impassioned; others are lyrical or playful. Like the baroque masters he revered, Brahms focuses the listener's attention on the ever-changing melodic and rhythmic ideas rather than on the repeated theme. Some variations sound completely new, even though most tones of the theme are retained. Brahms's delight in disguising a theme was noted by his contemporaries. When he grew a beard one summer, a friend joked that Brahms's face was now as hard to recognize under the beard as the theme in his variations.

The variations are connected to each other and maintain the theme's 8-bar form and triple meter. In variations 1 to 3, the theme is heard in the top or middle part, but from variation 4 to variation 11, the theme is presented in the bass, with countermelodies above it. From variation 12 on, the theme appears either in the top, middle, or bass part.

The movement can be outlined as three large sections plus coda:

| A | B | A' | Coda |
|---|---|----|------|
| Theme, Variations 1–11 | Variations 12–15 | Variations 16–30 | |

The rapid A section, in minor, is mostly forceful and intense. The B section brings a more relaxed mood, a slower tempo, and a major key in three of its four variations. Section A' returns to the quick tempo, minor key, and energetic mood of the opening section and is treated somewhat like a recapitulation. The opening variation of A', variation 16, is very similar to the original theme, and variations 24 and 25 are based on variations 1 and 2. Sections A, B, and A' all contain subgroups of variations that belong together because of similarities in melody, rhythm, texture, or orchestration. In the listening outline, these subgroups are indicated by brackets.

The impassioned coda begins with a climactic reappearance of the main theme in woodwinds and brasses. Then Brahms abandons the strict succession of 8-bar units and treats the theme more freely, presenting it in accelerated transformations in trombones, woodwinds, and full orchestra.

## Listening Outline To be read while music is heard

SYMPHONY NO. 4 IN E MINOR (1885),
BY JOHANNES BRAHMS

Fourth Movement: Allegro energico e passionato

Theme and variations (ground-bass or passacaglia form), triple meter ($\frac{3}{4}$ and $\frac{3}{2}$), E minor

2 flutes, 2 oboes, 2 clarinets, 2 bassoons, contrabassoon, 4 French horns, 2 trumpets, 3 trombones, timpani, 1st violins, 2d violins, violas, cellos, double basses

(Duration, 10:13)

A

THEME

57  8 0:00    Brasses and woodwinds, *f,* ascending theme, minor key.

VARIATION 1

58  9 0:17    Timpani rolls and horns, *f,* answered by syncopated theme in pizzicato violins, decrescendo.

VARIATION 2

0:32    Oboe, *mp,* legato melody, against theme in pizzicato cellos, *mp,* flutes join, crescendo.

VARIATION 3

0:48    Woodwinds, *f,* staccato melody, brasses, *f,* timpani roll.

VARIATION 4

1:03    Violins, *f,* lyrical melody, against theme in cellos and basses.

VARIATION 5

1:20    Violins, varied lyrical melody, against theme in pizzicato basses.

VARIATION 6

1:32    Violins continue melody against legato theme in basses, melody rises, crescendo to

VARIATION 7

1:48    High violin melody, *f,* forceful dotted rhythm (short-long, short-long), melody descends.

VARIATION 8

2:03    Rushing notes in violins, *f,* against theme in bass, decrescendo.

VARIATION 9

2:18    Suddenly loud, faster rushing notes in strings, suddenly soft, woodwinds, descending chromatic scale.

VARIATION 10

2:35    Sustained chords, *p,* strings answered by woodwinds.

VARIATION 11

2:57    Violins, *p,* staccato phrases, flutes *pp,* descending chromatic scale.

B

VARIATION 12

59  10 3:17    Extended legato flute solo, slower tempo, strings accompany, *p,* melody descends, decrescendo.

VARIATION 13

4:01    Clarinet phrases, *p,* answered by oboe, low strings, *pp,* major key, flute, descending oboe phrase introduces

┌ **VARIATION 14**
│    4:40      Trombones, *pp,* slow chords, strings accompany, descending horn phrase
│             introduces
└ **VARIATION 15**
     5:20      Oboe and brasses, *pp,* slow chords, strings accompany, descending flute phrase,
             ritardando, pause.

**A′**
  **VARIATION 16**
  60 11 6:05      Brasses and woodwinds, *ff,* original theme and tempo, minor key, high violins, *ff,*
             descending scale.
  **VARIATION 17**
     6:18      String tremolo, *p,* woodwinds, *mf.*
  **VARIATION 18**
     6:28      Horns and high woodwinds, *f,* ascending melody, crescendo.
┌ **VARIATION 19**
│    6:40      Violins, *f,* staccato phrases, answered by woodwinds, *f.*
└ **VARIATION 20**
     6:51      Violins and brasses, *f,* rapid staccato notes.
  **VARIATION 21**
     7:03      Timpani rolls, upward rushes in violins, *ff,* answered by trombones, *ff.*
  **VARIATION 22**
     7:16      Suddenly soft, woodwinds, staccato phrases, staccato strings, *pp.*
  **VARIATION 23**
     7:27      Suddenly loud, horns, ascending theme.
  **VARIATION 24**
     7:39      Timpani and brasses, *ff,* answered by high violins, *ff,* theme.
  **VARIATION 25**
     7:52      High violin tremolo, *ff,* legato melody punctuated by repeated chords in
             orchestra, *ff.*
┌ **VARIATION 26**
│    8:05      Suddenly soft, melody in horns, *p,* oboes and violas continue, *p.*
│  **VARIATION 27**
│    8:18      Woodwind sighs, *p,* accompanied by flowing phrases in strings.
└ **VARIATION 28**
     8:30      High woodwinds, lilting melody, strings accompany, *p.*
┌ **VARIATION 29**
│    8:42      Flute, *p,* rising phrases, pizzicato strings, violins, legato phrase.
└ **VARIATION 30**
     8:55      Suddenly loud, cellos and violins, downward phrase in imitation, crescendo
             timpani rolls, tempo slows.

**CODA**
     9:15      *a.* Brasses and woodwinds, *ff,* theme, faster tempo, woodwinds answered by
               brass chords.
     9:35      *b.* Trombones, *ff,* accelerated ascending theme, staccato, timpani rolls.

*marcato*

     9:43      *c.* Violins, *p,* crescendo.
     9:50      *d.* Woodwinds, *f,* accelerated ascending theme answered by orchestra, *ff.*
     9:57      *e.* Orchestra, *ff,* accelerated ascending theme, powerful ending chords.

# [14] GIUSEPPE VERDI

Giuseppe Verdi (1813–1901), the most popular of all opera composers, was born to a poor family in a tiny Italian village. He began studying music in a nearby town, Busseto, where he was taken into the home of a wealthy patron who later also supported his education in Milan. When he completed his studies, he became municipal music director in Busseto and married his patron's daughter; three years later he returned to Milan with the score of his first opera, *Oberto*.

*Oberto* was produced at La Scala (Milan's opera house) in 1839, had a modest success, and brought Verdi a contract for more operas. Then disaster struck: his wife and their two children died. Verdi managed to complete his next opera, but it was a failure and, in despair, he vowed to compose no more.

What changed his mind was a libretto about the ancient Jews exiled from their homeland. Verdi was an ardent nationalist who yearned for a free and united Italy and saw the Jews as a symbol of the oppressed Italians. He quickly composed *Nabucco* (*Nebuchadnezzar*, king of Babylon, 1842), which was a huge success. From then on, Verdi and his operas came to symbolize Italian independence. (The cry *Viva Verdi* also stood for the patriotic slogan "Vittorio Emmanuele, Re D'Italia"—*Victor Emmanuel, king of Italy.*)

In his late thirties, Verdi composed *Rigoletto* (1851), *Il Trovatore* (1853), and *La Traviata* (1853). Although the public loved them, critics were often scandalized by their subject matter—they seemed to condone rape, suicide, and free love. But Verdi was fiercely independent and himself lived openly with his second wife for ten years before marrying her.

After these successes had made him wealthy, Verdi bought an estate in Busseto; and in 1861 he was elected to the first parliament that convened after Italy had become a nation. In his later years he wrote *Aïda* (1871), *Otello* (1887), and—at the age of seventy-nine—his final opera, *Falstaff* (1893).

## VERDI'S MUSIC

Verdi composed not for the musical elite but for a mass public whose main entertainment was opera. He wanted subjects that were "original, interesting, . . . and passionate; passions above all!" Almost all his mature works are serious and end unhappily; they move quickly and involve extremes of hatred, love, jealousy, and fear, and his powerful music underlines the dramatic situations.

Giuseppe Verdi.

# THE ROMANTIC PERIOD

*The Large Enclosure Near Dresden* (1832), by the German painter Caspar David Friedrich. Romantic sensitivity to nature was revealed in landscape painting, which attained new importance. In Friedrich's landscapes, mystical feelings are often conveyed by a distant horizon.

*Liberty Leading the People* (1830), by Eugène Delacroix. Romantic painters and musicians often saw political revolution as a reflection of their own struggle for artistic freedom. Delacroix combined a realistic description of street fighting in Paris in the July Revolution of 1830 with a symbolic representation of liberty.

*Slave Ship* (1839), by Joseph Turner. In the seascapes of the English painter Turner, the sweep of waves expressed not only the power of nature but human passion as well.

*Third-Class Carriage* (1863–1865), by the French lithographer and painter Honoré Daumier. The industrial revolution caused vast social and economic changes and spurred interest in the poor. Daumier sympathetically portrayed people of the working class in a crowded train compartment.

Expressive vocal melody is the soul of a Verdi opera. There are many duets, trios, and quartets; and the chorus plays an important role. Verdi's style became less conventional as he grew older; his later works have greater musical continuity, less difference between aria and recitative, more imaginative orchestration, and richer accompaniments. His last three operas—*Aïda, Otello,* and *Falstaff*—are perhaps his greatest. *Falstaff,* his final work, is a comic masterpiece which ends with a carefree fugue to the words *All the world's a joke!*

## RIGOLETTO (1851)

Verdi dared to create an operatic hero out of a hunchback, a court jester named Rigoletto, whose only redeeming quality is an intense love for his daughter Gilda. Rigoletto's master, the licentious Duke of Mantua, has won Gilda's love while posing as a poor student. He seduces the innocent girl, causing Rigoletto to plot his death. Gilda loves the Duke even after learning about his dissolute character, and she ultimately sacrifices her own life to save his. Vice triumphs in this powerful drama.

## Act III:
### *La donna è mobile (Woman is fickle)*

Act III of *Rigoletto* contains one of the most famous and popular pieces in opera, the Duke's aria *La donna è mobile.* The scene is an inn where the Duke has come to meet Maddalena, the voluptuous sister of Sparafucile, a cutthroat whom Rigoletto has hired to kill the Duke. *La donna è mobile (Woman is fickle),* carefree and tuneful, expresses the Duke's pleasure-loving personality. Even before the premiere of *Rigoletto,* which was to take place in Venice, Verdi knew this aria would be a hit; so that it would not leak out during rehearsals and be sung by every Venetian gondolier, he waited until the last possible moment before giving the manuscript to the tenor who was to sing it.

Basic sets:
Side 11, band 4
CD 6 [13]

[13] 0:00
Aria. Orchestra introduces Duke's melody.

| | |
|---|---|
| *La donna è mobile* | Woman is fickle |
| *Qual piuma al vento,* | Like a feather in the wind, |
| *Muta d'accento* | She changes her words |
| *E di pensiero.* | And her thoughts. |
| *Sempre un amabile* | Always a lovable |
| *Leggiadro viso,* | And lovely face, |
| *In pianto o in riso,* | Weeping or laughing, |
| *È menzognero.* | Is lying. |
| *La donna è mobile, ecc.* | Woman is fickle, etc. |

| | |
|---|---|
| *È sempre misero* | The man's always wretched |
| *Chi a lei s'affida,* | Who believes in her, |
| *Chi le confida* | Who recklessly entrusts |
| *Mal cauto il core!* | His heart to her! |
| *Pur mai non sentesi* | And yet one who never |
| *Felice appieno* | Drinks love on that breast |
| *Chi su quel seno* | Never feels |
| *Non liba amore!* | Entirely happy! |
| *La donna è mobile, ecc.* | Woman is fickle, etc. |

# [ROMANTIC 15] GIACOMO PUCCINI

Giacomo Puccini (1858–1924), who created some of the best-loved operas, came from a long line of composers and church organists. During his student years at Milan University, he lived a hand-to-mouth existence; but the success of his first opera, shortly after his graduation, brought him commissions and an annual income from Italy's leading music publisher. In 1893, he became known throughout Italy for his opera *Manon Lescaut;* after 1896, he was wealthy and world-famous from the enormous success of *La Bohème. Tosca* (1900) and *Madame Butterfly* (1904) were also very popular; he died before finishing his last opera, *Turandot,* which was completed by a friend.

Puccini's marvelous sense of theater has given his operas lasting appeal. His melodies have short, memorable phrases and are intensely emotional; he used the orchestra to reinforce the vocal melody and to suggest mood. To achieve unity and continuity, he minimized the difference between aria and recitative and used the same material in different acts. Puccini was very much concerned with the literary and dramatic qualities of his librettos; he spent as much time polishing them as composing the music and often demanded endless changes from the librettists. Some of his operas (notably *Tosca*) reflect an artistic trend of the 1890s known as *verismo*—that is, *realism,* or the quality of being "true to life." But they also feature exoticism: *Madame Butterfly* is set in Japan and *Turandot* in China, and both have melodic and rhythmic elements derived from the music of those countries.

## LA BOHÈME (1896)

*La Bohème (Bohemian Life)* takes place in the Latin Quarter of Paris around 1830. Its hero is Rodolfo, a young poet who shares a garret with Marcello, a painter; Colline, a philosopher; and Schaunard, a musician. Mimi, the heroine, is a poor, tubercular seamstress who lives in the same building. The simple, touching plot has been aptly summarized as "boy meets girl, boy loses girl, boy and girl are reunited as girl dies of consumption in boy's arms and curtain falls." Everyone can relate to the characters and emotions of this enchanting opera. Though there are many realistic touches in this picture of bohemian life, it is seen through a romantic haze.

### Act I:

### Scene between Rodolfo and Mimi

Toward the end of Act I, Mimi and Rodolfo meet and fall in love. Her candle has blown out, and she knocks on his door asking for a light. After a short musical conversation, Mimi realizes she has lost her key, and they both search for it in the dark. When their hands touch, Rodolfo sings the aria *Che gelida manina (What a cold little hand)*. He sings about himself, his dreams, and his fantasies. Mimi responds with a poetic description of her simple life in the aria *Mi chiamano Mimì (They call me Mimì)*.

Puccini's sensuous melody casts a glow over the entire scene. His music has an improvisatory quality that is due to the many fluctuations of tempo. When Mimi enters, the orchestra murmurs a touching phrase, Mimi's theme, which suggests her fragility and tenderness. Each of the two arias begins simply, almost in conversation. Then the melody grows warmer until it reaches a climax in a broad, passionate phrase. The climactic phrase of Rodolfo's aria, beginning with the words *Talor dal mio forziere (My hoard of treasure is robbed by two thieves: a pair of beautiful eyes)*, is the love theme of the whole opera. Mimi's emotional high point is reached when she dreams about the end of winter *(Ma quando vien lo sgelo)*, when "the first kiss of April" is hers. Returning to reality at the end of her aria, she sings in conversational repeated tones.

**Brief sets:**
**Side 5, band 1**
**CD 3** [1]

Basic sets:
Side 12, band 1
CD 6 [16]

[1] [16] 0:00
Flute melody.

(Rodolfo closes the door, sets his light on the table, and tries to write. But he tears up the paper and throws the pen down.)

**Rodolfo**

*Non sono in vena.*                I'm not in the mood.

(A timid knock at the door.)

*Chi è la?*                          Who's there?                    Speechlike.

**Mimi**

*Scusi.*                             Excuse me . . .

Ilona Tokodny as Mimi and Dennis O'Neil as Rodolfo in a performance of *La Bohème* at the San Diego Opera.

|  |  |  |
|---|---|---|
|  | **Rodolfo** |  |
|  | *Una donna!* | A woman! |
|  | **Mimi** |  |
| Mimi's theme, *pp*, in orchestra. | *Di grazia, mi si è spento* | I'm sorry . . . my light |
|  | *Il lume.* | Has gone out. |
|  | **Rodolfo** |  |
|  | *Ecco.* | (opens) Here. |
|  | **Mimi** |  |
|  | (in the doorway, with a candlestick and a key) |  |
|  | *Vorrebbe . . .?* | Would you . . .? |
|  | **Rodolfo** |  |
|  | *S'accomodi un momento.* | Come in for a moment. |
|  | **Mimi** |  |
|  | *Non occorre.* | There's no need. |

**Rodolfo**

*La prego, entri.*                Please . . . come in.

(Mimi enters, has a fit of coughing.)

**Rodolfo**

*Si sente male?*                  You're not well?

**Mimi**

*No . . . nulla.*                 No . . . it's nothing.

**Rodolfo**

*Impallidisce!*                   You're pale!

**Mimi**

*È il respir . . . quelle scale . . .*    I'm out of breath . . . the stairs . . .

1:04
Oboe.

(She faints, and Rodolfo is just in time to support her and help her to a chair. The key and the candlestick fall from her hands.)

**Rodolfo**

*Ed ora come faccio?*             Now what shall I do?

(He gets some water and sprinkles her face.)

*Così.*                           So.
*Che viso d'ammalata!*            How ill she looks!

1:28
Staccato muted
strings.

(Mimi comes to.)

*Si sente meglio?*                Are you better now?

**Mimi**

*Sì.*                             Yes.

**Rodolfo**

*Qui c'è tanto freddo.*           It's so cold here.
*Segga vicino al fuoco.*          Come and sit by the fire.

(He helps her to a chair by the stove.)

*Aspetti . . . un po' di vino.*   Wait . . . some wine.

**Mimi**

*Grazie.*                         Thank you.

**Rodolfo**

*A lei.*                          Here.

**Mimi**

*Poco, poco.*                     Just a little.

**Rodolfo**

*Così.*                                           There.

**Mimi**

*Grazie.*                                         Thank you.

**Rodolfo**

*Che bella bambina!*                              What a lovely creature!

**Mimi**

*Ora permetta*                                    Now, please,
*Che accenda il lume.*                            Relight my candle.
*È tutto passato.*                                I'm better now.

**Rodolfo**

*Tanta fretta.*                                   Such a hurry.

**Mimi**

*Sì.*                                             Yes.

(Rodolfo lights her candle for her.)

**Mimi**

*Grazie. Buona sera.*                             Thank you. Good evening.

**Rodolfo**

*Buona sera.*                                     Good evening.

(Mimi goes out, then reappears at the door.)

2:28                        **Mimi**

A little faster.           *Oh! sventata, sventata,*        Oh! foolish me! . . .
Tuneful vocal              *La chiave della stanza*         Where have I left
melody.                    *Dove l'ho lasciata?*            The key to my room?

**Rodolfo**

*Non stia sull'uscio:*                            Don't stand in the door:
*Il lume vacilla al vento.*                       The wind makes your light flicker.

(Her candle goes out.)

**Mimi**

*Oh Dio! Torni ad accenderlo.*                    Heavens! Will you relight it?

(Rodolfo rushes to her with his light, but when he reaches the door, his candle
goes out, too. The room is dark.)

**Rodolfo**

*Oh Dio! Anche il mio s'è spento.*                There . . . Now mine's out, too.

**Mimi**

*Ah! E la chiave ove sarà?*          Ah! And where can my key be?

**Rodolfo**

*Buio pesto!*          Pitch dark!

**Mimi**

*Disgraziata!*          Unlucky me!

**Rodolfo**

*Ove sarà?*          Where can it be?

**Mimi**

*Importuna è la vicina . . .*          You've a bothersome neighbor . . .

**Rodolfo**

*Ma le pare!*          Not at all.

**Mimi**

*Importuna è la vicina . . .*          You've a bothersome neighbor . . .

**Rodolfo**

*Cosa dice, ma le pare!*          What do you mean? Not at all.

**Mimi**

*Cerchi.*          Search.

**Rodolfo**

*Cerco.*          I'm searching.

(They both grope on the floor for the key.)

**Mimi**

*Ove sarà?*          Where can it be?

**Rodolfo**

*Ah!*          Ah! (finds the key, pockets it)

**Mimi**

*L'ha trovata?*          Did you find it?

**Rodolfo**

*No.*          No.

**Mimi**

*Mi parve . . .*          I thought . . .

**Rodolfo**

*In verità!*          Truthfully!

|  | **Mimi** |
|---|---|
| *Cerca?* | Are you hunting? |

|  | **Rodolfo** |
|---|---|
| *Cerco.* | I'm hunting for it. |

3:50
Orchestra alone,
tempo slows.

(Guided by her voice, Rodolfo pretends to search as he draws closer to her. Then his hand meets hers, and he holds it.)

|  | **Mimi** |
|---|---|
| *Ah!* | (Surprised) Ah! |

(They rise. Rodolfo continues to hold Mimi's hand.)

2  17  4:14
Rodolfo's aria.

|  | **Rodolfo** |
|---|---|
| *Che gelida manina,* | What a cold little hand, |
| *Se la lasci riscaldar.* | Let me warm it. |

Harp.

| *Cercar che giova? Al buio* | What's the use of searching? |
|---|---|
| *Non si trova. Ma per fortuna* | We'll never find it now. |
| *È una notte di luna,* | But luckily there's a moon, |
| *E qui la luna l'abbiamo vicina.* | And she's our neighbor here. |
| *Aspetti, signorina,* | Just wait, my dear young lady, |
| *Le dirò con due parole chi son,* | And meanwhile I'll tell you |
| *Chi son, e che faccio, come vivo.* | In a word who and what I am. |
| *Vuole?* | Shall I? |

(Mimi is silent.)

| *Chi son? Chi son? Son un poeta.* | Who am I? I'm a poet. |
|---|---|
| *Che cosa faccio? Scrivo.* | My business? Writing. |
| *E come vivo? Vivo.* | How do I live? I live. |
| *In povertà mia lieta* | In my happy poverty |
| *Scialo da gran signore* | I squander like a prince |
| *Rima ed inni d'amore.* | My poems and songs of love. |
| *Per sogni e per chimere* | In hopes and dreams |
| *E per castelli in aria* | And castles in air, |
| *L'anima ho milionaria.* | I'm a millionaire in spirit. |
| *Talor dal mio forziere* | My hoard of treasure |

6:42
Love theme.

| *Ruban tutti i gioielli* | Is robbed by two thieves: |
|---|---|
| *Due ladri: gli occhi belli.* | A pair of beautiful eyes. |

| | |
|---|---|
| *Ventrar con voi pur ora* | They came in now with you |
| *Ed i miei sogni usati,* | And all my lovely dreams, |
| *Ed i bei sogni miei* | My dreams of the past, |
| *Tosto si dileguar!* | Were soon stolen away. |
| *Ma il furto non m'accora* | But the theft doesn't upset me, |
| *Poichè, poichè v'ha preso stanza* | Since the empty place was filled |
| *La speranza.* | With hope. |
| *Or che mi conoscete* | Now that you know me, |
| *Parlate voi. Deh parlate.* | It's your turn to speak. |
| *Chi siete? Vi piuccia dir?* | Tell me, please, who are you? |

**Mimi**

3 18 8:49
Mimi's aria.

| | |
|---|---|
| *Sì.* | Yes. |
| *Mi chiamano Mimí,* | They call me Mimi, |
| *Ma il mio nome è Lucia.* | But my real name is Lucia. |

| | |
|---|---|
| *La storia mia è breve.* | My story is brief. |
| *A tela o a seta* | I embroider silk and satin |
| *Ricamo in casa e fuori.* | At home or outside. |
| *Son tranquilla e lieta,* | I'm tranquil and happy, |
| *Ed è mio svago* | And my pastime |
| *Far gigli e rose.* | Is making lilies and roses. |
| *Mi piaccion quelle cose* | I love all things |
| *Che han si dolce malia,* | That have a gentle magic, |
| *Che parlano d'amor, di primavere,* | That talk of love, of spring, |
| *Che parlano di sogni e di chimere,* | That talk of dreams and fancies— |
| *Quelle cose che han nome poesia . . .* | The things called poetry . . . |
| *Lei m'intende?* | Do you understand me? |

**Rodolfo**

| | |
|---|---|
| *Sì.* | Yes. |

**Mimi**

| | |
|---|---|
| *Mi chiamano Mimí.* | They call me Mimi— |
| *Il perchè non so.* | I don't know why. |
| *Sola, mi fo il pranzo* | I live all by myself |
| *Da me stessa.* | And I eat all alone. |
| *Non vado sempre a messa,* | I don't often go to church, |
| *Ma prego assai il Signor.* | But I like to pray. |
| *Vivo sola, soletta,* | I stay all alone |
| *Là in una bianca cameretta;* | In my tiny white room, |
| *Guardo sui tetti e in cielo.* | I look at the roofs and the sky. |
| *Ma quando vien lo sgelo* | But when the thaw comes |
| *Il primo sole è mio,* | The first sunshine is mine, |
| *Il primo bacio* | The first kiss |
| *Dell'aprile è mio!* | Of April is mine! |
| *Il primo sole è mio!* | The first sunshine is mine! |
| *Germoglia in un vaso una rosa.* | A rose blossoms in my vase, |
| *Foglia a foglia l'aspiro.* | I breathe in its perfume, |
| *Così gentil è il profumo d'un fior.* | Petal by petal. So lovely, |
| *Ma i fior ch'io faccio, ahimè,* | So sweet is the flower's perfume. |
| *I fior ch'io faccio,* | But the flowers I make, |
| *Ahimè non hanno odore.* | Alas, have no scent. |
| *Altro di me non le saprei narrare.* | What else can I say? |
| *Sono la sua vicina* | I'm your neighbor, |
| *Che la vien fuori d'ora a importunare.* | Disturbing you at this impossible hour. |

## 16 RICHARD WAGNER

ROMANTIC

Few composers have had so powerful an impact on their time as Richard Wagner (1813–1883). His operas and artistic philosophy influenced not only musicians but also poets, painters, and playwrights. Such was his preeminence that an opera house of his own design was built in Bayreuth, Germany, solely for performances of his music dramas.

Wagner was born in Leipzig in a theatrical family. His boyhood dream was to be a poet and playwright, but at fifteen he was overwhelmed by Beethoven's music and decided to become a composer. He taught himself by studying scores, had almost three years of formal training in music theory, but never mastered an instrument. As a student at Leipzig University he dueled, drank, and gambled; and a similar pattern persisted later— he always lived shamelessly off other people and ran up debts he could not repay.

During his early twenties, Wagner conducted in small German theaters and wrote several operas. In 1839, he decided to try his luck in Paris, then the center of grand opera; he and his wife spent two miserable years there, during which he was unable to get an opera performed and was reduced to musical hackwork. But he returned to Germany in 1842 for the production of his opera *Rienzi* in Dresden; the work was immensely successful, and he was appointed conductor of the Dresden Opera. Wagner spent six years at this post, becoming famous as both an opera composer and a conductor.

When the revolutions of 1848 were sweeping across Europe, Wagner's life in Dresden had become difficult because of accumulated debts. Hoping that a new society would wipe these out and produce conditions favorable to his art, he participated in an insurrection and then had to flee to Switzerland. For several years he did no composing; instead, he worked out his theories of art in several essays and completed the librettos to *Der Ring des Nibelungen (The Ring of the Nibelung)*, a set of four operas based on Nordic myth which would occupy him for twenty-five years. He interrupted his work on the music for *The Ring* to compose *Tristan and Isolde* (1857–1859).

Wagner had several bad years after finishing *Tristan*. His opera *Tannhäuser* was a failure at the Paris Opera; *Tristan* was abandoned by the Vienna Opera; and he was hounded by creditors. In 1864, however, he was rescued by King Ludwig of Bavaria, an eighteen-year-old fanatical Wagnerite who put all the resources of the Munich Opera at his disposal. At this time, Wagner fell in love with Cosima von Bülow, who was Liszt's daughter and the wife of Hans von Bülow, Wagner's close friend and favorite conductor; she gave birth to two of Wagner's children while still married to von Bülow. Shortly after Wagner's first wife died, he married Cosima.

In Wagner, musical genius was allied with selfishness, ruthlessness, rabid German nationalism, and absolute self-conviction. He forged an audience for his complex music dramas from a public accustomed to conventional opera. The performance of the *Ring* cycle at Bayreuth in 1876 was perhaps the single most important musical event of the century; and—though some critics still found his music too dissonant, heavily orchestrated, and long-winded—he was generally acclaimed the greatest composer of his time. A year after completing *Parsifal* (1877–1882), his last opera, he died in Venice at age sixty-nine.

Richard Wagner.

## WAGNER'S MUSIC

For Wagner, an opera house was a temple in which the spectator was to be overwhelmed by music and drama. He wrote his own librettos, based on medieval Germanic legends and myths and with characters that are usually larger than life—heroes, gods, demigods. He called his works *music dramas* rather than operas, but today many people find his music more exciting than his rather static drama.

Within each act, there is a continuous musical flow (Wagner called this "unending melody") instead of traditional arias, recitatives, and ensembles, and there are no breaks where applause can interrupt. His vocal line, which he conceived as "speech song," is inspired by the rhythms and pitches of the German text. Wagner revolutionized opera by shifting the focus from voice to orchestra and treating the orchestra symphonically. His expanded and colorful orchestration expresses the drama and constantly develops, transforms, and intertwines musical ideas. (And the orchestral sound is so full that only very powerful voices can cut through it.) In the orchestra—and sometimes in the vocal parts—he uses brief, recurrent musical themes called *leitmotifs* (*leading motives*). A **leitmotif** is a short musical idea associated with a person, an object, or a thought in the drama.

The tension of Wagner's music is heightened by chromatic and dissonant harmonies—ultimately, these led to the breakdown of tonality and to the new musical language of the twentieth century.

## DIE WALKÜRE (THE VALKYRIE; 1856)

*Die Walküre (The Valkyrie)* is the second and most widely performed of the four music dramas in Wagner's gigantic cycle *Der Ring des Nibelungen (The Ring of the Nibelung)*. Despite its gods, giants, dwarfs (the Nibelungs), and magic fire, the *Ring* is really about Wagner's view of nineteenth-century society. He uses Nordic mythology to warn that society destroys itself through lust for money and power. It is fitting that Wagner first sketched the plot of the *Ring* in 1848, the year that brought Marx's *Communist Manifesto* and revolutions throughout Europe.

### Act I:

### Love scene (conclusion)

**Brief sets:**
**Side 5, band 2**
**CD 3** 4

Basic sets:
Side 12, band 2
CD 6 20

Wagner builds the first act of *Die Walküre* to an overwhelming climax in the passionate love scene which concludes it. To grasp this scene fully, it's helpful to know what has happened earlier in *The Ring*.

A Nibelung dwarf, Alberich, has stolen gold belonging to the Rhinemaidens, mermaids in the Rhine River. From this gold, the dwarf fashions a ring that can bestow immense power on anyone who wears it and is willing to renounce love. The dwarf, in turn, is robbed of his prize by the king of the gods, Wotan (*Wednesday* comes from *Wotan's day*.) Soon Wotan himself is forced to give up the ring; he then lives in fear that Alberich will get it back and use it to destroy him. Hoping to protect himself, he surrounds his castle, Valhalla, with a bodyguard of heroes. His daughters, goddesses called *Valkyries*, swoop over battlefields on horseback and bear away the dead bodies of the bravest warriors. The Valkyrie of the opera's title is Brünnhilde, Wotan's favorite daughter.

Seeking to create a hero who can help him regain the ring, Wotan takes a human wife and fathers the Volsung twins—a son, Siegmund; and a daughter, Sieglinde. The twins know their father as Wälse, unaware that he is the god Wotan. They are separated as children when a hostile clan kidnaps Sieglinde and kills their mother. Siegmund becomes an outlaw and Sieglinde is eventually forced to marry the warrior-chief Hunding, whom she hates. During the wedding feast in Hunding's home, Wotan appears, disguised as an old man dressed in gray. He thrusts a magic sword into the tree around which the house is built, and proclaims that the weapon belongs to the one who can draw it out. Hunding and his followers try but are unable to withdraw the sword.

The first act of *Die Walküre* begins as Siegmund, weaponless and pursued by enemies, unwittingly takes refuge in the house of Hunding, who is away hunting. Sieglinde and Siegmund almost immediately fall in love, unaware that they are brother and sister. Hunding returns and soon realizes that the stranger—who identifies himself as *Wehwalt (Woeful)*—is an enemy of his clan. He says that Siegmund is his guest for the night, but the next day they must do battle. Sieglinde gives her husband a sleeping potion and tells Siegmund that her shame and misery will be avenged by the hero who can withdraw the sword from the tree. As they embrace passionately, the door of the hut suddenly opens, allowing the moonlight of a beautiful spring night to shine upon them.

The following excerpt occurs at the end of the love scene, when Siegmund and Sieglinde gradually become aware of their amazing resemblance to each other and finally realize that they are brother and sister. Since her beloved no longer wants to be called *Wehwalt*, Sieglinde renames him *Siegmund (Victor)*. With a powerful effort, Siegmund withdraws the sword from the tree and the lovers rapturously embrace. (The offspring of this unlawful union will be Siegfried, the human hero of the *Ring* cycle. In the mythology and folklore of many lands, heros are often born of incestuous love.)

In the excerpt which we'll study, Wagner creates a continuous musical flow that depicts the surging passions of the lovers through frequent changes of tempo, dynamics, and orchestral color. Typically, the vocal lines range from speechlike to highly melodic and closely reflect the inflections and meaning of the text. For example, the word *Notung (Needful)*—the name of the sword—is powerfully emphasized when it is sung to the downward leap of an octave.

Several leitmotifs are heard, sometimes together. In this excerpt, the leitmotif *Valhalla*—Wotan's castle—is first presented when Sieglinde looks at Siegmund and later returns when she recalls how their father (Wotan disguised as the old man) gazed at her during her marriage feast. The very important *Sword* leitmotif is barely noticeable when it first appears, as Sieglinde refers to the fire in Siegmund's eyes. It is presented *pp*, in combination with the leitmotif *Volsung* (the people to which Siegmund and Sieglinde belong). Later, the sword motive is very prominent when it is proclaimed by the brasses as Siegmund draws the sword out of the tree and as the lovers embrace during the orchestral conclusion of the act. Other leitmotifs heard in our excerpt are *love* and *spring*.

(Sieglinde pushes Siegmund's hair back from his brow and looks at him with astonishment.)

### Sieglinde

| | |
|---|---|
| **4** **20** 0:00 |  |

*Wie dir die Stirn so offen steht,*      Look how your forehead broadens out,

*der Adern Geäst in den Schläfen sich schlingt!*      and the network of veins winds into your temples.

*Mir zagt es vor der Wonne, die mich entzückt!*      I tremble with the delight that enchants me.

**5** **21** 0:20
*Valhalla*, French horns, *p*.

*Ein Wunder will mich gemahen:*      It brings something strange to my mind:

*den heut zuerst ich erschaut,*      though I first saw you today,
*mein Auge sah dich schon!*      I've set eyes on you before.

### Siegmund

*Ein Minnetraum gemahnt auch mich:*      A dream of love comes to my mind as well:

*in heissem Sehnen sah ich dich schon!*      burning with longing I have seen you before.

### Sieglinde

*Im ·Bach erblick' ich mein eigen Bild*      In the stream I've seen my own likeness;

*und jetzt gewahr ich es wieder:*      and now I see it again.
*wie einst dem Teich es enttaucht,*      As once it appeared in the water
*bietest mein Bild mir nun du!*      so now you show me my likeness.

**Siegmund**

*Du bist das Bild, das ich in mir barg.*

You are the likeness that I hid in myself.

6 22 1:26
*Love*, voice.

Love

Du      bist      das      Bild

**Sieglinde**

*O still! Lass mich der Stimme lauschen:*
*mich dünkt, ihren Klang hört' ich als Kind.*
*Doch nein! Ich hörte sie neulich,*
*als meiner Stimme Schall*
*mir widerhallte der Wald.*

Hush! let me listen to your voice.
Its sound, I fancy, I heard as a child,

but no! I heard it recently—
when the echo of my voice sounded
back through the forest.

*Love*, French horn, *p*.

**Siegmund**

*O lieblichste Laute, denen ich lauschte!*

O loveliest sound for me to hear!

Volsung

*pp*

Sword

7 23 2:19
*Volsung*, low strings, *pp*, together with *Sword*, bass trumpet, *pp*.

**Sieglinde**

*Deines Auges Glut erglänzte mir schon:*

The fire in your eyes has blazed at me before,

*so blickte der Greis grüssend auf mich,*

So the old man gazed at me in greeting

*als der Traurigen Trost er gab.*

when to my sadness he brought comfort.

*An dem Blick erkannt' ihn sein Kind,*
*schon wollt' ich beim Namen ihn nennen!*

By his look his child recognized him,
I even wanted to call him by name.

*Wehwalt heisst du fürwahr?*

Are you really called Woeful?

2.28
*Valhalla*, French horns, *pp*, then strings, *pp*.

Pause.

**Siegmund**

*Nicht heiss ich so, seit du mich liebst:*

I am not called that since you love me:

*nun walt ich der hehrsten Wonnen!*

Now I am full of purest rapture.

245

### Sieglinde

*Und Friedmund darfst du froh dich nicht nennen?*

And "Peaceful" may you not, being happy, be named?

### Siegmund

*Nenne mich du, wie du liebst, dass ich heisse:*
*den Namen nehm ich von dir!*

Name me what you love to call me.

I take my name from you.

### Sieglinde

*Doch nanntest du Wolfe den Vater?*

But did you name Wolf as your father?

### Siegmund

*Ein Wolf war er feigen Füchsen!*
*Doch dem so stolz strahlte das Auge,*
*wie, Herrliche, hehr dir es strahlt,*
*der war: Wälse genannt.*

A Wolf he was to craven foxes!
But he whose proud eyes shone
as grandly as yours, you marvel,
his name was "Volsa."

### Sieglinde

*War Wälse dein Vater, und bist du ein Wälsung,*
*stiess er für dich sein Schwert in den Stamm,*
*so lass mich dich heissen, wie ich dich liebe:*
*Siegmund: so nenn ich dich!*

If "Volsa" was your father and you are a "Volsung,"
it was for you he thrust his sword in the tree—
so let me call you by the name I love:
Siegmund (Victor)—so I name you.

### Siegmund

*Siegmund heiss ich und Siegmund bin ich!*
*Bezeug es dies Schwert, das zaglos ich halte!*
*Wälse verhiess mir, in höchster Not*

*fänd' ich es einst: ich fass en nun!*

Siegmund I am called and Siegmund I am,
let this sword, which I fearlessly hold, bear witness.
Volsa promised me that in deepest distress

I should one day find it. Now I grasp it.

4:47

*Heiligster Minne höchste Not,*
*sehnender Liebe sehrende Not*
*brennt mir hell in der Brust,*
*drängt zu Tat und Tod:*

Holiest love's deepest distress,
yearning love's scorching desire,
burn bright in my breast,
urge me to deeds and death.

**8** **24** 5:13
Voice, downward
octave leaps.

*Notung! Notung! so nenn ich dich,*

"Needy," "Needy," I name you,

*Schwert.*
*Notung, Notung! neidlicher Stahl!*
*Zeig deiner Schärfe schneidenden Zahn:*

*heraus aus der Scheide zu mir!*

sword.
"Needy," "Needy," precious blade,
show your sharpness and cutting edge:

come from your scabbard to me!

(With a powerful effort, Siegmund pulls the sword from the tree, showing it to the astonished and delighted Sieglinde.)

9 25 5:42
*Sword*, trumpets, *ff.*

Sword
*ff*

| | |
|---|---|
| *Siegmund, den Wälsung, siehst du, Weib!* | You see Siegmund, the Volsung, woman! |
| *Als Brautgabe bringt er dies Schwert: so freit er sich die seligste Frau; dem Feindeshaus entführt er dich so.* | As wedding gift he brings this sword; so he weds the fairest of women; he takes you away from the enemy's house. |
| *Fern von hier folge mir nun,* | Now follow me far from here, |
| *fort in des Lenzes lachendes Haus:* | out into springtime's smiling house. |

6:00
*Volsung*, trumpets, *pp.*

10 26 6:29
*Spring*, voice.

fort in des Len - zes la - chen-des Haus;

| | |
|---|---|
| *dort schützt dich Notung, das Schwert,* | For protection you'll have "Needy" the sword, |
| *wenn Siegmund dir liebend erlag!* | even if Siegmund expires with love. |

**Sieglinde**

| | |
|---|---|
| *Bist du Siegmund, den ich hier sehe, Sieglinde bin ich, die dich ersehnt: die eigne Schwester gewannst du zu eins mit dem Schwert!* | Are you Siegmund whom I see here? I am Sieglinde who longed for you: your own sister you have won and the sword as well. |

**Siegmund**

| | |
|---|---|
| *Braut und Schwester bist du dem Bruder, so blühe denn Wälsungen-Blut!* | Wife and sister you'll be to your brother. So let the Volsung blood increase. |

(He draws her to him with passionate fervor.)

11 27 7:29
*Sword*, brasses, *ff.*
Passionate
orchestral
conclusion.

# THE TWENTIETH CENTURY

## VI

Twentieth-century painters distorted human figures and objects with extraordinary daring. In *The Juggler*, by Marc Chagall, a man with wings and a bird's head holds a clock case bent into a semicircle.

# [ 1 ] MUSICAL STYLES: 1900–1950

The years 1900 to 1913 brought radical new developments in science and art. During this period preceding World War I, discoveries were made that overturned long-held beliefs. Sigmund Freud explored the unconscious and developed psychoanalysis, and Albert Einstein revolutionized the view of the universe with his theory of relativity. Pablo Picasso's painting and sculpture distorted human figures and objects with unprecedented daring, showing them from several angles at once; Wassily Kandinsky's abstract paintings no longer tried to represent the visual world at all.

In music, too, the early twentieth century was a time of revolt. The years following 1900 saw more fundamental changes in the language of music than any time since the beginning of the baroque era. There were entirely new approaches to the organization of pitch and rhythm and a vast expansion in the vocabulary of sounds, especially percussive sounds. Some compositions broke with tradition so sharply that they were met with violent hostility. The most famous riot in music history occurred in Paris on May 29, 1913, at the premiere of Igor Stravinsky's ballet *Le Sacre du printemps (The Rite of Spring)*. Police had to be called in as hecklers booed, laughed, made animal noises, and actually fought with audience members who wanted to hear Stravinsky's evocation of primitive rites. One music critic complained that *The Rite of Spring* produced the "sensation of acute and almost cruel dissonance" and that "from the first measure to the last, whatever note one expects is never the one that comes." Another wrote, "To say that much of it is hideous in sound is a mild description. It has no relation to music at all as most of us understand the word."

Today, we are amused by the initial failure of some music critics to understand this composition, now recognized as a masterpiece. Chords, rhythms, and percussive sounds that were baffling in 1913 are now commonly heard in jazz, rock, and music for movies and television. But the hostile critics of the early 1900s were right in seeing that a great transformation in musical language was taking place.

From the late 1600s to about 1900, musical structure was governed by certain general principles. As different as the works of Bach, Beethoven, and Brahms may be, they share fundamental techniques of organizing pitches around a central tone. After 1900, however, no single system has governed the organization of pitch in all musical compositions. Each piece is more likely to have a system of pitch relationships unique to itself.

In the past, composers depended on the listener's awareness—conscious or unconscious—of the general principles underlying the interrelationship of tones and chords. For example, they relied on the listener's expectation that a dominant chord would normally be followed by a tonic chord. By substituting another chord for the expected one, a composer

(Collection, Museum of Modern Art, New York. Mrs. Simon Guggenheim Fund; oil on canvas, 6 feet 7 inches by 7 feet 3¾ inches)

*Three Musicians* (1921), by Pablo Picasso. In this cubist painting, the musicians and their instruments are flattened into planes. The year before he painted *Three Musicians*, Picasso had designed the costumes for *Pulcinella*, a ballet by his friend Igor Stravinsky. Picasso's portrait of Stravinsky is shown on page 268.

could create a feeling of suspense, drama, or surprise. Twentieth-century music relies less on preestablished relationships and expectations. Listeners are guided primarily by musical cues within an individual composition. This new approach to the organization of sound makes twentieth-century music fascinating. When we listen openly, with no assumptions about how tones "should" relate, modern music is an adventure.

## 1900–1950: AN AGE OF MUSICAL DIVERSITY

The range of musical styles during the first half of the twentieth century was vast. The stylistic diversity in the works of Claude Debussy, Igor Stravinsky, Arnold Schoenberg, Alban Berg, Anton Webern, Béla Bartók, Charles Ives, George Gershwin, and Aaron Copland—to name only the composers studied here—is a continuation and an intensification of the diversity of romantic music. Not only do twentieth-century composers seem to be using different languages, but radical changes of style occur even within the works of individual composers.

Such great variety of musical styles reflected the diversity of modern life and an expansion of musical sources. Through the work of scholars and performers, a wider range of music became available, and composers drew inspiration from folk and popular music, Asian and African music, and European art music from the Middle Ages through the nineteenth century.

Composers were especially attracted to unconventional rhythms, sounds, and melodic patterns in folk and popular music. Folk music was studied more systematically than before, partly because scholars could now record peasant songs; and one of the greatest twentieth-century composers, Béla Bartók, was also a leading authority on peasant music. Bartók's imagination was fired by the music of his native Hungary and other parts of eastern Europe; he considered it "the ideal starting point for a musical renaissance." Igor Stravinsky drew on Russian folk songs; Charles Ives used American revival hymns, ragtime, and patriotic songs.

Non-European music was also an important influence. Western composers were more receptive and sympathetic to Asian and African cultures than they had been earlier. Echoes of the gamelan—the Indonesian orchestra—can be heard in some of Debussy's works; and the novel rhythmic procedures of another Frenchman, Olivier Messiaen (1908–1992) grew out of his study of Indian music.

Another non-European influence was American jazz; musicians were fascinated by its syncopated rhythms, improvisational quality, and unique tone colors (unlike a string-dominated symphony orchestra, a jazz band emphasizes woodwinds, brasses, and percussion). Jazz elements were used as early as 1908 by Debussy (in *Golliwogg's Cakewalk* from the suite *Children's Corner*) and 1918 by Stravinsky (in *The Soldier's Tale*), but the influence of jazz peaked during the "jazz age" of the 1920s. For American composers, jazz represented a kind of musical nationalism, the search for an "American sound"; for Europeans, it represented musical exoticism. During the 1920s and 1930s, composers such as George Gershwin used jazz and popular elements within "classical" forms.

Modern composers could also draw inspiration from a wider historical range of music. During the twentieth century, music from remote times has been unearthed by scholars, published, performed, and recorded. Early masters have been rediscovered—for example, Perotin and Machaut from the medieval period, Josquin Desprez and Gesualdo from the Renaissance, and Purcell and Vivaldi from the baroque. And some important modern composers have been music historians (like Anton Webern) or performers of early music (like Paul Hindemith). Music from the past has been a fruitful source of forms, rhythms, tone colors, textures, and compositional techniques. Baroque dances, and forms like the passacaglia and concerto grosso, are being used again; and the long-forgotten harpsichord has been put to new use in works such as Ellen Taaffe Zwilich's *Concerto Grosso 1985*, which we'll study. Occasionally, modern composers use themes of earlier composers—Benjamin Britten (English, 1913–1976) based his *Young Person's Guide to the Orchestra* on a theme by Henry Purcell (about 1659–1695).

Supplementary sets:
Side 1, band 1
CD 1 1

However, all this does not imply that past styles are simply imitated: they are used with harmonies, rhythms, melodies, and tone colors that would have been inconceivable before the twentieth century.

Modern composers were also influenced by the music of the immediate past. Wagner, especially, was as potent an influence as Beethoven had been for the romantics; composers took Wagner's style as a point of departure or else reacted violently against all he stood for.

In addition, of course, composers have been affected by technological and social trends. For example, the twentieth century has seen dramatic changes in how music reaches its listeners: radio, television, and recordings have brought music to a much larger audience and vastly increased the amount and scope of music available. More women have been active as composers, music educators, virtuoso soloists, orchestra musicians, and conductors. Another trend is the vital role of American colleges and universities in our musical culture. They have reached countless students through music courses, housed most of the electronic studios, sponsored many performing groups, and trained and employed many composers, performers, and scholars. Thus, colleges and universities have indirectly become patrons of music, as the church and the aristocracy once were.

Finally, there has been a very significant change in the musical tastes of audiences. In the twentieth century, the concert and operatic repertory has been dominated by music from the past. This is a new situation in music history: before the nineteenth century, audiences demanded and got the latest music; and even during the romantic period, when interest in earlier music was high, concert programs consisted mainly of recent works. After 1900, however, listeners and performers were often baffled by the dissonances, percussive sounds, and irregular rhythms of some new music; conductors therefore tended to rely on traditional music and to favor contemporary works that were relatively accessible in style. During the 1950s and 1960s, more effort was made by individuals and organizations to present contemporary music, and to commission it. Yet few serious composers can live on commissions alone; most composers today are also teachers, conductors, or performers.

# CHARACTERISTICS OF TWENTIETH-CENTURY MUSIC

## Tone Color

During the twentieth century, tone color has become a more important element of music than it ever was before. It often has a major role, creating variety, continuity, and mood. In Webern's Orchestral Piece, Op. 10, No. 3 (1913), for example, the use of eerie, bell-like sounds at the beginning and end is vital to the form. If this composition were altered in tone color by being played on a piano, it would lose much. An orchestral work from an earlier period—say, Beethoven's Fifth Symphony—suffers less in a piano arrangement.

In modern music, noiselike and percussive sounds are often used, and instruments are often played at the very top or bottom of their ranges. Uncommon playing techniques have become normal. For example, the *glissando,* a rapid slide up or down a scale, is more widely used. Woodwind and brass players are often asked to produce a fluttery sound by rapidly rolling their tongues while they play. And string players frequently strike the strings with the stick of the bow, rather than draw the bow across the strings.

Percussion instruments have become prominent and numerous, reflecting the twentieth-century interest in unusual rhythms and tone colors. Instruments that have become standard during the 1900s include the xylophone, celesta, and wood block, to name a few. Composers occasionally call for noisemakers—typewriters, sirens, and automobile brake drums. A piano is often used to add a percussive edge to the sound of an orchestra. Modern composers often draw hard, drumlike sounds from the piano, in contrast to the romantics, who wanted the instrument to "sing." Besides expanding the percussion section of the orchestra, early twentieth-century composers wrote works for unconventional performing groups in which percussion plays a major role. Well-known examples are Stravinsky's *Les Noces* (*The Wedding,* 1914–1923), for vocal soloists, chorus, four pianos, and percussion; Bartók's Music for Strings, Percussion, and Celesta (1936); and Varèse's *Ionisation* (1931), which was one of the first works for percussion ensemble.

Modern orchestral and chamber works often sound transparent; individual tone colors are heard clearly. To bring out the individuality of different melodic lines that are played simultaneously, a composer will often assign each line to a different timbre. In general, there is less emphasis on blended sound than during the romantic period. Many twentieth-century works are written for nonstandard chamber groups made up of instruments with sharply contrasting tone colors. Stravinsky's *L'Histoire du soldat* (*The Soldier's Tale,* 1918), for example, is scored for violin, double bass, clarinet, bassoon, cornet, trombone, and percussion. Even orchestral works often sound as though they are scored for a group of soloists.

## Harmony

### Consonance and dissonance

The twentieth century brought fundamental changes in the way chords are treated. Up to about 1900, chords were divided into two opposing types: consonant and dissonant. A consonant chord was stable; it functioned as a point of rest or arrival. A dissonant chord was unstable; its tension demanded onward motion, or resolution to a stable, consonant chord. Traditionally, only the triad, a three-tone chord, could be consonant. All others were considered dissonant. In the nineteenth century, composers came to use ever more dissonant chords, and they treated dissonances with increasing freedom. By the early twentieth century, the traditional distinction between consonance and dissonance was abandoned in much music. A combination of tones that earlier would have been used to generate instability and expectation might now be treated as a stable chord, a point of arrival. In Stravinsky's words, dissonance "is no longer tied down to its former function. Having become an entity in itself, it frequently happens that dissonance neither prepares nor anticipates anything. Dissonance is thus no more an agent of disorder than consonance is a guarantee of security."

This "emancipation of the dissonance" does not prevent composers from differentiating between chords of greater or lesser tension. Relatively mild-sounding chords may be goals of motion, while harsher chords are used for transitional sounds. But no longer is there a general principle that determines whether a chord is stable or not. It is now entirely up to the composer's discretion. "We find ourself confronted with a new logic of music that would have appeared unthinkable to the masters of the past," wrote Stravinsky. "This new logic has opened our eyes to riches whose existence we never suspected."

### New chord structures

Before 1900, there were general principles governing chord construction: certain combinations of tones were considered chords, while others were not. At the core of traditional harmony is the triad. A triad might be made up of alternate tones of a major scale, such as the first *(do)*, third *(mi)*, and fifth *(sol)*. Within a triad, there are two intervals of a third, as in the following example:

Although the triad often appears in twentieth-century music, it no longer is so fundamental.

Some twentieth-century composers create fresh harmonies by placing one traditional chord against another. Such a combination of two chords heard at the same time is called a *polychord.*

Copland, *Appalachian Spring*

A polychord can be heard either as a single block of sound or as two distinct layers, depending on whether the two combined chords contrast in tone color and register.

Another development in twentieth-century music is the use of chordal structures *not* based on triads. One used commonly is the *fourth chord,* in which the tones are a fourth apart, instead of a third. (From *do* to *fa,* or from *re* to *sol,* is an interval of a fourth.)

Ives, *The Cage*

Harmonic resources have also been extended through the *tone cluster,* a chord made up of tones only a half step or a whole step apart. A tone cluster can be produced on a piano by striking a group of adjacent keys with the fist or forearm.

Ives, *The Majority*

## Alternatives to the Traditional Tonal System

Twentieth-century composers also explored alternatives to tonality, which had governed the organization of pitch since the 1600s. After 1900, the traditional tonal system was modified in many different ways, and some composers discarded it entirely. The new techniques of pitch organization are so varied as to resist easy generalization.

Some compositions have a central tone but are missing other traditional elements, such as the central major or minor scale, the tonic triad, or the dominant-tonic relationship. For instance, Stravinsky's *Serenade in A,* as its title suggests, revolves around the tone A but is not in a major or minor key; and some composers have used the ancient church modes, or scales borrowed from nonwestern countries, or scales they themselves invented. Twentieth-century pieces are often organized around a central chord other than the triad, and this basic chord may well be one that was considered a dissonance earlier. Melodies, sections, and entire compositions are rounded off not by a dominant-tonic cadence but by other chord progressions.

Another twentieth-century approach to pitch organization is *polytonality,* the use of two or more keys at one time. When only two different keys are used at once—as is most common—the technique is called *bitonality.* A famous bitonal passage occurs in Stravinsky's ballet *Petrushka,* when one clarinet plays in C major and another plays in F sharp major:

In general, the greater the contrast of tone color, register, and rhythm between the different layers of sound, the more we can hear the different keys.

A further departure from tradition is *atonality,* the absence of tonality or key. Atonality was foreshadowed in nineteenth-century works such as Wagner's *Tristan and Isolde,* where the pull of a central key is weakened by frequent modulations and by liberal use of all twelve tones in the chromatic scale. Arnold Schoenberg wrote the first significant atonal pieces around 1908. He avoided traditional chord progressions in these works and used all twelve tones without regard to their traditional relationship to major or minor scales. But atonality is not a specific technique of composition; each atonal work is structured according to its own needs. (Though the word *atonality* is imprecise and negative, no other term has yet come into general use.)

Before long, Schoenberg felt the need for a more systematic approach to atonal composition, and during the early 1920s he developed the *twelve-tone system,* a new technique of pitch organization. This system gives equal prominence to each of the twelve chromatic tones, rather than singling out one pitch as the tonal system does. For about twenty years, only Schoenberg and a few disciples used the twelve-tone system, but during the 1950s it came to be used by composers all over the world.

## Rhythm

The new techniques of pitch organization were accompanied by new ways to organize rhythm. The rhythmic vocabulary of music was expanded, with increased emphasis on irregularity and unpredictability. Rhythm is one of the most striking elements of twentieth-century music; it is used to generate power, drive, and excitement.

In the twentieth century, new rhythmic procedures are drawn from many sources, including folk music from all over the world, jazz, and European art music from the Middle Ages through the nineteenth century. Béla Bartók used the "free and varied rhythmic structures" of east European peasant music. The syncopations and complex rhythmic combinations of jazz fired the imagination of Stravinsky and Copland. And irregular phrase structures in Brahms's music inspired rhythmic innovations in Schoenberg's works.

Rapidly changing meters are characteristic of twentieth-century music, whereas baroque, classical, or romantic music maintains a single meter throughout a movement or section. Before the twentieth century, beats were organized into regularly recurring groups; the accented beat came at equal time intervals. Rhythmic irregularities such as syncopations or accents on weak beats were heard against a pervasive meter. But in many twentieth-century compositions, beats are grouped irregularly, and the accented beat comes at unequal time intervals. In some modern music the meter changes with almost every bar, so that we might count *1–2–3, 1–2–3–4–5, 1–2–3–4–5, 1–2–3, 1–2–3–4, 1–2–3–4–5, 1–2–3–4–5–6, 1–2–3–4–5, 1–2, 1–2–3–4–5–6:*

*Stravinsky, Ritual of Abduction from The Rite of Spring*

**Brief sets:**
**Side 5, band 4**
**CD 3** [26] **7:13**

Basic sets:
Side 12, band 3
CD 6 [35] 7:13

Count this again quickly to experience some of the rhythmic excitement of twentieth-century music, which often has a rapid and vigorous beat with jolting accents at unexpected times.

The rhythmic resources of twentieth-century music have also been expanded through the use of unconventional meters. Along with traditional meters such as duple and triple, modern composers use meters with five or seven beats to the measure. The pulses within a measure of any length may be grouped in irregular, asymmetrical ways. For example, eight quick pulses within a measure may be subdivided 3 + 3 + 2, or **1**–2–3–**4**–5–6–**7**–8, **1**–2–3–**4**–5–6–**7**–8. This meter, common in east European folk music, is used by Bartók in one of his *Six Dances in Bulgarian Rhythm.*

Twentieth-century music often uses two or more contrasting and independent rhythms at the same time, a procedure called **polyrhythm.** Each part of the musical texture goes its own rhythmic way, often creating accents that are out of phase with accents in the other parts. Different meters are used at the same time. For example, one instrument may play in duple meter (*1–2, 1–2*) while another plays in triple meter (*1–2–3, 1–2–3*). Although polyrhythm occasionally occurs in classical and romantic music, it became both more common and more complex after 1900. The polyrhythms of jazz strongly influenced composers in the 1920s and 1930s.

Rhythmic repetition of a group of pitches is a widely used unifying technique in twentieth-century music. Many modern compositions contain an *ostinato,* a motive or phrase that is repeated persistently at the same pitch throughout a section. The ostinato may occur in the melody or in the accompaniment. (The accompaniment for the above example from Bartók has an eight-note ostinato: **1**–2–3–**4**–5–6–**7**–8.) Ostinatos can be found in music from various periods and cultures. In twentieth-century music, they usually serve to stabilize particular groups of pitches.

## Melody

The new techniques of pitch and rhythmic organization had a strong impact on twentieth-century melody. Melody is no longer necessarily tied to traditional chords or major and minor keys. It may be based on a wide variety of scales, or may freely use all twelve chromatic tones and have no tonal center. Melody today often contains wide leaps that are difficult to sing. Rhythmic irregularity and changing meters tend to make twentieth-century melodies unpredictable. They often consist of a series of phrases that are irregular in length. In general, twentieth-century music relies less than classical and romantic music on melodies that are easy to sing and remember. Melody is as rich and varied as twentieth-century music itself; neither can be classified easily.

(Metropolitan Museum of Art, New York, H. O. Havemeyer Collection, bequest of Mrs. H. O. Havemeyer, 1929)

*La Grenouillère* (1869), by Claude Monet. Impressionist painters were concerned primarily with effects of light, color, and atmosphere.

# [ 2 ] IMPRESSIONISM AND SYMBOLISM

Many musical styles coexisted around the turn of the century. Among the most important was impressionism, best represented by the music of the French composer Claude Debussy (1862–1918). Musical impressionism is related to two slightly earlier artistic movements in France, which were catalysts for many developments during the twentieth century: impressionist painting and symbolist poetry.

In 1874, a group of French painters including Claude Monet (1840–1926), Auguste Renoir (1841–1919), and Camille Pissarro (1830–1903) had an exhibition in Paris. One Monet painting entitled *Impression: Sunrise* particularly annoyed an art critic, who mockingly called the entire show "the exhibition of the impressionists." The term *impressionist* stuck, but it eventually lost its derisive implication.

Today, most of us appreciate impressionist paintings, but during the 1870s they were seen as formless collections of tiny colored patches—which they are, when viewed closely, though from a distance the brush strokes become recognizable forms and shimmering colors. Impressionist painters were concerned primarily with effects of light, color, and atmosphere—with impermanence, change, and fluidity. Many of them worked outdoors rather than in a studio; they were fascinated by outdoor scenes from contemporary life (picnics in the woods, crowds on Parisian boulevards) and—most of all—by water. Using light, pastel colors, they depicted the ripples and waves of the ocean and the river Seine.

As the impressionists broke away from traditional techniques of painting, writers called *symbolists* rebelled against the conventions of French poetry. Like the painters, poets such as Stéphane Mallarmé (1842–1898), Paul Verlaine (1844–1896), and Arthur Rimbaud (1854–1891) emphasized fluidity, suggestion, and the purely musical, or sonorous, effects of words. Claude Debussy was a close friend of several symbolist poets; many of Verlaine's poems became texts for his songs, and Mallarmé's poem *L'Après-midi d'un faune (The Afternoon of a Faun)* inspired his most famous orchestral work.

# CLAUDE DEBUSSY

TWENTIETH CENTURY

3

The French impressionist composer Claude Debussy (1862–1918) linked the romantic era with the twentieth century. From the early age of ten until he was twenty-two he studied at the Paris Conservatory, where his teachers regarded him as a talented rebel. In 1884 he won the prestigious Prix de Rome, which subsidized three years of study in Rome; but he left after two years because he lacked musical inspiration away from his beloved Paris.

Influences on Debussy's work included several visits to Russia, where he worked as a pianist for Tchaikovsky's patroness, Nadezhda von Meck, and formed a lifelong interest in Russian music. He was also influenced by the Asian music performed at the Paris International Exposition of 1889, and by the ideas and music of Richard Wagner, which were having a profound effect in France and both attracted and repelled him.

(Culver Pictures)

Claude Debussy.

For years, Debussy led an unsettled life, earning a small income by teaching piano. His friends were mostly writers, like Stéphane Mallarmé, whose literary gatherings he attended regularly. He was little known to the musical public and not completely sure of himself, though he composed important works including his String Quartet (1893) and the tone poem *Prelude to "The Afternoon of a Faun"* (1894). But his opera *Pelléas and Mélisande* (1902) marked a turning point in his career: although the critics were sharply divided over it, it soon caught on, and he was recognized as the most important living French composer.

Debussy led a life filled with financial and emotional crises, constantly borrowing money (he had a craving for luxury) and having tempestuous love affairs. He was not gifted as a conductor and hated appearing in public, but to maintain his high standard of living he undertook concert tours and presented his music throughout Europe. He died in Paris in 1918.

## DEBUSSY'S MUSIC

Like the impressionist painters and symbolist poets, Debussy evoked fleeting moods and misty atmosphere, as the titles of his works suggest: *Reflets dans l'eau (Reflections in the Water)*, *Nuages (Clouds)*, and *Les Sons et les parfums tournent dans l'air du soir (Sounds and Perfumes Swirl in the Evening Air)*.

# IMPRESSIONISM

*Impression, Sunrise* (1874), by Claude Monet. At an exhibition in Paris in 1874, this painting annoyed a critic who viewed it as a formless collection of tiny colored patches. Using Monet's own title, he mockingly called the entire show the "exhibition of the impressionists." Like the impressionist painters, the French composer Claude Debussy was a master at evoking a fleeting mood and misty atmosphere.

(Dated on painting 1907. Oil on canvas, 59 1/4 inches by 6 feet 7/8 inch. Collection, The Museum of Modern Art, New York, Purchase.)

*Street Scene, Dresden* (1907), by Ernst Ludwig Kirchner. German expressionist painters used deliberate distortions and violent colors to communicate the tension and anguish of the human psyche. Expressionist composers include Arnold Schoenberg, Alban Berg, and Anton Webern.

*Painting No. 198* (above) and *Painting No. 200* (right), by Wassily Kandinsky (1914). Kandinsky stated that his abstract paintings were a "graphic representation of a mood and not of objects."

*Girl before a Mirror* (1932), by Pablo Picasso. The young girl on the left looks at an older, troubled reflection of herself. Picasso reinterpreted the traditional theme of a woman seeing a death's head in her mirror. Twentieth-century composers such as Stravinsky have also reinterpreted earlier musical forms and styles.

(Synthetic polymer on canvas, 124 by 140 inches. Collection of Whitney Museum of American Art, New York, Purchase, with funds from the Friends of the Whitney Museum of American Art. Photo, Geoffry Clements.)

*Flood* (1967), by Helen Frankenthaler. Working without a brush, Frankenthaler allows paint to soak and stain an unprimed canvas stretched on the floor.

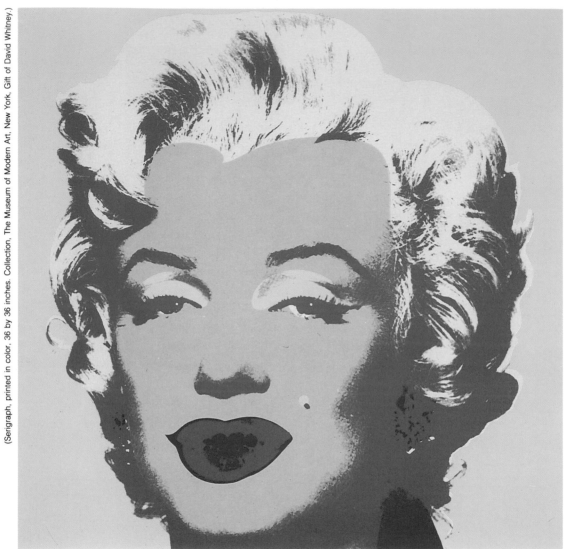

*Marilyn,* from *Ten Marilyns* (1967), by Andy Warhol. Pop artists like Warhol use ordinary subjects from everyday life and mass media.

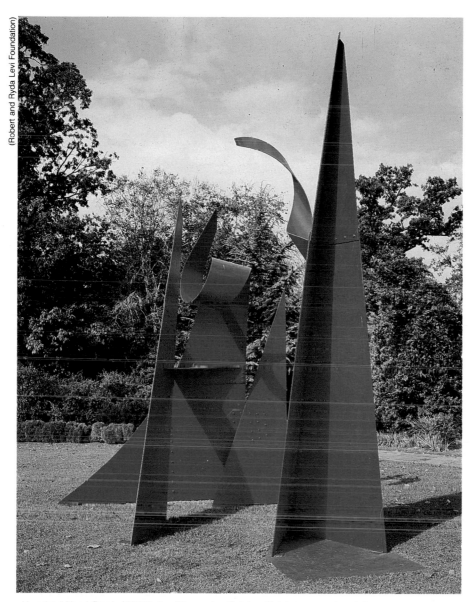

*Hundred-Yard Dash* (1969), by Alexander Calder. Calder created stabiles—large stable sculptures. He was also the originator of the mobile—a sculpture that moves with the aid of air currents.

*Thrusting Rocks* (1990), by David Hockney. One of the best-known contemporary painters, Hockney is also a leading designer of operatic sets and costumes.

Debussy was often inspired by literary and pictorial ideas, and his music sounds free and spontaneous, almost improvised. His stress on tone color, atmosphere, and fluidity is characteristic of *impressionism* in music.

Tone color truly gets unprecedented attention in his works; they have a sensuous, beautiful sound and subtle but crucial changes of timbre. The entire orchestra seldom plays together to produce massive sound; instead, there are brief but frequent solos. Woodwinds are prominent; strings and brasses are often muted. In his music for piano—which includes some of the finest piano works of the twentieth century—he creates hazy sonorities and uses a rich variety of bell- and gonglike sounds.

Debussy's treatment of harmony was a revolutionary aspect of musical impressionism. He tends to use a chord more for its special color and sensuous quality than for its function in a standard harmonic progression. He uses successions of dissonant chords that do not resolve. (As a young man, Debussy was asked which harmonic rules he followed; he replied, simply, "My pleasure.") He freely shifts a dissonant chord up or down the scale; the resulting parallel chords characterize his style.

Debussy, *La Cathédrale engloutie (The Sunken Cathedral)*

Debussy's harmonic vocabulary is large. Along with traditional three- and four-note chords, he uses five-note chords with a lush, rich sound. Chord progressions that were highly unorthodox when Debussy wrote them soon came to seem mild and natural.

"One must drown the sense of tonality," he wrote. Although he never actually abandoned tonality, he weakened it by avoiding progressions that would strongly affirm a key and by using scales in which the main tone is not emphasized. He turned to the medieval church modes and the pentatonic scales heard in Javanese music. A *pentatonic* scale is a five-tone scale, such as that produced by the five black keys of the piano in succession: F♯–G♯–A♯–C♯–D♯.

Debussy's most unusual and tonally vague scale is the *whole-tone scale*, made up of six different notes each a whole step away from the next (C–D–E–F♯–G♯–A♯–C). Unlike major and minor, the whole-tone scale has no special pull from *ti* to *do*, since its tones are all the same distance apart. And because no single tone stands out, the scale creates a blurred, indistinct effect.

Debussy, *Voiles (Sails)*

The pulse in Debussy's music is sometimes as vague as the tonality. This rhythmic flexibility reflects the fluid, unaccented quality of the French language, and in fact he set French to music very sensitively. He composed fifty-nine art songs, many of which are set to symbolist poems. His only opera, *Pelléas and Mélisande,* is an almost word-for-word setting of a symbolist play by Maurice Maeterlinck. It is the essence of musical impressionism: nebulous, mysterious, dreamlike, with a discreet, understated orchestral accompaniment.

Although not large, Debussy's output is remarkably varied; in addition to his opera and art songs it includes works for piano, orchestra, and chamber ensembles. Echoes of his music can be heard in the works of many composers of the years 1900–1920; but no other musician can so fairly be described as an impressionist. Even the composer most similar to him, his younger French contemporary Maurice Ravel (1875–1937), wrote music with greater clarity of form. Debussy's style was both a final expression of romanticism and the beginning of a new era.

## PRÉLUDE À "L'APRÈS-MIDI D'UN FAUNE" (PRELUDE TO "THE AFTERNOON OF A FAUN")

Brief sets:
Side 5, band 3
CD 3 [12]

Basic sets:
Side 13, band 3
CD 7 [5]

"The music of this Prelude," wrote Debussy regarding his *Prelude to "The Afternoon of a Faun,"* "is a very free illustration of the beautiful poem by Stéphane Mallarmé, *The Afternoon of a Faun."* This poem evokes the dreams and erotic fantasies of a pagan forest creature who is half man, half goat. While playing a "long solo" on his flute, the intoxicated faun tries to recall whether he actually carried off two beautiful nymphs or only dreamed of doing so. Exhausted by the effort, he falls back to sleep in the warm sunshine.

Debussy intended his music to suggest "the successive scenes through which pass the desires and dreams of the faun in the heat of this afternoon." The subtle, sensuous timbres of this miniature tone poem were new in Debussy's day. Woodwind solos, muted horn calls, and harp glissandos create a rich variety of delicate sounds. The dynamics are usually subdued, and the entire orchestra—from which trombones, trumpets, and timpani are excluded—rarely plays at one time. The music often swells sensuously, only to subside in voluptuous exhaustion.

The prelude begins with an unaccompanied flute melody; its vague pulse and tonality make it dreamlike and improvisatory. This flute melody is heard again and again, faster, slower, and against a variety of lush chords. Though the form of the prelude may be thought of as A B A', one section blends with the next. It has a continuous ebb and flow. The fluidity and weightlessness typical of impressionism are found in this music. We are never tempted to beat time to its subtle rhythms. The prelude ends magically with the main melody, played by muted horns, seeming to come from far off. The bell-like tones of antique cymbals finally evaporate into silence. With all its new sounds and musical techniques, the piece has been aptly described as a "quiet revolution" in the history of music.

## Listening Outline  To be read while music is heard

*PRÉLUDE À "L'APRÈS-MIDI D'UN FAUNE"*
(*PRELUDE TO "THE AFTERNOON OF A FAUN,"* 1894),
BY CLAUDE DEBUSSY

At a very moderate tempo, A B A' form, E major

3 flutes, 2 oboes, 1 English horn, 2 clarinets, 2 bassoons, 4 French horns, 2 harps, antique cymbals, 1st violins, 2d violins, violas, cellos, double basses

(Duration, 10:21)

A

| 12 | 5 | 0:00 | 1. *a.* Solo flute, *p*, main melody. |

Harp glissando; soft horn calls. Short pause. Harp glissando; soft horn calls.

| 13 | 6 | 0:54 | *b.* Flute, *p*, main melody; tremolo strings in background. Oboe, *p*, continues melody. Orchestra swells to *f*. Solo clarinet fades into |
| 14 | 7 | 1:57 | *c.* Flute, *p*, main melody varied and expanded; harp and muted strings accompany. Flute melody comes to quiet close. |
| | | 3:12 | 2. *a.* Clarinet; harp and cellos in background. |
| 15 | 8 | 3:41 | *b.* New oboe melody. |

Violins take up melody, crescendo and accelerando to climax. Excitement subsides. Ritardando. Clarinet, *p*, leads into

**B**
| 16 | 9 | 4:56

3. *a.* Woodwinds, *p*, legato melody in long notes. Crescendo.

5:31      *b.* Strings repeat melody; harps and pulsating woodwinds in background, crescendo. Decrescendo. Horns, *p*, solo violin, *p*, clarinet, oboe.

**A'**
| 17 | 10 | 6:46

4. *a.* Harp accompanies flute, *p*, main melody in longer notes. Oboe, staccato woodwinds.

7:21      *b.* Harp accompanies oboe, *p*, main melody in longer notes. English horn, harp glissando.

| 18 | 11 | 8:03

5. *a.* Antique cymbals, bell-like tones. Flutes, *p*, main melody. Solo violins, *pp*, in high register.

8:48      *b.* Flute and solo cello, main melody; harp in background.

9:15      *c.* Oboe, *p*, brings melody to close. Harps, *p*.

9:46      *d.* Muted horns and violins, *ppp*, beginning of main melody sounding far off. Flute, antique cymbals, and harp; delicate tones fade into silence.

TWENTIETH
CENTURY

# NEOCLASSICISM

From about 1920 to 1950, the music of many composers, including Igor Stravinsky and Paul Hindemith (1895–1963), reflected an artistic movement known as *neoclassicism.* Neoclassicism is marked by emotional restraint, balance, and clarity; neoclassical compositions use musical forms and stylistic features of earlier periods (particularly of the eighteenth century) to organize twentieth-century harmonies and rhythms.

Neoclassical composers—reacting against romanticism and impressionism—turned away from program music and the gigantic orchestras favored at the turn of the century; they preferred absolute music for chamber groups. The neoclassicists modeled many of their works after Bach's music, used clear polyphonic textures, and wrote fugues, concerti grossi, and baroque dance suites. (In fact, the term *neobaroque* might have been more appropriate for their work.) Most neoclassical music was tonal and used major and minor scales. Still, neoclassicism was more an attitude than a style, and neoclassical compositions sound completely modern—they play on the delightful tension between our expectations about old forms and their own novel harmonies and rhythms.

Neoclassicism was an important trend in other arts, too. The poet T. S. Eliot often quoted and alluded to earlier works; and Picasso (who designed sets for Stravinsky's first neoclassical work, *Pulcinella* in 1920) went through a phase during which his paintings showed the influence of ancient Greek art.

# IGOR STRAVINSKY [ TWENTIETH CENTURY 5 ]

Even during his lifetime, Igor Stravinsky (1882–1971) was a legendary figure. His once revolutionary works had already become modern classics, and he influenced three generations of composers and other artists. Cultural giants like Picasso and T. S. Eliot were his friends. President John F. Kennedy honored him at a White House dinner in his eightieth year.

Stravinsky was born in Russia, near St. Petersburg, grew up in a musical atmosphere, and studied with Nikolai Rimsky-Korsakov. He had his first important opportunity in 1909, when the great impresario Sergei Diaghilev heard his music. Diaghilev was the director of the Russian Ballet, an extremely influential troupe which employed great painters as well as dancers, choreographers, and composers. Diaghilev first asked Stravinsky to orchestrate some piano pieces by Chopin as ballet music and then, in 1910, commissioned an original ballet, *The Firebird*, which was immensely successful. A year later (1911), Stravinsky's second ballet, *Petrushka*, was performed, and Stravinsky was hailed as a modern master. When his third ballet, *The Rite of Spring*, had its premiere in Paris in 1913, a riot erupted in the audience—spectators were shocked and outraged by its pagan primitivism, harsh dissonance, percussiveness, and pounding rhythms—but it too was recognized as a masterpiece and influenced composers all over the world.

During World War I, Stravinsky sought refuge in Switzerland; after the armistice, he moved to France, his home until the onset of World War II, when he came to the United States. In the 1920s and 1930s he was an international celebrity, constantly touring in Europe and the United States; and his compositions—which had originally been inspired by Russian folk music—became cooler and more objective. During his years in the United States (he lived outside Los Angeles), his young musical assistant, Robert Craft, familiarized him with the works of Schoenberg, Berg, and Webern, and in the 1950s Stravinsky astonished his followers by adopting Schoenberg's twelve-tone system.

(Omikron/Photo Researchers)

Igor Stravinsky, in a sketch
by Picasso.

Unlike Schoenberg and Bartók, Stravinsky got well-paying commissions for his work and was an astute businessman; he also loved order and discipline and said that he composed "every day, regularly, like a man with banking hours." In his seventies and eighties he was still touring, conducting his rich and intense late works.

## STRAVINSKY'S MUSIC

Stravinsky's extensive output includes compositions of almost every kind, for voices, instruments, and the stage; and his innovations in rhythm, harmony, and tone color had an enormous influence.

His development shows dramatic changes of style. The three early ballets—*The Firebird* (1910), *Petrushka* (1911), and *The Rite of Spring* (1913)—call for very large orchestras and draw on Russian folklore and folk tunes. During World War I, he wrote for chamber groups, using unconventional combinations of instruments and incorporating ragtime rhythms and popular dances (an example is *The Soldier's Tale*, 1918). From about 1920 to 1951 (his "neoclassical" period), he was inspired largely by eighteenth-century music; his ballet *Pulcinella* (1920) was based partly on the music of Giovanni Battista Pergolesi (1710–1736), and his opera *The Rake's Progress* (1951) was modeled on Mozart. Stravinsky's neoclassical works emphasize restraint, balance, and wit and are far removed from the violence of *The Rite of Spring*. But his shift to the twelve-tone system in the 1950s was an even more dramatic change of approach, since until then all his music had had a clear tonal center. Inspired by Anton Webern (1883–1945), Stravinsky now wrote brief works in which melodic lines were "atomized" into short fragments in constantly changing tone colors and registers.

Despite such stylistic changes, however, all his music has an unmistakable "Stravinsky sound." Tone colors are dry and clear; the beat is strong. His work abounds in changing and irregular meters, and sometimes several meters are heard at once. Ostinatos—repeated rhythmic or melodic patterns—often unify sections of a piece. His treatment of musical form is also unique: rather than connecting themes with bridge passages, he makes abrupt shifts, but his music nevertheless sounds unified and continuous. The effectiveness of his rhythms, chords, and melodies often depends largely on his orchestration, in which highly contrasting tone colors are frequently combined. And his music has rich, novel harmonies—he makes even conventional chords sound unusual.

Stravinsky drew on a wide range of styles, from Russian folk songs to baroque melodies, from Renaissance madrigals to tango rhythms. He sometimes used existing music to create original compositions, but more often the music is entirely his own, while vaguely suggesting a past style.

## *LE SACRE DU PRINTEMPS (THE RITE OF SPRING, 1913)*

Few compositions have had so powerful an impact on twentieth-century music as *Le Sacre du printemps (The Rite of Spring)*, Stravinsky's third ballet score for the Russian Ballet. Its harsh dissonances, percussive orchestration, rapidly changing meters, violent offbeat accents, and ostinatos fired the imagination of many composers. The idea for *The Rite of Spring* came to Stravinsky as a "fleeting vision," while he was completing *The Firebird* in St. Petersburg in 1910. "I saw in imagination a solemn pagan rite: wise elders, seated in a circle, watching a young girl dance herself to death. They were sacrificing her to propitiate the god of spring." Later in life, Stravinsky revealed that the "most wonderful event" of every year of his childhood was the "violent Russian spring that seemed to begin in an hour and was like the whole earth cracking."

Stravinsky's interest in a so-called primitive or preliterate culture was shared by many artists and scholars in the early 1900s. In 1907, Picasso's violent and path-breaking painting *Les Demoiselles d'Avignon* reflected the influence of African sculpture. In 1913—the same year as *The Rite of Spring*—Freud published *Totem and Taboo*, a study of "resemblances between the psychic lives of savages and neurotics." But *primitivism*—the deliberate evocation of primitive power through insistent rhythms and percussive sounds—did not have a lasting impact on early twentieth-century music. Stravinsky never again wrote anything like *The Rite of Spring*; and with the exception of works like *Allegro barbaro* (1911), a piano piece by Bartók, few primitivistic compositions have entered the repertory.

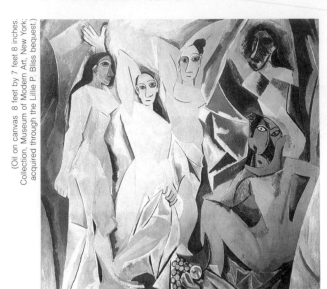

(Oil on canvas 8 feet by 7 feet 8 inches. Collection, Museum of Modern Art, New York; acquired through the Lillie P. Bliss bequest.)

*Les Demoiselles d'Avignon* (1907), by Picasso, reflects the influence of African sculpture.

*The Rite of Spring* consists of two large parts which are subdivided into sections with varying speeds. These subsections follow each other without pause. The titles of the dances suggest their primitive subject matter: Part I, *The Adoration of the Earth:* (1) *Introduction;* (2) *Omens of Spring: Dances of the Youths and Maidens;* (3) *Ritual of Abduction;* (4) *Spring Rounds;* (5) *Games of the Rival Tribes;* (6) *Procession of the Wise Elder;* (7) *Adoration of the Earth;* (8) *Dance of the Earth.* Part II, *The Sacrifice:* (1) *Introduction;* (2) *Mysterious Circles of the Young Girls;* (3) *Glorification of the Chosen Maiden;* (4) *Evocation of the Ancestors;* (5) *Ritual of the Ancestors;* (6) *Sacrificial Dance.* Each of the two large parts begins with a slow introduction and ends with a frenzied, climactic dance.

*The Rite of Spring* is written for an enormous orchestra including eight horns, four tubas, and a very important percussion section made up of five timpani, bass drum, tambourine, tam-tam, triangle, antique cymbals, and a guiro (a notched gourd scraped with a stick). The melodies of *The Rite of Spring* are folklike. They have narrow ranges like ancient Russian folk tunes and are made up of fragments that are repeated with slight changes in rhythm and pitch. Many individual chords are repeated, and each change of harmony produces a great impact. This melodic and harmonic repetition gives the music a ritualistic, hypnotic quality. Rhythm is a vital form-building element in *The Rite of Spring;* it has a life of its own, almost independent of melody and harmony. Today, *The Rite of Spring* is performed more frequently as a concert piece than as a ballet.

We'll now take a closer look at four sections of *The Rite of Spring:* the *Introduction, Dances of the Youths and Maidens,* and *Ritual of Abduction,* which open Part I; and the *Sacrificial Dance,* which concludes Part II.

## Part I:
### Introduction

For Stravinsky, the *Introduction* to Part I represented "the awakening of nature, the scratching, gnawing, wiggling of birds and beasts." It begins with the strangely penetrating sound of a solo bassoon straining at the top of its register. As though improvising, the bassoon repeats a fragment of a Lithuanian folk tune in irregular ways.

Soon other woodwind instruments join the bassoon with repeated fragments of their own. The impression of improvisation is strengthened by the absence of a clearly defined pulse or meter. Dissonant, unconventional chord structures are used. Toward the end of the *Introduction*, different layers of sounds— coming mostly from woodwinds and brasses—are piled on top of each other, and the music builds to a piercing climax. But suddenly, all sound is cut off; only the solo bassoon forlornly repeats its opening melody. Then the violins, playing pizzicato, introduce a repeated four-note "ticking" figure. This figure later serves as an ostinato in *Omens of Spring—Dances of the Youths and Maidens*, which immediately follows the *Introduction*.

**Brief sets:**
Side 5, band 4
CD 3 19

Basic sets:
Side 12, band 3
CD 6 28

## Part I:
### Omens of Spring—Dances of the Youths and Maidens

Sounding almost like drums, the strings pound out a dissonant chord. There are unexpected and irregular accents whose violence is heightened by jabbing sounds from the eight horns. The passage might be counted (with a rapid pulse): 1–2–3 -4, 1–2–3–4, 1 -2–3–4, 1–2–3–4, 1–2–3–4, **1**–2–3–4, **1**–2–3–4, **1**–**2**- 3–4. The unchanging dissonant harmony is a polychord that combines two different traditional chords. A succession of melodic fragments soon join the pounding chord and other repeated figures. The melodic fragments, played by brass and woodwind instruments, are narrow in range and are repeated over and over with slight variations. The rhythmic activity is constant and exciting, and gradually more and more instruments are added.

It's interesting to contrast Stravinsky's musical techniques in *Dances of the Youths and Maidens* with those of a classical movement in sonata form. A classical movement grows out of conflicts between different keys; this section of *The Rite of Spring* is based almost entirely on the repetition of a few chords. The themes in a classical movement are developed through different keys, varied, and broken into fragments that take on new emotional meanings. In *Dances of the Youths and Maidens*, Stravinsky simply repeats melodic fragments with relatively slight variation. To create movement and growth, he relies instead on variations of rhythm and tone color— a technique that can be traced back to nineteenth-century Russian musical tradition.

**Brief sets:**
Side 5, band 4
(continued)
CD 3 21 3:00

Basic sets:
Side 12, band 3
(continued)
CD 6 30

**Brief sets:**
**Side 5, band 4**
**(continued)**
**CD 3** 25 6:21

Basic sets:
Side 12, band 3
(continued)
CD 6 34

The frenzied *Ritual of Abduction* grows out of the preceding section and is marked by violent strokes on the timpani and bass drum. Enormous tension is generated by powerful accents and rapid changes of meter (see the music example on page 258). This section of *The Rite of Spring* closes with high trills in the strings and flutes.

# Listening Outline   To be read while music is heard

*LE SACRE DU PRINTEMPS (THE RITE OF SPRING, 1913),*
*BY IGOR STRAVINSKY*

Part I: *Introduction, Omens of Spring—Dances of the Youths and Maidens, Ritual of Abduction*

2 piccolos, 3 flutes, alto flute, 4 oboes, English horn, E flat clarinet, 3 clarinets, 2 bass clarinets, 4 bassoons, 2 contrabassoons, 8 French horns, small trumpet in D, 4 trumpets, 3 trombones, 3 tubas, timpani, bass drum, triangle, antique cymbals, 1st violins, 2d violins, violas, cellos, double basses

(Duration, 7:35)

*Introduction*
19 28 0:00

1. *a.* High solo bassoon, repeated folk-song fragment in changing meters, joined by French horn, *mp,* then clarinets and bass clarinets, *p.*

0:37  *b.* English horn, new melodic fragment; high bassoon; English horn, melodic fragment, bassoons accompany in faster rhythm.

1:01  *c.* Pizzicato strings, oboe, repeated notes introduce high clarinet melody.

1:12  *d.* Oboe phrase, *f,* high flutes accompany; English horn phrase, *mf,* bass clarinets accompany; flutes and English horn move in even rhythm; violin trill joins.

1:37  *e.* Pizzicato cello pulsations, rhythmic activity quickens, rapid shifts between large and small wind groups; clarinet, repeated descending phrase.

2:00  *f.* Oboe with rapid alto flute accompaniment; piercing high clarinet, *ff,* joins; music builds to *ff* climax, different layers of woodwind and brass sound piled on each other.

2:29
2. *a.* Sudden *p,* solo high bassoon, opening fragment; clarinet trill, joined by

20  29  2:40
    *b.* Pizzicato violins, "ticking" ostinato figure.

Low held tones in bass clarinet; high tones in violins; pizzicato violins, "ticking" ostinato figure.

*Omens of Spring—Dances of the Youths and Maidens*

21  30  3:00
3. *a.* Sudden *f,* strings, repeated dissonant polychord with punctuations in French horns, irregular accents, moderate tempo, duple meter.

3:09
    *b.* English horn, *mf,* "ticking" ostinato figure.

3:14
    *c.* Strings, *f,* repeated dissonant polychord with punctuations in French horns; piccolos, trumpets, oboes join.

3:25
    *d.* Bassoon trill, *mf,* introduces loud, rapid interjections in high trumpet and piccolos;

3:38
    *e.* Strings, *f,* repeated dissonant polychord with punctuations in French horns.

22  31  3:48
    *f.* Bassoons join with melodic fragment played staccato, string pulsations; trombone joins;

Bassoons repeat staccato melodic fragment; oboes, flute and trombone imitate;

4:19
    *g.* Sudden break in pulse, French horns, *f,* sustained tone, timpani strokes, tubas, *ff,* low sustained tone;

4:25
    *h.* High "ticking" ostinato figure descends to English horn, *mf,* trills in winds and strings; loud "ticking" ostinato in violins and trumpet.

23  32  4:45
    *i.* French horn, *mp,* joins with legato melody; flute answers;

descending figure in oboes and trumpet.

*j.* Legato melody in alto flute; legato melody in high flutes, pizzicato strings accompany.

*k.* Trumpets join with repeated-note melody; triangle joins.

*l.* Sudden *p,* strings and syncopated accents introduce piccolo, high legato melodic fragment; full orchestra, melodic figures repeated with long crescendo to

4. *a.* Sustained brass chord, violent strokes on timpani and bass drum; high trumpet, rapid-note fanfare, very fast tempo, changing meters.

*b.* Horn calls, *f,* alternate with piccolo and flutes, rapid-note fanfare; timpani, bass drum join; crescendo to

*c.* High woodwinds and brasses, *ff,* staccato passage in changing meters; horn calls; full orchestra, *ff.*

*d.* Timpani accents punctuate staccato phrases with changing meters in trumpets and high winds; timpani accents punctuate repeated rapid figure in strings.

*e.* Trill in violins, *ff,* accented chords; trill in flutes, *p.*

## Part II:
### *Sacrificial Dance*

The *Sacrificial Dance* is the overwhelming climax of the work. It consists of sections that can be outlined as follows: A B A′ C A″ (very brief) C A‴. In the opening section (A), explosive, percussive chords fight brutal blows on the timpani. The time signature changes with almost every bar: $\frac{3}{16} \frac{2}{16} \frac{3}{16} \frac{2}{8} \frac{2}{16} \frac{3}{16}$. The rapid pulse and irregular, jolting accents create intense excitement.

The second section (B) begins with a sudden drop in dynamic level as a single chord is repeated obsessively. Brief silences between these repeated chords urge the listener to supply accents.

Section C features brasses and percussive sounds from five timpani, a tam-tam (gong), and a bass drum. The *Sacrificial Dance* glorifies the power of rhythm, as does the entire *Rite of Spring.*

# EXPRESSIONISM

Much of twentieth-century music reflects an artistic movement called *expressionism,* which stressed intense, subjective emotion. It was largely centered in Germany and Austria from 1905 to 1925 and grew out of the emotional turbulence in the works of Wagner and late romantics like Richard Strauss and Gustav Mahler. Expressionist painters, writers, and composers explored inner feelings rather than depicting outward appearances. They used deliberate distortions to assault and shock their audience, to communicate tension and anguish. In a reaction against impressionism, they rejected conventional prettiness.

Expressionist painters, such as Ernst Ludwig Kirchner, Emil Nolde, Edvard Munch, and Oskar Kokoschka, often used jarring colors and grotesque shapes. Expressionist art also tends to be fragmentary— for example, the scenes of a play may be episodic and discontinuous. Expressionism was concerned with social protest: it conveyed the anguish of the poor and oppressed and the horrors of war. There was close communication among expressionist writers, painters, and musicians, and many were creative in several areas. The painter Wassily Kandinsky wrote essays, poetry, and plays; the composer Arnold Schoenberg painted.

In Sections 7, 8, and 9, we'll study four expressionist compositions: Schoenberg's Five Pieces for Orchestra, Op. 16 (1909), and *A Survivor from Warsaw* (1947); Alban Berg's opera *Wozzeck* (1917–1922); and Anton Webern's Five Pieces for Orchestra, Op. 10 (1911–1913). These works all avoid tonality and traditional chord progressions and stress harsh dissonance, fragmentation, extreme registers, and unusual instrumental effects. *A Survivor from Warsaw* and *Wozzeck* depict a nightmarish world and express a profound empathy with the poor and tormented.

# ARNOLD SCHOENBERG

Arnold Schoenberg (1874–1951), who was born in Vienna, was an almost entirely self-taught musician; he acquired his profound knowledge of music by studying scores, playing in amateur chamber groups, and going to concerts. After he lost his job as a bank clerk at age twenty-one, he devoted himself to music, earning a poor living conducting a choir of industrial workers and orchestrating popular operettas. Performances of his own early works met with hostility; but in 1904 he began to teach music theory and composition in Vienna, and he inspired love and loyalty in his students, two of whom—Alban Berg and Anton Webern—themselves became leading composers.

*The Scream* (1893), by the Norwegian expressionist Edvard Munch. Expressionist painters reacted against French impressionism; they often used jarring colors and grotesquely distorted shapes to explore the subconscious.

Around 1908 Schoenberg took the revolutionary step of abandoning the traditional tonal system. He was a man possessed ("I have a mission," he said; "I am but the loudspeaker of an idea"), and his productivity between 1908 and 1915 was incredible. For the next eight years, however, he searched for a way to organize his musical discoveries and published nothing. Then, in 1921, he told a student, "I have made a discovery which will ensure the supremacy of German music for the next hundred years," and shortly thereafter (1923–1925) he began publishing compositions using his new twelve-tone system. Although his music did not find a large audience, many important musicians respected it, and he received an important appointment at the Prussian Academy of Arts in Berlin.

After the Nazis seized power in Germany, Schoenberg, who was Jewish, was dismissed from his post; the same year—1933—he and his family came to the United States, where he joined the music faculty at the University of California in Los Angeles. Schoenberg felt neglected in America: his music was rarely performed and he was financially unsuccessful. But after his death, the twelve-tone system was used increasingly by composers throughout the world. It remains an important influence to this day.

## SCHOENBERG'S MUSIC

"I claim the distinction of having written a truly new music which, based upon tradition as it is, is destined to become tradition." This assertion by Schoenberg contains a great deal of truth: his musical language was indeed new, but it had evolved from the past and was eventually widely adopted.

His early works, like the string sextet *Verklärte Nacht* (*Transfigured Night*, 1899), show many features of the late romantic style. Some of them—such as the immense cantata *Gurrelieder* (*Songs of Gurre*, 1901)—use very large orchestras; dissonances and angular melodies create a feeling of subjectivity; chromatic harmony is prominent; and the central tonality is weakened as the music moves through remote keys. But from 1903 to 1907, he departed further from romanticism, and in the *Chamber Symphony*, Op. 9 (1906), he uses whole-tone scales and fourth chords.

### Atonality

Around 1908, Schoenberg began to write atonal music. *Atonality*—the absence of key—evolved from his earlier use of chromatic harmony and the chromatic scale; but in his atonal works, all twelve tones are used without regard for their traditional relationship to major and minor scales. Dissonances are "emancipated" from the necessity of resolving to consonances. Atonality does not imply a single system of composition: each atonal work has its own means of achieving unity, and a piece usually grows out of a few short motives transformed in many different ways.

Arnold Schoenberg.

Schoenberg's atonal compositions include Five Pieces for Orchestra, Op. 16 (1909), and *Pierrot lunaire*, Op. 21 *(Moonstruck Pierrot*, 1912); they are characterized by jagged melodies, novel instrumental effects, extreme contrasts of dynamics and register, and irregular phrases. *Pierrot lunaire* and some other works require an unusual style of vocal performance—**Sprechstimme** (literally, *speech-voice*)—halfway between speaking and singing. Schoenberg's atonal style was soon adopted by his students Berg and Webern; but their early atonal works tended to be short: without a musical system like tonality, extended compositions were possible only when there was a long text to serve as an organizing force.

## The Twelve-Tone System

In the early 1920s, Schoenberg developed a more systematic method of organizing atonal music; he called it the "method of composing with twelve tones." It is partly applied in Five Piano Pieces, Op. 23, and Serenade, Op. 24, and fully elaborated in Suite for Piano, Op. 25 (all composed from 1920 to 1923); and it enabled him to write more extended compositions, such as the monumental Variations for Orchestra (1928) and the unfinished opera *Moses und Aron (Moses and Aaron*, 1930–1932). From 1933 to 1951, in the United States, he used it in many rich and varied works.

The **twelve-tone system** is a twentieth-century alternative to tonality, a new way of organizing pitch in a composition. It is a systematized form of atonality which gives equal importance to each of the twelve chromatic tones. In a twelve-tone composition, the ordering or unifying idea is called a **tone row, set,** or **series** (for this reason, the method is also referred to as *serial technique* or *serialism*). The composer creates a unique tone row for each piece (the choice of rows is practically limitless, since there are 479,001,600 possible arrangements of the twelve tones), and the row is the source of every melody and chord in it. No pitch occurs more than once in the row; this prevents any tone from receiving too much emphasis.

A composition is built by manipulating the tone row, which may be presented in four basic forms: (1) forward (original form), (2) backward (retrograde), (3) upside down (inversion), and (4) backward and upside down (retrograde inversion). (See the illustrations on the opposite page, which show the row used in Suite for Piano, Op. 25.) Any of the four forms of a row may be shifted to any pitch level—that is, it can begin on any of the twelve tones while keeping the original pattern of intervals. Thus there are forty-eight (twelve times four) possible versions of a row. Each tone of a row may also be placed in any register; this enhances the flexibility of the system and may partially explain why so many twelve-tone melodies have very wide leaps. Finally, the tones of a row may be presented one after another (as a melodic line) or simultaneously (as chords). Also shown on the opposite page is the row from the Suite for Piano treated in two different ways.

Original and retrograde forms of a tone row.

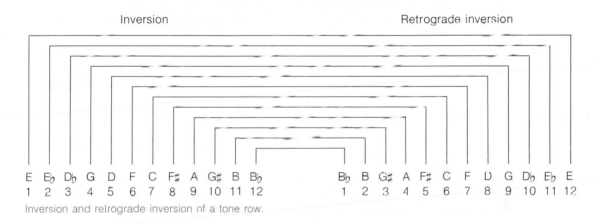

Inversion and retrograde inversion of a tone row.

Two treatments of the tone row from Schoenberg's Suite for Piano.

We'll now study Schoenberg's "freely" atonal *Five Pieces for Orchestra*, Op. 16 (1909), and the twelve-tone cantata *A Survivor from Warsaw*, Op. 46 (1947).

## FIVE PIECES FOR ORCHESTRA, OP. 16 (1909)

"I can promise you something really colossal, especially in sound and mood," wrote Schoenberg to the composer and conductor Richard Strauss after completing his Five Pieces for Orchestra, Op. 16, in 1909. These revolutionary pieces were the first atonal works for full orchestra. Though Schoenberg calls for an especially large orchestra, he treats it as a group of soloists. (In 1949, Schoenberg rearranged the Five Pieces for a conventional orchestra.) Many novel orchestral effects are exploited, and instruments are often used at the top or bottom of their ranges. The pieces embody Schoenberg's concept of a ***tone-color melody*** (***Klangfarbenmelodie***, in German), a succession of varying tone colors used as a musical idea in a composition.

Schoenberg added descriptive titles after he composed the music. Each piece is quite brief; at the time, Schoenberg unconsciously felt the need to "counterbalance extreme emotionality with extraordinary shortness." We'll study the first piece, *Vorgefühle (Premonitions)*.

### *Vorgefühle (Premonitions)*

Basic sets:
Side 14, band 1
CD 7 [16]

An amazing amount of musical activity takes place in the 2-minute span of *Premonitions*. It is "just an uninterrupted change of colors, rhythms, and moods," according to Schoenberg. The constant intensity and desperate energy of *Premonitions* are typically expressionistic.

[16] 0:00

The piece consists of two connected sections: an introductory part lasting about ½ minute, and a main part three times as long. The introduction sounds fragmentary and has a bewildering succession of musical ideas in different tempos, tone colors, dynamics, and registers. As though holding his full resources in reserve, Schoenberg uses only a few instruments at any one time. First, muted cellos introduce an abrupt upward motive (short-long-long, short-long-long):

The entire piece is built from rhythmic and melodic transformations of this idea.

The second part of *Premonitions* is rhythmically more continuous; it becomes increasingly complex in both texture and sound.

The cellos begin with a steady succession of rapid notes. They have a three-note figure that is repeated as a background ostinato throughout the piece.

17  0:27

The sound becomes increasingly loud and dense as more and more melodic fragments are piled on top of one another. After an earsplitting climax, the texture thins, and the volume decreases. *Premonitions* ends with a snarling chord played by trombones and tuba. (The snarling effect results from flutter-tonguing; each brass player rapidly rolls the tongue as if pronouncing *d-r-r-r*.) This chord is sustained in the background throughout most of *Premonitions*, and it unifies the flow of free associations in the piece.

## A SURVIVOR FROM WARSAW, OP. 46 (1947)

*A Survivor from Warsaw*, a dramatic cantata for narrator, male chorus, and orchestra, deals with a single episode in the murder of 6 million Jews by the Nazis during World War II. Schoenberg wrote the text himself, partly basing it on a direct report by one of the few survivors of the Warsaw ghetto. Over 400,000 Jews from this ghetto died in extermination camps or of starvation; many others perished during a heroic revolt against the Nazis in 1943. The narrator's text is spoken in English, except for some terrifying Nazi commands, which are shouted in German. The narrator's part is a kind of *Sprechstimme*, the novel speech-singing developed by Schoenberg. The rhythms of the spoken words are precisely notated, but their pitch fluctuations are indicated only approximately.

Brief sets:
Side 6, band 1
CD 3  27

Basic sets:
Side 14, band 2
CD 7  18

I cannot remember ev'rything,    I must have been un-conscious most of the time;

Besides English and German, the text includes Hebrew. These were the three languages of Schoenberg's life: German, his native tongue; English, his adopted language in the United States; and Hebrew, the language of his religious faith. The 6-minute cantata builds to an overwhelming conclusion when the male chorus sings in unison the Hebrew words of the prayer *Shema Yisroel (Hear, O Israel)*. For centuries this has been the prayer of Jewish martyrs in their last agonized moments.

*A Survivor from Warsaw* is a twelve-tone composition written in 1947, when Schoenberg was seventy-two. Its tense, expressionistic style recalls *Premonitions*, written almost forty years earlier. The music vividly sets off every detail in the text.

*A Survivor from Warsaw* opens with a brief orchestral introduction that captures the nightmarish atmosphere that prevailed as Nazi soldiers awakened the Warsaw Jews for transport to death camps. We hear a weirdly shrill reveille in the trumpet and fragmentary sounds in the military drum and high xylophone.

During the narrator's opening lines, Schoenberg already prepares for the concluding Hebrew prayer. As the narrator speaks of "the old prayer they had neglected for so many years," a French horn softly intones the beginning of the melody that is later proclaimed by the chorus.

An especially vivid musical description comes when the narrator describes how the Nazis counted their victims: "They began again, first slowly: One, two, three, four, became faster and faster. . . ." The music itself becomes faster and louder, building to the powerful entrance of the chorus.

The sung Hebrew contrasts dramatically with the spoken English and German that comes before, and it is the first extended melody in the work.

I cannot remember everything. I must have been unconscious most of the time; I remember only the grandiose moment when they all started to sing, as if prearranged, the old prayer they had neglected for so many years—the forgotten creed!

But I have no recollection how I got underground to live in the sewers of Warsaw so long a time.

The day began as usual. Reveille when it still was dark—get out whether you slept or whether worries kept you awake the whole night: you had been separated from your children, from your wife, from your parents, you don't know what happened to them; how could you sleep?

They shouted again: "Get out! The sergeant will be furious!" They came out; some very slow, the old ones, the sick men, some with nervous agility. They fear the sergeant. They hurry as much as they can. In vain! Much too much noise, much too much commotion and not fast enough!

The Feldwebel shouts: *"Achtung! Still gestanden! Na wird's mal, oder soll ich mit dem Gewehrkolben nachhelfen? Na jut; wenn Ihr's durchaus haben wollt!"* ("Attention! Stand still! How about it, or should I help you along with the butt of my rifle? Oh well, if you really want to have it!")

The sergeant and his subordinates hit everyone: young or old, strong or sick, guilty or innocent—it was painful to hear the groaning and moaning.

I heard it though I had been hit very hard, so hard that I could not help falling down. We all on the ground who could not stand up were then beaten over the head.

I must have been unconscious. The next thing I knew was a soldier saying, "They are all dead!" Whereupon the sergeant ordered to do away with us.

There I lay aside half conscious. It had become very still—fear and pain— Then I heard the sergeant shouting: *"Abzählen!"* ("Count Off!")

They started slowly, and irregularly: One, two, three, four, *"Achtung."* The sergeant shouted again: *"Rascher! Nochmals von vorn anfangen! In einer Minute will ich wissen wieviele ich zur Gaskammer abliefere! Abzählen!"* ("Faster! Once more, start from the beginning! In one minute I want to know how many I am going to send off to the gas chamber! Count off!")

They began again, first slowly: one, two, three, four, became faster and faster, so fast that it finally sounded like a stampede of wild horses, and all of a sudden, in the middle of it, they began singing the *Shema Yisroel*.

*Shema Yisroel Adonoy elohenoo Adonoy ehod. Veohavto es Adonoy eloheho beḥol levoveho oovehol nafsheho oovehol meodeho. Vehoyoo haddevoreem hoelleh asher onohee metsavveho hayyom al levoveho. Veshinnantom levoneho vedibbarto bom beshivteho beveteho oovelehteho baddereh ooveshohbeho oovekoomeho.* ("Hear, O Israel, the Lord our God, the Lord is One! And thou shalt love the Lord thy God with all thy heart, and with all thy soul, and with all thy might. And these words, which I command thee this day, shall be in thy heart. And thou shalt teach them diligently unto thy children, and speak of them when thou sittest in thy house, and when thou goest on the way, and when thou liest down, and when thou risest up.")

# 8 ALBAN BERG

Alban Berg (1885–1935), a student of Schoenberg, wrote music that is a unique synthesis of traditional and twentieth-century elements. Berg, who was born in Vienna, first attracted international attention in 1925, when his opera *Wozzeck* was premiered in Berlin; its atonality baffled many critics, but it made a powerful impression on the public and was soon performed throughout Europe and in the United States. Perhaps because of chronic ill health, Berg did not perform or conduct, and he composed relatively few works—these include the *Chamber Concerto,* for piano, violin, and thirteen winds (1925); the *Lyric Suite,* for string quartet (1926); the opera *Lulu* (1929–1935, orchestration not completed); and the Violin Concerto (1935).

## *WOZZECK* (1917–1922)

*Wozzeck* is the tragic story of a soldier who is driven to murder and madness by a hostile society. An antihero obsessed by strange visions, Wozzeck is persecuted by his sadistic captain, used as a guinea pig by a half-demented doctor, and betrayed by the woman with whom he lives, Marie. Wozzeck stabs Marie to death and drowns while trying to wash her blood from his hands.

Berg's musical imagination was fired in 1914 when he saw *Woyzeck,* a play by the German dramatist and revolutionary Georg Büchner (1813–1837). Though written in the early 1830s, the play is amazingly modern in its starkly realistic dialogue and disconnected scenes. Berg adapted the play into an opera while he was in the Austrian army during World War I. His own traumatic army experiences may well have deepened his sympathy for Wozzeck.

The opera's nightmarish atmosphere makes it a musical counterpart of expressionist painting and literature. Berg conveys the tensions and torments of the unconscious through harsh dissonances and grotesque distortions. The range of emotions and styles in the music is tremendous. Though most of *Wozzeck* is freely atonal—it does not use the twelve-tone system—major and minor keys occasionally add contrast. The vocal line includes speaking, shrieking, *Sprechstimme,* distorted folk songs, and melodies with wide leaps that are difficult to sing. The gigantic orchestra closely parallels the dialogue and stage action. Descriptive effects include vivid orchestral depiction of the moon rising, frogs croaking, and water engulfing the drowning Wozzeck. Berg's music rapidly shifts between very high and very low registers, between *ffff* and *pppp.*

*Wozzeck* has three acts, each with five scenes. Connecting the scenes are short orchestral interludes that comment musically on the preceding action and serve as preparation for what is to come. As in Wagner's music dramas, there is a continuous musical flow within each act, and characters are associated with specific musical ideas. A novel feature of *Wozzeck* is that the music for each scene is a self-contained composition with a particular form (passacaglia, sonata form, etc.) or of a definite type (military march, lullaby). The five scenes of the last act—we'll study Scenes 4 and 5—are organized as (1) variations on a theme, (2) variations on a single tone, (3) variations on a rhythmic pattern, (4) variations on a chord, and (5) variations on continuous running notes. But Berg did not intend for the listener to concentrate on or even be aware of these unifying techniques. He wanted the audience to be caught up in the opera's dramatic flow.

In Act II, Wozzeck has been driven to desperation by Marie's infidelity and by a savage beating from the man who has slept with her. Near the beginning of Act III, Wozzeck stabs Marie to death as they walk along a forest path near a pond.

## Act III: Scenes 4 and 5

### Scene 4: A path near a pond

Wozzeck returns to the scene of the crime to dispose of his knife. Berg's orchestra vividly evokes the dark forest scene as a background to Wozzeck's anguished shrieks. Rising harp tones suggest the blood-red moon coming up through the clouds. Wozzeck goes mad and drowns in the pond while trying to wash the blood from his hands. Soft chromatic slides depict the engulfing water as the Captain and the Doctor, Wozzeck's tormentors, indifferently comment that someone is drowning. As Wozzeck drowns, the slides become slower and narrower in range.

Basic sets.
Side 14, band 3
CD 7 [20]

The long orchestral interlude that follows is a deeply moving expression of grief for Wozzeck's tragic fate. It recalls the musical themes associated with his life. Berg described it as "a confession of the author stepping outside the dramatic events of the theater and appealing to the public as representing mankind." For this outpouring of compassion, Berg returns to tonality (the interlude is in D minor) and the musical language of late romanticism.

### Scene 5: A street before Marie's door

Children are playing in front of Marie's house; bright sunshine brings a glaring contrast to the darkness of the preceding scenes. One of the children cruelly tells Wozzeck's son: "Hey! Your mother is dead." The boy rides off on his hobby horse with the other children to see the body. The orchestra is reduced in size to produce delicate sounds that match the children's high voices, and a continuous rhythm symbolizes their utter indifference.

Side 14, band 3
(continued)
CD 7 [24]

The opera does not end with a conclusive chord. It simply breaks off as though to suggest that the tragedy could begin again.

**20** 0:00

Winds, *p*, repeated chord.

(Forest path by the pond. Moonlit night as before. Wozzeck staggers on hastily, and then stops as he searches for something.)

**Wozzeck**

Spoken
(*Sprechstimme*).

*Das Messer? Wo ist das Messer? Ich hab's dagelassen . . . Näher, noch näher. Mir graut's! Da regt sich was.*

Where is it? Where has the knife gone? Somewhere here I left it . . . Somewhere here, somewhere. Oh! Horror! There something moved!

Shouted.

*Still! Alles still und tot . . . Mörder! Mörder! Ha! Da ruft's. Nein, ich selbst.*

Still! All is still and dead! . . . Murder! Murder! Ah, who cried? No, 'twas me.

(Still searching, he staggers forward a few more steps, and comes on the corpse.)

*Marie! Marie! Was hast Du für eine rote Schnur um den Hals? Hast Dir das rote Halsband verdient, wie die Ohrringlein, mit Deiner Sünde! Was hängen Dir die schwarzen Haare so wild? Mörder! Mörder! Sie werden nach mir suchen . . . Das Messer verrät mich! Da, da ist's. So! Da hinunter. Es taucht ins dunkle Wasser wie ein Stein.*

Marie! Marie! What is that so like a crimson cord round your neck? And was that crimson necklace well earned, like the gold earrings: the price of sinning! Why hangs your fine black hair so wild on your head? Murder! Murder! For me they'll soon be searching . . . That knife will betray me! (*Seeks it feverishly.*) Ah! It's here! (*At the pond.*) Down to the bottom! (*Throws the knife in.*) It sinks through deep dark water like a stone.

**21** 1:44

Rising harp tones, *pp*.

(The moon comes up blood-red through the clouds.)

*Aber der Mond verrät mich . . . der Mond ist blutig. Will denn die ganze Welt es ausplaudern?!—Das Messer, es liegt zu weit vorn, sie finden's beim Baden oder wenn sie nach Muscheln tauchen. Ich find's nicht . . . Aber ich muss mich waschen. Ich bin blutig. Da ein Fleck . . . und noch einer. Weh! Weh!*

See how the moon betrays me . . . the moon is bloody! Must then the whole wide world be blabbing it?— The knife there, too near to the shore! They'll find it when bathing, maybe when they are mussel-gathering. (*He wades into the pond.*) It's gone now. I ought to wash my body. I am bloody. Here's a spot . . . and here . . . something. Woe! Woe!

*Ich wasche mich mit Blut! Das Wasser ist Blut . . . Blut . . .*

I wash myself with blood! The water is blood . . . blood . . .

**22** 2:38

Water music. Upward orchestral slides, *pp*. Rhythm gradually slows.

(He drowns.)

(After a short time the Doctor enters, followed by the Captain.)

**Captain**

*Halt!*                                              Stop!                                              Spoken.

**Doctor**
(Stands still.)
*Hören Sie? Dort!*                                   Do you hear? There!

**Captain**
(Stands still.)
*Jesus! Das war ein Ton.*                            Heavens! There was a sound.

**Doctor**
(Pointing to the pond.)
*Ja, dort!*                                          Yes, there!

**Captain**

*Es ist das Wasser im Teich. Das Wasser*             It is the water in the pond. The water
*ruft. Es ist schon lange Niemand*                   calls. It is a long time since anyone
*ertrunken. Kommen Sie, Doktor! Es ist*              was drowned. Come, Doctor, this is
*nicht gut zu hören.*                                not good to hear.

(He tries to drag off the Doctor.)

**Doctor**
(Stands still and listens.)
*Das stöhnt . . . als stürbe ein Mensch.*            It groans . . . like a dying man.
*Da ertrinkt Jemand!*                                There's someone drowning!

**Captain**

*Unheimlich! Der Mond rot und die*                   It's uncanny! The moon is red, and          Celesta.
*Nebel grau. Hören Sie? . . . Jetzt wieder*          the mist is grey. Do you hear? . . .
*das Ächzen.*                                        That groaning again.

**Doctor**

*Stiller, . . . jetzt ganz still.*                   It's getting softer . . . and now quite
                                                     gone.

**Captain**

*Kommen Sie! Kommen Sie schnell.*                    Come away! Quick!

(Drags the Doctor off with him.)

23 4:21
Extended orchestral
interlude.

Scene 5

(Street before Marie's door. Bright morning. Sunshine. Children are playing and
shouting. Marie's child is riding a hobby-horse.)

## Children

| | |
|---|---|
| *Ringel, Ringel, Rosenkranz, Ringelreih'n!* | Ring-a-ring-a-roses, all fall down! |
| *Ringel, Ringel, Rosenkranz, Rin . . .* | Ring-a-ring-a-roses, all . . . |

(They stop, and other children come rushing on.)

## One of them

| | |
|---|---|
| *Du Käthe! . . . Die Marie . . .* | Katie! . . . Marie . . . |

## Second Child

| | |
|---|---|
| *Was is?* | What is it? |

## First Child

| | |
|---|---|
| *Weisst' es nit? Sie sind schon Alle'naus.* | Don't you know? They've all gone out there. |

## Third Child
(To Marie's child.)

| | |
|---|---|
| *Du! Dein Mutter ist tot!* | Hey! Your mother is dead. |

## Marie's Child
(Still riding his horse.)

| | |
|---|---|
| *Hopp, hopp! Hopp, hopp! Hopp, hopp!* | Hop, hop! Hop, hop! Hop, hop! |

## Second Child

| | |
|---|---|
| *Wo is sie denn?* | Where is she now? |

## First Child

| | |
|---|---|
| *Draus' liegt sie, am Weg, neben dem Teich.* | Out there, on the path by the pond. |

## Third Child

| | |
|---|---|
| *Kommt, anschaun!* | Let's go and look! |

(All the children run off.)

## Marie's Child
(Continues to ride.)

| | |
|---|---|
| *Hopp, hopp! Hopp, hopp! Hopp, hopp!* | Hop, hop! Hop, hop! Hop, hop! |

(He hesitates a moment, and then rides off after the other children.)

24  7:53

Music breaks off.

288

# ANTON WEBERN

Anton Webern (1883–1945) was neglected during his lifetime, though his music influenced composers throughout the world during the 1950s and 1960s. He was born in Vienna; studied piano, cello, and music theory as a young man; and earned a doctorate in music history from the University of Vienna. While at the university, he studied composition privately with Schoenberg. His career was solid but unspectacular: he made a modest income conducting various choruses and orchestras, though the rare performances of his own works were usually met with ridicule. He was a shy man, devoted to his family, and a Christian mystic who loved to commune with nature.

Although his life seems ordinary enough, his death was a bizarre tragedy—he was shot by mistake by an American soldier toward the end of World War II.

## WEBERN'S MUSIC

Poetic lyricism pervades Webern's music, which is amazingly original in its brevity, quietness, and concentration. Most of his works are miniatures lasting only 2 or 3 minutes, and virtually all of his mature output can be played in less than 3½ hours—rarely has a composer exerted such worldwide influence on the basis of so little music.

About half of Webern's music is for solo voice or chorus; the rest is for chamber orchestra and small chamber groups. He wrote atonal works at about the same time as Schoenberg (starting in 1908–1909) and adopted the twelve-tone system soon after Schoenberg developed it. He also exploited Schoenberg's idea of a "melody built of tone colors." Webern's melodic lines are "atomized" into two-note or three-note fragments which may at first seem isolated but add up to a unified whole. He forces us to focus on the tone color, dynamic level, and register of each note. His textures are delicate and transparent; usually, not more than a few solo instruments play at once. In his twelve-tone works, there is often strict polyphonic imitation.

Composers in the 1950s and 1960s were fascinated by Webern's techniques and often imitated his deceptively "cool" sound. Works that appealed to very few during his lifetime became a source of inspiration after his death.

## FIVE PIECES FOR ORCHESTRA, OP. 10 (1911–1913)

Webern's unique style is fully revealed in his early, atonal Five Pieces for Orchestra, Op. 10, composed before he adopted the twelve-tone system. These five "expressions of musical lyricism," as Webern called them, are among the shortest orchestral compositions ever written. The fourth piece is only 6⅓ measures long and lasts less than 30 seconds. Webern's chamber orchestra of eighteen soloists includes unconventional instruments like the mandolin, guitar, cowbells, and harmonium (a small organ with metal reeds). Each piece (we'll consider the third) is scored for a different number and combination of instruments.

Melodic fragments are whispered by ever-changing solo instruments and framed by poetic silences. Tone-color melodies replace "tunes" in this music. There are few notes, but each is crucial. The tempo constantly fluctuates. Brasses and strings are usually muted.

### Third Piece:
### Very slow and extremely calm

**Brief sets:**
**Side 6, band 2**
**CD 3** 29

Basic sets:
Side 14, band 4
CD 7 25

With its bell sounds coming as though from far off, the third piece has a feeling of solitude and eerie stillness. The dynamics never rise above *pp*. The sustained bell-like sounds—produced by mandolin, celesta, guitar, harp, glockenspiel, cowbells, chimes, and harmonium—are heard both at the beginning and at the end. This creates a vague A B A' effect. Melodic fragments in ever-changing solo instruments are set apart from one another by brief moments of near silence.

# Listening Outline   To be read while music is heard

THIRD PIECE (1913) FROM FIVE PIECES FOR ORCHESTRA,
OP. 10 (1911–1913), BY ANTON WEBERN

Clarinet, muted French horn, muted trombone, harmonium, mandolin, guitar, celesta, harp, bass drum, snare drum, chimes, cowbells, violin, muted viola, muted cello.

Very slow and extremely calm

(Duration, 1:28)

| | |
|---|---|
| 29 25 0:00 | 1. *a.* Pulsating bell-like sounds, *ppp.*<br>  *b.* Violin, *pp*, pulsating bell-like sounds, *ppp.*<br>  *c.* Muted horn, *pp*, chimes, *ppp.* |
| 0:38 | 2. Quicker notes in clarinet. Muted viola. |
| 0:47 | 3. *a.* Pulsating bell-like sounds, *ppp.*<br>  *b.* Muted trombone, *ppp;* pulsating bell-like sounds, *ppp.* Snare-drum roll, extremely soft. |

# BÉLA BARTÓK

Béla Bartók (1881–1945), whose music is infused with the spirit of east European folk song, was born in Hungary. His mother gave him his first lessons on the piano, an instrument which was important in his career; he taught piano at his alma mater, the Budapest Academy of Music, from 1907 to 1934, and gave recitals throughout Europe. During the early 1900s, Bartók was influenced by the Hungarian nationalist movement and spent most of his free time in small villages recording peasant folk songs. He became an authority on peasant music, and his own music was profoundly influenced by it.

Though he was neglected in Hungary until the Budapest premiere of his ballet *The Wooden Prince* in 1917, Bartók was recognized early as an important composer abroad and had a successful career during the 1920s and 1930s. But he was violently anti-Nazi, and in 1940 he emigrated to the United States, where he was to spend the last five years of his life. This was a bleak period for him: he had little money, was in poor health, and felt isolated and neglected.

In 1943, while in a hospital in New York, he received an unexpected commission for the Concerto for Orchestra, now his best-known work; and its success resulted in several other commissions. Tragically, however, Bartók had only a year to live and could complete just two more compositions, the Sonata for Solo Violin (1944) and the Third Piano Concerto (1945). Soon after his death in New York in 1945, he became one of the most popular twentieth-century composers.

## BARTÓK'S MUSIC

"I do not reject any influence," wrote Bartók, "provided it be pure, fresh, and healthy"; but he emphasized that the "Hungarian influence is the strongest." He evolved a completely individual style that fused folk elements, classical forms, and twentieth-century sounds. He did arrange many folk tunes (often with highly dissonant accompaniments), but in most of his works he does not quote folk melodies—he uses original themes that have a folk flavor.

Bartók's genius found its most characteristic expression in instrumental music; he wrote many works for piano solo, six string quartets (which are among the finest since Beethoven's) and other chamber music, three piano concertos, two violin concertos, and several pieces for orchestra. His music embraces a wide range of emotions and is deeply expressive; and he revitalized and reinterpreted traditional forms such as the rondo, fugue, and sonata form.

(G. D. Hackett, New York)

Caught up in the nationalist movement that swept Hungary, Bartók spent most of his free time in tiny villages recording folk songs on a cylinder phonograph.

He always organized his works around a tonal center; but within this framework he often used harsh dissonances, polychords, and tone clusters (though some of his late works have a more traditional, less dissonant vocabulary). Rhythmically, his music is characterized by a powerful beat, unexpected accents, and changing meters. He was imaginative in his use of tone colors, particularly of percussion instruments—in Music for Strings, Percussion, and Celesta (1936), for example, he drew unusual sounds from the xylophone and timpani. Like many twentieth-century composers, he also drew percussive, drumlike sounds from the piano.

## CONCERTO FOR ORCHESTRA (1943)

The commission which led to the Concerto for Orchestra was offered to Bartók in 1943, while he was hospitalized in New York City. Serge Koussevitzky, the conductor of the Boston Symphony Orchestra, offered him a $1,000 commission for a new work. While recuperating at Saranac Lake, New York, Bartók was able to work "practically day and night" on his new composition. He finished it in six weeks. The Concerto for Orchestra was an enormous success at its premiere in Boston in 1944 and has since become Bartók's most popular work.

"The general mood of the work," wrote Bartók, "represents, apart from the jesting second movement, a gradual transition from the sternness of the first movement and the lugubrious death-song of the third, to the life-assertion of the last one." Bartók explained that the unusual title *Concerto for Orchestra* reflects the work's "tendency to treat the single orchestral instruments in a *concertant* or soloistic manner."

Indeed, the Concerto for Orchestra is a showpiece for an orchestra of virtuosos. It is romantic in spirit because of its emotional intensity, memorable themes, and vivid contrasts of mood. Though its melodies were original with Bartók, they have a distinct folk flavor. The concerto is an example of Bartók's mellow "late" style, which is characterized by more frequent use of traditional chords. In all five movements, time-honored procedures like A B A form, sonata form, and fugue are fused with twentieth-century rhythms and tone colors. We'll study the second movement, which is titled *Game of Pairs*.

### Second Movement: *Game of Pairs*
### Allegretto scherzando

The jesting second movement, *Game of Pairs,* which is in A B A' form, is a "game" involving different pairs of woodwind and brass instruments. The instruments of each pair move in parallel motion and are separated by a distinctive pitch interval. In the opening section (A), a chain of five melodies is played consecutively by pairs of bassoons, oboes, clarinets, flutes, and muted trumpets. The contrasting middle section (B) is a hymnlike melody softly played by brass instruments. When the opening section returns (A'), it has a more active accompaniment. The incisive sound of a side drum (without snares) is prominent throughout the movement. It plays syncopated solos at both the beginning and the end, as well as in the hymnlike middle section.

Brief sets:
Side 6, band 3
CD 3 30

Supplementary sets:
Side 7, band 2
CD 4 8

## Listening Outline   To be read while music is heard

CONCERTO FOR ORCHESTRA (1943), BY BÉLA BARTÓK

Second Movement: *Game of Pairs* (Allegretto scherzando)

A B A' form, duple meter ($\frac{2}{4}$)

2 flutes, 2 oboes, 2 clarinets, 3 bassoons, 4 French horns, 2 trumpets, 2 trombones, tuba, timpani, side drum, 2 harps, 1st violins, 2d violins, violas, cellos, double basses

(Duration, 6:06)

**A**

| | | |
|---|---|---|
| 30 8 | 0:00 | 1. Solo side drum (without snares), *mf.* |
| | 0:11 | 2. Two bassoons, *p,* accompanied by pizzicato strings. |
| 31 9 | 0:33 | 3. *a.* Two oboes, *p,* in higher register. Pizzicato strings accompany. |
| | | *b.* Low strings, pizzicato, while oboes sustain tones. |
| 32 10 | 1:01 | 4. *a.* Two clarinets. |
| | | *b.* Low strings, accented notes. |
| 33 11 | 1:22 | 5. *a.* Two flutes, *mf,* in higher register. |
| | | *b.* Low strings, pizzicato, while flutes sustain tones. |
| 34 12 | 2:04 | 6. Two muted trumpets, *p.* Muted string tremolos, *pp,* in background. |

**B**

| | | |
|---|---|---|
| 35 13 | 2:50 | 1. *a.* Brasses, *mf,* hymnlike legato melody. Side drum accompanies. |
| | | *b.* French horns, *p,* conclude hymnlike melody and sustain chord. |
| | | 2. Oboe, flute, and clarinet, *p,* lead to |

**A′**

| | | |
|---|---|---|
| 36 14 | 3:51 | 1. Two bassoons, *p,* opening melody. Staccato third bassoon in background. |
| | 4:13 | 2. *a.* Two oboes, *p,* in higher register. Clarinets and strings in background. |
| | | *b.* Low strings, pizzicato, while oboes sustain tones. |
| | 4:36 | 3. *a.* Two clarinets. Flutes and strings in background. |
| | | *b.* Low strings, accented notes. |
| | 4:56 | 4. *a.* Two flutes, *mf,* in higher register. Woodwinds and strings in background. |
| | | *b.* Low strings, pizzicato, while flutes sustain tones. |
| | 5:18 | 5. Two muted trumpets, *mf.* Harp glissandos and muted string tremolos in background. |
| | 5:55 | 6. Woodwinds, *p,* repeated chord; solo side drum, decrescendo, ends *Game of Pairs.* |

TWENTIETH
CENTURY

# 11 CHARLES IVES

The American composer Charles Ives (1874–1954) wrote startlingly original music that was far ahead of its time. He was born in Danbury, Connecticut, the son of a bandmaster who loved to experiment with unusual sounds ("Pa taught me what I know," he later recalled), and he studied composition at Yale University. But when he graduated, he entered the insurance business, having decided that he could keep his music "stronger, cleaner, bigger, and freer" if he did not try to make a living out of it. (He also said that he did not want to raise a family who would "starve on his dissonances.") Eventually he founded a successful insurance agency and became very wealthy.

Ives composed furiously after business hours, on weekends, and on holidays, in isolation from the musical world; he was completely unknown, none of his major works was publicly performed, and his scores accumulated in the barn of his Connecticut farm. World War I dampened his creative urge, however, and in 1918 he had a heart attack from which he never completely recovered; after 1921 he composed almost nothing but instead began to make his work known to the public.

(Omikron/Photo Researchers)

Charles Ives.

From 1920 to 1922, he privately printed and distributed his monumental *Concord* Sonata (1909–1915) for piano and his collection *114 Songs*; at first, they aroused little more than ridicule, but gradually a few young composers and performers recognized that Ives was enormously original. In 1939, the *Concord* Sonata received an ovation at its first complete New York performance; and by the 1940s, many considered Ives the first great composer from the United States. In 1947 he won a Pulitzer Prize for his Third Symphony (1904–1911), written some forty years earlier.

## IVES'S MUSIC

Though experimental, Ives's compositions are rooted deeply in the folk and popular music he knew as a boy: revival hymns, ragtime, village bands, church choirs, patriotic songs, and barn dances. He was inspired by the "unconventional" features of the American tradition—the village fiddler playing slightly out of tune, the cornetist a fraction ahead of the rest of the band, the church organist accidentally holding one chord while the choir sings another. His polyrhythms, polytonality, and tone clusters grew out of the music he knew. One boyhood experience in particular seems to have had an important influence: two bands playing different music passed each other as they marched by him in opposite directions. In later works Ives simultaneously presents musical events that seem unrelated: two bands play in different keys; consonant chords are set against dissonant chords; conflicting meters and rhythmic patterns are intertwined. To evoke memories, he often quotes snatches of familiar tunes, develops them, and integrates them within his music. Even the titles of his works suggest his New England heritage —for example, the movements of the *Concord* Sonata are *Emerson, Hawthorne, The Alcotts,* and *Thoreau;* and we'll study one movement from a set of orchestral pieces called *Three Places in New England.*

Ives's music has a wide range of emotions, styles, and techniques; it includes mild, consonant chords and earsplitting dissonances. (He scorned those who couldn't take dissonance: "Beauty in music," he wrote, "is too often confused with something that lets the ears lie back in an easy chair.") Much of his music is extraordinarily difficult to perform. His large and varied output includes five symphonies and other orchestral music; works for piano, chorus, and chamber ensembles; and over 200 songs.

## PUTNAM'S CAMP, REDDING, CONNECTICUT (1912), FROM *THREE PLACES IN NEW ENGLAND* (1908–?1914)

Basic sets:
Side 14, band 6
CD 7 [35]

*Putnam's Camp, Redding, Connecticut,* is part of *Three Places in New England,* a set of three movements for orchestra evoking American history, life, and landscape. Though completed around 1914, *Three Places in New England* was not performed until 1930, when it was booed and hissed at its premiere in Boston. Today, it is one of Ives's most popular works and a landmark in American music.

The daring and brilliant second movement, *Putnam's Camp,* is a child's impression of a Fourth of July picnic. Ives recaptures his boyhood memory of two marching bands clashing dissonantly as they play different tunes. Snatches of patriotic songs and folklike tunes written by Ives contribute to the piece's popular flavor.

In his preface to this score, Ives wrote, "Near Redding Center, Conn., is a small park preserved as a Revolutionary Memorial; for here General Israel Putnam's soldiers had their winter quarters in 1778–1779." One Fourth of July, "a child went there on a picnic held under the auspices of the First Church and the Village Cornet Band." The child wanders "away from the rest of the children past the camp ground into the woods. As he rests on the hillside of laurel and hickories, the tunes of the band and the songs of the children grow fainter. . . ." He falls asleep and dreams of the discouraged American soldiers breaking camp, marching out "with fife and drum to a popular tune of the day. Suddenly a new national note is heard. Putnam is coming over the hills from the center,—the soldiers turn back and cheer. The little boy awakes, he hears the children's songs and runs down past the monument to 'listen to the band' and join in the games and dances."

*Putnam's Camp* is in three sections (A B A') that parallel the composer's descriptive program. The first section, which is marked *quick step time,* captures the gaiety and confusion of a Fourth of July picnic in a nineteenth-century town. After a raucous, highly dissonant introduction, the strings play the main theme, a vigorous march that begins with conventional harmonies.

Introduction
[35] 0:00
Main theme
0:11

Such abrupt shifts between harsh dissonances and mild consonances are typical of Ives and are heard throughout *Putnam's Camp*. The piano, woodwinds, and brasses begin to compete for the listener's attention, and soon it sounds as though two bands are playing against each other. The mood becomes even more comic when a parody of the opening phrase of *Yankee Doodle* is quickly played by trumpet, flute, and violins.

36 1:06

The music then gradually becomes softer and slows to a halt, depicting the child as he falls asleep.

A mysterious high chord in the strings ushers in the middle section, which depicts the child's dream. Repeated piano and drum beats that seem out of phase with the rest of the orchestra begin one of the boldest parts of the score. Ives creates the impression of two bands playing at different tempos. (One band employs strings and woodwinds; the other has piano, drums, and trumpet.) Here the conductor must beat four bars with one hand against three bars in the other. The bands merge, and a flute plays *The British Grenadiers*, a favorite tune of the Revolutionary army. A sentimental tune in the strings leads to the riotous concluding section, in which the main march theme is combined with *The British Grenadiers* and other fragments. *Putnam's Camp* ends with an earsplitting dissonant chord.

Middle section
37 2:17

Concluding section
38 4:37

# GEORGE GERSHWIN

Popular songs and musical comedies as well as jazz-flavored orchestral works and opera won international fame for the American composer George Gershwin (1898–1937). His parents were Russian-Jewish immigrants, and he grew up on the lower east side of Manhattan. As a boy, he taught himself to play hit tunes on a neighbor's piano; when he was thirteen, he began studying with a teacher who recognized his talent and introduced him to piano works ranging from Bach to Liszt to Debussy.

At fifteen, he left school to become a pianist demonstrating new songs in the salesrooms of a music publisher; three years later, he started his own career as a songwriter, and in 1919 (at the age of twenty) he wrote *La, La, Lucille*, his first complete Broadway musical. The next year, his song *Swanee* was a tremendous hit; during the 1920s and 1930s he wrote one brilliant musical after another—including *Lady, Be Good* (1924), *Funny Face* (1927), and *Of Thee I Sing* (1931)—usually with his brother Ira as lyricist.

(Bettmann Archive)

George Gershwin.

Gershwin was not only a creator of the golden age of American musical theater but also a successful composer of music for the concert hall, beginning with the triumphant premiere of *Rhapsody in Blue* in 1924. He gave the first performance of his Concerto in F at Carnegie Hall in 1925 and traveled to Europe in the 1920s (meeting Berg in Vienna and Ravel and Stravinsky in Paris); part of his symphonic poem *An American in Paris* (1928) was composed on one of these visits. His most extended work is the opera *Porgy and Bess* (1935), which deals with the lives of poor black people in Charleston, South Carolina; it has been performed all over the world.

Gershwin was outgoing, a sportsman, an art collector and amateur painter, and irresistible to women; he was also wealthy, from royalties, concert fees, and his weekly radio show. During the last year of his life, he lived in Hollywood, where he wrote the music for several movies (and played tennis with Arnold Schoenberg in his spare time). He died of a brain tumor at the age of thirty-eight.

### RHAPSODY IN BLUE (1924)

Supplementary sets:
Side 7, band 3
CD 4 [15]

*Rhapsody in Blue,* Gershwin's most famous composition, is a one-movement work for piano and orchestra. The title reflects its free, rhapsodic form and blues flavor (see page 321 for a description of the blues). But it is not true jazz, though it employs jazzlike rhythms and melodies and the orchestration suggests the distinctive sounds of jazz. There are three main sections and a coda; the extended piano solos in the main sections reflect Gershwin's own dazzling pianism and his genius as an improviser.

*Rhapsody in Blue* opens with a now-famous clarinet solo that starts from 15 0:00 a low trill, climbs the scale, and then slides up to a high "wailing" tone. The blueslike opening theme, which grows out of the clarinet slide, is marked by the syncopations so typical of Gershwin's style.

It is followed by a repeated-note theme, presented by French horns, which 16 0:43 reappears many times.

The opening section continues with an extended piano solo, a return of the Trumpet theme<br>17 3:45 blues theme, and a marchlike trumpet theme.

A new jazzlike theme, introduced in the low register, begins the lively 18 5:08 second section, marked *con moto.*

The moderately slow third section is based on a lyrical, romantic melody 19 10:22 first presented by the violins. This memorable tune is combined with a countermelody played by the French horns.

20 14:00 *Rhapsody in Blue* concludes with a rapid coda which is ushered in by an accelerated transformation of the romantic melody.

# [13] AARON COPLAND

Aaron Copland (1900–1990), a leading American composer who died recently at the age of ninety, was born in Brooklyn; his parents (like Gershwin's) were Russian-Jewish immigrants. "No one ever talked music to me or took me to a concert," he recalled; but he discovered music on his own and at fifteen decided to become a composer. He was drawn to "modern" music, although his first teacher discouraged it; and in 1921 he went to France to study with Nadia Boulanger, an extraordinary woman who taught several generations of American composers and was sympathetic to contemporary trends.

Copland's music went through several phases. When he first returned to New York, he wanted to write works that would be "American in character"—and to him, *American* meant jazz. An example is his *Music for the Theater* (1925), a piece for small orchestra with elements of blues and ragtime; but this "jazz period" lasted only a few years. During the early 1930s he composed serious, very dissonant, sophisticated works (such as the highly regarded *Piano Variations*, 1930) that convey starkness, power, percussiveness, and intense concentration.

(Marianne Barcellora)

Aaron Copland.

In the late 1930s, he modified his style again, writing more accessible works for a larger audience. These were the depression years, when many composers rejected the idea of writing for an elite, and Copland now drew on American folklore—as in his ballets *Billy the Kid* (1938), *Rodeo* (1942), and *Appalachian Spring* (1944)—and on jazz, revival hymns, cowboy songs, and other folk tunes. His scores for films and his patriotic works (such as *A Lincoln Portrait,* 1942) also reached a mass public, and his name became synonymous with American music.

Copland accomplished the difficult feat of writing simple yet highly professional music. His textures are clear; his slow-moving harmonies—often almost motionless—seem to evoke the openness of the American landscape; and, though strongly tonal, his works embody twentieth-century techniques such as polychords, polyrhythms, changing meters, and percussive orchestration. He also used serial technique (that is, the manipulation of a tone row, or series) in such works as *Connotations* for orchestra (1962).

Aside from his numerous compositions, Copland made many other contributions to American music by directing composers' groups, organizing concerts, lecturing, writing books and articles, teaching, and conducting.

A scene from the original production of *Appalachian Spring.*

## *APPALACHIAN SPRING* (1943–1944)

*Appalachian Spring* originated as a ballet score for Martha Graham, the great modern dancer and choreographer. It took Copland about a year to finish the music. While composing *Appalachian Spring,* he thought, "How foolhardy it is to be spending all this time writing a thirty-five-minute score for a modern-dance company, knowing how short-lived most ballets *and* their scores are." But Copland arranged parts of the ballet as a suite for full orchestra (originally, the ballet used only thirteen instrumentalists) that won important prizes and brought his name to a large public. Today, *Appalachian Spring* is widely performed both as a ballet and as a concert piece.

The ballet concerns a "pioneer celebration in spring around a newly built farmhouse in the Pennsylvania hills" in the early 1800s. Its characters include a bride and groom, a neighbor, and a revivalist preacher with his followers. The rhythms and melodies are American-sounding and suggest barn dances, fiddle tunes, and revival hymns. But Copland uses only one actual folk tune in the score—a Shaker melody entitled *Simple Gifts.* (The Shakers were a religious sect established in America around the time of the

Revolution. They expressed religious fervor through shaking, leaping, dancing, and singing.) *Appalachian Spring* is bright and transparent, has a clear tonality, and is basically tender and calm in mood. The score's rhythmic excitement comes from delightful syncopations and rapid changes of meter. As in many twentieth-century works, the orchestra contains a piano and a large percussion section.

The ballet suite has eight sections, including a duo for the bride and groom, a fast dance for the revivalist preacher and his followers with "suggestions of square dances and country fiddlers," and a finale in which the couple are left "quiet and strong in their new house." We'll focus on Section 7, which originally accompanied "Scenes of daily activity for the Bride and her Farmer-husband."

### Section 7:
### Theme and Variations on *Simple Gifts*

Section 7 is a theme and five variations on the Shaker tune *Simple Gifts*. The melody's folklike simplicity reflects the Shaker text, which opens:

**Brief sets:**
**Side 6, band 4**
**CD 3** 37

Basic sets:
Side 15, band 1
CD 8 1

'Tis the gift to be simple, 'tis the gift to be free,
'Tis the gift to come down where we ought to be.

In each variation, Copland brings the tune back unadorned, creating variety and contrast through changes of tempo, tone color, dynamics, register, accompaniment, and key. Variation 2 sounds thoughtful and lyrical, as the tune is played more slowly, in a lower register, with polyphonic imitations. Variation 3 brings a brilliant contrast, as *Simple Gifts* is presented faster and staccato by trumpets and trombones. In each of the last two variations, Copland uses only part of the tune: its second part in the pastoral variation 4, and its first part in the majestic closing variation.

## Listening Outline  To be read while music is heard

*APPALACHIAN SPRING* (1943–1944; ORCHESTRAL ARRANGEMENT, 1945), BY AARON COPLAND

Section 7: Theme and Variations on *Simple Gifts*

Theme and variations, duple meter ($\frac{2}{4}$), A flat major

2 flutes, 2 oboes, 2 clarinets, 2 bassoons, 2 French horns, 2 trumpets, 2 trombones, timpani, triangle, glockenspiel, harp, piano, 1st violins, 2d violins, violas, cellos, double basses

(Duration, 2:58)

**THEME**

37  1  0:00

Clarinet, *p, Simple Gifts,* legato.

**VARIATION 1**

38  2  0:36

Oboe, *mp,* and bassoon, *mp, Simple Gifts,* slightly faster, in higher register.

**VARIATION 2**

39  3  1:02

High harp, piano, glockenspiel, *p,* introduce *Simple Gifts,* violas and trombone, *mf,* played half as fast, in lower register. *Simple Gifts* imitated in violins, *f,* then in cellos and basses, *f.* Woodwinds, *p,* brief transition to

**VARIATION 3**

40  4  1:50

Trumpets and trombones, *f, Simple Gifts,* twice as fast, staccato.

**VARIATION 4**

41  5  2:14

Woodwinds, *mf,* second part of *Simple Gifts,* slightly slower than variation 3, gentle and legato.

**VARIATION 5**

42  6  2:31

Full orchestra, *fff,* first part of *Simple Gifts,* played slowly and majestically, in high register.

# MUSICAL STYLES SINCE 1950

Since World War II, we have lived with instant communication—television, computers, and space satellites provide access to a virtually unlimited flow of information. Not only have we been bombarded by an incredible variety of stimuli, but there has also been a constant demand for novelty. New styles in fashion and the visual arts spread rapidly and then disappear.

In music as well, emphasis has been on novelty and change. Musical innovations since 1950 have been even more far-reaching than those of the earlier 1900s. There have been many new directions, and the range of musical styles and systems is wider than ever. As the American composer Hugo Weisgall observed, "Many composers today change their musical points of view with astonishing rapidity, composing this way and that, moving easily from complete traditionalism into the 'avant' *avant garde*."

## CHARACTERISTICS OF MUSIC SINCE 1950

Accurately describing the relatively recent past is a difficult task. Yet any overview of music since 1950 must include these major developments:

1. Increased use of the *twelve-tone system*
2. *Serialism*—use of the techniques of the twelve-tone system to organize rhythm, dynamics, and tone color
3. *Chance music*, in which a composer chooses pitches, tone colors, and rhythms by random methods, or allows a performer to choose much of the musical material
4. *Minimalist music*, characterized by a steady pulse, clear tonality, and insistent repetition of short melodic patterns
5. Works containing deliberate *quotations* from earlier music.
6. A *return to tonality* by some composers
7. *Electronic music*
8. *"Liberation of sound"*—greater exploitation of noiselike sounds
9. *Mixed media*
10. New concepts of *rhythm* and *form*

Since 1950, long-playing records, audiotape, and compact disks have spread these new musical ideas far and wide.

## Increased Use of the Twelve-Tone System

A striking development after World War II (1945) was the gradual abandonment of tonality in favor of the twelve-tone system. From the early 1920s—when Schoenberg invented the system—to about 1950, most composers still wrote music with a tonal center. Few were attracted to the new method, because it was associated with Schoenberg's expressionist style, which had gone out of fashion. During the 1950s, however, the twelve-tone system was adopted by many composers, including Stravinsky, who had been the leading composer of tonal music.

The most important reason for this dramatic shift was probably composers' discovery that the system was a compositional technique rather than a special musical style, and that diversity and individuality were possible within it. The system also had the advantage of stimulating unconventional approaches to melody, harmony, and form: Aaron Copland said once, "I began to hear chords that I wouldn't have heard otherwise."

Many composers of the 1950s and 1960s wrote music that was stylistically reminiscent of Webern, whose lean, "modern" sound appealed to the postwar generation. (Schoenberg's works, by contrast, were considered too "romantic" and traditional in form.)

## Extensions of the Twelve-Tone System: Serialism

The twelve-tone system was originally used to organize pitch; but during the later 1940s and 1950s, its techniques were also used to organize rhythm, dynamics, tone color, and other dimensions of music. For example, a rhythmic or dynamic series might be manipulated like a twelve-tone row. Use of a series—an ordered group of musical elements—to organize several dimensions of a composition is called *serialism.* Proponents of serialism include Milton Babbitt (American, b. 1919), Karlheinz Stockhausen (German, b. 1928), and Pierre Boulez (French, b. 1925). Their methods produce totally controlled and organized music; but the complex relationships in it are often difficult to perceive, and the actual sound may seem random and chaotic.

## Chance Music

*Chance,* or *aleatory, music* (from the Latin *alea,* or *game of dice*) is the opposite of serialism. In chance music, composers choose pitches, tone colors, and rhythms by random methods, such as flipping a coin or having the performers choose the ordering of the musical material or even much of the material itself. For example, performers might be told to play certain passages in any order they like, or to invent rhythmic patterns for a given group of pitches.

The most famous and influential creator of chance music was the American John Cage (1912–1992), who said, "I try to arrange my composing means so that I won't have any knowledge of what might happen. . . . My purpose is to eliminate purpose." Cage's approach is illustrated by his *Imaginary Landscape No. 4* (1951) for twelve radios. The score gives precise instructions to the performers—two at each radio—for turning the dials to affect wavelength and volume, but these instructions disregard local station frequencies and the time of performance, and Cage chose them by throwing dice. With Cage's work as an example, some serial composers (including Boulez and Stockhausen) introduced elements of chance into their compositions during the mid-1950s.

Chance music makes a complete break from traditional values in music—it asserts, in effect, that one sound or ordering of sounds is as acceptable as another.

## Minimalist Music

Minimalism—an artistic movement which began in the mid-1960s—was partly a reaction against the complexity of serialism and the randomness of chance music. *Minimalist music* is characterized by steady pulse, clear tonality, and insistent repetition of short melodic patterns. Its dynamics, textures, and harmony stay constant for long stretches of time, creating a trancelike or hypnotic effect. Leading minimalist composers, such as Terry Riley (b. 1935), Steve Reich (b. 1936), Philip Glass (b. 1937), and John Adams (b. 1947), have been profoundly influenced by nonwestern thought and music. Their work grew out of the same intellectual climate as minimalist art, which features simple forms, clarity, and understatement.

Minimalist composers have generally tried to reach the widest possible audience; Reich and Glass, for example, have ensembles which perform in both auditoriums and rock clubs. A turning point in the public acceptance of minimalist music came in New York in 1976, when Reich's *Music for 18 Musicians* received an ovation in Town Hall and Glass's opera *Einstein on the Beach* sold out the Metropolitan Opera House. After the early 1970s, minimalist music became progressively richer in harmony, tone color, and texture, as is exemplified in Adams's opera *Nixon in China*, which we'll study.

## Musical Quotation

Since the mid-1960s, many composers have made extensive use of quotations from earlier music, usually fairly familiar works of the eighteenth, nineteenth, and twentieth centuries. *Quotation music* often represents a conscious break with serialism as well as an attempt to improve the communication between composer and listener. The quoted material usually conveys a symbolic meaning or is varied, transformed, and juxtaposed with other music. For example, in the outer movements of *Concerto Grosso 1985*, which we'll study, Ellen Taaffe Zwilich juxtaposes parts of a Handel sonata with original passages. One section of *Sinfonia* (1968), a composition for voices and orchestra by Luciano Berio (Italian, b. 1925), is based on the scherzo of Mahler's Second Symphony, with fragments of music by Bach, Debussy, Ravel, Berlioz, Schoenberg, and others superimposed. Often, composers juxtapose heterogeneous material; George Crumb (American, b. 1929) has said that in writing his song cycle *Ancient Voices of Children* (1970), he "was conscious of an urge to fuse various unrelated stylistic elements, . . . Flamenco with a Baroque quotation . . . or Mahler with a breath of the orient."

Basic sets:
Side 15, band 4
CD 8 [9]

Occasionally, modern composers also imitate earlier styles. In the String Quartet No. 3 (1972) by George Rochberg (American, b. 1918), there are atonal sections but also passages in the styles of Beethoven and Mahler.

## Return to Tonality

Paralleling the use of musical quotation is the return to tonality in some recent music. Some works are entirely tonal; others, although basically atonal, contain traditional chord progressions that give a fleeting sense of stability. Tonality could be a fascinating "new" option for composers trained in the twelve-tone system.

## Electronic Music

Since the development of tape studios, synthesizers, and computers in the 1950s and 1960s (see Part I, page 24), composers have had potentially unlimited resources for the production and control of sound. Electronic music is as diverse as nonelectronic music. Its spectrum includes rock, chance music, and serial compositions.

Electronic instruments let composers control tone color, duration, dynamics, and pitch with unprecedented precision. Composers are no longer limited by human performers. For the first time, they can work *directly* in their own medium—sound. There is no more need for intermediaries, that is, performers. The audiotape of a composition *is* the composition. Thus, a composer alone is now responsible for putting into music the subtle variations of rhythm, tone color, and dynamics that once rested with the performer.

Many composers have felt a need to "humanize" their electronic music by combining it with live performers. This can be done in several ways. Some pieces use one or more live performers and taped sounds. The taped sounds may be electronic pitches or noises, or they may be previously recorded sounds of live performers. In some cases, performers may be involved in a duet with themselves, or with electronically manipulated versions of their own performances. In combining live performers with taped sounds, composers face the problem of synchronizing sounds that

308

change from performance to performance—those of the live musicians—and the taped sounds, which don't vary. Recently, some composers have dealt with this problem by creating interactive works for performers and computer. In such compositions, the computer is programmed by the composer to respond in musically meaningful ways to the live performance.

There are also works for traditional instruments and digital synthesizers and samplers that are performed "live." In addition, traditional instruments may also be "electrified" through amplification. Composers use "electric" pianos and violins, for instance.

## "Liberation of Sound"

Composers today use a wider variety of sounds than ever before, including many that were once considered undesirable noises. Edgard Varèse (whose *Poème électronique* we'll study) calls this the "liberation of sound, . . . the right to make music with any and all sounds."

Electronic music may include environmental sounds, such as thunder, and electronically generated hisses and blips. But composers also draw novel sounds from voices and nonelectronic instruments. Singers may be asked to scream, whisper, laugh, groan, sneeze, etc., or to sing phonetic sounds rather than words. Wind and string players may tap, scrape, and rub the bodies of their instruments. A brass or woodwind player may hum while playing, to produce two pitches at once; a pianist may reach inside the piano to pluck a string and then run a chisel along it. The greatest expansion and experimentation have involved percussion instruments, which outnumber strings and winds in many recent compositions. Traditional percussion instruments are struck with new types of beaters, and unconventional instruments—tom-toms, bongos, slapsticks, maracas, and so on—are widely used.

In the search for novel sounds, increased use has been made of *microtones,* intervals smaller than the half step. (Microtones have long been used in nonwestern music but have only recently become important in western music.) Composers such as Krzysztof Penderecki (Polish, b. 1933) create sounds bordering on electronic noise through tone clusters—closely spaced tones played together and heard as a mass, block, or band of sound. The directional aspect of sound has taken on new importance; loudspeakers or groups of instruments may be placed at opposite ends of the stage, in the balcony, or at the back and sides of the auditorium.

Because standard notation makes no provision for many of these innovations, such as noiselike sounds, recent music scores may contain graphlike diagrams, new note shapes and symbols, and novel ways of arranging notation on the page (see the illustration on the following page, from George Crumb's *Ancient Voices of Children*).

Scores for recent music often contain notes in new shapes, or new symbols, as well as novel ways of arranging notation on the page. Here is a page from the score of *Ancient Voices of Children,* by George Crumb.

## Mixed Media

Electronic music is often presented with visual counterparts such as slide projections, films, light shows, gestures, and theatrical actions; Varèse's *Poème électronique*, for instance, combined electronic sounds with images projected on walls. But multimedia works are not confined to electronic music. Other types of recent music sometimes require performers to be actors as well as sound producers, as in *Ancient Voices of Children* (1970) by George Crumb. Mixed-media presentations are generally intended to break down the ritual surrounding traditional concerts and increase communication between composer and audience.

## Rhythm and Form

Rhythm and form have undergone some of the most striking changes in music since 1950. Earlier in the century, composers often changed meters or used unconventional ones such as $\frac{7}{8}$ and $\frac{5}{8}$. Today, some composers abandon the concepts of beat and meter altogether. This is a natural outcome of electronic music, which needs no beat to keep performers together. In nonelectronic music, too, the composer may specify duration in absolute units such as seconds rather than in beats, which are relative units. In some recent music, there may be several different speeds at the same time.

More than ever, each piece of music follows its own laws, and its form grows out of its material. Many composers no longer write music in the traditional forms, such as A B A, sonata form, or rondo. Indeed, form may unfold with little or no obvious repetition of material.

# MUSIC SINCE 1950: THREE REPRESENTATIVE PIECES

TWENTIETH CENTURY

15

## *POÈME ÉLECTRONIQUE (ELECTRONIC POEM),* BY EDGARD VARÈSE

Edgard Varèse (1883–1965), one of the great innovators of twentieth-century music, was born in France but spent most of his life in the United States. As early as 1916, he dreamed of freeing music from the limitations of traditional instruments and expanding the vocabulary of sounds. During the 1920s and 1930s, Varèse pioneered in the exploration of percussive and noiselike sounds, and he wrote the first important work for percussion ensemble (*Ionisation,* 1931).

Brief sets
(opening segment):
Side 6, band 5
CD 3 43

Basic sets
(complete piece):
Side 15, band 2
CD 8 7

But it was the new electronic developments of the 1950s that enabled Varèse to realize his vision of the "liberation of sound." In 1958, at the age of seventy-five, he composed *Poème électronique,* one of the earliest masterpieces of electronic music created in a tape studio. The 8-minute work was designed to be heard within the pavilion of the Philips Radio Corporation at the 1958 Brussels World Fair. Varèse obtained unique spatial effects by projecting sound from 425 loudspeakers placed all over the interior surfaces of the pavilion. The composer worked in collaboration with the architect Le Corbusier, who selected the series of images—photographs, paintings, and writing—that were projected on the walls as the music was heard. However, Varèse did not make any attempt to synchronize the sounds with the images chosen by Le Corbusier, which included "birds and beasts, fish and reptiles, . . . masks and skeletons, idols, girls clad and unclad, cities in normal appearance and then suddenly askew," as well as atomic mushroom clouds.

Because it was created in a tape studio, *Poème électronique* exists in only a single "performance" whose duration (8 minutes) is fixed on audiotape. Varèse's raw sound material—tones and noises—came from a wide variety of sources, including electronic generators, church bells, sirens, organs, human voices, and machines. The sounds are often electronically processed in a such a way that they cannot be precisely identified. In the listening outline, the effect of such sounds is conveyed by words placed in quotation marks; for example, "wood blocks" or "chirps." Varèse unifies *Poème électronique* through a distinctive group of three rising tones heard several times. Tension is created by suspenseful pauses lasting from 2 to 7 seconds. Varèse organizes his sounds into an electronic poem that seems weird, yet is amazingly logical and compelling. The listening outline describes the opening 2 minutes and 36 seconds of this work, a segment which begins and ends with low bell tolls.

## Listening Outline  To be read while music is heard

*POÈME ÉLECTRONIQUE (ELECTRONIC POEM;* 1958), BY EDGARD VARÈSE (1883–1965)

Excerpt: Opening Segment

**Tape studio**

(Duration, Brief sets, 2:43; Basic sets, 8:00)

[43] [7]  0:00    1. Low bell tolls. "Wood blocks." Sirens. Fast taps lead into high, piercing sounds. 2-second pause.

| | |
|---|---|
| 0:43 | 2. "Bongo" tones and higher grating noises. Short "squawks." Three-tone group stated three times. |
| 1:11 | 3. Low sustained tones with grating noises. Sirens. Short "squawks." Three-tone group. 2-second pause. |
| 1:40 | 4. Short "squawks." High "chirps." Variety of "shots," "honks," "machine noises." Sirens. Taps lead to |
| 2:36 | 5. Low bell tolls. |

## CONCERTO GROSSO 1985
## (TO HANDEL'S SONATA IN D MAJOR
## FOR VIOLIN AND CONTINUO, FIRST MOVEMENT),
## BY ELLEN TAAFFE ZWILICH

The American composer Ellen Taaffe Zwilich (b. 1939) won the 1983 Pulitzer Prize for Music for her Symphony No. 1. Zwilich was born in Miami, Florida, the daughter of an airline pilot. She studied at Florida State University and at the Juilliard School and played for several years as a professional violinist in the American Symphony Orchestra under the direction of Leopold Stokowski. She has composed an impressive series of widely performed instrumental works, including the String Quartet (1974), Chamber Symphony (1979), String Trio (1982), Double Quartet for Strings (1984), Symphonies No. 2 (1985) and No. 3 (1992), Concerto for Piano and Orchestra (1986), and *Symbolon* (1988). Her Symphony No. 3 was commissioned as part of the celebration of the hundred-fiftieth anniversary of the New York Philharmonic orchestra.

*Concerto Grosso 1985* was commissioned by the Washington Friends of Handel to commemorate Handel's three-hundredth birthday. Each of its five movements uses thematic material drawn from the opening movement of Handel's Sonata for Violin and Continuo in D Major. Zwilich has said: "I performed the [Handel] many years ago, and I especially love the opening theme of the first movement. . . . Throughout [*Concerto Grosso 1985*], I found myself using compositional techniques typical of the baroque period, including terraced dynamics, repeated phrases . . . techniques I would not normally use, but I felt inspired to do so because of the fact that this piece was based on Handel." Like the concerti grossi of Handel and Bach, Zwilich's composition is written for a small orchestra including a harpsichord and gives solo instruments prominent roles.

The five movements of *Concerto Grosso* 1985 are arranged symmetrically: the finale is similar to the opening movement, and the fourth movement parallels the second. The two outer movements include entire passages from the Handel sonata, whereas the three inner movements employ no quotations but freely develop its opening melodic motive. We'll focus on the first movement, a clear example of "quotation music."

(Cori Wells Braun)

Ellen Taaffe Zwilich.

## First Movement:

### Maestoso (majestic)

Brief sets:
Side 6, band 6
CD 3  44

Basic sets:
Side 15, band 5
CD 8  10

The maestoso repeatedly alternates quotations from Handel with passages that could have been written only in the twentieth century. Though abrupt, these contrasts somehow add up to a unified whole. Partly, this is because the newly composed sections are often based on a speeded-up variation of Handel's opening four-note motive.

In addition, Zwilich's own music uses compositional techniques associated with the baroque. Long pedal points in the bass give a firm definition of key to melodic lines that use dissonances freely in a twentieth-century manner. And these melodic lines include the repeated rhythmic pattern short-short-long, short-short-long that is often found in music by Bach and Handel.

# Listening Outline To be read while music is heard

*CONCERTO GROSSO 1985*
(TO HANDEL'S SONATA IN D MAJOR FOR VIOLIN AND CONTINUO, FIRST MOVEMENT),
BY ELLEN TAAFFE ZWILICH

Maestoso (majestic), quadruple meter ($\frac{4}{4}$), D major

Flute, 2 oboes, bassoon, 2 French horns, harpsichord, 1st violins, 2d violins, violas, cellos, double basses

(Duration, 2:41)

44 10 0:00    **1.** *a.* Orchestra in unison, *f*, single sustained tone presented three times.
        *b.* Violins, *f*, vigorous phrase, short-short-long rhythm, sustained tone in bass;

        vigorous phrase repeated softly.

45 11 0:34       *c.* Handel quotation, strings and harpsichord, *mp*,

        interrupted by

0:55    **2.** *a.* Vigorous phrase developed in strings and woodwinds; crescendo to *f*; short string phrases with abrupt pauses.
        *b.* Handel quotation continued, oboe *mf*, accompanied by harpsichord and strings.

1:31    **3.** *a.* Vigorous phrase in violins, *f*, imitated in flute, *f*; vigorous phrase in violins, *f*.
        *b.* Handel quotation continued, *f*; trills in strings and woodwinds; harpsichord; melody closes.

2:03    **4.** *a.* Vigorous phrase in violins, flute, and oboes; crescendo to *ff*.
2:13        *b.* Woodwinds, high sustained dissonant chords; low strings, fragments of vigorous string phrase, *ff*. Ends on sustained dissonant chord, *f*.

315

## *NIXON IN CHINA* (1987), BY JOHN ADAMS

John Adams (b. 1947) is a leading American composer who has described himself as "a minimalist bored with minimalism." Like other minimalists, he writes music with a steady, driving pulse, clear tonality, constant repetition of melodic and rhythmic patterns, and a slow rate of change. But his works are enriched by lyrical, expressive melodies and varied orchestral colors. A conductor as well as composer, he taught and directed the New Music Ensemble at the San Francisco Conservatory of Music from 1972 to 1982 and was composer in residence with the San Francisco Symphony Orchestra during 1982–1985. His works include *Harmonium* (1980), for chorus and orchestra; *Light over Water* (Symphony for Brass and Synthesizers, 1983); *Harmonielehre* (1985) for orchestra; and the operas *Nixon in China* (1987), which we'll study, and *The Death of Klinghoffer* (1991).

*Nixon in China* takes place from February 21 to 25, 1972, when Richard Nixon, then president of the United States, made a historic trip to Beijing to meet the Chinese leader, Chairman Mao Tse-Tung, and work toward the establishment of diplomatic relations between the two countries. The opera is extraordinary because it deals with a media event involving famous people contemporary with the composer. Its libretto, by Alice Goodman, is written in eight-syllable couplets and is based on news reports, television broadcasts, biographies, and memoirs. The main characters are the two leaders; their wives, Pat Nixon and Chiang Ch'ing; the American Secretary of State, Henry Kissinger, who is a former Harvard professor; and the Chinese Prime Minister, Chou En-Lai.

### Act I: Opening of Scene 2 (Chairman Mao's Study)

Brief sets:
Side 6, band 7
CD 3 46

Basic sets:
Side 15, band 6
CD 8 12

In this scene, Nixon, Kissinger, Mao, and Chou En-Lai chat about such topics as Chiang Kai-shek (then head of the Chinese government in exile on Taiwan), Mao's books (which are "read at Harvard"), and Kissinger's reputation in "foreign affairs."

The opening orchestral passage, heard while the leaders enter Mao's study, is a characteristic example of minimalist music, with high repeated rhythmic figures pulsating over low, syncopated notes played on a Yamaha HX-1 synthesizer. Rhythmic pulsations in the orchestra accompany the singers throughout the scene. To convey the effect of a simultaneous translation, every word that Mao sings is also sung at the same time by his three female secretaries, who are given different melodies with slower rhythms.

(Jim Caldwell/Houston Grand Opera)

President Richard Nixon, Chairman Mao Tse-Tung, and Mao's three secretaries in Act I, scene 2, of *Nixon in China*, as performed by the Houston Grand Opera.

46 12
Orchestral introduction, high pulsations over low, syncopated tones of synthesizer.

**Mao**
I can't talk very well. My throat—

**Nixon**
I'm nearly speechless with delight
Just to be here.

**Mao**
We're even then.
That is the right way to begin.
Our common old friend Chiang Kai-shek
With all his virtues would not look
Too kindly on all this. We seem
To be beneath the likes of him.
You've seen his latest speech?

### Nixon

You bet.
It was a scorcher. Still, he's spit
Into the wind before, and will
Again. That puts it into scale.
You shouldn't despise Chiang.

### Mao

No fear
Of that. We've followed his career
For generations. There's not much
Beneath our notice.

### Chou

We will touch
On this in our communiqué.

### Mao

(addressing Kissinger)
Ah, the philosopher! I see
Paris can spare you then.

### Kissinger

The Chair-
Man may be gratified to hear
He's read at Harvard. I assign
All four volumes.

### Mao

Those books of mine
Aren't anything. Incorporate
Their words within a people's thought
As poor men's common sense and try
Their strength on women's nerves, then say
They live.

### Nixon

The Chairman's books enthralled
A nation, and have changed the world.

### Mao

I could not change it. I'd be glad
To think that in the neighborhood
Of Peking something will remain.

### Nixon

Let us turn our talk towards Taiwan,
Vietnam and the problems there.
Japan—

**Mao**
Save that for the Premier.
My business is philosophy.
Now Doctor Kissinger—

**Kissinger**
Who me?

**Mao**
—Has made his reputation in
Foreign affairs.

**Nixon**
My right hand man.
You'd never think to look at him
That he's James Bond.

**Chou**
And all the time
He's doing undercover work.

**Kissinger**
I had a cover.

**Mao**
In the dark
All diplomats are gray.

**Chou**
Or *gris* [*gray* in French]
When their work takes them to *Paris*.

**Kissinger**
I pull the wool over their—                     Sung
                                                simultaneously.
**Mao**
He pulls the wool over their lap.

**Nixon**
He's a consummate diplomat.
Girls think he's lukewarm when he's hot.

**Mao**
You also dally with your girls?

**Nixon**
His girls, not mine.

**Kissinger**
He never tells.

**Chou**
And this is an election year.

# [16] JAZZ

About the time Schoenberg and Stravinsky were changing the language of music in Europe, a new musical style called *jazz* was being developed in the United States.* It was created by musicians—predominantly African Americans—performing in the streets, bars, brothels, and dance halls of New Orleans and other southern cities. *Jazz* can be described generally as music rooted in improvisation and characterized by syncopated rhythm, a steady beat, and distinctive tone colors and performance techniques. Although the term *jazz* became current in 1917, the music itself was probably heard as early as 1900. We do not know exactly when jazz started or how it sounded at first, because this new music existed only in performance, not musical notation. Moreover, very little jazz was captured on recordings before 1923, and none at all before the Original Dixieland Jazz Band recorded in 1917.

Since its beginnings, jazz has developed a rich variety of substyles such as New Orleans style (or Dixieland), swing, bebop, cool, free jazz, and jazz rock. It has produced such outstanding figures as Louis Armstrong, Duke Ellington, Benny Goodman, Charlie Parker, and John Coltrane. Its impact has been enormous and worldwide, affecting not only many kinds of popular music, but the music of such composers as Maurice Ravel, Darius Milhaud, and Aaron Copland. For a long time, jazz was basically music for dancing; but since the 1940s, many jazz styles have been intended for listening.

## ROOTS OF JAZZ

Early jazz blended elements from many musical cultures, particularly west African, American, and European. West African influences included an emphasis on improvisation, drumming, percussive sounds, and complex rhythms, as well as a feature known as *call and response*. In much west African vocal music, a soloist's phrases are repeatedly answered by a chorus; similarly, in jazz, **call and response** occurs when a voice is answered by an instrument, or when one instrument or group of instruments is answered by another instrument or group.

---

*An excellent recorded anthology of jazz is the *Smithsonian Collection of Classic Jazz,* available from Smithsonian Books and Recordings (P.O. Box 10229, Des Moines, Iowa 50381–0229) as a set of seven records (no. 1846), five cassettes (no. 1847), or five compact disks (no. 1848).

Actually, the call-and-response pattern of jazz was derived more directly from African American church services in which the congregation vocally responds to the preacher's "call." Other American influences on jazz were the rich body of music that blacks developed here—including work songs, spirituals, gospel hymns, and dances like the cakewalk—and the music of white America. Nineteenth-century American and European musical traditions became elements in the background of jazz. In addition to hymns, popular songs, folk tunes, dances, and piano pieces, the American band tradition was a major influence. Many marching band instruments were used in early jazz bands, and band music helped shape the forms and rhythms of early jazz. A leading American composer of band music was John Philip Sousa (1854–1932)—nicknamed the "march king"—whose works include *The Stars and Stripes Forever.*

*Basic sets:*
*Side 1, band 5*
*CD 1* 16

Along with band music, the immediate sources of jazz were ragtime and the blues.

## Ragtime

*Ragtime* (1890s to about 1915) is a style of composed piano music developed primarily by black pianists who played in southern and midwestern saloons and dance halls. It is generally in duple meter ($\frac{2}{4}$) and performed at a moderate march tempo; the pianist's right hand plays a highly syncopated melody while the left hand steadily maintains the beat with an "oom-pah" accompaniment. The "king of ragtime" was Scott Joplin (1868–1917), whose most famous pieces include *Maple Leaf Rag* and *The Entertainer.*

*Maple Leaf Rag*
*Basic sets:*
*Side 15, band 7*
*CD 8* 13

## The Blues

The *blues* (developed in the 1890s) is a style of vocal music, originating among African Americans, that involves "bent" notes and slides of pitch; "blue" notes are produced by slightly lowering, or flatting, the third, fifth, and seventh notes of the major scale. The intensely personal lyrics consist of several 3-line stanzas, each set to a harmonic framework that usually lasts for 12 *bars,* or measures, and is thus known as *12-bar blues.* This pattern uses three basic chords: tonic (I), *subdominant* (IV, based on the fourth note of the scale, *fa*), and dominant (V). These are ordered: tonic (4 bars)–subdominant (2 bars)–tonic (2 bars)–dominant (2 bars)–tonic (2 bars). Each stanza is sung to the same series of chords, although other chords may be inserted. The music is in quadruple meter ($\frac{4}{4}$).

Jazz instrumentalists imitate the performing style of blues singers and use the harmonic pattern of 12-bar blues as a basis for improvisation. This 12-bar pattern is repeated over and over while new melodies are improvised above it.

(Granger Collection)

Scott Joplin, the "king of ragtime."

(CBS Records)

Bessie Smith, the "empress of the blues."

Notable blues figures include W. C. Handy (1873–1958), who wrote *Memphis Blues* (1912) and *St. Louis Blues* (1914); and the singer Bessie Smith (1894–1937), known as the "empress of the blues." Her *Lost Your Head Blues* is a marvelous example of blues form and performance style.

Basic sets:
Side 15, band 8
CD 8 17

## ELEMENTS OF JAZZ

### Tone Color

Jazz is generally played by a small group (or *combo*) of three to eight players, or by a "big band" of ten to fifteen. The backbone of a jazz ensemble is its rhythm section, which is comparable to the basso continuo in baroque music. The ***rhythm section,*** usually made up of piano, plucked double bass (bass), percussion, and—sometimes—banjo or guitar, maintains the beat, adds rhythmic interest, and provides supporting harmonies.

The main solo instruments of jazz include the cornet, trumpet, saxophone (soprano, alto, tenor, baritone), piano, clarinet, vibraphone, and trombone. Jazz emphasizes brasses, woodwinds, and percussion rather than the bowed strings that dominate symphonic music. A jazz performance usually involves both solo and ensemble sections. For example, a full ensemble might be followed by a trumpet solo and then by a clarinet solo or a duet for saxophone and trumpet.

The distinctive sounds of jazz are easy to recognize but hard to describe. They result from the particular way tones are attacked, "bent," and released; from the type of vibrato employed; and from a variety of pitch inflections that might be described as "smears," "scoops," "falloffs," and "shakes."

## Improvisation

At the heart of jazz lies improvisation. Jazz musicians create a special electricity as they simultaneously create and perform, making decisions at lightning speed. The fertility of great improvisers is staggering. Their recorded performances represent only a tiny fraction of the music they create almost nightly. Of course, not all jazz is improvised, and most contains both improvised and composed sections. Yet it is improvisation that contributes most to the freshness and spontaneity of jazz.

A jazz improvisation is usually in theme-and-variations form. The theme is often a popular song melody in A A B A form made up of 32 bars. The improviser varies this original melody by adding embellishments and changing its pitches and rhythms. Some jazz improvisations are based on a harmonic pattern, or series of chords. This harmonic pattern will be repeated over and over while the improviser creates melodies above it. In jazz, each statement of the basic harmonic pattern or melody is called a *chorus.*

A jazz performance usually includes improvised solos by various members of the ensemble. In addition, there may be sections of *collective* improvisation, during which several musicians make up different melodies simultaneously. Their music is held together by the underlying chords.

## Rhythm, Melody, and Harmony

Syncopation and rhythmic swing are two of the most distinctive features of jazz. We say that jazz performers "swing" when they combine a steady beat with a feeling of lilt, precision, and relaxed vitality. In most jazz styles, the beat is provided by the percussionist (on drums or cymbals) and by the bass player. There are usually four beats to the bar. Accents often come on the weak beats: 1–**2**–3–**4.** Many kinds of syncopated rhythms result when accented notes come *between* the beats. Jazz musicians also create a swing feeling by playing a series of notes slightly unevenly. For example, the second note of a pair of eighth notes will be shorter than the first:

But the rhythms of jazz are so irregular that it is difficult to notate them accurately. A performer must deviate from the notated rhythms to get a true jazz feeling. And as jazz has evolved, rhythms have become ever more irregular and complex.

Jazz melodies are as flexible in pitch as in rhythm. They employ a major scale in which the third, fifth, and seventh notes are often lowered, or flatted. These "bent," or "blue," notes came into jazz through the vocal blues. Jazz uses chord progressions like those of the traditional tonal system. But over the years, the harmonic vocabulary of jazz—like its rhythm—has become increasingly complex and sophisticated.

## JAZZ STYLES

### New Orleans Style

Jazz in *New Orleans style* (or *Dixieland*), as its name suggests, was developed in New Orleans, which was the major center of jazz from 1900 to 1917. It was typically played by five to eight performers: a *front line* of melodic instruments (cornet or trumpet; clarinet; and trombone) and a supporting rhythm section (drums; chordal instruments such as piano, banjo, and guitar; and a single-line low instrument such as a tuba or plucked bass). The front-line players would improvise several contrasting melodic lines at once, producing a kind of polyphonic texture; and their syncopations and rhythmic independence created a marvelous sense of excitement. This collective improvisation, in which each instrument had a special role, was the most distinctive feature of New Orleans jazz, though as the style evolved during the 1920s (mainly in Chicago), solo playing came to be more emphasized. New Orleans jazz was usually based on a march, a church melody, a ragtime piece, a popular song, or 12-bar blues.

*Dippermouth Blues*
Basic sets:
Side 16, band 1
CD 8 [18]

Notable figures of New Orleans jazz include Ferdinand "Jelly Roll" Morton and Joseph "King" Oliver; Oliver's *Dippermouth Blues* (1923) is a fine example of instrumental blues and New Orleans style. Especially important is the trumpeter and singer Louis "Satchmo" Armstrong (1900–1971). *Hotter Than That*, in a rendition by Louis Armstrong and His Hot Five, was studied in Part I, Section 1 (see the discussion and listening outline on pages 6–7); since the emphasis is on improvisatory solos, it shows how New Orleans style developed in Chicago in the 1920s. Listen for the exciting vocal and instrumental solos (items 2, 3, 4, 5, and 6*a*), the syncopations of Armstrong's vocal melody (item 4), and the dissonant guitar chord at the end.

(Photo Files)

New Orleans style (or Dixieland) was typically played by five to eight performers. King Oliver (standing, at left rear) is shown here with his Creole Jazz Band in 1923. The band included Louis Armstrong (seated, center) and Lil Hardin (at the piano).

## Swing

A new jazz style called *swing* developed in the 1920s and flourished from 1935 to 1945 (the "swing era"). It was played mostly by big bands; the typical *swing band* had about fifteen players in three sections—saxophones, brasses (trumpet and trombone), and rhythm (piano, percussion, guitar, and bass). A band of that size needed music which was more composed than improvised and also *arranged*, that is, notated in written-out parts for the musicians. With swing, the arranger became an important figure in jazz.

Melodies were often performed by entire sections of a swing band, either in unison or in harmony. The main melody was frequently accompanied by saxophones and brasses playing short, repeated phrases called *riffs.* The saxophone became one of the most important solo instruments, and percussionists also had a more prominent and spectacular role.

The swing era produced hundreds of "name" bands—both black and white—like those of Count Basie, Glenn Miller, Tommy Dorsey, and Benny Goodman (the "king of swing"). Duke Ellington (1899–1974) was perhaps the most important composer, arranger, and conductor. One of his most distinctive works is *Concerto for Cootie* (1940), designed to display

Basic sets:
Side 16, band 3
CD 8 [20]

Duke Ellington and his orchestra in 1943. Ellington was perhaps the most important swing composer, arranger, and conductor.

the variety of tone colors that Cootie Williams could draw from the trumpet. Some swing bands included leading musicians like the saxophonists Coleman Hawkins and Lester Young and featured singers like Billie Holiday, Ella Fitzgerald, and Frank Sinatra.

## Bebop

*Bebop,* or *bop* (developed in the early 1940s), was a complex style, usually for small jazz groups, and meant for attentive listening rather than dancing. It had sophisticated harmonies and unpredictable rhythms, and its performers were a special "in" group. A typical bebop ensemble might have a saxophone and a trumpet supported by a rhythm section of piano, bass, and percussion. The role of the rhythm instruments was different from that in earlier jazz—the beat was marked mainly by a pizzicato bass, with the drum supplying occasional irregular accents (*bombs*) and the pianist's left hand supplying chords at irregular intervals. Melodic phrases were often varied in length, and chords might have six or seven notes rather than the four or five characteristic of earlier jazz. A bop performance generally began and ended with a statement of the main theme (often derived from a popular song or 12-bar blues) by a soloist, or by two soloists in unison; the remainder of the piece was made up of solo improvisations based on the melody or harmonic structure.

Notable bebop performers included the trumpeter Dizzy Gillespie (1917–1993) and the pianist Thelonious Monk (1917–1982). The alto saxophonist Charlie "Bird" Parker (1920–1955) was a towering figure among bebop musicians and an important influence on instrumentalists. Parker's *KoKo* (1945) illustrates bebop style and his own improvisatory genius.

Basic sets:
Side 16, band 4
CD 8 [21]

## Cool Jazz

*Cool jazz* (which emerged in the late 1940s and early 1950s) was related to bop, but far calmer and more relaxed. Cool jazz pieces also tended to be longer than bebop and relied more on arrangements; and they sometimes used instruments new to jazz, including the French horn, flute, and cello. The tenor saxophonists Lester Young (1909–1959) and Stan Getz (b. 1927), the pianist Lennie Tristano (1919–1978), and the trumpeter and bandleader Miles Davis (1926–1991) were important figures.

## Free Jazz

Until about 1960, improvised jazz variations tended to keep the length and chord structure of the original theme, if not its melody. But during the 1960s, some musicians created *free jazz,* a style that was not based on regular forms and established chord patterns. *Free Jazz,* recorded in 1960 by Ornette Coleman (b. 1930) with several other musicians improvising individually and collectively, is an example: it can be compared to the chance music of John Cage and his followers. Another free-jazz musician was John Coltrane (1926–1967), who was influential as an improviser, tenor and soprano saxophonist, and composer.

## Jazz Rock (Fusion)

Rock music became a potent influence on jazz during the late 1960s, the 1970s, and the 1980s. This influence led to *jazz rock,* or *fusion,* a new style combining the jazz musician's improvisatory approach with rock rhythms and tone colors. A jazz rock group typically has acoustic instruments (which may have electric attachments) along with synthesizers and electric piano, guitar, and bass (which takes a melodic role). The percussion section is larger than that in earlier jazz groups and often includes instruments from Africa, Latin America, or India. A distinctive feature is the insistent repetition of rhythmic figures.

Miles Davis, a leading musician in cool jazz, was also important in jazz rock; Herbie Hancock, Chick Corea, Joe Zawinul, and Wayne Shorter—who made recordings with Davis—became pacesetters of jazz rock in the 1970s and 1980s.

# [17] THE AMERICAN MUSICAL

Along with jazz and rock, the *musical* is one of the most important American contributions to twentieth-century popular culture. Shows like *Oklahoma!*, *South Pacific*, *West Side Story*, and *My Fair Lady* are performed and enjoyed all over the world.

## MUSICAL THEATER

### Elements of the Musical

A *musical,* or *musical comedy,* is a type of theater that fuses script, acting, and spoken dialogue with music, singing, and dancing and with scenery, costumes, and spectacle. Most musicals are in fact comedies, though some are serious. Many have been produced in theaters around Broadway in New York (hence the term *Broadway musical*), but successful musicals reach nationwide and even worldwide audiences, often becoming films.

Generally, a musical is in two acts, of which the second is shorter and brings back some of the melodies heard earlier. Traditionally, the songs consisted of an introductory section (the *verse)* and a main section (the *chorus)* in A A B A form (32 bars). Hit songs like *Ol' Man River* (from *Showboat*) and *Some Enchanted Evening* (from *South Pacific*) often have lasting appeal, detached from their original theatrical context.

The American musical embraces a variety of styles, yet it is a distinct type of musical theater, separate from opera. In contrast to opera, it tends to use simpler harmonies, melodies, and structures; it has more spoken dialogue; and its songs have a narrower pitch range. Also, the musical is an even more collaborative effort: one composer may create the songs, but other musicians are responsible for orchestration, the overture, connective musical passages, and ballets; and the book and lyrics are usually written by several people. Still, certain works, such as Stephen Sondheim's *Sweeney Todd* (1979), fall somewhere between musicals and operas; and some, like Sondheim's *A Little Night Music* (1973), are eventually performed by opera companies.

### Development of the Musical

Sources of the American musical include various musical and dramatic forms of the late nineteenth and early twentieth centuries, such as operetta, vaudeville, and the revue. *Operetta,* or *comic opera,* combines song, spoken dialogue, and dance with sophisticated musical techniques. Examples are the operettas of the Englishmen W. S. Gilbert and Arthur Sullivan, such as *The Mikado* (1885); and those of the American Victor Herbert, such as *Babes in Toyland* (1903) and *Naughty Marietta* (1910). A more popular antecedent was *vaudeville,* a variety show with songs, comedy, juggling, acrobats, and animal acts, but no plot. The *revue,* a variety show without a plot but with a unifying idea, was often satirical; it featured chorus girls and comedians.

The years from about 1920 to 1960 saw a golden era of the American musical, created by songwriters and composers like Irving Berlin (1888–1989), Jerome Kern (1885–1945), George Gershwin (1898–1937), Cole Porter (1893–1964), Richard Rodgers (1902–1979), Frank Loesser (1910–1969), and Leonard Bernstein (1918–1990). Plots became more believable and wider in range; song and dance were better integrated with the story, and musical techniques became more sophisticated.

During the 1920s and 1930s, despite unrealistic "boy-meets-girl" stories, lyrics were clever and witty, as in Cole Porter's song "You're the Top" (1934):

> You're the top! You're the Colosseum.
> You're the top! You're the Louvre Museum.
> You're a melody from a symphony by Strauss.
> You're a Bendel bonnet, a Shakespeare sonnet, you're Mickey Mouse. . . .

A pathbreaking musical with a serious plot was *Show Boat* (1927, music by Jerome Kern and lyrics by Oscar Hammerstein II), which treated interracial romance. Its songs—including *Ol' Man River* and *Why Do I Love You?*—revealed character and were smoothly woven into the action. In the 1930s, some musicals satirized social and political institutions; one example is George and Ira Gershwin's *Of Thee I Sing* (1931), which poked fun at American presidential elections. In the late 1930s, ballet became more significant and was used to carry the action forward. For example, the climax of the musical *On Your Toes* (1936) was a ballet choreographed by George Balanchine (1904–1989) called *Slaughter on Tenth Avenue. Oklahoma!* (1943)— the first in a memorable series by Richard Rodgers and the lyricist Oscar Hammerstein II—was a landmark in the integration of dance, songs, and plot; its ballets, created by Agnes de Mille and inspired by square dances, were important for the progress of the story. After World War II, more and more musicals were set in foreign lands, such as Siam (*The King and I;* 1951), France (*Fanny;* 1954), England (*My Fair Lady;* 1956), and Russia (*Fiddler on the Roof;* 1964). Postwar musicals also began to explore new kinds of serious subjects, such as teenage gang warfare in *West Side Story* (1957).

*Oklahoma!* was a landmark in the history of American musical theater. Shown here is the 1950 touring production.

After 1960, some composers of Broadway shows continued to write traditional songs—a conservative trend that was also seen in many revivals of classic musicals. However, other composers departed from the traditional A A B A form; and often their songs were so much a part of the context that they were unlikely to become hits on their own. The musical was relatively unaffected by the "rock revolution" of the 1960s, except for a few rock musicals such as *Hair* (1967) and *Jesus Christ Superstar* (1971)—the latter by the British musician Andrew Lloyd Webber (b. 1948), who later created *Cats* (1982) and *Phantom of the Opera* (1987). The unusual prominence of English composers on the American musical scene is also reflected in *Les Misérables* (1986) and *Miss Saigon* (1989). Perhaps the most original contributor to American musical theater since the 1960s is the composer-lyricist Stephen Sondheim (b. 1930), who first became known as the lyricist for *West Side Story*. Many of his works are "concept musicals," based more on an idea than on a traditional plot; they include *Company* (1970); *Sunday in the Park with George* (1984); and his most ambitious work, *Sweeney Todd, the Demon Barber of Fleet Street* (1979), which blurs the boundary between musicals and opera. His musical style fuses elements of the traditional Broadway song with elements of Stravinsky, Copland, and Bernstein.

## LEONARD BERNSTEIN

The extraordinarily versatile Leonard Bernstein (1918–1990) was a twentieth-century culture hero—conductor, pianist, author, lecturer, and composer of orchestral and vocal works, including *West Side Story*. Bernstein was born in Lawrence, Massachusetts; graduated from Harvard University; and studied piano and conducting at the Curtis Institute in Philadelphia. In 1943, he was appointed assistant conductor of the New York Philharmonic orchestra and his spectacular career was launched when a guest conductor became ill: Bernstein took the podium on a few hours' notice with no rehearsal; the concert, which was broadcast on nationwide radio, was hailed as a "dramatic musical event" on the front page of the *New York Times*.

"I have a deep suspicion that every work I write, for whatever medium, is really theater music in some way." Bernstein's words apply not only to his musicals, operas, and ballets and his theater piece *Mass* (1971), but also to his choral work *Chichester Psalms* (1965) and his three programmatic symphonies—*Jeremiah* (1942), *The Age of Anxiety* (1949), and *Kaddish* (1963). His music is clearly tonal, enlivened by syncopations, irregular meters, and jazz and dance rhythms. Like Stravinsky and Copland, both of whom influenced him, Bernstein wrote successful ballets, including *Fancy*

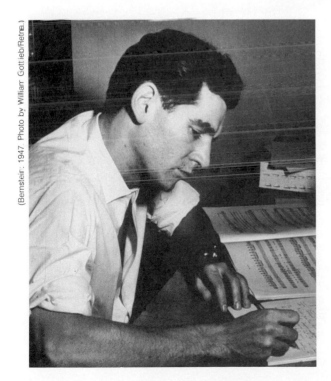

(Bernstein. 1947. Photo by William Gottlieb/Retna.)

Leonard Bernstein.

(Eileen Darby)

Tony and Maria meet on the fire escape in a scene from *West Side Story*.

*Free* (1944) and *Facsimile* (1946). Dance is very important and dramatic in his musicals *On the Town* (1944), *Wonderful Town* (1953), and *West Side Story* (1957). Bernstein accomplished the difficult feat of bridging the worlds of "serious" and popular music. He died in 1990, mourned by people all over the world.

## WEST SIDE STORY (1957)

On January 6, 1949, the choreographer Jerome Robbins first suggested to Leonard Bernstein that they collaborate on a modern version of Shakespeare's *Romeo and Juliet*, to be set in the slums of New York. Bernstein was very enthusiastic about the "idea of making a musical that tells a tragic story in musical-comedy terms, using only musical-comedy techniques, never falling into the 'operatic' trap. Can it succeed? . . . I'm excited. If it can work—it's the first." *West Side Story*— with music by Bernstein, book by Arthur Laurents, and lyrics by Stephen Sondheim —was created seven years later.

*West Side Story* deals with the conflict between gang rivalry and youthful love. The feud between the lovers' families in Shakespeare's *Romeo and Juliet* is transformed into warfare between two teenage street gangs: the Jets, native-born Americans led by Riff; and the Sharks, Puerto Ricans led by Bernardo. The plot revolves around a fight ("rumble") between the gangs and the doomed love of Tony (Romeo), a former member of the Jets; and Maria (Juliet), Bernardo's sister. Tony kills Bernardo after a vain attempt to break up the fight. Later he is shot by one of the Sharks and dies in Maria's arms.

Though it included rough street language and ended unhappily, *West Side Story* was a tremendous popular success and became an Oscar-winning musical film (1961). It was an unprecedented fusion of song and drama with electrifyingly violent choreography (by Jerome Robbins and Peter Gennaro). Compared with the average Broadway show, *West Side Story* contained more music, more complex and unconventional music, and a wider range of styles, from vaudeville (*Gee, Officer Krupke*) and Latin rhythms (*America*) to bebop fugue (*Cool*) and quasi-operatic ensemble (*Tonight*).

### *Tonight* Ensemble

In the *Tonight* ensemble, Bernstein projects several different emotions at the same time: Riff, Bernardo, and their gangs excitedly planning for the upcoming fight; Anita—Bernardo's girlfriend—looking forward to the "kicks" she's "gonna get"; and Tony and Maria anticipating the joy of being together. Riff, Bernardo, and Anita sing quick, staccato tones in a narrow range, whereas Tony and Maria sing the legato, soaringly lyrical *Tonight* melody, heard in an earlier "balcony scene" on Maria's fire escape. Bernstein lets us hear the voices separately before combining them in an ensemble. Such dramatic ensembles were uncommon in musicals, which tended to feature solo songs with "hit" potential.

Brief sets:
Side 6, band 8
CD 3 47

Basic sets:
Side 16, band 5
CD 8 22

# Listening Outline  To be read while music is heard

*TONIGHT* ENSEMBLE FROM *WEST SIDE STORY* (1957), BY LEONARD BERNSTEIN

Riff, Bernardo, Anita, Tony, Maria, gang members, orchestra

Fast and rhythmic.

(Duration, 3:39)

0:00
0:07

1. *a.* Orchestra, menacing staccato melody with syncopations introduces
   *b.* Riff, Bernardo, and their gangs alternate and then sing together quick, staccato phrases with syncopations.

The Jets are gon-na have their day _____ To - night. _____

1:07
1:25

   *c.* Anita repeats previous phrases.
   *d.* Tony, lyrical *Tonight* melody.

To - night, to - night Won't be just an - y

night, To - night there will be no morn - ing star. _____

2:18
2:23
2:40

2. *a.* Orchestra, *ff.*
   *b.* Riff, quick staccato phrases.
   *c.* Maria, lyrical *Tonight* melody, with Riff's staccato phrases, and brief interjections *(All right, Tonight)* by Tony and Anita. Tony joins Maria on *Tonight* melody.

3:29

   *d.* Voices join on sustained high tones *(Tonight), ff;* orchestral conclusion.

334

# ROCK

The mid-1950s saw the growth of a new kind of popular music that was first called *rock and roll* and then simply *rock*. Though it includes diverse styles, **rock** tends to be vocal music with a hard, driving beat, often featuring electric guitar accompaniment and heavily amplified sound. Early rock grew mainly out of *rhythm and blues,* a dance music of African Americans that fused blues, jazz, and gospel styles. Rock also drew upon *country and western,* a folklike, guitar-based style associated with rural white Americans. In little more than a decade, rock evolved from a simple, dance-oriented style to music that was highly varied in its tone colors, lyrics, and electronic technology.

## DEVELOPMENT OF ROCK

In the late 1940s, rhythm and blues became the dominant style among African Americans. The rhythm and blues of the 1950s differed from earlier blues in its more powerful beat and its use of the saxophone and electric guitar. Among the leading performers were Little Richard, Chuck Berry, and vocal groups such as the Platters. During the 1950s many rhythm-and-blues hits were issued by white performers in versions with less sexually explicit lyrics.

The earliest of the important rock and roll groups was Bill Haley and His Comets, whose *Rock Around the Clock* (1954) was the first big hit of the new style. To many people, the new music seemed rebellious in its loudness, pounding beat, and sexual directness; and the image of youthful rebellion was also projected by Elvis Presley, who reigned as "king" of rock and roll.

During the 1960s, much of the rock music by black performers was called *soul,* a term that emphasized its emotionality, its gospel roots, and its relationship to the black community. Soul musicians included James Brown, Ray Charles, and Aretha Franklin. *Motown* (after the name of a record company) was a type of soul music that blended rhythm and blues with popular music; among its stars were Diana Ross and the Supremes, and Stevie Wonder.

A new era began in 1964 with the American tour of the Beatles, an English rock group who have so far been the most influential performers in the history of rock. The Beatles—the singer-guitarists Paul McCartney, John Lennon, and George Harrison, and the drummer Ringo Starr (all born in the early 1940s)—came to dominate the popular music scene in the United States, along with the Rolling Stones (also English). Under their influence, rock musicians explored a wider range of musical sources and sounds, including electronic effects, "classical'" and nonwestern instruments, and unconventional chord progressions. Rock in the 1960s also absorbed elements of folk music and expressed contemporary social issues; *Blowin' in the Wind*, by the songwriter and singer Bob Dylan, is a well-known example. The diversity of rock styles of this period—which produced the first rock musical (*Hair*) and the first rock opera (*Tommy*)—is reflected in the terms *folk rock, jazz rock, classical rock, psychedelic rock,* and *acid rock.*

The 1970s saw a continuation of many 1960s styles, the revival of early rock and roll, and the rise of a dance music called *disco.* In addition to veteran performers, new stars emerged, such as Linda Ronstadt, Billy Joel, Bruce Springsteen, and Donna Summer. A blend of country music and rock called *country rock* became popular; other musical styles included *reggae* (from the West Indies), *funk* (featuring electrification and jazzlike rhythms), and *punk,* or *new wave* (a primitive form of rock and roll). Some groups performed *classical rock* (rock arrangements of earlier serious music), and jazz rock reached a wider audience than ever before through groups like Chicago; Weather Report; and Blood, Sweat, and Tears.

In the early 1980s, new wave bands from Britain such as Police, Culture Club, and Eurhythmics were popular in the United States—a "second British invasion" comparable to that of the Beatles. Though their styles varied, most of these groups used electronic technology (synthesizers and computers) and featured outlandish-looking performers. *Heavy metal* bands such as Quiet Riot, Iron Maiden, Black Sabbath, and Guns 'n' Roses played a type of basic rock with sexually explicit lyrics, bizarre costumes, and tremendous volume. *Rapping (rap music)*—a kind of rhythmic talking accompanied by a disk jockey who alternates between recordings on two turntables—developed among young urban blacks. Groups such as the Talking Heads and Police drew inspiration from "exotic" sources like African music and Jamaican reggae. African popular music was a significant trend of the 1980s, and Youssou N'Dour of Senegal became an international star.

## ELEMENTS OF ROCK

### Tone Color

The electric-guitar sound of rock is very different from the brass-reed sound of the "big band" heard in earlier popular music. Rock music is powerfully amplified, and the guitar is often manipulated electronically to produce a wide range of tone colors. Along with singers (who also play instruments), a rock group typically includes two electric guitars (lead and rhythm), electric bass, percussion, and keyboard instruments such as piano, electric piano, and synthesizer. Some groups also include one or more trumpets, trombones, or saxophones.

(Larry Busacca/Retna Ltd.)

Guns 'n' Roses.

As rock evolved during the 1960s, a wide range of instruments—from the harpsichord to the Indian sitar—were occasionally added to the basic rock group, particularly for recording sessions. Rock recordings use such diverse sounds as electronic blips, crowd noises, and a fifty-piece orchestra. During the 1970s and 1980s, rock musicians exploited the ever-expanding capacities of synthesizers and computers. Sophisticated electronic technology made it possible for a few performers to sound like a large ensemble.

The singing style of rock is drawn largely from black, folk, and country-and-western music. Although singing styles vary, they all are different from the crooning sound cultivated by earlier popular vocalists. Rock singers shout, cry, wail, growl, and use guttural sounds, as well as *falsetto*, a method of singing used by males to reach notes higher than their normal range. Nonsense syllables and repeated chants (such as *Yeah! Yeah! Yeah!*) are also featured.

## Rhythm

Rock is based on a very powerful beat in quadruple ($\frac{4}{4}$) meter with strong accents on the second and fourth beats of the bar. The rhythmic excitement is heightened because each beat is subdivided into 2 equal notes. This produces 8 faster pulses, which are superimposed on the 4 basic beats. To

(Don McCullin/Magnum)

The Beatles.

get the effect, count out the following: 1-and-**2**-and-3-and-**4**-and. Rock of the 1960s and 1970s often combined complicated rhythms with this basic pattern; for example, the bass player might emphasize the offbeats—the *ands*. During the late 1970s and 1980s, some rock music became more rhythmically complex, as performers drew inspiration from the polyrhythms of African music.

## Form, Melody, and Harmony

Rock music is usually in 12-bar blues form (see Section 16), in 32-bar A A B A form, or in variants of these forms. Earlier popular songs usually consisted of 4- or 8-bar phrases, but rock melodies sometimes contain phrases that are irregular in length. Rock songs tend to have short melodic patterns that are repeated several times. They are occasionally built on modes, rather than on traditional major or minor scales.

The harmonic progressions of rock are usually quite simple, often consisting of just three or four basic chords. Sometimes, the harmony can be restricted deliberately to only two chords, as in *Eleanor Rigby*, by John Lennon and Paul McCartney. Rock often uses chord progressions that are rare in earlier popular music.

## *LUCY IN THE SKY WITH DIAMONDS*, FROM *SGT. PEPPER'S LONELY HEARTS CLUB BAND* (1967), BY THE BEATLES

*Sgt. Pepper's Lonely Hearts Club Band*, a landmark of rock music, was one of the first rock recordings to be presented as a unified song cycle: its thirteen songs are linked by the device of a music hall show with a dazzling succession of acts. The impact of this record comes largely from its tremendous range of sounds and electronic effects—audience noises, barnyard sounds, weird orchestral tone clusters, and instruments such as the harpsichord, harp, and sitar. There is also a wide range of musical styles, including traditional rock and roll, a parody of a 1920s music-hall tune, an old-fashioned melodramatic ballad, and the exotic sounds of Indian music.

*Lucy in the Sky with Diamonds*, the third song of the cycle, evokes a world of daydream and fantasy. But the dreamlike mood is shattered by a brusque refrain. Apart from its introduction, the song is made up of three sections that are repeated: A, B, and C. Sections A and B are relatively soft, gently pulsating, and in triple meter. In contrast, section C (the refrain *Lucy in the sky*) is loud, heavily accented, and in quadruple meter.

# NON-WESTERN MUSIC

## VII

All over the world, music is an indispensible accompaniment to daily activities, magic rites, and ceremonies marking important phases of life. In this funeral ceremony of the Onitsha people of Nigeria, the chief blows an elephant tusk trumpet, an instrument symbolizing royalty.

# [1] MUSIC IN NONWESTERN CULTURES

Nonwestern music reflects and expresses the diversity of the world's languages, religions, geographical conditions, social and economic systems, values, beliefs, and ways of life. Each culture has its own characteristic instruments, performance practices, tonal systems, and melodic and rhythmic patterns. Nonwestern societies also differ in their range of musical styles: some have only folk music, some have both folk and popular music, and some have complex classical music as well. Thus nonwestern music can offer a wide range of listening experiences and cultural insights. Moreover, nonwestern traditions have been an important source of inspiration for twentieth-century western music. For example, they have influenced the French composer Claude Debussy, the British rock star George Harrison, and the African American jazz artist John Coltrane.

## CHARACTERISTICS OF NONWESTERN MUSIC

Although nonwestern music is extremely varied, some features are common to most traditions: music is closely linked with religion, dance, and drama; it can be both entertainment and an accompaniment to everyday activities, magic rites, and ceremonies; and it is often used to communicate messages and relate traditions.

### Oral Tradition

Nonwestern music is usually transmitted orally from parent to child or from teacher to student. Compositions and performance techniques are learned by rote and imitation. Music notation is far less important in nonwestern than in western culture: many musical cultures do not have notation; and when notation exists, it traditionally serves only as a record, not for teaching or performance.

### Improvisation

Improvisation—usually based on traditional melodic phrases and rhythmic patterns—is basic to much nonwestern music. Often, it is a highly disciplined art that requires years of training. Indian and Islamic musicians, for instance, create music within a framework of many melody types, each associated with a specific mood, a specific set of tones, and characteristic phrases. Although in some cultures the traditional songs and instrumental pieces are performed similarly from generation to generation (as in Japan, where improvisation in classical music is practically nonexistent), in other cultures pieces are treated with great flexibility (in Iran and sub-Saharan Africa, performers freely vary melodies and add sections).

## Voices

In most nonwestern cultures, singing is the main way of making music. Each tradition has its own preferred vocal timbres: for example, middle eastern and north African singers cultivate a nasal, intense, strained tone while singers in sub-Saharan Africa prefer a more relaxed, open-throated sound. Vocal techniques include shouting, crying, whispering, sighing, humming, yodeling, and singing through the teeth.

## Instruments

Nonwestern instruments produce a wealth of sounds and come in many sizes, shapes, and materials. Scholars usually group these instruments into four categories, based on what actually generates the sound:

1. *Membranophones* are instruments— basically, drums—whose sound generator is a stretched skin or other membrane.
2. *Chordophones* are instruments—such as harps—whose sound generator is a stretched string.
3. *Aerophones* are instruments—such as flutes and trumpets—whose sound generator is a column of air.
4. *Idiophones* are instruments—such as bells, gongs, scrapers, rattles, and xylophones—whose own material is the sound generator (no tension is applied).

The musical style of a culture is an important factor in its choice of instruments. For example, chordophones (strings) are prominent in Islamic and Indian classical music, in which highly ornamented melodies require instruments with great flexibility of pitch. Idiophones and membranophones (such as bells, rattles, and drums) are characteristic in sub-Saharan Africa, where rhythm is strongly emphasized and music is closely linked with dancing.

A second factor is geography, which determines the availability of raw materials. Bronze idiophones are prominent in southeast Asia; Indonesian orchestras (gamelans) include bronze gongs, chimes, and xylophones. Instruments made of animal skins and horns are common in parts of sub-Saharan Africa, where these materials are easily found. Among the Aniocha Ibos of Nigeria, for example, drums are made of animal skins, and some aerophones (winds) are made from elephant tusks. Where raw materials are scarce, as in the deserts of Australia, instruments may be few.

A third factor in choice of instruments is religion: often, instruments are symbolic and are linked with specific gods and goddesses (for instance, they may be shaped like birds, animals, or fish).

### Melody, Rhythm, and Texture

In Asia, the near east, and north Africa, most music emphasizes melody and rhythm, rather than harmony or polyphony. Texture is often monophonic: the melody is unaccompanied, or it is supported by percussion or (in India and the near east) by a drone—one or more sustained tones. In some regions (such as north Africa, the middle east, southeast Asia, and the far east) all parts may perform the same basic melody, with differing ornamentation or rhythm—a texture called *heterophony* (see Section 3). Homophonic and polyphonic textures tend to be more common in sub-Saharan Africa than in Asia.

Many scales are used in nonwestern music. Most often, they contain five, six, or seven tones. Nonwestern melodies commonly employ intervals smaller or larger than those standard in the west. Microtones—intervals smaller than the western half step—are frequent in India and the near east. And much nonwestern music employs very complex rhythms; drummers in India and sub-Saharan Africa spend years learning their sophisticated art.

## INTERACTION BETWEEN NONWESTERN AND WESTERN MUSIC

Because of increased urbanization, adoption of western technology, and access to radios, films, recordings, and western instruments, twentieth-century nonwestern music has been influenced by American and European music. In large cities in Africa, Asia, and the near east, western elements often appear in popular music—such as west African *high life*, which combines European instruments with the characteristic African steady rhythm. Some composers combine traditional elements with western forms and styles. And in many areas, western and traditional music exist side by side. Yet there are vast areas where traditional music still prevails, and many governments subsidize traditional performers groups to preserve their heritage.

In the following sections, traditional music of sub-Saharan Africa and Japan will be studied as a sample of the wealth of nonwestern music.

# MUSIC IN SUB-SAHARAN AFRICA

The African continent can be subdivided into north Africa (Morocco, Algeria, Tunisia, Egypt, etc.) and sub-Saharan Africa, the area south of the Sahara Desert (Ghana, Nigeria, Mozambique, Angola, and many other countries). North Africa is predominantly Moslem and Arabic-speaking, and its music is closely related to that of the middle east. This section focuses on the music of sub-Saharan Africa, sometimes called "black Africa"; throughout the section, the word *Africa* generally refers to sub-Saharan Africa.

Sub-Saharan Africa, which is environmentally and culturally diverse, has several thousand peoples with different religions, different customs, and over 700 different languages. Though urban growth and industrialization are now transforming sub-Saharan Africa, many Africans still hold to traditional ways of life. Most are polytheists, live in villages, and have traditional occupations like agriculture and cattle raising.

Though the music of sub-Saharan Africa is as diverse as its people, most of it features complex rhythms and polyrhythms, percussive sounds, and a wide variety of instrumental ensembles. Vocal music is often performed by a soloist and a responding chorus. Of course, the different cultures of Africa have influenced each other. For example, in parts of sub-Saharan Africa, such as Ghana and northern Nigeria, musical styles have been influenced by Arabic culture.

## MUSIC IN SOCIETY

Music permeates African life. It is used to entertain; as part of dances, plays, religious ceremonies, and magic rites; and to mark such events as birth, puberty, marriage, and death. There are work songs; specific songs or dances to treat the ill; litigation songs; songs praising leaders, criticizing authority, and recounting history; and many songs for particular occasions (for example, among the Fon—a people in Dahomey in west Africa—children sing a special song when they lose their first tooth). Singing and instrumentation are so interwoven into life that the abstract word *music*—as understood in the west—is not used by most African peoples, though there are words for *song*, *dance*, and *poetry*.

African music is closely associated with dancing; both arts are basic to many ceremonies, rituals, and celebrations. Dancers often sing or play rattles or other idiophones that are held or tied to the body.

345

(John Moss/Black Star)

African music is closely associated with dancing. While moving, a dancer often sings or plays an instrument.

African music is also intimately linked with language. Many languages are "tone languages," in which a word can have several different meanings, depending on its relative pitch. Tone languages permit the use of music for communication: drummers, trumpeters, and other musicians convey messages and tell stories by imitating the rhythms and pitch fluctuations of words. "Talking drums"—capable of two or more different pitches—are often used to send musical messages.

In Africa, music is a social activity in which almost everyone participates. It is usually performed outdoors, and there is spontaneous music making as well as performances by social and music groups at ceremonies and feasts. There is no musical notation; musical tradition, like folklore and history, is transmitted orally.

## ELEMENTS OF AFRICAN MUSIC

### Rhythm and Percussion

Rhythm and percussion are highly emphasized in African music, reflecting the close link between music and dance. African music tends to feature complex polyrhythms; usually, several different rhythmic patterns are played simultaneously and repeated over and over, and each instrument goes its own rhythmic way. Dancers may choose any of several rhythmic patterns to follow—one dancer may follow the pattern played by a bell while a second follows a rattle and a third follows a drum.

Percussion ensembles consist mainly of drums, xylophones, or rattles carefully chosen to provide contrasts of tone color and pitch. The human body itself is often used as a percussion instrument—hand clapping, foot stamping, and slapping the thigh or chest are common.

### Vocal Music

African singers use a wide variety of sounds. Even within a single performance a singer may shift from an open, relaxed tone to one that is tighter and more constricted. Singers may whisper, hum, grunt, shout, imitate animal noises, and yodel (move quickly from a chest voice to a falsetto).

In a characteristic performance style known as *call and response,* the phrases of a soloist are repeatedly answered by those of a chorus. An exciting overlap often results when the leader resumes singing before the chorus has finished responding. Singers are often accompanied by percussion ostinatos (repeated rhythmic patterns). Typically, short musical phrases are repeated over and over to different words.

### Texture

African music (unlike that of many other nonwestern cultures) is often homophonic or polyphonic. Several voice parts may sing the same melody at different pitch levels, occasionally producing a series of parallel chords. Some African peoples also perform polyphonic music in which the different melodic lines are quite independent.

## AFRICAN INSTRUMENTS

A great variety of instruments and instrumental ensembles are found in Africa. Ensembles have two to twenty or more players and may consist of instruments of indefinite pitch (bells, rattles, log drums), definite pitch (flutes, trumpets, xylophones, plucked lutes), or a combination of both (flutes, drums, bells).

### Idiophones

The most common instruments in Africa are idiophones, such as bells, rattles, scrapers, xylophones, and log drums. Most are struck or shaken, but others are scraped, rubbed, plucked, or stamped against the ground. Many—like rattles, bells, and stone clappers—are instruments of indefinite pitch. A few—like the xylophone and *mbira*, or *thumb piano*—are tuned instruments.

Xylophones are particularly important; they are played solo, in small groups, and in larger orchestras and exist in different sizes ranging from soprano to double bass (in some areas, one large xylophone is played by several performers simultaneously). Xylophones have from about ten to over twenty slats, sometimes with gourd resonators. Spider webs are often placed over small holes in the resonators to create a buzzing sound.

The *mbira (sansa, kalimba,* or *thumb piano)* is a melodic idiophone that can produce elaborate melodies; vocalists often use it to accompany themselves. Eight to over thirty metal or bamboo tongues, attached to a sounding board or box, are plucked with the thumbs and forefingers.

Another important idiophone is the slit drum, a hollowed-out log with a long slit on top used as both a "talking drum" and a musical instrument. Some slit drums are small enough to be held in the hand, while others are tree trunks over 20 feet long. Variations in the width of the slit allow two and sometimes four different tones to be produced.

### Membranophones

Drums with stretched skins or other membranes are extremely important in African culture. They are essential to many ceremonies; they are used for dancing and regulating the pace of work; "talking drums" are used to send messages; and drums are often considered sacred or magical. The manufacture of drums is usually accompanied by special rites, and drums are sometimes housed in special shrines, given food, and offered sacrifices. Drums are often regarded as the property of a group, not an individual, and they often symbolize power and royalty.

Drums are usually played in groups of two to four, though some ensembles are made up of as many as fifteen drums, played by four to six performers. The drums are often tuned to different pitches and create melodic music similar to that of xylophone ensembles. The chief drummer is typically free to improvise within a traditional framework; the other drummers repeat certain rhythmic patterns. African drummers are among the most sophisticated in the world, producing complicated rhythms and a wide range of tone colors and pitches.

Drums come in many sizes, shapes, and forms. There are drums shaped like cones, cylinders, kettles, barrels, goblets, and hourglasses. They are made from logs, gourds, and clay. They may have one or two drum heads made from animal skins. Some drums produce a single sound; others—

like the hourglass-shaped *pressure drum* (which often imitates the spoken "tone language")—can produce a variety of pitches. Devices used for special effects include seeds or beads inside a closed drum and pieces of metal or small bells attached to a drum's rim.

## Aerophones and Chordophones

The most common African aerophones (winds) are flutes, whistles, horns, and trumpets. Reed instruments are less widespread. Flutes are usually made of bamboo, cane, or wood; horns and trumpets are made from animal horns, elephant tusks, wood, bamboo, and gourds.

Most chordophones (strings) are plucked or struck, perhaps because percussive sounds are preferred. One of the most widely used chordophones is the musical bow, whose string is plucked or struck with a stick. Some musical bows have a gourd resonator; with others, the player's mouth is the resonator.

We'll now study two examples of music from sub-Saharan Africa.

## SONG FROM ANGOLA

A call-and-response pattern dominates this song from Angola, which consists of four statements of the pattern ababc. The performance involves brief solos for male voice (a), even shorter choral responses (b), and longer phrases for chorus alone or for chorus together with the soloist (c). Notice how the soloist's voice—somewhat tense and nasal in quality—becomes increasingly intertwined with the chorus. In the background, several drummers perform different rhythms simultaneously.

Brief sets:
Side 6, band 9
CD 3 |49|

Basic sets:
Side 16, band 6
CD 8 |24|

---

# Listening Outline  To be read while music is heard

SONG FROM ANGOLA

Solo male voice, chorus, drums

(Duration, 1:25)

|49| |24| 0:00  1. Drums introduce solo; choral response; solo; choral response; longer choral phrases.

0:21  2. Solo; choral response; solo; choral response; longer choral phrases solo tone interjected.

0:41  3. Solo; choral response; solo; choral response; soloist with longer choral phrases.

1:03  4. Solo continues into choral response; solo; choral response; soloist with longer choral phrases.

Brief sets:
Side 6, band 10
CD 3 50

Basic sets:
Side 16, band 7
CD 8 25

Percussive sounds and complex polyrhythms are featured in *Mitamba Yalagala Kumchuzi*, a dance song of the Zaramo people in Tanzania. First we hear percussion instruments—tin rattles and tuned goblet drums and cylindrical drums—producing a variety of rhythms, pitches, and tone colors. Then the percussion instruments are joined by a group of voices singing a dance melody.

## Listening Outline  To be read while music is heard

*MITAMBA YALAGALA KUMCHUZI*

Voices, 5 tuned goblet drums, 4 tuned cylindrical drums, tin rattles

(Duration, 1:30)

50 25 0:00    1. Goblet drums, cylindrical drums, tin rattles, complex polyrhythms against basic pulse.
0:43    2. Group of voices with dance melody, percussion accompanies.

NONWESTERN

# 3  KOTO MUSIC OF JAPAN

The musical culture of Japan embraces both folk music and a thousand-year tradition of classical music—sacred and secular works, theater music, vocal and instrumental music, and works for orchestra, chamber ensemble, and soloists—using many styles, forms, instruments, and musical techniques. We shall explore some of its characteristic features by focusing on the koto, a plucked string instrument whose importance in Japanese music is comparable to that of the piano in western music.

### THE KOTO

The *koto* has thirteen silk or nylon strings—each with a movable bridge—stretched over a hollow sound board about 6 feet long; the player tunes the strings by adjusting the placement of the bridges. The strings are plucked with ivory *plectra* worn on the thumb, index finger, and middle finger of the right hand and may also be struck and scraped with the plectra to produce various tone colors and musical effects.

Right-hand playing techniques include a slide across the strings (resembling the glissando on western string instruments) and a rapid shaking of a single string (like a tremolo). The player may raise the pitch of a string by pressing it down on the left side of its bridge. Left-hand pressure is also used to obtain ornamental pitch slides and "bent" tones.

## HISTORICAL BACKGROUND

The koto (like Buddhism, woodblock printing, and much else in Japanese culture) originally came from China—it reached Japan between 650 and 750, brought by Chinese and Korean musicians who came to play in the Japanese court orchestra. It was used in Japanese court music and also, by the tenth century, as a solo instrument, though the earliest surviving solo music dates from the sixteenth century. This music, heard mostly in temples, was performed only by Buddhist priests, Confucian scholars, and aristocrats.

Most masterpieces of traditional koto music were composed during the Edo period (1615 to 1868; the name comes from the capital city, Edo—now Tokyo), when Japan isolated itself from foreign cultures and its merchant class stimulated new developments in the arts, such as color woodblock prints and kabuki theater. The early Edo period saw the rise of koto music intended for entertainment rather than religious rites. It was composed not by scholars or priests but by blind professional musicians who belonged to a special guild; the highest rank bestowed by this guild was *kengyō, master of koto.* Yatsuhashi Kengyō (1614–1685) is known as the founder of modern koto music.

## KOTO MUSIC

The koto is used for solos and duets, for vocal accompaniments, and in combination with one or more other instruments (with or without voice). An important chamber ensemble consists of koto and voice, *shakuhachi* (an end-blown bamboo flute with five holes), and *shamisen* (an instrument with three plucked strings, also spelled *samisen*).

The most important type of music for solo koto is *danmono*, a theme-and-variations form: the theme, presented in the first section, is then varied in sections with increasingly faster tempos; new melodic material is placed between phrases of the original theme. Danmono pieces were composed during the seventeenth and eighteenth centuries; *Rokudan (Six Sections)*, attributed to Yatsuhashi Kengyō, is the most famous. Another form is *tegotomono*, a song cycle with extended instrumental interludes, developed during the eighteenth century and performed today by an ensemble of voice, koto, shamisen, and shakuhachi.

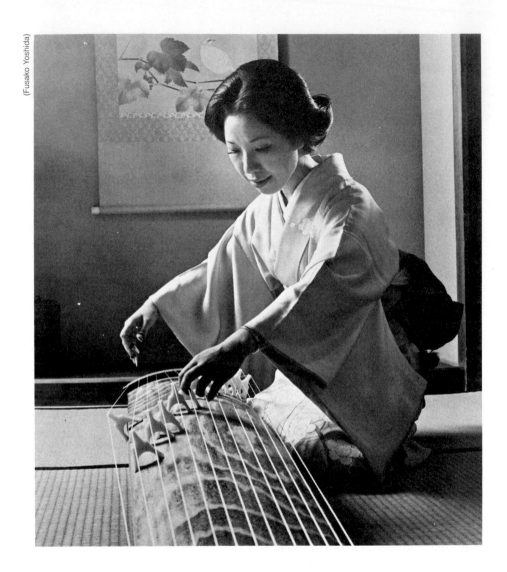

Fusako Yoshida,
a "master of koto."

The koto repertory is made up of traditional pieces passed down from teacher to student and learned by rote. Most koto music is based on pentatonic (five-tone) scales that correspond to A–B–C–E–F or E–F–A–B–C on the piano. The precise quality of each tone is of great importance—the performer strives to give each the proper dynamic level, tone color, pitch inflection, and ornamentation.

When the koto is part of a chamber ensemble, no instrument (or voice) may outshine the others; instruments and voices blend without losing their individual qualities. Such chamber music usually has *heterophonic texture:* all parts perform the same basic melody, but with differing ornamentation or rhythm. However, the parts are sometimes so independent that the texture becomes polyphonic.

## GODAN-GINUTA (NINETEENTH CENTURY), BY MITSUZAKI KENGYŌ

*Godan-Ginuta,* by Mitsuzaki Kengyō (?–1853), is one of the earliest and most brilliant pieces conceived as a duet for two koto. As its title indicates, *Godan-Ginuta* is composed of five sections (*godan* means *five sections*) and evokes the sound of cloth beating against a wooden block called a *kinuta* (*ginuta*). Japanese women once used the kinuta to clean and soften cloth in autumn, and so the music of *Godan-Ginuta* is associated with that season.

In this duet, the koto are tuned to different scales, and one instrument is pitched 5 steps higher than the other. The two koto are of about equal importance and often engage in a lively dialogue with rapid give-and-take. Variety is created through changes between monophonic, heterophonic, and polyphonic textures. Typical of koto music are the many tones which are "bent" upwards or downwards. Also characteristic are the duple meter and the flexible tempo, which is often held back or pressed forward. The rhythm of *Godan-Ginuta* is particularly exciting and features much syncopation. We'll now focus on the opening section of the piece, which is included in the recordings.

*Godan-Ginuta* opens with the two koto playing long notes in unison. These tones represent the sound of the kinuta. As the section unfolds, the tempo quickens and the rhythm becomes increasingly animated. Toward the middle we hear a characteristic koto sound: rapid scrapes of the plectrum along the top of the string. This section of *Godan-Ginuta* ends with a point of repose when a long note is played in unison by the two koto.

**Brief sets:**
**Side 6, band 11**
**CD 3 [51]**

Basic sets:
Side 16, band 10
CD 8 [28]

## Listening Outline   To be read while music is heard

GODAN-GINUTA (NINETEENTH CENTURY), BY MITSUZAKI KENGYŌ

Opening Section

Duple meter ($\frac{2}{4}$)

2 koto

(Duration, 2:49)

| | | |
|---|---|---|
| [51] [28] 0:00 | 1. *a.* | Downward skips, long notes in unison. |
| 0:10 | *b.* | Quicker notes, dialogue between two koto; low register. |
| 1:01 | 2. *a.* | Downward skip, long notes in unison; faster tempo, more active rhythms. |
| 1:33 | *b.* | Scrapes alternate with repeated notes. |
| 1:54 | *c.* | Rhythmic motive rapidly tossed between two koto. |
| 2:00 | *d.* | Two koto play together, tempo accelerates. |
| 2:35 | *e.* | Two koto in unison; downward skip, long notes in unison end section with a point of repose. |

# APPENDIXES

# GLOSSARY AND EXAMPLE LOCATOR

**Note:** Musical examples are given for most of the terms in the glossary. Examples indicate (as appropriate) composer; title; movement (mvt); page (p) where discussed or page where listening outline (LO) appears; item on listening outline; words in vocal text; side, band, CD, and track numbers (track numbers are in small boxes); and timings (in minutes and seconds, 0:00). Unless otherwise specified, all references to recordings are to the brief sets of three cassettes or CDs. Additional abbreviations are: basic sets of eight cassettes, LPs, and CDs = basic sets; supplementary sets of four cassettes, LPs, and CDs = supp sets; first, second, third, fourth, etc., = 1st, 2d, 3d, 4th, etc.

*A B form*   See *two-part form.*

*A B A form*   See *three-part form.*

*Absolute music*   Instrumental music having no intended association with a story, poem, idea, or scene; nonprogram music.

*A capella*   Choral music without instrumental accompaniment.
>   Example   Josquin Desprez, *Ave Maria;* p 68; side 1, band 8; CD 1 **27**

*Accent*   Emphasis of a note, which may result from its being louder (dynamic accent), longer, or higher in pitch than the notes near it.

*Accelerando*   Becoming faster.
>   Example   Liszt, *Transcendental Étude* No. 10 in F Minor; p 204; LO 4*b*; side 4, band 2; CD 2 **41**; 1:49

*Accompanied recitative*   Speechlike melody that is sung by a solo voice accompanied by the orchestra.
>   Example   Handel, *Messiah, Comfort Ye,* starting at *The voice of him;* basic sets side 4, band 5; CD 2 **26**; 2:39

*Accordion*   Instrument consisting of a bellows between two keyboards (pianolike keys played by the right hand, and buttons played by the left hand) whose sound is produced by air pressure which causes free steel reeds to vibrate.

*Adagio*   Slow.
>   Example   Beethoven, Sonata in C Minor, Op. 13 *(Pathétique);* 2d mvt; basic sets side 8, band 3; CD 4 **37**

*Aerophone*   Any instrument—such as a flute or trumpet—whose sound is generated by a vibrating column of air.

*Aleatory music*   See *chance music.*

*Allegretto*   Moderately fast.
>   Example   Mozart, *Eine kleine Nachtmusik,* 3d mvt; p 135; side 2, band 9; CD 1 **71**

**Allegro**   Fast.

Example   Vivaldi, *La Primavera (Spring)*, Concerto for Violin and String Orchestra, 1st mvt; p 99; side 2, band 2; CD 1 $\boxed{40}$

**Alto (contralto)**   Female voice of low range.

Example   Josquin Desprez, *Ave Maria*, opening words *Ave Maria* presented by sopranos, then imitated by altos; p 68; side 1, band 8; CD 1 $\boxed{27}$

**Andante**   Moderately slow, a walking pace.

Example   Haydn, Symphony No. 94, 2d mvt; p 131; side 2, band 8; CD 1 $\boxed{65}$

**Answer**   Second presentation of the subject in a fugue, usually in the dominant scale.

Example   Bach, Organ Fugue in G Minor, p 91; LO 1*b*; side 1, band 11; CD 1 $\boxed{36}$; 0:18

**Aria**   Song for solo voice with orchestral accompaniment, usually expressing an emotional state through its outpouring of melody; found in operas, oratorios, and cantatas.

Example   Puccini, *La Bohème, Mi chiamano Mimi*; p 233; side 5, band 1; CD 3 $\boxed{3}$; 8:19

**Arioso**   A vocal solo more lyrical than a recitative and less elaborate than an aria.

**Arpeggio**   See *broken chord*.

**Art song**   Setting of a poem for solo voice and piano, translating the poem's mood and imagery into music, common in the romantic period.

Example   Schubert, *Erlkönig (The Erlking)*; p 187; side 3, band 5; CD 2 $\boxed{24}$

**Atonality**   Absence of tonality, or key, characteristic of much twentieth-century music.

Example   Webern, *Five Pieces for Orchestra*, 3d piece; p 290; side 6, band 2; CD 3 $\boxed{29}$

**Augmentation**   Variation of a fugue subject in which the original time values of the subject are lengthened.

**Bar**   Another term for *measure*, often used in jazz.

**Baritone**   A male voice lower than a tenor and higher than a bass.

Example   Schubert, *Erlkönig (The Erlking)*; p 187; side 3, band 5; CD 2 $\boxed{24}$

**Bass**   (1) Male voice of low range. (2) See *double bass*.

Example   Mozart, *Don Giovanni*, Introduction, Leporello's *Notte e giorno faticar*; p 147; side 3, band 2; CD 2 $\boxed{5}$

**Bass clarinet**   Member of the clarinet family, having a low range. Its shape is curved at the end before flaring into a bell.

**Bass clef**   Symbol on the staff indicating relatively low pitch ranges, such as those played by a pianist's left hand.

**Bass drum**   Percussion instrument of indefinite pitch, the largest of the orchestral drums.

Example   Stravinsky, *The Rite of Spring, Ritual of Abduction*; p 272; LO 4*a*; side 5, band 4; CD 3 $\boxed{25}$; 6:21

***Bass fiddle***   See *double bass*.

***Basso continuo (figured bass)***   Baroque accompaniment made up of a bass part together with numbers (figures) indicating the chords to be played above it. Usually the basso continuo is played by two instruments, a keyboard plus a low melodic instrument.
   Example   Bach, *Brandenburg* Concerto No. 5 in D Major, 1st mvt, opening ritornello; pp 87 and 82; LO 1*a*; side 1, band 10; CD 1 |31|

***Basso ostinato***   See *ground bass*.

***Bassoon***   Double-reed woodwind instrument, made of wood, having a low range.
   Example   Bartók, Concerto for Orchestra, 2d mvt; p 293; LO 2; side 6, band 3; CD 3 |30|

***Beam***   Horizontal line connecting the flags of several eighth notes or sixteenth notes in succession, to facilitate reading these notes.

***Beat***   Regular, recurrent pulsation that divides music into equal units of time.

***Bebop (bop)***   Complex jazz style, usually for small groups, developed in the 1940s and meant for attentive listening rather than dancing.
   Example   Parker, *KoKo*; basic sets side 16, band 4; CD 8 |21|

***Bitonality***   Approach to pitch organization using two keys at one time, often found in twentieth-century music.

***Blues***   Term referring both to a style of performance and to a form; an early source of jazz, characterized by flatted, or "blue," notes in the scale; vocal blues consist of 3-line stanzas in the form a a' b.
   Example   Smith, *Lost Your Head Blues*; basic sets side 15, band 8; CD 8 |17|

***Bop***   See *bebop*.

***Bow***   Slightly curved stick strung tightly with horsehair, used to play string instruments.

***Brass instrument***   Instrument, made of brass or silver, whose sound is produced by the vibrations of the player's lips as he or she blows into a cup- or funnel-shaped mouthpiece. The vibrations are amplified and colored in a tube that is flared at the end.

***Bridge (transition)***   In the exposition of the sonata form, a section which leads from the first theme in the tonic, or home, key to the second theme, which is in a new key.
   Example   Beethoven, Symphony No. 5 in C Minor, 1st mvt; p 166; LO exposition 2; side 3, band 4; CD 2 |17|; 0:21

***Broken chord (arpeggio)***   Sounding of the individual tones of a chord in sequence rather than simultaneously.
   Example   Haydn, Symphony No. 94, 2d mvt; p 132; LO theme, 1st seven notes; side 2, band 8; CD 1 |65|

***Cadence***   (1) Resting place at the end of a phrase in a melody. (2) Progression, often from the dominant chord to the tonic chord, giving a sense of conclusion.
   Example   Mozart, *Eine kleine Nachtmusik*, 3d mvt; p 135; LO 1, end of stately melody; side 2, band 9; CD 1 |71|

*Cadenza*   Unaccompanied section of virtuoso display for the soloist in a concerto, usually appearing near the end of the first movement, and sometimes in the last movement.

Example   Mozart, Piano Concerto in A Major, K. 488, 1st mvt; p 156; LO recapitulation 5c; side 3, band 3; CD 2 **15** ; 9:03

*Call and response*   (1) In jazz, a pattern wherein one voice or instrument is answered by another voice, instrument, or group of instruments. (2) Performance style in which the phrases of a soloist are repeatedly answered by those of a chorus, often found in African and other nonwestern music.

Example   Song from Angola (Gangele Song); p 349; side 6, band 9; CD 3 **49**

*Camerata*   In Italian, *fellowship* or *society;* a group of nobles, poets, and composers who began to meet regularly in Florence around 1575 and whose musical discussions prepared the way for the beginning of opera.

*Cantata*   Composition in several movements, usually written for chorus, one or more vocal soloists, and orchestra. The church cantata for the Lutheran service in Germany during the baroque period often includes chorales.

*Cantus firmus*   Melody—often a Gregorian chant—used as the basis of a polyphonic composition.

Example   Machaut, *Notre Dame* Mass, Agnus Dei; p 63; side 1, band 7; CD 1 **24**

*Castrato*   Male singer castrated before puberty to retain a high voice range; the most important category of vocal soloists in opera during the baroque period.

*Celesta*   Percussion instrument of definite pitch, with metal bars that are struck by hammers controlled by a keyboard.

*Cello (violoncello)*   String instrument with a range lower than that of the viola and higher than that of the double bass.

Example   Berlioz, *Fantastic Symphony*, 5th mvt, cellos doubled an octave lower by double basses; p 214; LO 7a; side 4, band 3; CD 2 **48** ; 5:21

*Chamber music*   Music employing a small group of musicians, with one player to a part.

*Chance (aleatory) music*   Music composed by the random selection of pitches, tone colors, and rhythms; developed in the 1950s by John Cage and others.

*Chimes*   Percussion instrument of definite pitch, with suspended metal tubes that are struck with a hammer.

Example   Berlioz, *Fantastic Symphony*, 5th mvt; p 214; LO 4a; side 4, band 3; CD 2 **46**

*Chorale*   Hymn tune sung to a German religious text.

Example   Bach, Cantata No. 140, mvt 7; p 109; side 2, band 4; CD 1 **48**

*Chorale prelude*   Short composition for organ, based on a hymn tune and often used to remind the congregation of the melody before the hymn is sung.

*Chord*   Combination of three or more tones sounded at once.

Example   Bizet, *Farandole* from *L'Arlésienne* Suite No. 2, p 47; LO 1a (opening chord); side 1, band 3; CD 1 **11**

***Chordophone***   Instrument—such as a harp or lute—whose sound is generated by a stretched string.

***Chorus***   In jazz, a statement of the basic harmonic pattern or melody.

***Chromatic harmony***   Use of chords containing tones not found in the prevailing major or minor scale but included in the chromatic scale (which has twelve tones); often found in romantic music.

***Chromatic scale***   Scale including all twelve tones of the octave; each tone is a half step away from the next one.
> **Examples**   Chopin, Nocturne in E Flat Major, Op. 9, No. 2; p 198; LO 2*b*; side 4, band 1; CD 2 **37**; 1:18
> Berlioz, *Fantastic Symphony*, 5th mvt; p 214; LO˙2*b*; side 4, band 3; CD 2 **45**; 2:25

***Church modes***   Scales containing seven tones with an eighth tone duplicating the first an octave higher, but with different patterns of whole and half steps from major and minor scales; used in medieval, Renaissance, and twentieth-century music and in folk music.
> **Example**   *Alleluia: Vidimus stellam;* p 58; side 1, band 6; CD 1 **21**

***Clarinet***   Single-reed woodwind instrument with a beak-shaped mouthpiece, cylindrical in shape with a slightly flared bell.
> **Example**   Copland, *Appalachian Spring*, Section 7: Theme and Variations on *Simple Gifts*; p 303; LO theme; side 6, band 4; CD 3 **37**

***Clavichord***   Baroque keyboard instrument in which sound is produced by means of brass blades striking strings, capable of making gradual dynamic changes, but within a narrow volume range.

***Clef***   Symbol placed at the beginning of the staff to show the exact pitch of each line and space.

***Climax***   Highest tone or emotional focal point in a melody or a larger musical composition.

***Coda***   In a sonata-form movement, a concluding section following the recapitulation and rounding off the movement by repeating themes or developing them further.
> **Example**   Beethoven, Symphony No. 5 in C Minor, 1st mvt; p 166; LO coda; side 3, band 4; CD 2 **23**; 5:54

***Complete cadence***   Definite resting place, giving a sense of finality, at the end of a phrase in a melody.
> **Example**   Mozart, *Eine kleine Nachtmusik*, 3d mvt; p 135; LO 1, end of stately melody; side 2, band 9; CD 1 **71**

***Computer***   Tool used to synthesize music, to help composers write scores, to store samples of audio signals, and to control synthesizing mechanisms.

***Concert overture***   Independent composition for orchestra in one movement, usually programmatic and in sonata form, often found in the romantic period.

***Concerto***   Extended composition for instrumental soloist and orchestra, usually in three movements: (1) fast, (2) slow, (3) fast.

*Concerto grosso*  Composition for several instrumental soloists and small orchestra; common in late baroque music.
 Example  Bach, *Brandenburg* Concerto No. 5 in D Major; p 86; side 1, band 10; CD 1 ⬚31

*Conductor*  Leader of a performing group of musicians.

*Consonance*  Tone combination that is stable and restful.

*Contrabassoon*  Double-reed woodwind instrument with a register one octave lower than the bassoon's.

*Contralto*  See *alto*.

*Contrast*  Striking differences of pitch, dynamics, rhythm, and tempo that provide variety and change of mood.

*Cool jazz*  Jazz style related to bebop, but more relaxed in character and relying more heavily on arrangements; developed around 1950.

*Cornet*  Brass instrument similar in shape to the trumpet, with a mellower tone.

*Countermelody*  Melodic idea that accompanies a main theme.
 Example  Haydn, Symphony No. 94, 2d mvt; p 132; LO variation 3; side 2, band 8; CD 1 ⬚68; 3:20

*Counterpoint*  Technique of combining two or more melodic lines into a meaningful whole.

*Countersubject*  In a fugue, a melodic idea that accompanies the subject fairly constantly.
 Example  Bach, Organ Fugue in G Minor; p 91; LO 1*b*; side 1, band 11; CD 1 ⬚36; 0:18

*Crescendo (cresc.)*  Gradually louder.
 Example  Bizet, *Farandole* from *L'Arlésienne* Suite No. 2, p 47; LO 2*a*; side 1, band 3; CD 1 ⬚12; 0:33

*Cymbals*  Percussion instrument of indefinite pitch, consisting of a pair of metal plates, played by striking the plates against each other.
 Example  Wagner, *Lohengrin*, Prelude to Act III; p 6; LO 1*a*; side 1, band 1; CD 1 ⬚1

*Da capo*  In Italian, *from the beginning;* an indication usually meaning that the opening section of a piece is to be repeated after the middle section.
 Example  Mozart, *Eine kleine Nachtmusik*, 3d mvt; p 135; side 2, band 9; CD 1 ⬚71

*Da capo aria*  Aria in A B A form; after the B section, the term *da capo* is written; this means *from the beginning* and indicates a repetition of the opening A section.

*Decrescendo*  Gradually softer.
 Example  Wagner, *Lohengrin*, Prelude to Act III; p 6; LO 3*c*; side 1, band 1; CD 1 ⬚4; 2:47

*Development*  Second section of a sonata-form movement, in which themes from the exposition are developed and the music moves through several different keys.
 Example  Beethoven, Symphony No. 5 in C Minor, 1st mvt; p 166; LO development; side 3, band 4; CD 2 ⬚21; 2:57

***Diminuendo***   See *decrescendo*.

***Diminution***   Variation of a fugue subject in which the original time values of the subject are shortened.

***Dissonance***   Tone combination that is unstable and tense.

***Dixieland***   See *New Orleans jazz*.

***Dominant chord***   Triad built on the fifth note of the scale, which sets up tension that is resolved by the tonic chord.
  Example   Vivaldi, *La Primavera (Spring)*, Concerto for Violin and String Orchestra, 1st mvt; p 100; LO 1a, end of first phrase; side 2, band 2; CD 1 [40]

***Dotted note***   Note with a dot to the right of it. This dot increases the note's undotted duration by half.

***Dotted rhythm***   Long-short rhythmic pattern in which a dotted note is followed by a note that is much shorter.
  Example   Liszt, *Transcendental Étude* No. 10 in F Minor; p 204; LO 2a; side 4, band 2; CD 2 [39]; 0:42

***Double bass ("bass fiddle"; bass)***   Largest string instrument, having the lowest range of the string family.
  Example   Berlioz, *Fantastic Symphony*, 5th mvt, double basses doubled an octave higher by cellos; p 214; LO 1a; side 4, band 3; CD 2 [44]

***Double-reed woodwinds***   Instruments whose sound is produced by two narrow pieces of cane held between the player's lips; these pieces vibrate when the player blows between them.

***Double stop***   See *stop*.

***Downbeat***   First, or stressed, beat of a measure.
  Example   Bizet, *Farandole* from *L'Arlésienne* Suite No. 2; p 47; LO 1a, opening chord; side 1, band 3; CD 1 [11]

***Duple meter***   Pattern of 2 beats to the measure.
  Example   Tchaikovsky, *Nutcracker* Suite, *Dance of the Reed Pipes;* p 50; side 1, band 4; CD 1 [16]

***Dynamic accent***   Emphasis that a note receives when a performer plays it more loudly than the notes around it.

***Dynamics***   Degrees of loudness or softness in music.

***Electronic instrument***   Instrument whose sound is produced, modified, or amplified by electronic means.

***Embellishments***   Ornamental tones that are either improvised by the performer or indicated in the music by signs or notes in small print.

***English horn***   Double-reed woodwind instrument, slightly larger than the oboe and with a lower range, straight in shape with an egg-shaped bell.
  Example   Tchaikovsky, *Nutcracker* Suite, *Dance of the Reed Pipes;* p 50; LO 1c; side 1, band 4; CD 1 [16]

***Ensemble***   In opera, a piece sung by three or more solo singers.
  Example   Mozart, *Don Giovanni*, Introduction, andante, starting *Ah, soccorso;* p 147; side 3, band 2; CD 2 [7]; 4:09

**Episode** Transitional section in a fugue between presentations of the subject, which offers either new material or fragments of the subject or countersubject.
Example Bach, Organ Fugue in G Minor; p 91; LO 1e; side 1, band 11; CD 1 |37|; 1:14

**Étude** In French, *study;* a piece designed to help a performer master specific technical difficulties.
Example Liszt, *Transcendental Étude* No. 10 in F Minor; p 204; side 4, band 2; CD 2 |38|

**Exoticism** Use of melodies, rhythms, or instruments that suggest foreign lands; common in romantic music.

**Exposition** First section of a sonata-form movement, which sets up a strong conflict between the tonic key and the new key; and between the first theme (or group of themes) and the second theme (or group of themes).
Example Beethoven, Symphony No. 5 in C Minor, 1st mvt; p 166; LO exposition; side 3, band 4; CD 2 |16|

**Expressionism** Musical style stressing intense, subjective emotion and harsh dissonance, typical of German and Austrian music of the early twentieth century.
Example Schoenberg, *A Survivor from Warsaw;* p 281; side 6, band 5; CD 3 |27|

**Figured bass** See *basso continuo.*

**Flag** Wavy line attached to the stem on a note, indicating how long that note is to be held relative to the notes around it.

**Flat sign** Symbol which notates a pitch one half step lower than the pitch that would otherwise be indicated.

**Flute** Woodwind instrument, usually made of metal, with a high range, whose tone is produced by blowing across the edge of a mouth hole.
Example Tchaikovsky, *Nutcracker* Suite, *Dance of the Reed Pipes;* p 50; LO 1b; side 1, band 4; CD 1 |16|

**Form** Organization of musical ideas in time.

**Forte (f)** Loud.
Examples Mozart, *Eine kleine Nachtmusik,* 3d mvt; p 135; LO 1; side 5, band 2; CD 3 |7|
Vivaldi, *La Primavera (Spring),* Concerto for Violin and String Orchestra, 1st mvt; p 100; LO 1a; side 2, band 2; CD 1 |40|

**Fortepiano** Eighteenth-century or early-nineteenth-century piano, which differs from the modern piano in sound and construction.
Example Mozart, Piano Concerto in A Major, K. 488, 1st mvt; p 156; LO second exposition 1a; side 3, band 3; CD 2 |12|; 2:03

**Fortissimo (ff)** Very loud.
Example Wagner, *Lohengrin,* Prelude to Act III; p 6; LO 1a; side 1, band 1; CD 1 |1|

**Fourth chord** Chord in which the tones are a fourth apart, instead of a third; used in twentieth-century music.

**Free jazz** Jazz style which departs from traditional jazz by not being based on regular forms or on established chord patterns; developed during the 1960s.

***French horn***   Brass instrument of medium range, whose tube is coiled into a roughly circular shape and fitted with valves; commonly used in symphony orchestras and in bands. (Sometimes called simply a *horn*.)
> **Examples**   Smetana, *The Moldau*; p 219; LO 3a; side 4, band 4; CD 2 ⟦52⟧; 2:50
> Beethoven, Symphony No. 5 in C Minor, 1st mvt; p 166; LO exposition 3a; side 3, band 4; CD 2 ⟦18⟧; 0:46

***French overture***   Common opening piece in baroque suites, oratorios, and operas; usually in two parts: the first slow, with characteristic dotted rhythms, full of dignity and grandeur; the second quick and lighter in mood, often starting like a fugue.
> **Example**   Handel, *Messiah*, Overture; basic sets side 4, band 4; CD 2 ⟦23⟧

***Front line***   In Dixieland or New Orleans jazz, the group of melodic instruments which improvise on a melody, supported by the rhythm section.

***Fugue***   Polyphonic composition based on one main theme, or subject.
> **Example**   Bach, Organ Fugue in G Minor; p 90; side 1, band 11; CD 1 ⟦36⟧

***Fusion***   See *jazz rock*.

***Glissando***   Rapid slide up or down a scale.
> **Example**   Debussy, *Prelude to the Afternoon of a Faun*; p 265; side 5, band 3; LO 1a; CD 3 ⟦12⟧

***Glockenspiel***   Percussion instrument of definite pitch, made up of flat metal bars set in a frame and played by striking with small metal hammers.
> **Example**   Copland, *Appalachian Spring*, Section 7: Theme and Variations on *Simple Gifts*; p 303; LO variation 2; side 6, band 4; CD 3 ⟦39⟧; 1:02

***Gong (tam-tam)***   Percussion instrument of indefinite pitch, made up of a large flat metal plate that is suspended and struck with a mallet.

***Grand staff***   Combination of the treble and bass staves, used in keyboard music to encompass the wide range of pitches produced by both hands.

***Grave***   Very slow, solemn.
> **Example**   Beethoven, Piano Sonata in C Minor, Op. 13 *(Pathétique)*, slow introduction; basic sets side 8, band 2; CD 4 ⟦30⟧

***Gregorian chant***   Melodies set to sacred Latin texts, sung without accompaniment; the official music of the Roman Catholic church.
> **Example**   *Alleluia: Vidiumus stellam*; p 58; side 1, band 6; CD 1 ⟦21⟧

***Ground bass (basso ostinato)***   Variation form in which a musical idea in the bass is repeated over and over while the melodies above it constantly change; common in baroque music.
> **Examples**   Purcell, *Dido and Aeneas, Dido's Lament*; basic sets side 2, band 8; CD 1 ⟦57⟧
> Brahms, Symphony No. 4 in E Minor, 4th mvt; p 227; LO variations 4–8; side 4, band 5; CD 2 ⟦57⟧; 1:02

***Guitar***   Plucked string instrument with six strings stretched along a fretted fingerboard.
> **Example**   Armstrong, *Hotter Than That*; p 7; LO 4–5; side 1, band 2; CD 1 ⟦8⟧ and ⟦9⟧; 1:19

*Half step*   Smallest interval traditionally used in western music; for example, the interval between *ti* and *do*.

*Harmonics*   Very high-pitched tones, like a whistle's, produced in bowed string instruments by lightly touching the string at certain points while bowing.

*Harmony*   How chords are constructed and how they follow each other.

*Harp*   Plucked string instrument, consisting of strings stretched within a triangular frame.
> Example   Debussy, *Prelude to the Afternoon of a Faun;* p 265; side 5, band 3; LO 1a; CD 3 |12| and LO 4a; CD 3 |17|; 6:46

*Harpsichord*   Keyboard instrument, widely used from about 1500 to 1775, whose sound is produced by plectra which pluck its wire strings. The harpsichord has been revived during the twentieth century.
> Example   Bach, *Brandenburg* Concerto No. 5 in D Major, 1st mvt; p 87; LO 8c; side 1, band 10; CD 1 |35|

*Heterophonic texture*   Simultaneous performance of the same basic melody by two or more voices or instruments, but in versions that differ in ornamentation or rhythm; common in nonwestern music.

*Home key*   See *tonic key.*

*Homophonic texture*   Term describing music in which one main melody is accompanied by chords.
> Examples   Chopin, Nocturne in E Flat Major, Op. 9, No. 2; p 197; side 4, band 1; CD 2 |35|
> Bizet, *Farandole* from *L'Arlésienne* Suite No. 2, p 47; LO 1a; side 1, band 3; CD 1 |11|

*Horn*   See *French horn.*

*Idée fixe*   Single melody used throughout a long work to represent one idea.
> Example   Berlioz, *Fantastic Symphony;* p 214; LO 2b; side 4, band 3; CD 2 |45|; 1:47

*Idiophone*   Instrument—such as bells, a gong, a scraper, a rattle, or a xylophone—whose sound is generated by the instrument's own material with no applied tension.

*Imitation*   Presentation of a melodic idea by one voice or instrument that is immediately followed by its restatement by another voice or instrument, as in a round.
> Examples   Josquin Desprez, *Ave Maria,* opening words *Ave Maria;* p 68; side 1, band 8; CD 1 |27|
> Bach, Organ Fugue in G Minor; p 91; LO 1; side 1, band 11; CD 1 |36|

*Impressionism*   Musical style which stresses tone color, atmosphere, and fluidity, typical of Debussy (flourished 1890–1920).
> Example   Debussy, *Prelude to the Afternoon of a Faun;* p 264; side 5, band 3; CD 3 |12|

*Improvisation*   Creation of music at the same time as it is performed.
> Example   Armstrong, *Hotter Than That;* p 6; side 1, band 2; CD 1 |5|

*Incidental music*   Music intended to be performed before and during a play, setting the mood for the drama.

*Incomplete cadence*    Inconclusive resting point at the end of a phrase which sets up expectations for phrases to follow.
Example   Vivaldi, *La Primavera (Spring)*, Concerto for Violin and String Orchestra, 1st mvt; p 100; LO 1a (end of opening phrase); side 2, band 2; CD 1 ⎡40⎤

*Interval*    "Distance" in pitch between any two tones.

*Inversion*    Variation of a melodic idea (such as a fugue subject) in which each interval of the idea is reversed in direction.

*Jazz*    Music rooted in improvisation and characterized by syncopated rhythm, a steady beat, and distinctive tone colors and performance techniques. Jazz was developed in the United States predominantly by black musicians and gained popularity in the early twentieth century.
Example   Armstrong, *Hotter Than That*; p 6; side 1, band 2; CD 1 ⎡5⎤

*Jazz rock (fusion)*    Style which combines the jazz musician's improvisatory approach with rock rhythms and tone colors; developed in the 1960s.

*Kettledrums*    See *timpani.*

*Key (tonality)*    Central note, scale, and chord within a piece, in relationship to which all other tones in the composition are heard.

*Key signature*    Sharp or flat signs immediately following the clef sign at the beginning of a piece of music, indicating the key in which the music is to be played.

*Keyboard instrument*    Instrument—such as the piano, organ, or harpsichord—played by pressing a series of keys with the fingers.

*Keynote (tonic)*    Central tone of a melody or larger piece of music. When a piece is in the key of C major, for example, C is the keynote.

*Klangfarbenmelodie*    See *tone-color melody.*

*Koto*    Instrument with thirteen silk or nylon strings stretched over a hollow sound board about 6 feet long; each string is tuned by adjusting the placement of a movable bridge. The koto is important in Japanese music.
Example   Mitsuzaki Kengyō, *Godan Ginuta;* p 353; side 6, band 11; CD 3 ⎡51⎤

*Largo*    Very slow, broad.
Example   Chopin, Prelude for Piano in C Minor; basic sets side 1, band 2; CD 1 ⎡5⎤

*Leap*    Interval larger than that between two adjacent tones in the scale.
Example   Chopin, Nocturne in E Flat Major, Op. 9, No. 2, upward leap at beginning of main melody; p 198; LO 1a; side 4, band 1; CD 2 ⎡35⎤

*Ledger lines*    Short, horizontal lines above or below the staff, used to indicate a pitch that falls above or below the range indicated by the staff.

*Legato*    Smooth, connected manner of performing a melody.
Example   Bach, Organ Fugue in G Minor; p 91; LO 1a; side 1, band 11; CD 1 ⎡36⎤

*Leitmotif*    Short musical idea associated with a person, object, or thought, characteristic of the operas of Wagner.
Example   Wagner, *Die Walküre*, Act 1, love scene, *sword;* p 242; side 5, band 2; CD 3 ⎡9⎤; 5:42

**Librettist**  Dramatist who writes the libretto, or text, of an opera.

**Libretto**  Text of an opera.

**Madrigal**  Composition for several voices set to a short secular poem, usually about love, combining homophonic and polyphonic textures and often using word painting; common in Renaissance music.
Example  Weelkes, *As Vesta Was Descending;* p 72; side 1, band 9; CD 1 30

**Major key**  Music based on a major scale.
Examples  Mozart, *Eine kleine Nachtmusik,* 3d mvt; p 135; side 2, band 9; CD 1 71
Contrast between major and minor keys is illustrated in Tchaikovsky, *Nutcracker* Suite, *Dance of the Reed Pipes;* p 50; LO 1 (major) and 2 (minor); side 1, band 4; CD 1 16 and 17

**Major scale**  Series of seven different tones within an octave, with an eighth tone repeating the first tone an octave higher, consisting of a specific pattern of whole and half steps; the whole step between the second and third tones is characteristic.
Example  Handel, *Messiah, Ev'ry Valley Shall Be Exalted,* downward major scale on first appearance of *-ley shall be exalted;* p 113; side 2, band 5; CD 2 49

**Marimba**  Percussion instrument with tuned wooden bars, similar to the xylophone, but larger and having cylindrical acoustic resonators.

**Mass**  Sacred choral composition made up of five sections: Kyrie, Gloria, Credo, Agnus Dei; Sanctus, and Agnus Dei.
Example  Machaut, *Notre Dame* Mass, Agnus Dei; p 63; side 1, band 7; CD 1 24

**Mass ordinary**  Roman Catholic church texts which remain the same from day to day throughout most of the year: Kyrie, Gloria, Credo, Sanctus, and Agnus Dei.

**Measure**  Rhythmic group set off by bar lines, containing a fixed number of beats.

**Melody**  Series of single tones that add up to a recognizable whole.

**Membranophone**  Instrument—basically, a drum—whose sound is generated by a stretched skin or other membrane.

**Meter**  Organization of beats into regular groups.

**Meter signature**  See *time signature.*

**Metronome**  Apparatus which produces ticking sounds or flashes of light at any desired constant speed.

**Mezzo forte (mf)**  Moderately loud.
Example  Berlioz, *Fantastic Symphony;* p 214; LO 1*b;* side 4, band 3; CD 2 44 ; 0:27

**Mezzo piano (mp)**  Moderately soft.
Example  Stravinsky, *The Rite of Spring;* p 272; LO 1*a;* side 3, band 19; CD 5 4

**Mezzo soprano**  Female voice lower than a soprano and higher than an alto.

**Microtone**  Interval smaller than a half step.

**Middle C**  The note C nearest to the center of the piano keyboard, notated as the pitch on the ledger line below the treble clef and above the bass clef.

*Minimalist music*   Music characterized by steady pulse, clear tonality, and insistent repetition of short melodic patterns; its dynamic level, texture, and harmony tend to stay constant for fairly long stretches of time, creating a trancelike or hypnotic effect; developed in the 1960s.
> Example   Adams, *Nixon in China*, Act I, scene 2; p 316; side 6, band 7; CD 3 46

*Minor key*   Music based on a minor scale.
> Examples   Bach, Suite No. 2 in B Minor, *Badinerie;* p 51; side 1, band 5; CD 1 19
> Contrast between minor and major keys is illustrated in Bizet, *L'Arlésienne* Suite No. 2; p 47; LO 1 (minor) and 2 (major); side 1, band 3; CD 1 11 and 13

*Minor scale*   Series of seven tones within an octave, with an eighth tone repeating the first tone an octave higher, consisting of a specific pattern of whole and half steps; the half step between the second and third tones is characteristic.
> Example   Smetana, *The Moldau;* p 219; LO 2; side 4, band 4; CD 2 51; 1:00

*Minuet*   See *minuet and trio.*

*Minuet and trio (minuet)*   Compositional form—derived from a dance—in three parts: minuet (A), trio (B), minuet (A). Often employed as the third movement of classical symphonies, string quartets, and other works, it is in triple meter ($\frac{3}{4}$ time), and usually in a moderate tempo.
> Example   Mozart, *Eine kleine Nachtmusik*, 3d mvt; p 135; side 2, band 9; CD 1 71

*Moderato*   Moderate tempo.
> Example   Tchaikovsky, *Nutcracker* Suite, *Dance of the Reed Pipes;* p 50; side 1, band 4; CD 1 16

*Modified strophic form*   Form in which two or more stanzas of poetry are set to the same music while other stanzas have new music; found in art songs of the romantic period.

*Modulation*   Shift from one key to another within the same piece.
> Example   Mozart, Symphony No. 40 in G Minor, 1st mvt; modulation from G minor to B flat major; p 129; LO exposition; side 2, band 7; CD 1 56

*Monophonic texture*   Single melodic line without accompaniment.
> Example   *Alleluia: Vidiumus stellam,* p 58; side 1, band 6; CD 1 21

*Motet*   Polyphonic choral work set to a sacred Latin text other than that of the mass; one of the two main forms of sacred Renaissance music.
> Example   Josquin Desprez, *Ave Maria;* p 68; side 1, band 6; CD 1 21

*Motive*   Fragment of a theme, or short musical idea which is developed within a composition.
> Example   Beethoven, Symphony No. 5 in C Minor, 1st mvt, first four notes; p 166; LO exposition 1a; side 3, band 4; CD 2 16

*Movement*   Piece that sounds fairly complete and independent but is part of a larger composition.

*Musical texture*   How many layers of sound are heard at once, what kinds of layers they are, and how they are related to each other.

*Musical (musical comedy)*   Type of American theater created to entertain through fusion of a dramatic script, acting, and spoken dialogue with music, singing, and dancing, and with scenery, costumes, and spectacle.

**Example** Bernstein, *West Side Story, Tonight* ensemble; p 333; side 6, band 8; CD 3 47

*Mute* Device used to veil or muffle the tone of an instrument. In string instruments, the mute is a clamp which fits onto the bridge; in brass instruments, it is a funnel-shaped piece of wood, metal, or plastic which fits into the bell.

*Nationalism* Inclusion of folk songs, dances, legends, and other national material in a composition to associate it with the composer's homeland; characteristic of romantic music.

*Natural sign* Symbol used in notation of pitch to cancel a previous sharp or flat sign.

*Neoclassicism* Musical style marked by emotional restraint, balance, and clarity, inspired by the forms and stylistic features of eighteenth-century music, found in many works from 1920 to 1950.

*New Orleans (Dixieland) jazz* Jazz style in which the melodic instruments (the *front line*) improvise several contrasting melodic lines at once, with a rhythm section that clearly marks the beat and provides a background of chords; usually based on a march or church melody, a ragtime piece, a popular song, or 12-bar blues.
**Example** Armstrong, *Hotter Than That*; p 6; side 1, band 2; CD 1 5

*Nocturne* In French, *night piece*; a composition, usually slow, lyrical, and intimate in character, often for piano solo.
**Example** Chopin, Nocturne in E Flat Major, Op. 9, No. 2; p 197; side 4, band 1; CD 2 35

*Notation* System of writing down music so that specific pitches and rhythms can be communicated.

*Note* In notation, a black or white oval to which a stem and flags can be added.

*Oboe* Double-reed woodwind instrument with a relatively high range, conical in shape with a small flared bell.
**Example** Wagner, *Lohengrin*, Prelude to Act III; p 6; LO 2; side 1, band 1; CD 1 3; 1:16

*Octave* Interval between two tones in which the higher tone has twice the frequency of the lower tone.
**Example** Handel, *Messiah, Hallelujah* Chorus, downward and upward octave leaps to the words *God omni(potent)*; p 114; side 2, band 6; CD 1 51

*Opera* Drama that is sung to orchestral accompaniment, usually a large-scale composition employing vocal soloists, chorus, orchestra, costumes, and scenery.

*Oratorio* Large-scale composition for chorus, vocal soloists, and orchestra, usually set to a narrative text, but without acting, scenery, or costumes; often based on biblical stories.

*Organ (pipe organ)* Keyboard instrument with many sets of pipes controlled from two or more keyboards, including a pedal keyboard played by the organist's feet. The keys control valves from which air is blown across or through openings in the pipes. (The electric organ is an electronic instrument that is sometimes designed to imitate the sound of a pipe organ.)
**Example** Bach, Organ Fugue in G Minor; p 90; side 1, band 11; CD 1 36

*Organ point*    See *pedal point*.

*Organum*    Medieval polyphony that consists of Gregorian chant and one or more additional melodic lines.
>    Example    Perotin, *Alleluia: Nativitas;* basic sets side 2, band 1; CD 1 ⟨40⟩

*Ostinato*    Motive or phrase that is repeated persistently at the same pitch, used in twentieth-century music to stabilize a group of pitches.
>    Example    Stravinsky, *The Rite of Spring, Introduction* and *Omens of Spring;* p 272; LO 2*b;* side 5, band 4; CD 3 ⟨20⟩ ; 2:40

*Overture (prelude)*    Short musical composition, purely orchestral, which opens an opera and sets the overall dramatic mood. Orchestral introductions to later acts of an opera are called *preludes.*

*Passacaglia*    See *ground bass*.

*Pedal point (organ point)*    Single tone, usually in the bass, which is held while the other voices produce a series of changing harmonies against it; often found in fugues.

*Pentatonic scale*    Scale made up of five different tones, used in folk music and music of the far east.

*Percussion instrument*    Instrument of definite or indefinite pitch whose sound is produced by striking by hand, or with a stick or hammer, or by shaking or rubbing.

*Phrase*    Part of a melody.
>    Example    Vivaldi, *La Primavera (Spring),* Concerto for Violin and String Orchestra, 1st mvt, opening phrase of ritornello; p 100; LO 1*a;* side 2, band 2; CD 1 ⟨40⟩

*Pianissimo (pp)*    As softly as possible.
>    Example    Haydn, Symphony No. 94 *(Surprise),* 2d mvt; p 132; LO theme, section a repeated; side 2, band 8; CD 1 ⟨65⟩

*Piano*    Widely used keyboard instrument of great range and versatility, whose sound is produced by felt-covered hammers striking against steel strings.
>    Example    Chopin, Nocturne in E-Flat Major; p 197; side 4, band 1; CD 2 ⟨35⟩

*Piano (p)*    Soft.
>    Example    Wagner, *Lohengrin,* Prelude to Act III; p 6; LO 2; side 1, band 1; CD 1 ⟨3⟩ ; 1:16

*Piccolo*    Smallest woodwind instrument, having the highest range; a smaller version of the flute.
>    Example    Stravinsky, *The Rite of Spring, Omens of Spring;* p 272; LO 3*l;* side 5, band 4; CD 3 ⟨24⟩ ; 5:37

*Pipe organ*    See *organ*.

*Pitch*    Relative highness or lowness of a sound.

*Pitch range*    Distance between the highest and lowest tones that a given voice or instrument can produce.

*Pizzicato*    Means of playing a string instrument by which the strings are plucked, usually with a finger of the right hand.
>    Example    Tchaikovsky, *Nutcracker* Suite, *Dance of the Reed Pipes;* p 50; LO 1*a–b;* side 1, band 4; CD 1 ⟨16⟩

**Polonaise**   Composition in triple meter with a stately character, often for piano solo; originally a Polish court dance.

Example   Chopin, Polonaise in A Flat Major, Op. 53; p 200; basic sets side 9, band 4; CD 5 [10]

**Polychord**   Combination of two chords sounded at the same time, used in twentieth-century music.

Example   Stravinsky, *The Rite of Spring, Omens of Spring*; p 272; LO 3a; side 5, band 4, CD 3 [21]; 3:00

**Polyphonic texture**   Performance of two or more melodic lines of relatively equal interest at the same time.

Examples   Bach, Organ Fugue in G Minor, illustrates polyphonic texture based on imitation; p 90; side 1, band 11; CD 1 [36]
Bach, Cantata No. 140, 4th mvt, starting with entry of tenors, illustrates polyphonic texture based on the simultaneous presentation of different melodies; p 107; side 2, band 3; CD 1 [46]

**Polyrhythm**   Use of two or more contrasting and independent rhythms at the same time, often found in twentieth-century music and the music of sub-Saharan Africa.

Example   *Mitamba Yalagala Kumchuzi*; p 350; side 6, band 10; CD 6 [50]

**Polytonality**   Approach to pitch organization using two or more keys at one time, often found in twentieth-century music.

**Postlude**   Concluding section; the section at the end of an art song which sums up its mood, played by the piano alone.

Example   Robert Schumann, *Im wunderschönen Monat Mai*; basic sets side 9, band 1; CD 5 [1]

**Prelude**   (1) Short piece usually serving to introduce a fugue or other composition; a short piece for piano. (2) See *overture.*

Example   Chopin, Prelude in E Minor for Piano; basic sets side 1, band 9; CD 1 [25]

**Prestissimo**   As fast a tempo as possible.

Example   Beethoven, String Quartet in C Minor, Op. 18, No. 4, 4th mvt; p 137; LO 7; side 3, band 1; CD 2 [4]; 3:31

**Presto**   Very fast tempo.

**Primitivism**   Evocation of primitive power through insistent rhythms and percussive sounds.

Example   Stravinsky, *The Rite of Spring, Omens of Spring*; p 271; side 5, band 4; CD 3 [21]

**Program**   Explanatory comments specifying the story, scene, or idea associated with program music.

**Program music**   Instrumental music associated with a story, poem, idea, or scene, often found in romantic music.

**Program symphony**   Symphony (a composition for orchestra in several movements) related to a story, idea, or scene, in which each movement usually has a descriptive title; often found in romantic music.

Example   Berlioz, *Fantastic Symphony*, 5th mvt; p 213; side 4, band 3; CD 2 [44]

**Progression**   Series of chords.

*Prompter*   Person who gives cues and reminds singers of their words or pitches during an opera performance. The prompter is located in a box just over the edge of center stage, which conceals him or her from the audience.

*Quadruple meter*   Pattern of 4 beats to the measure.
   Example   Vivaldi, *La Primavera (Spring)*, Concerto for Violin and String Orchestra, 1st mvt; p 100; side 2, band 2; CD 1 | 40 |

*Quadruple stop*   See *stop*.

*Quintuple meter*   Pattern of 5 beats to the measure.

*Quotation music*   Works which make extensive use of quotations from earlier music; common since the mid-1960s.
   Example   Zwilich, *Concerto Grosso 1985*, 1st mvt; p 314; side 6, band 6; CD 3 | 44 |

*Ragtime*   Style of composed piano music, generally in duple meter with a moderate march tempo, in which the pianist's right hand plays a highly syncopated melody while the left hand maintains the beat with an "oom-pah" accompaniment. Ragtime was developed primarily by African American pianists and flourished from the 1890s to about 1915.
   Example   Joplin, *Maple Leaf Rag*; basic sets side 15, band 7; CD 8 | 13 |

*Range*   See *pitch range*.

*Recapitulation*   Third section of a sonata-form movement, in which the first theme, bridge, second theme, and concluding section are presented more or less as they were in the exposition, with one crucial difference: all the principal material is now in the tonic key.
   Example   Mozart, Symphony No. 40 in G Minor, 1st mvt; p 129; LO recapitulation; side 2, band 7; CD 1 | 62 | and | 63 |

*Recitative*   Vocal line in an opera, oratorio, or cantata that imitates the rhythms and pitch fluctuations of speech, often serving to lead into an aria.
   Example   Mozart, *Don Giovanni*, introduction; p 147; side 3, band 2; CD 2 | 8 |; 5:19

*Recorder*   Family of woodwind instruments whose sound is produced by blowing into a "whistle" mouthpiece, usually made of wood or plastic.
   Example   Andrea Gabrieli, Ricercar in the Twelfth Mode; p 73; basic sets side 2, band 5; CD 1 | 48 |

*Reed*   Very thin piece of cane, used in woodwind instruments to produce sound as it is set into vibration by a stream of air.

*Register*   Part of the total range of an instrument or voice. The tone color of the instrument or voice may vary with the register in which it is played or sung.

*Repetition*   Reiteration of a phrase, section, or entire movement, often used to create a sense of unity.

*Resolution*   Progression from a dissonance to a consonance.

*Rest*   In notation of rhythm, a symbol to indicate the duration of silence in the music.

*Retrograde*   Variation of a fugue subject in which the subject is presented by beginning with its last note and proceeding backward to the first.

***Rhythm***  Ordered flow of music through time; the pattern of durations of notes and silences in music.

***Rhythm section***  Instruments in a jazz ensemble which maintain the beat, add rhythmic interest, and provide supporting harmonies. The rhythm section is usually made up of piano, plucked double bass, percussion, and sometimes banjo or guitar.

***Ricercar***  Polyphonic instrumental composition which makes extensive use of imitation, often found in Renaissance music.
   Example   Andrea Gabrieli, Ricercar in the Twelfth Mode; p 73; basic sets side 2, band 5; CD 1 48

***Riff***  In jazz, a short repeated phrase that may be an accompaniment or a melody.

***Ritardando***  Becoming slower.
   Example   Liszt, *Transcendental Étude* No. 10 in F Minor; p 204; LO 5; side 4, band 2; CD 2 42; 2:04

***Ritornello***  In Italian, *refrain;* a repeated section of music usually played by the full orchestra, or tutti, in baroque compositions.
   Example   Bach, *Brandenburg* Concerto No. 5 in D Major, 1st mvt; p 87; LO 1a; side 1, band 10; CD 1 31

***Ritornello form***  Compositional form usually employed in the baroque concerto grosso, in which the tutti plays a ritornello, or refrain, alternating with one or more soloists playing new material.
   Examples   Bach, *Brandenburg* Concerto No. 5 in D Major, 1st mvt; p 86; side 1, band 10; CD 1 31
   Vivaldi, *La Primavera (Spring),* Concerto for Violin and String Orchestra, 1st mvt; p 99; side 2, band 2; CD 1 40

***Rock***  First called *rock and roll,* a style of popular vocal music which developed in the 1950s, characterized by a hard, driving beat and featuring electric guitar accompaniment and heavily amplified sound.

***Romance***  In nineteenth-century music, a short lyrical piece for piano or solo instrument with piano accompaniment.
   Example   Clara Schumann, Romance in G Minor for Violin and Piano; p 194; side 3, band 6; CD 2 30

***Rondo***  Compositional form featuring a main theme (A) which returns several times in alternation with other themes, such as A B A C A and A B A C A B A. Rondo is often the form of the last movement in classical symphonies, string quartets, and sonatas.
   Example   Beethoven, String Quartet in C Minor, Op. 18, No. 4, 4th mvt; p 136; side 3, band 1; CD 2 1

***Rubato***  Slight holding back or pressing forward of tempo to intensify the expression of the music, often used in romantic music.
   Example   Chopin, Nocturne in E Flat Major, Op. 9, No. 2; p 198; LO 2a; side 4, band 1; CD 2 37

***Saxophone***  Family of single-reed woodwind instruments.
   Example   Parker, *KoKo;* basic sets side 16, band 4; CD 8 21

***String quartet***　Composition employing two violins, one viola, and one cello; usually consisting of four movements. (Also, the four instrumentalists.)
　Example　Beethoven, String Quartet in C Minor, Op. 18, No. 4, 4th mvt; p 136; side 3, band 1; CD 2 **1**

***Strophic form***　Vocal form in which the same music is repeated for each stanza of a poem.
　Example　Robert Schumann, *Im wunderschönen Monat Mai*; p 192; basic sets side 9, band 1; CD 5 **1**

***Style***　Characteristic way of using melody, rhythm, tone color, dynamics, harmony, texture, and form in music.

***Subdominant***　Fourth note *(fa)* of the scale, or the triad (chord) based on this note.

***Subject***　Theme of a fugue.
　Example　Bach, Organ Fugue in G Minor; p 91; LO 1a; side 1, band 11; CD 1 **36**

***Suite***　In baroque music, a set of dance-inspired movements that are all written in the same key but differ in tempo, meter, and character.
　Example　Bach, Suite No. 3 in D Major; p 103; basic sets side 4, bands 1–3; CD 2 **17**, **19**, **21**

***Swing band***　Typically, a large band made up of fourteen or fifteen musicians grouped in three sections: saxophones, brasses, and rhythm. They play swing, a jazz style which was developed in the 1920s and flourished between 1935 and 1945.
　Example　Ellington, *Concerto for Cootie*; basic sets side 16, band 3; CD 8 **20**

***Symphonic poem (tone poem)***　Programmatic composition for orchestra in one movement, which may have a traditional form (such as sonata or rondo) or an original, irregular form.

***Symphony***　Orchestral composition, usually in four movements, typically lasting between 20 and 45 minutes, exploiting the expanded range of tone color and dynamics of the orchestra.

***Syncopation***　Accenting of a note at an unexpected time, as between two beats or on a weak beat. Syncopation is a major characteristic of jazz.
　Examples　Vivaldi, *La Primavera (Spring)*, Concerto for Violin and String Orchestra, 1st mvt; p 100; LO 1a, closing phrase of ritornello; side 2, band 2; CD 1 **40**
　Liszt, *Transcendental Étude* No. 10 in F Minor; p 204; LO 1a; side 4, band 2; CD 2 **38**

***Synthesizer***　System of electronic components which can generate, modify, and control sound; used to compose music and to perform it.
　Example　Adams, *Nixon in China*, Act I, scene 2; p 316; side 6, band 7; CD 3 **46**

***Tambourine***　Percussion instrument of indefinite pitch, consisting of a skin stretched across a shallow cylinder, with small circular plates set into the cylinder which jingle when the skin is struck or the cylinder is shaken.
　Example　Bizet, *L'Arlésienne* Suite No. 2, *Farandole*; p 47; LO 2a, introducing dance theme in woodwinds; side 1, band 3; CD 1 **13**; 0:33

***Tam-tam***　See *gong*.

***Tape studio***　Studio with tape recorders and other equipment used to create electronic music by modifying and combining recorded sounds.
　Example　Varèse, *Poème électronique*; p 311; side 6, band 9; CD 3 **33**

*Tempo*   Basic pace of the music.

*Tempo indication*   Words, usually at the beginning of a piece of music, often in Italian, which specify the pace at which the music should be played.

*Tenor*   Male voice of high range.
 Example   Handel, *Messiah, Ev'ry Valley;* p 113; side 2, band 5; CD 1 49

*Terraced dynamics*   Abrupt alternation between loud and soft dynamic levels; characteristic of baroque music.
 Example   Vivaldi, *La Primavera (Spring),* Concerto for Violin and String Orchestra, 1st mvt; p 100; LO 1a; side 2, band 2; CD 1 40

*Thematic transformation*   Alteration of the character of a theme by means of changes in dynamics, orchestration, or rhythm, when it returns in a later movement or section; often found in romantic music.
 Example   Liszt, *Transcendental Étude* in F Minor; p 204; compare lyrical theme at LO 2a and processional theme at LO 3; side 4, band 2; CD 2 39 and 40 ; 0:42 and 1:14

*Theme*   Melody which serves as the starting point for an extended piece of music.
 Example   Mozart, Symphony No. 40, 1st mvt; p 129; LO 1; side 2, band 7; CD 1 56

*Theme and variations*   Form in which a basic musical idea (the theme) is repeated over and over and is changed each time in melody, rhythm, harmony, dynamics, or tone color. Used either as an independent piece or as one movement of a larger work.
 Examples   Haydn, Symphony No. 94 in G Major *(Surprise),* 2d mvt; p 131; side 2, band 8; CD 1 65
 Copland, *Appalachian Spring,* section 7, Theme and Variations on *Simple Gifts;* p 303; side 6, band 8; CD 3 37

*Three-part form (A B A)*   Form that can be represented as statement (A); contrast (B); return of statement (A).
 Examples   Tchaikovsky, *Nutcracker* Suite, *Dance of the Reed Pipes;* p 50; side 1, band 4; CD 1 16
 Clara Schumann, Romance in G Minor for Violin and Piano; p 194; side 3, band 6; CD 2 30

*Through-composed form*   Vocal form in which there is new music for each stanza of a poem.
 Example   Schubert, *Erlkönig (The Erlking);* p 187; side 3, band 5; CD 2 24

*Tie*   In notation of rhythm, an arc between two notes of the same pitch indicating that the second note should not be played but should be added to the duration of the first.

*Timbre*   See *tone color.*

*Time signature (meter signature)*   Two numbers, one above the other, appearing at the beginning of a staff or the start of a piece, indicating the meter of the piece.

*Timpani (kettledrums)*   Percussion instruments of definite pitch, shaped like large kettles with calfskin or plastic stretched across the tops, usually played with sticks with felt heads.
 Example   Smetana, *The Moldau;* p 219; LO 7; side 4, band 4; CD 2 55 ; 8:46

*Tonality*   See *key.*

*Tone*   Sound that has a definite pitch, or frequency.

*Tone cluster*   Chord made up of tones only a half step or a whole step apart, used in twentieth-century music.
   **Example**   Penderecki, *Threnody for the Victims of Hiroshima*, opening; supp sets side 8, band 3; CD 4 |28|

*Tone color (timbre)*   Quality of sound that distinguishes one instrument or voice from another.

*Tone-color melody*   Succession of varying tone colors serving as a musical idea in a composition, used by Schoenberg and his followers.
   **Example**   Webern, *Five Pieces for Orchestra*, 3d piece; p 290; side 6, band 2; CD 3 |29|

*Tone poem*   See *symphonic poem.*

*Tone row (set, series)*   Particular ordering of the twelve chromatic tones, from which all pitches in a twelve-tone composition are derived.
   **Example**   Schoenberg, *A Survivor from Warsaw*, to the Hebrew words of *Shema Yisroel;* p 281; side 6, band 1; CD 3 |28|

*Tonic*   See *keynote.*

*Tonic chord*   Triad built on the first, or tonic, note of the scale, serving as the main chord of a piece and usually beginning and ending it.
   **Example**   Bizet, *L'Arlésienne* Suite No. 2, *Farandole*, opening chord; p 47; LO 1a; side 1, band 3; CD 1 |11|

*Tonic key (home key)*   Central key of a piece of music, usually both beginning and ending the piece, regardless of how many other keys are included.

*Transition*   See *bridge.*

*Treble clef*   Notation of a staff to indicate relatively high pitch ranges, such as those played by a pianist's right hand.

*Tremolo*   Rapid repetition of a tone, produced in string instruments by quick up-and-down strokes of the bow.
   **Examples**   Vivaldi, *La Primavera (Spring)*, Concerto for Violin and String Orchestra, 1st mvt; p 100; LO 3b; side 2, band 2; CD 1 |43|; 1:40
   Berlioz, *Fantastic Symphony*, 5th mvt; p 214; LO 1a; side 4, band 3; CD 2 |44|; 1:47

*Triad*   Most basic of chords, consisting of three alternate tones of the scale, such as *do, mi, sol.*

*Triangle*   Percussion instrument of indefinite pitch, consisting of a triangular length of metal suspended from a hook or cord, played by striking with a metal rod.
   **Example**   Smetana, *The Moldau*; p 219; LO 4a; side 4, band 4; CD 2 |53|

*Trill*   Musical ornament consisting of the rapid alternation of two tones that are a whole or half step apart.
   **Example**   Vivaldi, *La Primavera (Spring)*, Concerto for Violin and String Orchestra, 1st mvt; p 100; LO 1b; side 2, band 2; CD 1 |43|; 0:30

*Triple meter*   Pattern of 3 beats to the measure.
   **Example**   Mozart, *Eine kleine Nachtmusik*, 3d mvt; p 135; side 2, band 9; CD 1 |71|

*Triple stop*  See *stop*.

*Triplet*  In notation of rhythm, three notes of equal duration grouped within a curved line with the numeral 3, lasting only as long as two notes of this same length would normally last.

*Trio sonata*  Baroque composition which has three melodic lines: two high ones, each played by one instrument; and a basso continuo, played by two instruments.
Example   Corelli, Trio Sonata in E Minor; p 98; supp sets side 2, bands 1–4; CD 1 34 – 37

*Trombone*  Brass instrument of moderately low range, whose tube is an elongated loop with a movable slide, commonly used in symphony orchestras, bands, and jazz ensembles.
Example   Armstrong, *Hotter Than That;* p 7; LO 6a; side 1, band 2; CD 1 9 ; 2:17

*Trumpet*  Brass instrument with the highest range, commonly used in symphony orchestras, bands, and jazz and rock groups.
Examples   Armstrong, *Hotter Than That;* p 7; LO 2; side 1, band 4; CD 1 10
Copland, *Appalachian Spring,* section 7, Theme and Variations on *Simple Gifts;* p 303; LO variation 3; side 6, band 8; CD 3 40

*Tuba*  Largest brass instrument, having the lowest range, commonly used in symphony orchestras and bands.
Example   Berlioz, *Fantastic Symphony;* p 214; LO 4a; side 4, band 3; CD 2 46 ; 1:17

*Tutti*  In Italian, *all;* the full orchestra, or a large group of musicians contrasted with a smaller group; often heard in baroque music
Example   Bach, *Brandenburg* Concerto No. 5 in D Major, 1st mvt; p 87; LO 1a; side 1, band 10; CD 1 31

*12-bar blues*  In vocal blues and jazz, a harmonic framework that is 12 bars in length, usually involving only three basic chords: tonic (I), subdominant (IV), and dominant (V).
Example   Smith, *Lost Your Head Blues;* basic sets side 15, band 8; CD 8 17

*Twelve-tone system*  Method of composing in which all pitches of a composition are derived from a special ordering of the twelve chromatic tones (tone row or set); developed by Schoenberg in the early 1920s.
Example   Schoenberg, *A Survivor from Warsaw;* p 281; side 6, band 1; CD 3 27

*Two-part form (A B)*  Form that can be represented as statement (A) and counterstatement (B).
Examples   Bach, Suite No. 2 in B Minor, *Badinerie;* p 51; side 1, band 5; CD 1 19
Haydn, Symphony No. 94 in G Major *(Surprise),* 2d mvt, theme; p 132; LO theme; side 2, band 8; CD 1 65

*Unison*  Performance of a single melodic line by more than one instrument or voice at the same pitch or in different octaves.
Examples   Handel, *Messiah, Hallelujah* Chorus, to the words *For the Lord God;* p 114; side 2, band 6; CD 1 51
Beethoven, Symphony No. 5 in C Minor, 1st mvt; p 166; LO 1a; side 3, band 4; CD 2 16

*Upbeat*  Unaccented pulse preceding the downbeat.
Example   Chopin, Nocturne in E Flat Major, Op. 9, No. 2, opening note; p 197; LO 1a; side 4, band 1; CD 2 35

***Variation***    Changing some features of a musical idea while retaining others.

***Vibraphone***    Percussion instrument of definite pitch with metal bars, similar to the marimba, with tubular metal resonators driven by electronic impulses.

***Vibrato***    Small fluctuations of pitch which make the tone warmer, produced in string instruments by rocking the left hand while it presses the string down.
  **Example**    Clara Schumann, Romance in G Minor for Violin and Piano; p 194; side 3, band 6; CD 2 [30]

***Viola***    String instrument with a lower range than the violin and a higher range than the cello.
  **Example**    Bizet, *L'Arlésienne* Suite No. 2, *Farandole*; p 47; LO 1*b*; side 1, band 3; CD 1 [12]; 0:16

***Violin***    String instrument with the highest range of the string family.
  **Example**    Clara Schumann, Romance in G Minor for Violin and Piano; p 194; side 3, band 6; CD 2 [30]

***Violoncello***    See *cello*.

***Virtuoso***    Performing artist of extraordinary technical mastery.

***Vivace***    Lively tempo.
  **Example**    Wagner, *Lohengrin*, Prelude to Act III; p 6; side 1, band 1; CD 1 [1]

***Voice categories of opera***    Voice ranges which include coloratura soprano, lyric soprano, dramatic soprano, lyric tenor, dramatic tenor, basso buffo, and basso profundo, among others.

***Whole step***    Interval twice as large as the half step; for example, the interval between *do* and *re*.

***Whole-tone scale***    Scale made up of six different tones, each a whole step away from the next, which conveys no definite sense of tonality; often found in the music of Debussy and his followers.

***Woodwind instrument***    Instrument whose sound is produced by vibrations of air in a tube; holes along the length of the tube are opened and closed by the fingers, or by pads, to control the pitch.

***Word painting***    Musical representation of specific poetic images—for example, a falling melodic line to accompany the word *descending*—often found in Renaissance and baroque music.
  **Example**    Weelkes, *As Vesta Was Descending*; p 72; side 1, band 9; CD 1 [30]

***Xylophone***    Percussion instrument of definite pitch, consisting of flat wooden bars set in a frame and played by striking with hard plastic or wooden hammers.

# CHRONOLOGY [ APPENDIX **2** ]

## MIDDLE AGES (450–1450)

| Musicians | Artists and Writers | Historical and Cultural Events |
|---|---|---|
| | | Sack of Rome by Vandals (455) |
| | | Reign of Pope Gregory I (590–604) |
| | | First Crusade (1096–1099) |
| Perotin (late twelfth century) | | Beginning of Notre Dame Cathedral in Paris (1163) |
| | | King John signs Magna Carta (1215) |
| | Dante (1265–1321) | |
| | Giotto (1266–1337) | |
| Guillaume de Machaut (c. 1300–1377) | | |
| | Boccaccio (1313–1375) | |
| | Chaucer (c. 1343–1400) | Hundred Years' War (1337–1453) |
| | | Black death (1348–1350) |

## RENAISSANCE (1450–1600)

| Musicians | Artists and Writers | Historical and Cultural Events |
|---|---|---|
| Guillaume Dufay (c. 1400–1474) | | Fall of Constantinople (1453) |
| Josquin Desprez (c. 1440–1521) | Leonardo da Vinci (1452–1519) | Gutenberg Bible (1456) |
| | | Columbus discovers America (1492) |
| | Michelangelo (1475–1564) | |
| | Raphael (1483–1520) | Martin Luther's ninety-five theses (1517) |
| | Titian (c. 1477–1576) | |
| | François Rabelais (c. 1494–c. 1553) | |
| Andrea Gabrieli (c. 1520–1586) | | |

| Musicians | Artists and Writers | Historical and Cultural Events |
|---|---|---|
| Giovanni Pierluigi da Palestrina (c. 1525–1594) | | Council of Trent (1545–1563) |
| Roland de Lassus (1532–1594) | Michel de Montaigne (1533–1592) | |
| William Byrd (1543–1623) | | |
| Giovanni Gabrieli (c. 1555–1612) | | |
| Thomas Morley (1557–1603) | Cervantes (1547–1616) | Elizabeth I, queen of England (1558–1603) |
| | William Shakespeare (1564–1616) | |
| | | Spanish Armada defeated (1588) |
| Thomas Weelkes (1575–1623) | | |

---

## BAROQUE (1600–1750)

| Musicians | Artists and Writers | Historical and Cultural Events |
|---|---|---|
| | | Jamestown founded (1607) |
| Claudio Monteverdi (1567–1643) | | |
| | Peter Paul Rubens (1577–1640) | Thirty Years' War (1618–1648) |
| Heinrich Schütz (1585–1672) | | |
| | Gian Lorenzo Bernini (1598–1680) | |
| | Rembrandt (1606–1669) | |
| | John Milton (1608–1674) | |
| Jean-Baptiste Lully (1632–1687) | Molière (1622–1673) | Louis XIV reigns in France (1643–1715) |
| | Baruch Spinoza (1632–1677) | |
| Arcangelo Corelli (1653–1713) | | |
| Henry Purcell (c. 1659–1695) | Jonathan Swift (1667–1745) | Newton, *Principia Mathematica* (1687) |
| François Couperin (1668–1733) | | |
| Antonio Vivaldi (1678–1741) | | Louis XV reigns in France (1715–1774) |
| Johann Sebastian Bach (1685–1750) | Jean Antoine Watteau (1684–1721) | |
| George Frideric Handel (1685–1759) | | |

## CLASSICAL (1750–1820)

| Musicians | Artists and Writers | Historical and Cultural Events |
|---|---|---|
| | Voltaire (1694–1778) | Maria Theresa reigns in Austria (1740–1780) |
| | | Frederick the Great reigns in Prussia (1740–1786) |
| | Benjamin Franklin (1706–1790) | Publication of the French *Encyclopedia* begins (1751) |
| Christoph Gluck (1714–1787) | Jean Jacques Rousseau (1712–1778) | |
| | | Seven Years' War (1756–1763) |
| Carl Philipp Emanuel Bach (1714–1788) | | Winckelmann's *History of the Art of Antiquity* (1764) |
| | Immanuel Kant (1724–1804) | |
| Joseph Haydn (1732–1809) | | |
| | Goya (1746–1828) | |
| | Jacques Louis David (1748–1825) | |
| | Johann Wolfgang von Goethe (1749–1832) | Louis XVI reigns in France (1774–1792) |
| Wolfgang Amadeus Mozart (1756–1791) | | American Declaration of Independence (1776) |
| Ludwig van Beethoven (1770–1827) | | French Revolution begins (1789) |
| | | Eli Whitney invents cotton gin (1792) |
| | | Napoleon becomes first consul of France (1799) |
| | | Battle of Waterloo (1815) |

## ROMANTIC (1820–1900)

| Musicians | Artists and Writers | Historical and Cultural Events |
|---|---|---|
| | William Wordsworth (1770–1850) | |
| | J. M. W. Turner (1775–1851) | |
| Carl Maria von Weber (1786–1826) | | |
| Gioacchino Rossini (1792–1868) | | |

| Musicians | Artists and Writers | Historical and Cultural Events |
|---|---|---|
| Franz Schubert (1797–1828) | Heinrich Heine (1797–1856) | |
| | Eugène Delacroix (1798–1863) | |
| | Honoré de Balzac (1799–1850) | Revolutions in France, Belgium, Poland (1830) |
| Hector Berlioz (1803–1869) | Victor Hugo (1802–1885) | |
| | George Sand (1804–1876) | First Reform Bill in Britain (1832) |
| Felix Mendelssohn (1809–1847) | Edgar Allan Poe (1809–1849) | |
| Frédéric Chopin (1810–1849) | | Revolutions of 1848; Marx and Engels, *The Communist Manifesto* (1848) |
| Robert Schumann (1810–1856) | | |
| | | Darwin's *Origin of Species* (1859) |
| Franz Liszt (1811–1886) | | American Civil War (1861–1865) |
| | Charles Dickens (1812–1870) | |
| Richard Wagner (1813–1883) | | Franco-Prussian War (1870) |
| Giuseppe Verdi (1813–1901) | | |
| Clara Wieck Schumann (1819–1896) | | |
| César Franck (1822–1890) | Fyodor Dostoyevsky (1821–1881) | |
| Anton Bruckner (1824–1896) | | |
| Bedřich Smetana (1824–1884) | Leo Tolstoy (1828–1910) | |
| | Emily Dickinson (1830–1886) | |
| Johannes Brahms (1833–1897) | Edouard Manet (1832–1883) | |
| Georges Bizet (1838–1875) | Paul Cézanne (1839–1906) | |
| Modest Mussorgsky (1839–1881) | | |
| Peter Ilyich Tchaikovsky (1840–1893) | Claude Monet (1840–1926) | First group exhibition of impressionists in Paris (1874) |
| Antonin Dvořák (1841–1904) | Stéphane Mallarmé (1842–1898) | |
| John Philip Sousa (1854–1932) | | |
| Giacomo Puccini (1858–1924) | Friedrich Nietzsche (1844–1900) | Bell invents telephone (1876) |
| Gustav Mahler (1860–1911) | | |
| | Vincent Van Gogh (1853–1890) | |
| Richard Strauss (1864–1949) | | Spanish-American War (1898) |

## TWENTIETH CENTURY

| Musicians | Artists and Writers | Historical and Cultural Events |
|---|---|---|
| | | Freud, *The Psychopathology of Everyday Life* (1904) |
| Claude Debussy (1862–1918) | Wassily Kandinsky (1866–1944) | Einstein, special theory of relativity (1905) |
| Scott Joplin (1868–1917) | | |
| | Henri Matisse (1869–1954) | |
| | Marcel Proust (1871–1922) | |
| Arnold Schoenberg (1874–1951) | Gertrude Stein (1874–1946) | |
| | | World War I (1914–1918) |
| Charles Ives (1874–1954) | | Russian Revolution begins (1917) |
| Maurice Ravel (1875–1937) | | |
| Béla Bartók (1881–1945) | Pablo Picasso (1881–1973) | |
| | James Joyce (1882–1941) | Beginning of Great Depression (1929) |
| | Virginia Woolf (1882–1945) | |
| Igor Stravinsky (1882–1971) | | |
| | Franz Kafka (1883–1924) | Franklin D. Roosevelt inaugurated (1933) |
| Anton Webern (1883–1945) | | Hitler Chancellor of Germany (1933) |
| Edgard Varèse (1883–1965) | | |
| Alban Berg (1885–1935) | | |
| | T. S. Eliot (1888–1965) | World War II (1939–1945) |
| Sergei Prokofiev (1891–1953) | | |
| Bessie Smith (1894–1937) | | |
| Paul Hindemith (1895–1963) | | |
| Roger Sessions (1896–1985) | | |
| George Gershwin (1898–1937) | William Faulkner (1897–1962) | |
| E. K. ("Duke") Ellington (1899–1974) | Henry Moore (1898–1986) | |
| | Ernest Hemingway (1899–1961) | |
| Louis Armstrong (1900–1971) | Louise Nevelson (1900–1988) | |
| Aaron Copland (1900–1990) | Isaac Bashevis Singer (1904–1991) | |
| Ruth Crawford-Seeger (1901–1953) | | |
| Miriam Gideon (b. 1906) | Willem de Kooning (b. 1904) | |
| Dmitri Shostakovich (1906–1975) | Jean Paul Sartre (1905–1980) | |

| Musicians | Artists and Writers | Historical and Cultural Events |
|---|---|---|
| Elliott Carter (b. 1908) | David Smith (1906–1965) | |
| Olivier Messiaen (1908–1992) | | Atomic bomb destroys Hiroshima (1945) |
| John Cage (1912–1992) | | |
| | | Korean war begins (1950) |
| Benjamin Britten (1913–1976) | Jackson Pollock (1912–1956) | |
| Billie Holiday (1915–1959) | Albert Camus (1913–1960) | |
| | Saul Bellow (b. 1915) | |
| | Robert Motherwell (1915–1991) | |
| Milton Babbitt (b. 1916) | Andrew Wyeth (b. 1917) | |
| Leonard Bernstein (1918–1990) | | |
| Charlie Parker (1920–1955) | Alexander Solzhenitsyn (b. 1918) | |
| | Roy Lichtenstein (b. 1923) | American involvement in Vietnam increases dramatically (1965) |
| | Norman Mailer (b. 1923) | |
| Pierre Boulez (b. 1925) | James Baldwin (1924–1987) | American astronauts land on moon (1969) |
| John Coltrane (1926–1967) | Allen Ginsberg (b. 1926) | |
| Miles Davis (1926–1991) | John Hollander (b. 1928) | |
| Karlheinz Stockhausen (b. 1928) | Helen Frankenthaler (b. 1928) | Resignation of President Nixon (1974) |
| George Crumb (b. 1929) | Andy Warhol (1931–1987) | End of American involvement in Vietnam (1975) |
| Joe Zawinul (b. 1932) | David Hockney (b. 1937) | |
| Krzysztof Penderecki (b. 1933) | | United States and China establish diplomatic relations (1979) |
| Mario Davidovsky (b. 1934) | | Revolution in Iran (1979) |
| Steve Reich (b. 1936) | | Ronald Reagan inaugurated (1981) |
| Philip Glass (b. 1937) | | Wars in Lebanon and the Falkland Islands (1982) |
| Charles Wuorinen (b. 1938) | | Ronald Reagan inaugurated for second term (1985) |
| Ellen Taaffe Zwilich (b. 1939) | | Nuclear accident at Chernobyl, Soviet Union (1986) |
| John Lennon (1940–1980) | | George Bush inaugurated (1989) |
| | | Reunification of Germany (1990) |
| John Adams (b. 1947) | | Persian Gulf war (1991) |
| | | Dissolution of Soviet Union; formation of Commonwealth (1991) |
| | | Bill Clinton inaugurated (1993) |

# COMPLETE LIST OF RECORDING PACKAGES

| | BASIC SETS | | BRIEF SETS | | SUPPLEMENTARY SETS | |
|---|---|---|---|---|---|---|
| | 8 CDS | 8 LPs/ 8 Cassettes | 3 CDs | 3 Cassettes | 4 CDs | 4 LPs/ 4 Cassettes |
| **ELEMENTS** | CD TRACK | Side/Band | CD TRACK | Side/Band | CD TRACK | Side/Band |
| Wagner: *Lohengrin*, Prelude to Act III | 1 [1] | 1/1 | 1 **1** | 1/1 | | |
| Chopin: Prelude in C Minor for Piano, Op. 28, No. 20 | 1 [5] | 1/2 | | | | |
| Stravinsky: *Firebird* Suite, Finale | 1 [8] | 1/3 | | | | |
| Armstrong: *Hotter Than That* | 1 [10] | 1/4 | 1 **5** | 1/2 | | |
| Sousa: *The Stars and Stripes Forever* | 1 [16] | 1/5 | | | | |
| Gershwin: *I Got Rhythm* | 1 [20] | 1/6 | | | | |
| Brubeck: *Unsquare Dance* | 1 [21] | 1/7 | | | | |
| Arlen: *Over the Rainbow* | 1 [22] | 1/8 | | | | |
| Chopin: Prelude in E Minor, Op. 28, No. 4 | 1 [25] | 1/9 | | | | |
| Bizet: *Farandole* from *L'Arlésienne* Suite No. 2 | 1 [26] | 1/10 | 1 **11** | 1/3 | | |
| Tchaikovsky: *Dance of the Reed Pipes* from *Nutcracker* Suite | 1 [31] | 1/11 | 1 **16** | 1/4 | | |
| Bach: *Badinerie* from Suite No. 2 in B Minor | 1 [34] | 1/12 | 1 **19** | 1/5 | | |
| Britten: *The Young Person's Guide to the Orchestra* (Variations and Fugue on a Theme by Purcell) | | | | | 1 [1] | 1/1 |
| **MIDDLE AGES** | | | | | | |
| *Alleluia: Vidimus stellam* | 1 [38] | 1/13 | 1 **21** | 1/6 | | |
| *Estampie* | 1 [39] | 1/14 | | | | |
| Perotin: *Alleluia: Nativitas* | 1 [40] | 2/1 | | | | |
| Machaut: *Agnus Dei* from *Notre Dame* Mass | 1 [41] | 2/2 | 1 **24** | 1/7 | | |
| Machaut: *Je suis aussi* | | | | | 1 [26] | 1/2 |
| **RENAISSANCE** | | | | | | |
| Josquin Desprez: *Ave Maria . . . virgo serena* | 1 [44] | 2/3 | 1 **27** | 1/8 | | |
| Palestrina: Kyrie from *Pope Marcellus* Mass | | | | | 1 [29] | 1/3 |
| Weelkes: *As Vesta Was Descending* | 1 [47] | 2/4 | 1 **30** | 1/9 | | |
| Morley: *Now Is the Month of Maying* | | | | | 1 [32] | 1/4 |
| Andrea Gabrieli: *Ricercar in the Twelfth Mode* | 1 [48] | 2/5 | | | | |
| Praetorius: *La Bourée* | 1 [52] | 2/6 | | | | |
| Giovanni Gabrieli: *Plaudite*, Motet in Twelve Parts for Three Choirs | | | | | 1 [33] | 1/5 |

| | BASIC SETS | | BRIEF SETS | | SUPPLEMENTARY SETS | |
|---|---|---|---|---|---|---|
| | 8 CDS | 8 LPs/ 8 Cassettes | 3 CDs | 3 Cassettes | 4 CDs | 4 LPs/ 4 Cassettes |
| **BAROQUE** | CD TRACK | Side/Band | CD TRACK | Side/Band | CD TRACK | Side/Band |
| Monteverdi: *Tu se' morta* from *Orfeo*, Act II | 1 56 | 2/7 | 1 **39** | 2/1 | | |
| Purcell: *Dido's Lament* from *Dido and Aeneas* | 1 57 | 2/8 | | | | |
| Corelli: Trio Sonata in E Minor, Op. 3, No. 7 | | | | | | |
|   first movement (grave) | | | | | 1 34 | 2/1 |
|   second movement (allegro) | | | | | 1 35 | 2/2 |
|   third movement (adagio) | | | | | 1 36 | 2/3 |
|   fourth movement (allegro) | | | | | 1 37 | 2/4 |
| Vivaldi: *La Primavera (Spring),* Concerto for Violin and String Orchestra, Op. 8, No. 1, from *The Four Seasons* | | | | | | |
|   first movement (allegro) | 1 59 | 2/9 | 1 **40** | 2/2 | | |
|   second movement (largo e pianissimo sempre) | | | | | 1 38 | 2/5 |
|   third movement (*Danza pastorale*) | | | | | 1 39 | 2/6 |
| Bach: Organ Fugue in G Minor (*Little Fugue*) | 1 64 | 2/10 | 1 **36** | 1/11 | | |
| Bach: *Brandenburg* Concerto No. 5 in D Major | | | | | | |
|   first movement (allegro) | 2 1 | 3/1 | 1 **31** | 1/10 | | |
|   second movement (affetuoso) | 2 6 | 3/2 | | | | |
|   third movement (allegro) | 2 7 | 3/3 | | | | |
| Bach: Mass in B Minor | | | | | | |
|   *Crucifixus* | | | | | 1 40 | 2/7 |
|   *Et Resurrexit* | | | | | 1 41 | 2/8 |
| Bach: Cantata No. 140, *Wachet auf, ruft uns die Stimme* | | | | | | |
|   first movement (chorus and orchestra) | 2 10 | 3/4 | | | | |
|   fourth movement (tenor chorale) | 2 13 | 3/5 | 1 **45** | 2/3 | | |
|   fifth movement (recitative for bass) | | | | | 1 42 | 2/9 |
|   sixth movement (duet for bass and soprano) | | | | | 1 43 | 2/10 |
|   seventh movement (chorale) | 2 16 | 3/6 | | | | |
| Bach: from Suite No. 3 in D Major, S. 1068 | | | | | | |
|   Air | 2 17 | 4/1 | | | | |
|   Bourée | 2 19 | 4/2 | | | | |
|   Gigue | 2 21 | 4/3 | | | | |
| Handel: *Messiah* | | | | | | |
|   Sinfonia for Orchestra (French Overture) | 2 22 | 4/4 | | | | |
|   *Comfort Ye, My people* | 2 25 | 4/5 | | | | |
|   *Ev'ry Valley Shall Be Exalted* | 2 27 | 4/6 | 1 **49** | 2/5 | | |
|   *For unto Us a Child Is Born* | 2 28 | 4/7 | | | | |
|   *Hallelujah* Chorus | 2 31 | 4/8 | 1 **50** | 2/6 | | |

**CLASSICAL**

| | 8 CDS | 8 LPs/ 8 Cassettes | 3 CDs | 3 Cassettes | 4 CDs | 4 LPs/ 4 Cassettes |
|---|---|---|---|---|---|---|
| Haydn: Trumpet Concerto in E Flat Major; third movement (allegro) | 2 37 | 4/9 | | | | |
| Haydn: Symphony No. 94 in G Major (*Surprise*) | | | | | | |
|   first movement (adagio; vivace assai) | | | | | 2 1 | 3/1 |
|   second movement (andante) | 3 1 | 5/1 | 1 **65** | 2/8 | | |
|   third movement (minuet) | | | | | 2 9 | 3/2 |
|   fourth movement (finale) | | | | | 2 12 | 3/3 |

388

| | BASIC SETS | | BRIEF SETS | | SUPPLEMENTARY SETS | |
|---|---|---|---|---|---|---|
| | 8 CDS | 8 LPs/ 8 Cassettes | 3 CDs | 3 Cassettes | 4 CDs | 4 LPs/ 4 Cassettes |
| | CD TRACK | Side/Band | CD TRACK | Side/Band | CD TRACK | Side/Band |

## CLASSICAL

| | CD TRACK | Side/Band | CD TRACK | Side/Band | CD TRACK | Side/Band |
|---|---|---|---|---|---|---|
| Mozart: *Eine kleine Nachtmusik*, K. 525; third movement (minuet) | 3 [7] | 5/2 | 1 **[71]** | 2/9 | | |
| Mozart: Piano Concerto in A Major, K. 488 | | | | | | |
| first movement (allegro) | 3 [10] | 5/3 | 2 **[9]** | 3/3 | | |
| second movement (adagio) | | | | | 2 [15] | 3/4 |
| third movement (allegro assai) | | | | | 2 [18] | 3/5 |
| Mozart: *Don Giovanni*, K. 527; Act I | | | | | | |
| Introduction (opening scene) | 3 [17] | 5/4 | 2 **[5]** | 3/2 | | |
| "Catalog" aria (*Madamina*) | 3 [21] | 5/5 | | | | |
| *Là ci darem la mano* | 3 [23] | 5/6 | | | | |
| Mozart: *Dies irae*, from Requiem, K. 626 | 3 [27] | 6/1 | | | | |
| Mozart: Symphony No. 40 in G. Minor, K. 550 | | | | | | |
| first movement (molto allegro) | 3 [28] | 6/2 | 1 **[56]** | 2/7 | | |
| second movement (andante) | 3 [37] | 6/3 | | | | |
| third movement (menuetto) | 3 [40] | 6/4 | | | | |
| fourth movement (allegro assai) | 3 [43] | 6/5 | | | | |
| Beethoven: Symphony No. 5 in C Minor, Op. 67 | | | | | | |
| first movement (allegro con brio) | 4 [1] | 7/1 | 2 **[16]** | 3/4 | | |
| second movement (andante con moto) | 4 [9] | 7/2 | | | | |
| third movement (allegro) | 4 [15] | 7/3 | | | | |
| fourth movement (allegro) | 4 [19] | 7/3 | | | | |
| Beethoven: String Quartet in C Minor, Op. 18, No. 4; fourth movement (rondo) | 4 [26] | 8/1 | 2 **[1]** | 3/1 | | |
| Beethoven: Piano Sonata in C Minor, Op. 13 (*Pathétique*) | | | | | | |
| first movement (grave; allegro molto e con brio) | 4 [30] | 8/2 | | | | |
| second movement (adagio cantabile) | 4 [37] | 8/3 | | | | |
| third movement (rondo: allegro) | 4 [41] | 8/4 | | | | |
| Beethoven: String Quartet in F Major, Op. 18, No. 1; first movement (allegro con brio) | | | | | 2 [23] | 4/1 |

## ROMANTIC

| | CD TRACK | Side/Band | CD TRACK | Side/Band | CD TRACK | Side/Band |
|---|---|---|---|---|---|---|
| Schubert: *Erlkönig* | 4 [45] | 8/5 | 2 **[24]** | 3/5 | | |
| Schubert: *Die Forelle* | 4 [51] | 8/6 | | | | |
| Schubert: Piano Quintet in A Major, D. 667 (*Trout*); fourth movement (andantino) | 4 [53] | 8/7 | | | | |
| Robert Schumann: *Im wunderschönen Monat Mai* from *Dichterliebe*, Op. 48 | 5 [1] | 9/1 | | | | |
| Robert Schumann: *Aufschwung* from *Fantasiestücke*, Op. 12 | 5 [2] | 9/2 | | | | |
| Clara Wieck Schumann: Romance in G Minor for Violin and Piano, Op. 22, No. 2 | 5 [5] | 9/3 | 2 **[30]** | 3/6 | | |
| Chopin: Polonaise in A Flat Major, Op. 53 | 5 [10] | 9/4 | | | | |
| Chopin: Nocturne in E Flat Major, Op. 9, No. 2 | 5 [14] | 9/5 | 2 **[35]** | 4/1 | | |
| Chopin: Étude in C Minor, Op. 10, No. 12 (*Revolutionary*) | | | | | 2 [31] | 4/2 |
| Liszt: *Transcendental Étude* No. 10 in F Minor | 5 [17] | 9/6 | 2 **[38]** | 4/2 | | |

|  | BASIC SETS | | BRIEF SETS | | SUPPLEMENTARY SETS | |
|---|---|---|---|---|---|---|
|  | 8 CDS | 8 LPs/<br>8 Cassettes | 3 CDs | 3 Cassettes | 4 CDs | 4 LPs/<br>4 Cassettes |
|  | CD TRACK | Side/Band | CD TRACK | Side/Band | CD TRACK | Side/Band |

## ROMANTIC

| | 8 CDS CD TRACK | Side/Band | 3 CDs CD TRACK | Side/Band | 4 CDs CD TRACK | Side/Band |
|---|---|---|---|---|---|---|
| Mendelssohn: Concerto for Violin and Orchestra in E Minor, Op. 64 | | | | | | |
|   first movement (allegro molto appassionato) | 5 [23] | 9/7 | | | | |
|   second movement (andante) | | | | | 3 [23] | 6/2 |
|   third movement (allegro non troppo; allegro molto vivace) | | | | | 3 [26] | 6/3 |
| Berlioz: *Symphonie fantastique* | | | | | | |
|   first movement (excerpt, *idée fixe*) | | | | | 2 [32] | 4/3 |
|   fourth movement (*March to the Scaffold*) | 5 [28] | 10/1 | | | | |
|   fifth movement (*Dream of a Witches Sabbath*) | 5 [32] | 10/2 | 2 [44] | 4/3 | | |
| Mussorgsky, *Boris Godunov; Coronation* Scene | | | | | 2 [33] | 4/4 |
| Tchaikovsky: *Romeo and Juliet,* Overture-Fantasy | 5 [38] | 10/3 | | | | |
| Smetana: *The Moldau* | 6 [1] | 11/1 | 2 [50] | 4/4 | | |
| Dvořák: Symphony No. 9 in E Minor *(From the New World)* | | | | | | |
|   first movement (adagio; allegro molto) | | | | | 3 [1] | 5/1 |
|   second movement (largo) | | | | | 3 [8] | 5/2 |
|   third movement (scherzo: molto vivace) | | | | | 3 [13] | 5/3 |
|   fourth movement (allegro con fuoco) | | | | | 3 [19] | 6/1 |
| Brahms: Symphony No. 4 in E Minor, Op. 98; fourth movement (allegro energetico e passionato) | 6 [8] | 11/2 | 2 [57] | 4/5 | | |
| Brahms: *A German Requiem,* fourth movement *(How Lovely Is Thy Dwelling Place)* | 6 [12] | 11/3 | | | | |
| Verdi: *Rigoletto,* Act III, *La donna è mobile* and Quartet | 6 [13] | 11/4 | | | | |
| Puccini: *La Bohème,* Act I, excerpt (Mimi's entrance through conclusion of act) | 6 [16] | 12/1 | 3 [1] | 5/1 | | |
| Wagner: *Die Walküre,* Act I, scene 3 (love scene, conclusion) | 6 [20] | 12/2 | 3 [4] | 5/2 | | |
| Mahler: Symphony No. 1, third movement *(Funeral March)* | | | | | 2 [36] | 4/5 |

## TWENTIETH CENTURY

| | 8 CDS CD TRACK | Side/Band | 3 CDs CD TRACK | Side/Band | 4 CDs CD TRACK | Side/Band |
|---|---|---|---|---|---|---|
| Stravinsky: *Le Sacre du printemps* | | | | | | |
|   Part I, *Introduction, Omens of Spring—Dances of the Youths and Maidens, Ritual of Abduction* | 6 [28] | 12/3 | 3 [19] | 5/4 | | |
|   Part II, *Sacrificial Dance* | 7 [1] | 13/1 | | | | |
| Stravinsky: *Symphony of Psalms;* first movement | 7 [4] | 13/2 | | | | |
| Stravinsky: *Petrushka;* Act I, scene 1 | | | | | 4 [1] | 7/1 |
| Debussy: *Prélude à "L'Après-midi d'un Faune"* *(Prelude to "The Afternoon of a Faun")* | 7 [5] | 13/3 | 3 [12] | 5/3 | | |
| Debussy: *Voiles* from Preludes for Piano, Book I | | | | | 4 [21] | 8/1 |
| Ravel: *Bolero* | 7 [12] | 13/4 | | | | |

| | BASIC SETS | | BRIEF SETS | | SUPPLEMENTARY SETS | |
|---|---|---|---|---|---|---|
| | 8 CDS | 8 LPs/ 8 Cassettes | 3 CDs | 3 Cassettes | 4 CDs | 4 LPs/ 4 Cassettes |
| **TWENTIETH CENTURY** | CD TRACK | Side/Band | CD TRACK | Side/Band | CD TRACK | Side/Band |
| Schoenberg: Five Pieces for Orchestra, Op. 16, first piece: *Vorgefühle* | 7 16 | 14/1 | | | | |
| Schoenberg: *A Survivor from Warsaw*, Op. 46 | 7 18 | 14/2 | 3 27 | 6/1 | | |
| Berg: *Wozzeck;* Act III, scenes 4 and 5 | 7 20 | 14/3 | | | | |
| Webern: Five Pieces for Orchestra, Op. 10, third piece (very slow and extremely calm) | 7 25 | 14/4 | 3 29 | 6/2 | | |
| Bartók: Concerto for Orchestra first movement | 7 26 | 14/5 | | | | |
| second movement | | | 3 30 | 6/3 | 4 8 | 7/2 |
| Ives: *Putnam's Camp, Redding, Connecticut,* from *Three Places in New England* | 7 35 | 14/6 | | | | |
| Gershwin: *Rhapsody in Blue* | | | | | 4 15 | 7/3 |
| Copland: *Appalachian Spring,* Section 7 (Theme and Variations on *Simple Gifts*) | 8 1 | 15/1 | 3 37 | 6/4 | | |
| Carter: Sonata for Flute, Oboe, Cello, and Harpsichord, first movement (risoluto) | | | | | 4 26 | 8/2 |
| Penderecki: *Threnody: For the Victims of Hiroshima* | | | | | 4 28 | 8/3 |
| Varèse: *Poème électronique* (complete piece on basic sets; excerpt on brief sets) | 8 7 | 15/2 | 3 43 | 6/5 | | |
| Babbitt: *Composition for Synthesizer* (excerpt) | 8 8 | 15/3 | | | | |
| Crumb: *Ancient Voices of Children, From Where Do You Come, My Love, My Child?* | 8 9 | 15/4 | | | | |
| Zwilich: *Concerto Grosso 1985;* first movement (maestoso) | 8 10 | 15/5 | 3 44 | 6/6 | | |
| Adams: *Nixon in China,* Act I, scene 2, opening | 8 12 | 15/6 | 3 46 | 6/7 | | |

## JAZZ

| | | | | | | |
|---|---|---|---|---|---|---|
| Joplin: *Maple Leaf Rag* | 8 13 | 15/7 | | | | |
| Smith: *Lost Your Head Blues* | 8 17 | 15/8 | | | | |
| Oliver: *Dippermouth Blues* | 8 18 | 16/1 | | | | |
| Berlin: *Blue Skies* | 8 19 | 16/2 | | | | |
| Ellington: *Concerto for Cootie* | 8 20 | 16/3 | | | | |
| Parker: *Koko* | 8 21 | 16/4 | | | | |

## THE AMERICAN MUSICAL

| | | | | | | |
|---|---|---|---|---|---|---|
| Bernstein: *West Side Story, Tonight* ensemble | 8 22 | 16/5 | 3 47 | 6/8 | | |

## NONWESTERN MUSIC

| | | | | | | |
|---|---|---|---|---|---|---|
| Song from Angola (Gangele song) | 8 24 | 16/6 | 3 49 | 6/9 | | |
| *Mitamba Yalagala Kumchuzi* | 8 25 | 16/7 | 3 50 | 6/10 | | |
| *Hinganyengisa Masingita* | 8 26 | 16/8 | | | | |
| *Maru-Bihag,* excerpt | 8 27 | 16/9 | | | | |
| Mitsuzaki Kengyō: *Godan Ginuta* (excerpt) | 8 28 | 16/10 | 3 51 | 6/11 | | |

# ACKNOWLEDGMENTS

## PART-OPENING PHOTOGRAPHS

I.   Innervision
II.   Glasgow University Library
III.   A. C. Cooper, by gracious permission of the Queen
IV.   Carnavalet Museum, Paris; Giraudon/Art Resource
V.   Lauros-Giraudon/Art Resource
VI.   Art Institute of Chicago; gift of Mrs. Gilbert W. Chapman; oil on canvas, 1943, 109.9 by 79.1 cm.
VII.   Peter Buckley/Photo Researchers

## MUSIC AND MUSICAL TEXTS

Adams, John, and Alice Goodman. *Nixon in China*. Music copyright © 1987 Red Dawn Music BMI. Libretto © Alice Goodman 1990. Reprinted by permission of Michael Imison Playwrights Ltd.

Bach, Johann Sebastian. *Cantata No. 140: Wachet auf, ruft uns die Stimme* translated by Gerhard Herz. In Roger Kamien (ed.), *The Norton Scores*. Copyright 1970, W. W. Norton & Company, Inc.

Bartók, Béla. *Mikrokosmos* from *Six Dances in Bulgarian Rhythm*, Vol. 6, Nos. 148–153. © copyright 1940 by Hawkes & Son (London) Ltd.; copyright renewed. Reprinted by permission of Boosey & Hawkes, Inc.

Berg, Alban. *Wozzeck*, Act III, Scenes 4–5. Translation by Eric Blackall and Vida Harford. © 1923, 1931 by Universal Edition A. G., Wien. English translation © 1952 by Alfred A. Kalmus, London. Copyright renewed. All rights reserved. Used by permission of European American Music Distributors Corporation, sole U.S. agent for Universal Edition.

Bernstein, Leonard, and Stephen Sondheim. *Tonight* from *West Side Story*. Copyright © 1957 (renewed) Leonard Bernstein and Stephen Sondheim, Jalni Publications, Inc., U.S. and Canadian publisher. G. Schirmer, Inc., worldwide print rights and publisher for the rest of the world. International copyright secured. All rights reserved. Used by permission.

Copland, Aaron. *Appalachian Spring*. Copyright © 1946 by Aaron Copland; copyright renewed. Reprinted by permission of The Estate of Aaron Copland, copyright owner; and Boosey & Hawkes, Inc., sole licensees.

Gershwin, George. *Rhapsody in Blue*. © 1924 (renewed) W B Music Corp. All rights reserved. Used by permission.

Haydn, Franz Josef. Symphony No. 94 in G. Major (*Surprise*) from critical edition of *Haydn, Complete Symphonies* by H. C. Robbins Landon, Vol. XI. © 1965 by Haydn-Mozart Presse, Salzburg. All rights reserved. Used by permission of European American Music Distributors Corporation, sole U. S. agent for Haydn-Mozart Presse.

Ives, Charles. *The Cage*. © Copyright 1955 by Peer International Corporation. International copyright secured. Used by permission.

Mozart, Wolfgang Amadeus. *Don Giovanni*, Act I. Translation by William Murray. Used by permission of Angel Records.

Porter, Cole. *You're the Top* from *Anything Goes*. Words and music by Cole Porter. © 1934 (renewed) Warner Bros. Inc. All rights reserved. Used by permission.

Puccini, Giacomo. *La Bohème*, Act I, Scene 1. Translation by William Weaver from *Seven Puccini Librettos in New English Translations by William Weaver*. © 1981, 1986 W. W. Norton & Company.

Schoenberg, Arnold. Suite Op. 25 for piano, 1920–1923. Copyright by Universal Edition. Copyright renewed 1952 by Gertrude Schoenberg. Used by permission of Belmont Music Publishers, Pacific Palisades, CA 90272.

Schoenberg, Arnold. *A Survivor from Warsaw*. Copyright © 1949 by Boelke-Bomart, Inc. Used by permission.

Schubert, Franz. *Der Erlkönig* translation from Philip L. Miller (ed.), *The Ring of Words*. Copyright © 1966 by Doubleday, a division of Bantam Doubleday Dell Publishing Group, Inc. Reprinted by permission of Doubleday and Philip L. Miller.

Schumann, Clara Wieck. Romanze in G Minor for Violin and Piano, Op. 22, No. 2. Used by permission of Brietkopf & Härtel GmbH.

Schumann, Robert. *Im wunderschönen Monat Mai* from *Dichterliebe*, translation from Philip L. Miller (ed.), *The Ring of Words*, published by Doubleday & Company. Used by permission of Philip L. Miller.

Stravinsky, Igor. *Petrouchka*, original 1911 version. Copyright © by Edition Russe de Musique. Copyright assigned to Boosey & Hawkes, Inc. Revised edition copyright © 1947, 1948 by Boosey & Hawkes; copyright renewed. Reprinted by permission of Boosey & Hawkes, Inc.

Stravinsky, Igor. *The Rite of Spring*. Copyright © 1921 by Edition Russe de Musique (Russischer Musikverlag); copyright renewed. Copyright assigned 1947 to Boosey & Hawkes, Inc. Reprinted by permission of Boosey & Hawkes, Inc.

Verdi, Giuseppe. *Rigoletto*, translation by William Weaver from *Seven Verdi Librettos*. © 1963 by William Weaver. Reprinted by permission of Doubleday, a division of Bantam Doubleday Dell Publishing Group, Inc., and the William Morris Agency.

Wagner, Richard. *Die Walküre*, Act I, conclusion. Copyright William Mann. (This translation was commissioned and originally published by The Friends of Covent Garden.) Used by permission of Erika Mann.

Zwilich, Ellen Taaffe. *Concerto Grosso 1985*. © copyright 1985 by Mobart Music Publications, Inc. Used by permission.

## QUOTATIONS

Reich, Steve. Interview with D. Sterrit, *Tradition Reseen*, *Christian Science Monitor*, 23 October 1980. Used by permission of Steve Reich.

Zwilich, Ellen Taaffe. Commentary on *Concerto Grosso 1985*. © copyright 1985 by Mobart Music Publications, Inc. Used by permission.

# INDEX

401

Postlude, 185, 371
Preclassical music, 118
Prelude, 371
  choral prelude, 105, 359
  fugue, 90
  opera, 6(LO), 49, 90
Prélude à ''L'Après-midi d'un faune''
    (Prelude to ''The Afternoon of a
    Faun''), 262, 264–266(LO)
Premonitions (Vorgefühle) from Five Pieces
    for Orchestra, Op. 16
    (Schoenberg), 280–282
Presley, Elvis, 335
Pressure drum, 349
Prestissimo (tempo), 29, 371
Presto (tempo), 29
Primavera, La (Spring), Concerto for
    Violin and String Orchestra, Op.
    8, No. 1 from The Four Seasons
    (Vivaldi), 99–100(LO)
Primitivism, 269, 371
Prix de Rome (Rome Prize), 210, 261
Processional theme, 204
Program, 208, 371
Program music, 99, 181, 208–209, 371
  (See also specific composers)
Program symphony, 209, 371
Progression, 38, 371
Prompter, 372
Prussian Academy of Arts, 277
Psaltery, 61
Psychedelic rock, 336
Puccini, Giacomo, 178, 181, 232–240
  La Bohème (Bohemian Life), 213–240
    Che gelida manina (What a cold little
      hand), 233, 238–239
    Mi chiamano Mimi (They call me
      Mimi), 233, 239–240
Punk (new wave) music, 336
Purcell, Henry, 78, 253
  Dido and Aeneas, 84
    Dido's Lament (When I am laid in
      earth), 84
Putnam, Israel, 296
Putnam's Camp, Redding, Connecticut
    from Three Places in New England
    (Ives), 296–297

Quadruple meter, 28, 35, 321, 372
Quadruple stop (string technique), 13,
    375
Quiet Riot (group), 336
Quintuple meter, 29, 372
Quotation music, 305, 307–308,
    314–316(LO), 372

Radio, twentieth-century music and,
    253, 307
Ragtime, 321, 372
Range, 3
Rapping (rap music), 336
Ravel, Maurice, 264, 298, 308, 320
Rebec, 61
Recapitulation (sonata form), 125, 126,
    372
Recitative, 94, 232, 372

Recorder, 10, 13, 14, 73, 83, 372
Recordings of music, 253, 337
Reed (woodwind instruments), 13, 372
Reformation, Protestant, 66
Reggae, 336
Register, 8, 372
Reich, Steve, 307
Religious music (see Sacred music)
Rembrandt van Rijn, 78
Renaissance music, 64–74, 253, 269
  characteristics of, 66–68
  harmony, 67–68
  imitation in, 67–70, 72
  instrumental, 73–74
  instruments, 73
  madrigal, 71–73, 269, 367
  mass, 70–71, 367
  melody, 68
  mood in, 67
  motet, 68–70, 368
  musical texture, 67–68, 70–71, 80
  pitch in, 67
  rhythm, 68, 80
  sacred, 67–71
  secular, 71–74
  vocal, 67, 71–73
  word painting, 67
Renoir, Auguste, 261
Repetition, 36–37, 48, 49, 372
  in baroque music, 80
  in classical recapitulation, 126
  in minuet and trio, 134
Resolution, 39, 372
Rest (notation), 33, 372
Retrograde:
  in fugue, 90, 372
  in twelve-tone system, 278, 279
Return, 49
Reverberators, 25
Revolutionary Étude (Étude in C Minor,
    Op. 10, No. 12) (Chopin), 200
Revue, 329
Rhapsody in Blue (Gershwin), 298–300
Rhythm, 2, 26–30, 62, 373
  accent, 26, 29, 258, 326, 356
  in baroque music, 80, 84
  in Bartók, 292, 293
  beat, 26, 27, 258, 337–338, 358
  ''bombs,'' 326
  in classical music, 122
  in Debussy, 264
  dotted, 33, 362
  in Gregorian chant, 57–58, 61, 62
  in jazz, 323–325
  measured, 62
  in nonwestern music, 344, 347
  notation, 32–33
  in organum, 62, 80, 370
  ostinato, 259, 269, 370
  polyrhythm, 259, 301, 347
  in Renaissance music, 68, 80
  in rock, 337–338
  in romantic music, 225
  in Stravinsky, 269
  syncopation, 26, 29, 63, 252, 258, 323,
    376

Rhythm (Cont.):
  tempo, 29–30, 183, 377
  in twentieth-century music, 250,
    258–259, 305, 311
  (See also Meter)
Rhythm and blues, 335
Rhythm section, 322, 373
Ricercar, 74, 373
Ricercar in the Twelfth Mode (Gabrieli),
    73–74
Riffs, 325
Rigoletto (Verdi), 230, 231, 333
  Donna è mobile, La (Woman Is Fickle),
    231–232
Riley, Terry, 307
Rimbaud, Arthur, 261
Rimsky-Korsakov, Nikolai, 181, 217, 267
Ritardando (tempo), 30, 183, 373
Rite of Spring, The (Le Sacre du printemps)
    (Stravinsky), 250, 267–270
  Introduction, 270, 271, 272–273(LO)
  Omens of Spring—Dances of the Youths
    and Maidens, 270, 271,
    273–274(LO)
  Ritual of Abduction, 258, 270, 272,
    274(LO)
  Sacrificial Dance, 270, 274
Ritornello, 373
Ritornello form, 85–88, 99–100(LO),
    107–108, 113, 373
Ritual of Abduction from Le Sacre du
    printemps (The Rite of Spring)
    (Stravinsky), 258, 270, 272,
    274(LO)
Robbins, Jerome, 333
Rochberg, George, 308
Rock (rock and roll), 309, 335–339, 373
  development of, 335–336
  elements of, 336–339
  harmony in, 338–339
  instruments, 337
  melody, 338–339
  meter in, 337
  musical form, 338–339
  nonwestern, 336
  orchestra, 336
  rhythm, 337–338
  tone color, 336–337
Rococo art, 118, 119
Rodgers, Richard, 329
Rolling Stones (group), 335
Rollins, Sonny, 16
Romance (Romanze), 194, 373
Romance in G Minor for Violin and
    Piano, Op. 22, No. 2 (Clara
    Wieck Schumann), 194–196(LO)
Romantic music, 174–247, 253, 258
  characteristics of, 179–184
  chromatic harmony, 182–183
  dynamics, 183
  exoticism, 180–181, 232, 363
  expressive aims of, 180
  key, 183
  middle class and, 178–179, 179, 186
  mood in, 182–183, 185
  musical form, 183–184

DEMCO